ANDRÉ MALRAUX

André Malraux

JEAN LACOUTURE

Translated from the French by
ALAN SHERIDAN

PANTHEON BOOKS
A Division of Random House, New York

First American Edition

English translation copyright © 1975 by Alan Sheridan

All rights reserved under International and Pan-American Copyright Conventions. Published in the United States by Pantheon Books, a division of Random House, Inc., New York, and simultaneously in Canada by Random House of Canada Limited, Toronto. Originally published in France by Editions du Seuil, Paris. Copyright © 1973 by Editions du Seuil. Translation (abridged for English edition) first published in Great Britain by Andre Deutsch Limited, London.

Library of Congress Cataloging in Publication Data

Lacouture, Jean.
    André Malraux.

    Includes bibliographical references and index.
    1. Malraux, André, 1901-   —Biography.
PQ2625.A716Z686813   1975   843'.9'12   75-10361
ISBN 0-394-48367-7

Manufactured in the United States of America

Perhaps you will say: 'Are you sure this legend is true?' Does it matter what the reality outside me may be if it has helped me to live, to feel sure that I am and what I am?

CHARLES BAUDELAIRE
Petits poèmes en prose. Les Fenêtres

Contents

Illustrations

Acknowledgements

THIS book could not have been written without the help, information and documentation provided by a large number of people, beginning with André Malraux himself. As soon as he was informed of the project, M. Malraux agreed to see me and, in the course of four conversations, answered most of my questions. Not only did he express himself with his usual brilliance and with genuine openness (about everything that did not concern his private life), but he never made the slightest attempt to check what I had written: indeed, he claims never to read what is written about him.

I was also given the invaluable help of Clara Malraux, whose four volumes of memoirs are essential reading for anyone wishing to understand André Malraux, of Florence Resnais, their daughter, and Alain, the writer's nephew and son-in-law and a friend of mine. I also wish to acknowledge the encouragement and help given me by André Malraux's oldest and most faithful friends, Louis and Germaine Chevasson and the late Marcel Brandin.

The welcome I have received at Gallimard's, Malraux's principal publisher, from the founder of the firm himself, its present head, Marcel Arland and his colleagues on the *NRF*, Jean Grosjean, Roger Grenier and Marie-Claude de Saint-Seine, went well beyond normal professional courtesy. I received a similar welcome at Bernard Grasset's, André Malraux's previous publishers. And if all the treasures of the Bibliothèque Doucet were not at my disposal it certainly was not the fault of M. François Chapon, who was unfailingly obliging.

The following friends, companions, rivals, admirers or critics of André Malraux agreed to see me or wrote to me: Alexandre Alexeieff, Alice Alley, Max Aub (who died some months later), Pierre Bockel, Emmanuel Berl, Mme Francine Albert Camus, André Chamson, Pierre Cot, Rosine Delclaux, Antoine Diener-Ancel, Alfred Fabre-Luce, Brigitte Friang, Louis Guilloux, Generals Guillermaz and Jacquot, Walter Langlois, Georges Gabory, Georges Henein, Dolorès Ibarruri ('La Pasionaria'), Arthur Koestler, René Jugie, Georges Manue, Pierre Naville, Gaston Palewski, Julien Segnaire, Philippe Soupault, Manès Sperber, Georges Soria, Herbert Southworth, Louis Vallon, André Vandegans and Fernando Valera, head of the Spanish government in exile.

I particularly wish to thank Claude Mauriac, Gaëtan Picon and Roger Stéphane, who not only have written penetrating and indispensable books on Malraux, but have very generously given me access to their documentation: my friends Jean Daniel, Julien Besançon and Henry Tanner, who allowed me to reproduce extracts from unpublished interviews with André Malraux; and Georges Borchardt, who was at the origin of this bold enterprise. Two particularly attentive readers, Paul-André Lesort and Georges Buis, have been good enough to point out a number of errors and shortcomings. In the writing of this book I owe a particular debt of gratitude to Simone Lescuyer, Claude Lemaître, Denise Barcilon and Simonne Lacouture.

J.L.

Book 1

======

DIFFERENCE

PART I

DERISION

---

1 A son of the war

ON THE evening of 10 November 1918, a young man was walking through the Tuileries Gardens in Paris. He was just seventeen. He had left school and was free of all attachments – family, friends, or career. A man dashed up to him, shouting: 'The armistice has been signed!' In fact, the document was not signed until fifteen hours later.

André Malraux was already in the grips of history in the making. And already, he tells us, he felt alone in the midst of the universal joy that burst out at the news of the German defeat and what was believed to be the victory of France and her allies. In a life that was to swing constantly between solitude and fraternity, between difference and communion, he set out with this profound feeling of apartness.

He was to experience many revolutions and wars before he finally discovered the fraternity that was to be his life's ambition. But there he was, an adolescent, scarcely aware of himself, in the grips of a history that was to shape his whole life.

'What distinguished us from our mentors, at twenty, was the presence of history. *We* were surrounded by corpses; for *them* nothing had happened. *We* were people whose fields had been ploughed up by history, as if by tanks . . .' These words were spoken to me by André Malraux, at Verrières-le-Buisson, one day in the summer of 1972.

He is not indifferent to the fact that there are Flemings among his recent forebears: there is something in his temperament of the fierceness of a carnival giant, something in his gaze of the open sea, the dreams of Bosch, Breughel and Ensor. He loves long sea voyages, spent writing on deck or by the light of a porthole. And the fact that he was born in Montmartre, at a time when Utrillo was painting, Bruant singing, Reverdy emerging as a poet, lends a certain style to his voice, his gestures, his walk.

But what really matters, as far as Malraux is concerned, is not *where*, but *when* he became aware of himself and of the world. The most absurd, and, so far, the bloodiest of wars was drawing to a close – and European society found itself face to face with its millions of dead victims and its millions of blinded, maimed, gassed, or simply stunned survivors, with the overthrow of its values, the ruin of its finances, and the crumbling of its monuments.

Malraux was sixteen when the Bolsheviks seized power in Petrograd. He was not yet seventeen when the streets and squares of Paris, London and New York thronged with the Armistice celebrations. He was not yet eighteen when, in March 1919, the Third International was created. He was not yet nineteen when Tristan Tzara launched his first Dada Manifesto, not yet twenty when the French Communist Party was founded at Tours, when Mussolini transformed his *fascii* into a political party with the avowed aim of seizing power, and when, on the other side of Europe, around Odessa, the Red Army was smashing the last remnants of Wrangel's White Guards.

But in 1920 an eighteen-year-old Frenchman did not have to look so far to be seized by a fever of revolt, rejection or action. The France that the victors of 11 November had bequeathed to his generation was a great dismembered, brainless body, drunk with pride.

A million and a half dead – almost a third of whom were men aged between eighteen and twenty-five; nearly three million wounded – six hundred and fifty thousand of whom were to remain permanently disabled; one seventh of the national territory laid waste. Poincaré and Clemenceau embraced on the parade-ground at Metz; a feeble old politician cried: 'The Bosch will pay . . .'; and Kaiser Wilhelm was asked to go back to growing roses in his gardens at Doorn.

In this convulsed France of 1919 where, in the Galerie des Glaces at Versailles, the victors tried to cash the dividends of the holocaust, and where the generals responsible for the insane butchery of Verdun and the Somme were laden with honours, worshipped like demigods and listened to like oracles, a young man, without illusions and without prejudices, was discovering for himself the relations between art and life, the pleasures of freedom, ambition, friendship and the exhilaration of dawning intelligence.

For generations the Malrauxs had lived in Dunkirk. They belonged among the craftsmen of the lower-middle-class: the men tended to be joiners, the women to marry sailors. It is said that André's great grandfather, and even his grandfather, Alphonse, who died in 1909, spoke not French but the Flemish dialect. In *La Voie royale*, then in *Les Noyers de l'Altenburg*, and, lastly, in the *Antimémoires*, André Malraux, usually so reticent with revelations about himself or his family, describes this stubborn, spirited old man, a shipowner and a master-cooper, who, in revolt against the Church for granting certain concessions in the Lenten rules, refused to set foot in his parish church again and tried to follow the Mass standing among the nettles outside. Here are a few lines of this portrait in its third and final 'state' – always supposing that in passing from avowed fiction to self-proclaimed autobiography, André Malraux is moving towards a truer truth, which is perhaps a naïve supposition, and in some sense the subject of the *Antimémoires*:

> This grandfather is mine . . . He was a shipowner, of whom I drew a somewhat closer likeness in the grandfather of the hero of *La Voie Royale* – specifically his old Viking's death. Although he was prouder of his master-cooper's certificate than of his fleet, most of which had already been lost at sea, he liked to keep up the rites of his youth, and had split his skull open with a blow from a double-edged axe while symbolically putting the finishing touch to the figurehead of his last boat in accordance with tradition.[1]

Alphonse Malraux died in 1909, aged sixty-eight, leaving five children: two girls and three boys. The youngest of the sons, Fernand, was then thirty and was already separated from his first wife, Berthe Lamy, a farmer's daughter from the Jura. He was a strong, handsome man, very much in love with life, the possessor of a fine moustache and a shapely pair of legs. Something of a Maupassant hero, so little ill-treated by women, it seems, that he tired of his wife. Berthe and Fernand Malraux were married in 1900 and divorced fifteen years later. They separated four years after the birth of their only son, André, on 3 November 1901, at 73 rue Damrémont, at the foot of the Butte Montmartre. Two more boys, Roland and Claude, were born to a second marriage to a Mlle Godard.

Little is known about the social position of André's father. He has been described as a rather eccentric inventor of gadgets (his eldest son has said that he invented the non-skid tyre) and in *La Voie royale* reference is made to 'discoveries' made by Grabot's father, who 'invents tie-holders, starters for engines, anti-splash tap-nozzles . . .' At other times, Fernand Malraux is presented as the representative in France of 'an American bank'. Which bank? No further details are available. There can be little doubt that he dabbled on the Stock Exchange. What we do know, from Clara Malraux, is that he was a man overflowing with vitality, gaiety and high spirits, with at least three new ideas a day, few principles and a good heart. A jovial 'failure' who seems to have reached his peak in his role as a tank officer in 1917–18, and found his life thereafter so insipid that, finally, in 1930, he put an end to it.

Berthe Lamy, his first wife and André's mother, was a tall, slender, rather good-looking woman. After her divorce, she went back to her Italian mother, who, although she ran a wholesale grocery business, lived in a style more suited to an aristocrat. Clara Malraux speaks admiringly of Grand'mère Adrienne. She remembers her once saying, in her inimitable way, 'When I was young, people came out to fight in the streets!'[2] This was her way of referring to social injustice. So it was with his Grand'mère Adrienne, his mother and his aunt that André Malraux grew up, at Bondy, one of the most outlying, most dismal suburbs of Paris. There, not far from the Ourcq canal, these three ladies ran a small, but profitable business at 16 rue de la Gare.

'Almost all the writers I know love their childhood; I hate mine'[3]! – this is one of the first sentences of the *Antimémoires*, and one of the most scandalous. It is something of an understatement to say that writers love their childhood: most of them idolize it. To repudiate one's childhood is almost tantamount to insulting one's mother, and few have done this so specifically as Malraux in an interview with Emmanuel d'Astier in 1967: 'I didn't like my youth. Youth is a feeling that drags you back. I didn't have a childhood . . .'[4]

He was nearly five when, in October 1906, he went to the École de Bondy, in the rue Saint-Denis, a private school whose level of teaching left something to be desired. The headmaster and an assistant master called Malaval divided their eighteen-odd pupils between them. The following year, André Malraux noted the arrival at the school of a dark-eyed neighbour called Louis Chevasson – he was to remain, sixty-five years later, Malraux's most constant friend.

Perhaps because he shared it to some extent, Louis Chevasson now denies that André's childhood was really unhappy. 'No, no. André didn't mind at all being spoilt by women. His mother was quite delightful, and he saw his father nearly every week in Paris, often with his mother. It has been suggested that his nervous tics were the result of being badly treated at school. That's ridiculous! André has always had these tics. As for the poverty he's supposed to have lived in – it's a complete fabrication. The grocery business in the rue de la Gare did very well indeed and our friend never lacked for anything.' But Clara Malraux observes that André's mother used to tell him that his protruding ears were a disfigurement and that he was very ugly. Such a thing could leave its mark on a sensitive child.

André, thin and pale, with his unruly hair and large ears, left primary school with a good academic record. He was good at history and French; he was even good at the sciences. The young Malraux was already a dominant personality. Malaval, his teacher, was somewhat ahead of his time: he would ask his pupils to take part in the awarding of marks. The pupils' work was laid out on a desk and it was often the future author of *Les Conquérants* who settled matters. At the local library, where he spent hours ferreting among the shelves, he would help the assistant in his work, and it was not long before he was advising readers which books to borrow and suggesting titles that the library should buy.

He took little interest in sport: just some rifle shooting, at which he later claimed to excel. On Thursdays, which was traditionally a holiday for French schoolchildren, the boys would go for walks in the Bois de Villemonble – the Forêt de Bondy of the medieval tales – which was then very dense and mysterious, the perfect setting for imaginary exploits. They read Dumas and Walter Scott and filled their heads with fantastic dreams. Then, one day, war broke out. André, Louis and their schoolfriends were to live the war, at thirteen, like a fabulous spectacle that was there beside them.

Fernand Malraux was at the front. But neither his sons nor his closest friends seem to have had any feelings of nationalistic fervour. Fathers being away, the distant echoes of battle, the excitement of arrivals and departures around the nearby station, the mobilization of a teacher, all helped to create a holiday atmosphere – unexpected freedom, spiced with a sense of living through history. And the few privations brought about through rationing served merely to heighten the atmosphere of adventure in which one lived.

The first important books in André's life, after *The Three Musketeers*, the books that marked the transition from childhood to adolescence were, first, Flaubert's *Bouvard et Pécuchet* and *Salammbô*!, then the novels of Victor Hugo and Balzac. The library at Bondy had only two of Shakespeare's plays, *Macbeth* and *Julius Caesar*: André Malraux read them.

Anyway, plays are not to be read, but seen. Chevasson and Malraux were thirteen and fourteen when they first went to the theatre: they saw Racine's *Andromaque* at the Comédie Française and Molière's *Le Médecin malgré lui* at the Odéon. For a time, André dreamt of becoming an actor. They were already captivated by the cinema. On public holidays, a tent was set up in the Place de Bondy and in 1912 *Les Misérables* was shown. The whole family went. Later, westerns were shown and, in 1916, the first Chaplin films.

But it was books that interested the young Malraux most – books to read, but also books to be unearthed, exchanged, sold. On Thursdays and Sundays, either to scrape together enough money for the theatre or cinema, or simply for the sheer pleasure of it, André and Louis would make a tour of the book-

stalls along the Seine or in the narrow side streets off the Boul'
Mich'. Each of them did one side of the street. Two hours later,
they'd meet to pool their spoils and go off to the Librairie Crès,
at the corner of the rue Danton and the boulevard Saint-
Germain, where they collected their cash. At first it was a game,
then a small source of income: soon it became a sort of job, the
only job he was to have for twenty years.

The day before his fourteenth birthday, in October 1915,
André Malraux left his schoolfriends at Bondy, but not his
home, to which he returned every evening, and went to the
École Primaire Supérieure in the rue de Turbigo, which was to
become the Lycée Turgot at the end of the war. It was there
that he formed his second great friendship, with Marcel
Brandin.

These apparently easy-going young men, with their appetite
for life still keen, were not to remain for long indifferent to
political concerns. The vicissitudes of the last year of the war,
from the autumn of 1917, were a constant subject of discussion
in the school playground. The tragic communiqués of the
winter, the news of the Petrograd uprising, the entry of the
Americans on the European scene, the treaty of Brest-Litovsk,
the terrible British losses on the Somme, the accession to power
of Clemenceau – how could one fail to react to such news when
one was sixteen? The adolescents of that time were not those of
1968, but they sometimes had the same temperament.

Malraux's young friends tended to pacifism. They were
'leftish' in a Jacobin sort of way. The 'treason' of the Bolsheviks
was considered 'unacceptable', the Kaiser was lampooned,
Foch, now the Allied Commander-in-Chief, was regarded as a
great man. Thus from his first incursions into politics, André
Malraux's thinking was imbued with Jacobin ambiguity. Like
Michelet, he had a hatred for war and a passion for the glory of
arms – a passion that did not, however, drive this adolescent of
seventeen to enlist, as it did others of his age. Marcel Brandin,
for example, tried to get himself accepted for the army. In fact,
the young Malraux would have needed his father's permission,
which, according to his friends at the time, would certainly have
been refused.

In 1918, he abandoned the pedantic, pedestrian teaching that was then being dispensed at the rue de Turbigo and tried to enter the Lycée Condorcet. He was refused and so gave up any idea of taking the *bachot*, with its passport to a secure future. As the long holiday of the war years came to a close, the young Malraux embarked on another.

The young man of seventeen who was leaving war and school behind him was serious and reserved, full of ambition and restless energy, in search of the world and of himself.

Quoting Malraux in his *Journal* (27 March 1930), Julien Green writes: 'Between eighteen and twenty, life is like a market where one buys values, not with money, but with acts. Most men buy nothing . . .' Malraux threw himself on to this 'market' enthusiastically.

From 1919 to 1921, this boy, almost entirely alone, without the support of family or friends, more or less uprooted, with no faith, no real convictions, no connections, no certificates or degrees, no properly based education, rich only in his burning intelligence, an extraordinary ragbag accumulation of knowledge, an appetite for beauty and glory and a great power of attraction, was to gain access to that tiny world which, from the Place du Tertre to the rue Campagne-Première, produced practically everything that was being written, painted and composed in Paris, and well beyond.

> Long before I was sixteen, I wanted to become a great writer. But my friends and I were convinced that to be a great writer, or a great painter, one must be *maudit*, an outcast. One had to go hungry, in the best traditions of Baudelaire and the Symbolists . . . In my aspirations, the feeling of revolt was much stronger than a desire for notoriety.[5]

Since one had to exist and make one's mark in this vain, absurd world, why not try one's hand at what one knew best? The young Malraux knew about one thing at least – books. From the age of ten, when he began to work his way through the stock of the local library and ransack the bookstalls of the Quai Voltaire, he had read widely and voraciously. With the help of his prodigious memory, his ability to savour the page, to plunder it for a turn of phrase, with his taste for the elaborate, the eccentric, the unusual, he had built up a culture of his own of encyclopedic scope and proportions.

Towards the end of 1917, an odd character called René-Louis Doyon had opened a bookshop in the galerie de la Madeleine, at the corner with the rue Boissy d'Anglas. Under the sign of 'La Connaissance', this shop specialised in the buying and selling of rare books. After a difficult beginning, Doyon had managed to find a clientèle: the fall in the value of currency had led the local bourgeois residents to invest their money in less precarious commodities. A rare edition of Mallarmé or Huysmans was worth more than a portfolio of Russian stocks and shares. But these articles had to be sought out.

Eighteen months after Doyon's bookshop opened, the young Malraux, who had already made two or three incursions into this magic cave and delighted in the air of refinement that reigned there – he was now calling himself 'the Mandarin' and signing his writings with this name – came and offered his services. Already a very talented dealer, he was well equipped to supply Doyon with the rare articles he sought – a Chateaubriand first edition perhaps, or a de Sade.

For nearly a year, André Malraux acted as Doyon's chief buyer, earning enough money in the end to leave his family's gloomy apartment at Bondy and move first to the Hôtel Lutetia, in the boulevard Raspail, then to a small bedsitter in the rue Brunel, near the Étoile. His father, whom the war had not cured of his jovial instability, gave him money from time to time, but André refused to ask his mother for anything. He hated having to count every penny, and to his natural generosity was added a taste for ostentation.

Through their interchange first of books, then of ideas and opinions, the ingenious Doyon discovered in Malraux the man he needed to carry out a more ambitious project: for a long time he had dreamt of founding a review. Now, with the help of his young friend, this could be done. In January 1920 there emerged the first number of *La Connaissance*, in which André Malraux published his first article 'Les origines de la poésie cubiste' (*La Connaissance*, no. 1), before moving on to work for another publisher, Simon Kra, who owned the Éditions du Sagittaire.

It was a strange firm. Kra's son, Lucien, was an ex-juggler who, under the name of Jack Ark, had performed at the Olympia music hall in happier, pre-war days. In the book trade his gifts as an illusionist worked wonders. The young Malraux took to this serious practical-joke business like a fish to water. He discovered two little-known fragments by de Sade, *Les Amis du crime* and *Le Bordel de Venise*, and prepared a generously illustrated edition, which, for that reason, sold extremely well. Indeed, Malraux was becoming more and more interested in illustration: he became a friend of Galanis, who took him out of the world of semi-clandestine small presses and directed his energies to more respectable horizons.

But after Doyon and Kra, Malraux was to cross the path of a third buccaneer of letters, Florent Fels, who founded the review *Action*. Fels didn't always behave very well towards Malraux, but one cannot dispute the vitality, ingenuity and diversity of his review. Its pages were regularly filled with work by such names as Max Jacob, Cendrars, Aragon, Cocteau, Radiguet, Eluard, Tzara, Artaud, as well as the composer Erik Satie, the painter Derain, and the new Russian writers Gorky, Ehrenburg, Blok and Karleja.

It was a 'left-wing' review, of course – if one views as left-wing (and at the time the left itself certainly did) the radical questioning of bourgeois values and the established order. It might be said that its position was closer to anarchism, except that it counted among its contributors men like Gorky, Blok and Ehrenburg, then regarded as 'Bolshevik writers'. Victor Serge, who had moved from anarchism to support for the Soviet Union, was also a contributor. In the atmosphere of the 'sanitary cordon' around the USSR that reigned in 1920–1, to publish Gorky was tantamount to spreading the virus and waving the Red Flag.

Did Malraux see things in this light? Perhaps not. His own work on the review was of the most apolitical kind. But he knew what was going on around him: socially, *Action* gave off a smell of sulphur. Malraux was certainly to see the real thing, three years later, in Indo-China.

From the first number, Fels made his position clear: he published an article entitled 'In Praise of Landru' (at the time of the trial of the so-called 'French Bluebeard') by Georges Gabory, then the most flamboyant of André Malraux's friends. Gabory was not given to half-measures. Praising Landru as a 'precursor', and criticising him only for using 'outworn methods', he proclaimed the right to murder for superior individuals, for 'all those who hold their heads above the human sea'.

It was not until the third number, in April 1920, that Malraux published anything of his own in *Action*. Two months after the publication of his first piece, in *La Connaissance* (he was still working with Doyon), he set out to reveal 'La genèse des *Chants de Maldoror*'. The surprising thing about this short piece is not so much the carefree way in which Malraux handles the documentation – he is not, and will never be, an archivist – but the acidity of his attitude towards Lautréamont, then regarded as little less than a god by the younger writers. He speaks ironically of this 'railway clerk's Baudelaireanism' and concludes his article with the abrupt question, 'What is the literary value of a method?' What seems to have interested Malraux above all in this precursor of Surrealism was his life-style. The article begins with three significant words: 'Hating his family . . .' Isn't that the clue to what Malraux and Lautréamont have in common? Malraux didn't exactly hate his family, but he understood very well why a man might do so.

In later numbers, one finds other pieces by the young Malraux – 'Mobilités', 'Prologue', 'Le pompier du jeu de massacre', the first fragment of a later collection of writings. His work at this time was cast very much in the manner of Max Jacob and Laforgue. And the study entitled 'Aspect d'André Gide', begun in *Action* no. 12 (the last), and unfortunately interrupted – the rest should have appeared over two more numbers – earned him a letter from Gide himself, who praised his 'unusual penetration and perspicacity'.[6] We shall return to this later.

Action played an important part in the life of the young Malraux. Although he did not meet there with Max Jacob, Galanis, or Fernand Fleuret, his first masters, the review did introduce him to a group of people who represented the best, the most vital literature of his time, and provided him with a living alternative to the bits and pieces of knowledge he could have picked up in libraries. It was there, too, that he met Clara, and the first friends who were not simply good listeners: the scholarly Pascal Pia, who was to cross his path many times in the future, and Georges Gabory. The author of 'In Praise of Landru' had acquired a notoriety that impressed Malraux for a time. For over a year (1920–1), the period of young André's most extreme 'dandyism', right up to his marriage to Clara, they were inseparable.

According to Gabory, it was always Malraux who paid on their outings together. Gabory, who had no money at all, was astonished that his friend was already rich, or at least always had money, 'which he spent, unlike most people with money, whether writers or not'. Malraux took him out to lunch at Larue's or Marguery's, or at Noel Peters's, a then fashionable, exotically decorated restaurant in the passage de l'Opéra: '. . . *Sole normande* and *Chateaubriand aux pommes* . . . Pouilly fuissé, Pommard or Corton . . . brandy, a Havana, euphoria . . .' And Gabory remembers a club in the place de Ravignan, *La petite Chaumière*, which was frequented by the best-known 'queens' of the day: 'We were young, Malraux and I, easily attracted by the spectacle of depravity, whether real or pretended. Malraux had lent Sade's *Juliette ou les prospérités du vice* to Gabory, who had somewhat bolder ideas on the subject of eroticism than his own. Clara tells how Gabory defined himself as a *'lesbien'*, a he-Lesbian![7]

With his silk-lined cloaks and a rose in his button-hole, Malraux was still at the stage of a vaguely subversive, but mysteriously ostentatious dandyism. This kind of attitude would normally have taken him to one of the established publishers and, perhaps, to an American-style marriage into oil wells or copper mines. But there was more to Malraux than that – and he had other friends. There was René Latouche, for example, a clerk from Clichy-la-Garenne, who, indeed, had introduced him to Georges Gabory. He was a small, lame young man who thought of nothing but literature. Why did he decide to take his own life one day in the marshlands of Brittany? Malraux was very fond of him: seven years later, after experiencing a great many ups and downs in his own life, and having made many other friends, it was to him that he dedicated *Les Conquérants*.

At this time Malraux also met Marcel Arland, who was to become one of the guiding lights of the *Nouvelle Revue Française*, and Daniel-Henry Kahnweiler. The great promoter of Cubism was of German nationality and for that reason had spent the war years in Switzerland. On his return to Paris in 1920, he found that his collections had been sequestrated. In September 1920, he opened a new gallery and it was there that Max Jacob introduced him to the young Malraux, who, having more or less broken with Lucien Kra, agreed at once to take over the de-luxe editions that Kahnweiler was planning. In a few months, books by Max Jacob, Radiguet, Satie and Reverdy were published and the first book by André Malraux – and in what company for a nineteen-year-old beginner – illustrated by Juan Gris, Georges Braque, Fernand Léger . . .

The great dealer was to be not only Malraux's first publisher (in association with André Simon). He was also an admirable promoter and aesthetic guide. The young man did not have to meet Kahnweiler before coming to love painting, especially painting that is addressed to the intelligence. But without Kahnweiler would he have learnt to appreciate Derain and Picasso, Braque and Léger as he did?

But the greatest influence of all on the young Malraux was Max Jacob – Max the enchanter, Max the swindler, Max the inventor, charming, outrageous, indignant, facetious, touching by turns.

Over these immediate post-war years, marked by the Dada exhibition, the flowering of jazz, the appearance of Radiguet, the reign of Cocteau, the exploits in the boxing ring of Georges Charpentier and the lessons of Dr Freud, this tiny figure exercised an indefinable, limitless influence. Over and above talent – and his was great – the little man with the huge eyes beneath the Romanesque arches of his coal-black eyebrows possessed something else, something rarer, that we might call imagination – a mixture of restlessness and flair, anxiety and vital optimism, lack of balance and a sense of harmony that made him an incomparable master of demolition, and of architecture.

A virulent clown, the sarcastic prior of some very mendicant order, with only one hate in the world: Symbolism, with its nebulous, shapeless sententiousness. But in formal matters he was more demanding than even Mallarmé or Valéry. He was, between the disappearance of Apollinaire and the appearance of Breton, the master of French poetry. As such, Malraux saw him, admired him, followed him, and sometimes made himself his docile echo.

'When Malraux came to offer Max Jacob the first fruits of his mind, according to the ritual observed by newcomers to the circle, he was so well dressed – kid gloves, cane with tassel, pearl tie-pin – that he might have been taken for a Sunday visitor . . .' That was in November 1919.

Georges Gabory, who relates this incident,[8] does not say whether Max made fun of so much affectation, but he probably did not: although he wore what looked like a sack himself, he did not scorn those who put on their best clothes in his honour. Moreover, he was far from indifferent to the beauty of young men, and although he must have soon realised that the young man with the tie-pin was not of those beloved by old Buonarotti, he certainly found the precociously Baudelairean gaze of his eighteen-year-old visitor to his taste.

They continued to see a great deal of one another. Malraux would walk up the Butte Montmartre to the little house in the rue Gabrielle where the poet lived, in a condition bordering on poverty. Arm-in-arm, they would redescend to 'La mère Anceau's', a cheap restaurant, where, seated at a table covered in oil-cloth, they would sip their *mominette* (absinthe) and regale themselves with Max's favourite dish, *navarin aux pommes* (mutton stew with potatoes). André Malraux preferred the damask tablecloth at Larue's or the china service at Noel Peters's to the thick glasses and paper napkins of 'Mère Anceau's'. He was not always able to conceal his preferences, which brought him a certain amount of ragging from his companions.

Everything Malraux wrote at this period, right up to his departure for Indo-China, is placed under the sign of Max. From his first article devoted to 'Cubist poetry' – of which the author of *Le Cornet à dés* was obviously the inspiration as well as the principal subject – to his first book, *Lunes en papier*, expressly dedicated to Max Jacob, Malraux drew everything, directly or indirectly, from the little man of the rue Gabrielle. But what other guide could a young man, in love with literature, with aesthetic innovation, with liberation of the mind and freedom of behaviour, have sought in 1919?

André Malraux himself answered this question in June 1972:

At twenty, we underwent certain aesthetic influences – the most important was that of Apollinaire, which was taken over in a sense by Max Jacob – and influences of a quite different kind, stemming essentially from Nietzsche, who, for us, was something of a giant . . .

Laforgue and Lautréamont also meant a great deal to us. Above all there was Corbière – a terrific fellow. But he was almost impossible to find in those days. When I met Breton he hadn't read *Les Amours jaunes.* I had, of course . . .

The Surrealists? My distance from them was mainly topographical. My first rather dotty books, like *Lunes en papier,* came before the movement. When the movement got going I was in Indo-China, quite otherwise engaged. So I wasn't in on it. By the time I got back, the Surrealists had won their battle. What was the point of joining a fight that was already over and won? In fact, for us, in those early post-war years, the three great French writers were Claudel, Gide and Suarès . . .[9]

So that was how André Malraux appeared at twenty (and still appears fifty years later, as a result of some choice that is difficult to date), on the eve of a marriage that was not to leave his cultural world unaffected and of adventures that were to change his life.

A prudently subversive dandy, a selfconsciously 'lunatic' poet, an ingenious critic, a scholar of incredible erudition, a seeker after unusual sensations, an aesthete of tireless curiosity, he threw himself into the movement centred around the 'Boeuf sur le Toit' to an excessive degree, yet placed above everything those highly disciplined painters, Braque and Derain.

At this point when, with his twentieth year, that period of two years that he claimed to be that of 'the acquisition of values' had come to an end, what had he done, what had become of André

Malraux, this semi-self-taught young man, with a semi-absent
father, with no degree, a semi-publisher of long-lost books,
semi-author of small bits and pieces, semi-poor, but given to
extravagant gestures?

He was a dandy, but still a bookworm; he was ambitious, but
in a Stendhalian rather than a Balzacian way – he wished not so
much to succeed as to assert himself against his modest background, his lack of roots, the break-up of his family and the
absurdity of time. What had he 'asserted' since he had given up
school – though not his schoolfriends – and embarked on that
aimless life, wandering from bookshop to bar, from library to
museum, that endless holiday, interrupted by odd periods of
feverish study and indiscriminate reading that had taken the
place for him of the university, and which enabled him to learn
more about Sophocles, Michelet and Caravaggio than he
would have heard in the rue des Écoles?

He had, it is true, attended lectures at the École des langues
orientales in the rue de Lille – a lecture in Chinese here, another
in Persian there – but he was never actually enrolled. He even
tried the École du Louvre, but soon abandoned the somewhat
elementary lessons for other, more challenging pursuits.
Above all, he read, he read insatiably, he wandered through
the galleries and museums, he made contacts. Without having written anything of note, there he was at the centre of
the tiny planet of books, writers and critics, a restorer of failing
reputations, a resurrector of the forgotten, something of an
arbiter, something of a sycophant, a prompter in a shadow
theatre in which he believed less than any of the others, but in
which he was gradually building up a 'personality' for himself
rather than a true self.

Three texts seem to reveal what might be called his 'pink and
black' period, the period when his critical intelligence and his
frantic search for synthesis pierce through the selfconscious
whimsy typical of a young writer of the time: his first article,
published in the January 1920 number of *La Connaissance*, on
'the origins of Cubist poetry'; his first book, *Lunes en papier*,
published in the spring of 1921; and his first essay, 'On the
Painting of Galanis', presented at an exhibition in March 1922.
There will be our evidence.

When Symbolism, having reached the stage of senility as a literary movement, was splashing about in the lapping waves that preceded its final dissolution, young men who had no wish to publish flabby (but 'acceptable') poems, mere trifles weighed down by a prodigious battery of footnotes, set out in search of an artist capable of producing a body of work whose new aesthetic could be discovered without plagiarism.

These were the first lines of the *La Connaissance* article on Cubist poetry – the first lines published by André Malraux.

There is a period quality about them that seems rather dated today. Like most of the writing published by the very young – he was only eighteen at the time – it is overwritten and over-allusive. But the rest of the piece has both verve and penetration.

Pointing out that Rimbaud's influence on the Symbolists was 'slight', and approving that of Apollinaire, who inaugurated a 'modern poetry of wit in which the object (instead of standing for something else) sometimes achieved autonomy', he ends by singling out three writers who, following in the footsteps of this 'instigator', emerge as the inventors of Cubist poetry: Max Jacob, Pierre Reverdy and Blaise Cendrars.

Max Jacob brought to Cubism a delicate irony, an almost crazy mysticism, a sense of the oddity of everyday things and a destruction of the possibility of any logical ordering of facts.

Of all the Cubists, Pierre Reverdy was the most certain of what he wanted and the most obscure for the uninitiated . . . The ordinary poem is a *development*; the poem inaugurated by Reverdy was a synthesis . . . he inflicted on his works a surgical stripping down . . .

After publishing *Pâques*, a poem of a grave, almost painful beauty, sometimes reminiscent of Rimbaud . . . Cendrars brought out three slim volumes in which one finds an original view, above all a paroxystic expression of modern life obtained without verbalism. Since then, Cendrars has published *Neuf poèmes élastiques*, in which this expression has become more marked and is mingled with an odd sense of humour . . .

Lunes en papier, which Malraux began to write early in 1920 and which he published in April 1921, when he was not yet nineteen, in a series that included works by Max Jacob, Reverdy, Satie and Radiguet, is a sort of fairy-tale inside out, a dream journey, a mechanical ballet, an allegorical masquerade: a poster for 1921 in which one finds everyone and no one, a little period object, the type of literary curiosity likely to interest scholars and specialists in the 'decadent' fringes of the Dada movement.

It was Daniel-Henry Kahnweiler (on the advice of his chief editor, André Malraux) who published *Lunes en papier*. The work appeared under the imprint of the 'Galerie Simon' (Simon was a partner of Kahnweiler's). It was printed in a very large format (about $13\frac{1}{2}$ x 9 inches), on very good quality paper, with a fine, very dark Cubist woodcut by Fernand Léger on the cover, much graver in mood than the text inside. On the half-title page was a dedication – to Max Jacob – and this announcement:

> A little book in which are related some of man's lesser-known struggles and also a journey among familiar, but strange objects. All told in a truthful manner and decorated with woodcuts, also very veracious, by Fernand Léger.

The young Malraux had developed a taste for certain Montmartre evenings in the place Ravignan. He actually spent more time with his friend Chevasson at the Tabarin music hall than at the Petite Chaumière. It was there, according to Gabory, that Malraux picked up the girl he was living with. It was there, too, in the profusion and glitter of coloured lamps, in the shabby gaudy little revues, with their cancan and their magicians, that Malraux found the idea of representing the world as a spectacle of masks, grimaces and illusion – André Malraux did not have a very exalted idea of the world in 1920. That Death in dinner jacket and those giggling, playful creatures belong to the blackest, most uncompromising nihilism.

We ought to quote a few lines from this almost unknown text:

> Whenever a heart was plucked out, its tail bled a little: but it healed and, light and slender as an arrow, a long stem grew

out of it like a soap bubble out of a pipe, and went and planted itself in the earth . . . So many birds fell and so many layers of lacquer glazed the river that it was soon a lock of golden hair in which the highlights glided and shifted continually . . .

An animal scent, sharp as ether, accompanied the wisps of of hair as they passed by; when one of the sins breathed it, it seemed to him as if fruits made of flesh wafted to his lips, and when he bit into these fruits they burst and spattered sweet blood over his face . . .

But there is also a tragic note that foreshadows the true Malraux: 'We find the world bearable only because we are used to bearing with it. It is imposed upon us when we are too young to defend ourselves.'

Malraux now speaks of this first book of his with majestic unselfconsciousness: 'I wrote *Lunes en papier* when I was twenty: a *gloire de café*.'[10]

Of all these adolescent exercises, all this apprentice work, all this Malraux before Malraux, what has survived best is the first essay that the young man devoted to the plastic arts. Asked by his friend Galanis in March 1922 to write a preface for an exhibition of his works at the La Licorne gallery, in the rue La Boétie, the young Malraux found his true style, his true mode of thinking, at a stroke. Here, in a few lines, is almost everything that the author of *Les Voix du Silence* was to develop thirty years later:

From the fact that a particular culture may provide an artist with certain means of self-expression, may even guide his choice in the expression of his means, one can only deduce logically that expression is subordinated to birth. It is out of the conjunction of the Greek genius, the French genius and the Italian genius that this art [Galanis'] is born . . . No artist is created entirely out of the French tradition; no Greek artist is entirely created out of the Greek tradition. We can feel only by comparison. He who knows *Andromaque* and *Phèdre* will gain a better idea of the French genius by reading *A Midsummer Night's Dream* than by reading all the other tragedies by Racine. The Greek genius will be better understood by comparing a Greek statue with an Egyptian or Asiatic statue than by an acquaintance with a hundred Greek statues.

Has André Malraux written anything else about art, over the past fifty years, than those last two sentences, which emerge with a strange, urgent force from a previously rather heavy prose? At twenty, he was already possessed of the art of seeing, a system of evaluation, a technique and a knowledge of the plastic arts that were as astonishing as they were effective. This young man in search of everything had at least discovered the art of seeing.

2 Clara

'A YOUNG man was sitting among the thirty other guests at a banquet table and it was he who for years and years was to mean more to me than anyone else on earth. Because of him I was to relinquish everything, as the Gospel requires those that love to leave father and mother . . .[1]

The woman writing about her youth forty years later was then called Clara Goldschmidt. She was twenty, of German origin, hardly a recommendation in those early post-war years, and Jewish, which didn't help either twenty years after the Dreyfus case. Her father had died shortly before the outbreak of war. Her family, which was rich but not excessively so, came from Magdeburg, where, returning each year for the summer holidays, the little girl had experienced an antisemitism more virulent than that she was to undergo in France (before 1940). It should be noted, however, that one of her brothers, while fighting at the front in 1917, learnt that steps were being taken to denaturalise him and his family.

Yet it was a family that had managed to emerge from its fears and find temporary security. Thanks to the generosity of an uncle who had made a fortune in the leather trade, they lived in a fairly large, two-storey house in the avenue des Chalets, at Auteuil, near where Jaurès had once lived: the Goldschmidt children remembered playing with the children of the Socialist leader.

Clara lived with her mother and two brothers in a fairly free-and-easy atmosphere. Though she herself had remained religious in a fairly vague way, Mme Goldschmidt gave her daughter

no religious education. Clara had been very spoilt by her father
– in that world, daughters were stamped by the double hallmark
of uselessness and joy, of everything in life that escaped the law
of necessity: happiness was their justification. Her mother had
maintained this tradition and (apart from an understandable
reaction after the unfortunate Cambodia affair) Mme Goldschmidt was never to waver in the understanding she showed
her daughter and, later, her daughter's companion. That understanding was more than a sign of the times: it came from a
generous individual.

In 1921, Clara, with her beautiful grey-green eyes, her figure
a little on the short side, her acute intelligence, an avid, omni-
vorous desire for the things of the mind, her friends those that
one would expect of an upper-middle-class Jewish girl at the
time, with all the advantages and disadvantages that this implies, was already something of a character in her own right.
She had contributed (at first as a translator) to the review *Action*
which had just published her translation of a poem by Johannes
Becher. Indeed, it was as fellow contributors to this review that
she and André Malraux met at a dinner organised by Florent
Fels in a restaurant near Palais-Royal.

André was not sitting next to Clara, but next to one of her
friends, who was by no means unimpressed by him. Clara took
note of him:

> They were talking – or, to be more exact, he was talking.
> He was a very tall thin youth and his eyes were too large,
> their pupils did not quite fill the immense rounded globes; a
> white line showed under the washed-green iris. Later I was
> to say to him, 'Your eyes have reached their limit'; later I
> was to think of his sailor ancestors, who must have had that
> faraway, absorbed, gaze; and later I thought – stupidly
> enough no doubt – 'He can't look people in the eye.'

After the dinner, Clara and her friend accompanied the boy
with the over-large eyes and the poet Ivan Goll to a nearby
nightclub, 'Le Caveau révolutionnaire'. 'It was under red,
white and blue garlands, symbolizing revolution that I exchanged my first words with my future companion,' Clara
remarks, adding that he danced badly and only asked her to

dance at the end of the evening, after confiding to her that her friend had asked him not to pay any attention to the girl with the grey-green eyes. 'Was it true?' Clara asks. 'Or was he already bending the truth a little?'

A few days later, they met again at Claire and Ivan Goll's, a meeting-place for painters and poets of the *Action* group, like Chagall and Delaunay. They sat together near a window, whispering. She was amused by his voice, 'with its slight Parisian accent, which said very quickly curiously obscure things'; he seemed convinced that she was an initiate of the same sect as himself. He talked about the medieval poets, whom he adored at the time, and the French satirical poets; and she talked about Hölderlin and Novalis. And they met on common ground with Nietzsche, Dostoevsky and Tolstoy (she notes that he hadn't yet read *War and Peace* – she had). He spoke of Spain and El Greco; she of Italy and 'her' painters. 'I am going back to Italy in August,' she remarked. 'I'll go with you,' he answered. They had been brought together – it had all happened with almost pre-ordained ease.

He took her to his favourite museums, and introduced her to the work of Lautrec. She showed him the strange wonders of the Musée du Trocadéro, which were later to play an important role in his life. She took him round the Bois de Boulogne, taught him to row. They went to the races – they both had a passion for gambling. The young man said to his girl friend: 'I only know one person as intelligent as you – Max Jacob.'

And Clara adds, half in jest: 'He really did have a taste for erudition: indeed what was there that he didn't have a taste for? Later he said to me, "If I had not met you I might have become a mere bookworm." ' She was, and still is, ready to believe this. 'Who can tell? As our years turned out, he became (the future will judge whether it was for a long time or a short) a wonderful soldier of fortune and a great writer, at the same time an amateur of genius. Obsessed by Nietzsche, of course, and that even before we knew each other. And dividing people into the "amusing" and "unamusing" as early as that, too, and accusing the Surrealists of taking themselves seriously.'[2]

There's a lot of insight in what Clara says, and a certain sharpness of tone, too. She wrote her book after a somewhat

stormy period, alone and cut off from Malraux's time of glory.
But there is no bitterness, no rancour and, above all, no hitting
below the belt. It is clear that she was aware of the young man's
weaknesses, as well as his gifts, from the beginning, and knew
what she was letting herself in for. She still saw him more as a
'bookworm' than as a true scholar, 'ingenious' rather than
'cultured' – and a misogynist to boot. But she also saw that this
semi-opportunist of art was consumed by something that was
at once a passion for beauty, a taste for freedom, a thirst for
intellectual intercourse and true courage.

It was a Sunday.

Clara had dressed with great care: 'Why had I dressed like
that? To give him pleasure. I felt that he loved luxury and
pretty things . . .'[3] He took her to a 'low dance hall' in the rue
Broca, where they didn't pass unnoticed . . . a pimp got Clara
to dance with him. And then it was the young man's turn:

> It was rather as though I were alone on a boat with this
> young man whom nothing, I thought, would ever satisfy.
> He wanted everything – at least that is what I imagined – and
> I, too, I wanted everything, beginning with him . . . We left:
> we were going to walk side by side in the street. The door
> banged behind us. Some men coming out of the dance hall
> jostled past us as from behind. 'Look out!' said my com-
> panion. I stood out too clearly in that almost unlighted
> street . . . The outlines of the men began coming towards
> us . . . My friend thrust me behind him with his left arm, and
> he kept it stretched out to protect me better. He plunged his
> right hand into his pocket, and after the others had fired
> there came a revolver shot from our side. It all happened
> very quickly: then there was silence. And there was my
> protector's left hand, that I was holding in mine – wounded,
> our first close embrace . . .
>
> In the cab I felt him close to me, but perhaps not closer
> than when that harmony had sprung up between us at the
> reciting of the poem. We had gone through our first series of
> trials: we had experienced danger and courage together, and
> solidarity, union, in the face of others . . .[4]

The reader must bear in mind that this high-flown account

concerns two wide-eyed adolescents, that those gunshots, at nineteen, broke something unreal and childish and brought these two dreamers a little way beyond their dreams, into the immediate presence of short-lived pain and real danger.

'Everything remained plain and straightforward between us; and it was still so in his room on that Fourteenth of July when the rockets tore open the sky outside – a bridal bouquet . . .'[5] The next afternoon, the young man did not turn up at his appointment, not because he did not care for 'tomorrow's faces', but because he had gone to ask his father's permission to marry, which was 'refused pointblank'. Because Clara was of German origin? Because André was too young? Nobody really knows.

As Clara's mother got off the train that was about to take her daughter to Florence, André slipped into the place left vacant beside the girl. A fellow traveller, and a friend of Clara's elder brother, realised the situation and André got on his high horse: 'I suggested a little duel!' After all, they were setting out for the country of d'Annunzio!

From Florence they sent a telegram to the Goldschmidts announcing their forthcoming marriage. To which her mother replied: 'Return immediately without your friend.'[6] Naturally, they did no such thing. And they moved from Giottos to Ucellos, from the Signoria to the Uffizi, from the banks of the Arno to San Miniato, like everybody else. The young man dazzled his companion by the acuity of his eye, his visual voracity, the virtuosity of his scholarship and his prodigious memory. In a museum he would rush to the finest exhibit, to the Donatello or the Cimabue, 'as if he was in danger', taking it in very rapidly – too rapidly – and finding possible meanings in it. There, in a state of sensual exaltation, he could drink deep of all the things he had talked about for years without having seen them.

Clara, who refused to be entranced by Venice, in order to assert her own personality in the face of her guide, discovered that half her companion's mind was in the future, he 'always compared what was in front of him with what he had not yet seen but could imagine'. (Of course, the towers of San Gimi-niano had to remind him of New York!) 'Every stage of our journey meant a desire for the next: Was that the essence of his being – this movement from one desire towards another . . . What lonely childhood was my presence banishing? What humiliations was I wiping out? What hope suddenly arising in him was he putting into his love? At that moment it seemed to me that for him our love was as it were a conversion, a break from his previous relationship with the world.'[7]

A break? Whatever it was, the company of a human being whom he loved with carnal intelligence and shared experience led him out of the tense solitude among the crowd in which he had lived up till then, among friends he had to astonish, mandarins he had to please and possible rivals that had to be pushed aside. Clara cured him neither of dandyism, nor of careerism, still less of pedantry, but the figure was to step out of the canvas upon which he had flattened himself, as a somewhat contrived eccentric, into a three-dimensional world, involving risk, everyday human relations, social responsibilities and economic constraints.

They returned to Paris. At home, Clara's mother asked her, quite simply: 'Are you happy?' Her brother's attitude was more rigid: 'You have dishonoured us. I am leaving for America!' In fact, he stayed in Paris. André's father became resigned to the marriage and observed: 'She dresses very simply for a Jewess.' Clara wanted to accompany her civil marriage with 'something in the religious line . . . like Laforgue.' 'All right,' said André, 'but we'll go to the Protestant church, a synagogue, the Catholic church, to a mosque, a pagoda . . .' She protested. 'You'll end up in a convent,' he concluded. As they were leaving the town hall, Aunt Jeanne remarked to Clara: 'You ought to have picked the father. He is much nicer than the son . . .' They agreed to divorce in six months.

What did she know about him? 'I asked no questions, ever. Though a few illusions, a few inconsistencies, a few "pathetic trimmings" . . . I could make out a sad childhood, one that was not far away from poverty, perhaps . . . My rich-bitch instinct quickly pierced through a certain amount of bluff. Nobody had to tell me that his mother had never lived at Claridge's, as he asserted, nor that his grandmother had a little grocer's shop at Bondy. I . . . did my best to accept that truth should wear different faces for him and for me . . .'[8]

They set off again, from Strasbourg to Prague, where they were moved by their meeting with some old rabbis, and to Vienna, where the spectacle of the 'joyless streets' in the working-class districts brought back to Clara memories of Jaurès and Romain Rolland. (At which André remarked: 'You're one of those people who want to kill everybody for the good of a few!' Malraux in 1922 . . . It was, of course, the time of Kronstadt.)

At Magdeburg they were the guests of Clara's grandfather, who congratulated himself on having worked so well for both countries during the war – he had had grandsons in both armies. He read Heine so well – according to this boy who had come from France without knowing a word of German –that he made a firm friend. In Berlin, they made enthusiastic discoveries of *The Cabinet of Dr Caligari*, Spengler and Freud – and Clara picked up *The Psychoanalytical Diary of a Little Girl*, which she translated two years later. From Antwerp, where they were fascinated by the matter-of-fact behaviour of the prostitutes, they went on to Bruges, then to Ostend, where André Malraux, somewhat intimidated, called on one of the men who had most obsessed his imagination, James Ensor. At Ensor's, he told an astonished Clara, he had seen living sirens – and Clara believed him, momentarily. André, half believing his own stories, remained dazzled by the shellfish shop that had been run by the painter's mother, and which the painter himself had kept intact.

Back in Paris, they picked up the threads where they had left off, but in a somewhat one-sided way. The friends they saw were almost invariably his friends – André did not care for her best friends, the Golls – and above all Marcel Arland, to whom, on the eve of the wedding, André had written: 'I'm getting married. See you in three weeks.' But before settling down, the young Malraux had to dispose of an awkward possibility that hung over him: military service.

Summoned by the authorities to Strasbourg, André and his wife set off for Alsace with Clara's young brother, who had friends there. André Malraux learnt that he had been drafted into the hussars (for which recruits must not exceed a maximum height of 5′ 6″ – he was 5′ 11″). He had his head shaved, but found no dolman – the short jacket worn by the hussars –

that would fit him, while the trousers looked like shorts on
him. He complained of heart trouble, which turned out to be
justified, since he had managed to swallow an enormous
quantity of caffeine. At last, to his relief, he was told by a
major (who was reprimanded by the brother-in-law for his
pains) that he had something better to do than disguise himself
as a giant hussar in the barracks of the Robertsau. He was
turned down for the army on medical grounds.

The next problem was what they were to live on. In André's
view, there were three ways of earning a living: the cinema
industry, the publishing of erotic literature and the Stock
Exchange. After their visit to Berlin and their delighted discovery of the Expressionist work of Lang, Wiene and Murnau,
Malraux invested some of his money in buying films, which,
with the help of Ivan Goll, he claimed he would distribute in
France. But he was constantly being refused the certificates
necessary for their distribution. In the end he gave up and con-
tented himself with private showings of his favourite films.

The publishing of erotic works of literature was nothing new
to the young Malraux. Clara explains that since their wandering
life was scarcely compatible with his earlier work as a publisher's editor, he soon settled for 'the production of bawdy
texts, with no less bawdy illustrations . . . I found nothing
shocking in that enterprise . . . And anyway it amused me all
the more in that it involved an element of danger . . . Ever since
I was twenty or so, I have always lived in such a way that if
some representative of the law knocked on my door there'd be
at least one good reason to incriminate me: the presence of
some poor girl recovering from an abortion, opium or opium-
addict, forbidden books, illegal tracts, some man or woman on
the run, foreigners without papers . . .'[9]

With the decline in the erotic book publishing business, due
largely to the departure of Pia on military service, the main
source of income for the young couple in those years (1922–3)
was the Stock Exchange. Shortly after they were married, Clara
learned from André that everything they possessed (most of it
was hers anyway) had been used to buy shares: from then on,
when they were not travelling, a good part of their time was
spent in following the ups and downs in the shares they had

bought – practically all in a Mexican mining company, the Pedrazzini, which, ever since his father had given him the opportunity of attending one of its annual general meetings, had excited the young man's imagination. Their fortune grew and enabled them to lead the lives of wandering aesthetes that suited them so well. Between journeys abroad, they would go the rounds of the merchant banks, following the upward trends of Mexican shares. One evening, in a cinema, André whispered to Clara that they were practically millionaires . . .

Yet at the beginning of 1923 they learnt that they were ruined: their Mexican shares were worthless. All that remained of 'their past glory', says Clara, was a piece of paper. Two years of idle freedom, stylish living and aesthetic wanderings ended with this financial disaster.

The broodingly forceful young man of 1919 seems, in marrying, in allying himself with a bourgeois family, in sharing his life with a young woman accustomed to luxury, to have turned into a drawing-room illusionist. He had lost nothing of his dazzling zest, he had extended his intellectual register and he had become something other than a bookworm – all this was true. But his love of shocking people and his distaste for sustained effort had become more marked in his passage from the shop in the rue Blanche to the apartments of Auteuil, from the walks on the Butte Montmartre to the merchant banks around the Opéra, from the long walks through Paris to nights spent in sleeping-cars on his way to Venice or Brussels.

Between eighteen and twenty, André Malraux had acquired, in a haphazard but passionate way, the 'values' by which he wished to live. In the following two years, he seems rather to have dissipated them. His life with Clara had brought other rewards too, of course, and the immense perspectives that she had opened up for him on to German culture, on to the Expressionism of the 1920s, with Ivan and Claire Goll, for example, on to Italy and a certain kind of Italian painting – Giotto, Fra Angelico – which he had not previously cared for, her art of listening without losing all critical sense, the emulation of intelligence she introduced into his life, the sharpening of appetite she brought him – all this amounted to a broader, more mature outlook. But for the moment, this dandy, wishing at all costs to astonish, seems to have deflected the restless genius that was within him away from art and towards financial speculation, art tourism and a keen interest in business.

But what was he writing during this period? It was certainly not worthless, but it was hardly better than the apprentice scribblings published in 1920 by *La Connaissance* or *Lunes en papier*. At the time this little book was published, shortly before his marriage, the young Malraux had undertaken to write a new piece that he called 'Journal d'un pompier du jeu de massacre', part of which was published in *Action* in the late summer of 1921. He was also seeking his way on other levels, and the love of rigour, of a certain kind of order, which he admired in the work of Derain and Galanis, led him into some strange political excursions. Indeed, it was in 1923 that he wrote a preface to *Mademoiselle Monk* by Charles Maurras, the ideologist of the monarchist Right – he, Malraux, who was still linked with the review *Action,* which published Victor Serge and Gorky.

'Don't bother yourself with that,' Malraux told me in 1972. 'It's of no interest. Florent Fels was looking for an author, young if possible, to write a preface for this book. I agreed to do so by way of an exercise. I might equally well have written about Hegel . . .'[10]

Of course. But the text written by this young man is no mere 'exercise'. One cannot speak of wholehearted agreement, but there is an undoubted admiration. 'To pass from intellectual anarchism to the *Action Française*,' he writes of Maurras, 'is not to contradict oneself, but to construct . . . His work is a series of constructions intended to create or to maintain a harmony . . . He makes one admire order, because all order represents beauty and strength . . . In Greece and Italy, he loved with passion only what was to determine the mode of the French genius. Charles Maurras is one of the most powerful intellects at work today . . .'

In any case, the meeting between Malraux and Maurras was not the result of a bizarre invention on the part of Florent Fels. Clara notes that from the time of their escapade in Florence in 1921, André had read and got her to read passages from Maurras' *Anthinéa*. Antisemitic as its author was, she was considerably influenced by this work. 'The man who found "*Salut belle guerrière!*",' she wrote generously, 'can only be my enemy by mistake . . .'[11]

Mademoiselle Monk is not simply a book written in praise of Hellenism: it is a piece of political writing, and a very fine piece, in which Maurrasism is expressed with all too clear severity and weight. Malraux, who refers openly to *Action Française*, sees very clearly into this appeal for strong government and the affirmation of dominant personalities. Was this a forerunner of the temptation he felt in 1947 for an authoritarian régime based on a young generation inspired by ideas of 'order', 'energy' and 'beauty'? No, of course not. But there is just a touch of it there.

He is as ambiguous as ever. Almost simultaneously, in *Le Disque Vert*, he published an article entitled 'Ménalque' in praise of the anti-Maurras, Gide. What Malraux admired in Gide – and he admired Gide above all other contemporaries – was his combination of classical rigour and provocative freedom of mind, creative constraint and defiance.[12]

His indeterminate dislocated, 'moon-struck' side had, since his marriage, been transformed into an easy, not to say authoritative manner. But in many respects he was still an adolescent, dominated by his wife, and perhaps his tendency to verbal fireworks and to the dramatic gesture found a spur in a situation that must at times have seemed humiliating to him. Perhaps he overcompensated for such feelings. Clara Malraux has often admitted to feeling inferior to her dazzling companion. The reverse was also the case, at least until the end of 1933 and the sudden rise to fame of the author of *La Condition humaine*.[13]

What, then, did Malraux want? What was he looking for, apart from a convenient way of life? Virtually free of all family ties, professional obligations, ideological commitment, moral guidelines, he had emerged, at seventeen, in the little, inventive, anarchistic, cosmopolitan world of *avant-garde* literature, in the midst of Max Jacob, *Action* and Kahnweiler. He had traded in erotic literature, manipulated without excessive scruple documents of literary history, played the Stock Exchange and lived, at Montmartre and thereabouts, the life of a resourceful dandy.

He was already, in the bourgeois, pejorative sense of the word, an adventurer – and his wife's family, and even his hardly conformist wife, saw him as such. His marriage, which was at once a challenge to custom and a homage to the proprieties, had more to do with challenge than with the proprieties. This common enterprise, which so often has the effect of domesticating adventurers burdened with providing for the needs of the home, tended, in his case, to revive his audacity and to stir his wandering imagination rather than a concern for the everyday.

But one implicit compensation was at work within him. Whereas, draped in his velvet cloak, a rose in his buttonhole, cane in hand, he conducted himself in private life as a character of the anti-society, as a rebel and a flouter of proprieties, traditions and the established order, the intellectual was tending to move away from literary adventure, spontaneous poetry and automatic writing, towards a neoclassicism to which he felt drawn by the instinct for order and constraint that remained obstinately within him. He was already moving in the direction of the *NRF*, which, without ceasing to be a centre of innovation, was to become the bastion of what remained of French classicism.

The Malraux of 1923 was a dismembered, vacillating figure: a man who behaved in society as a *déclassé* and an artist moving ever closer to classical ideals of order. How could he resolve these contradictions? How could he find a new centre of gravity? Through forward flight, through defiance and danger. Through adventure, which combined the madness required to undertake it in the first place and the need to organise it in the second; the disorder of the situation and the order of the gesture; the uncertainty of the result and the discipline required in attaining it.

In adventure, which he was later to call the 'realism of romance',[14] Malraux the man set out to realise the romantic ideals that had imbued his adolescence.

PART II

DIVERTISSEMENT

---

3 The small change of revolt

CLARA and André had just learned of their financial ruin.

'You surely don't suppose I'm going to work,' said André.
'No, but . . . what . . .'
'You know the route from Flanders to Spain taken by the pilgrims to the shrine of St James of Compostela? . . . This route was studded with cathedrals, most of which have survived relatively intact. But in addition to these great churches there must have been innumerable small chapels, many of which have disappeared . . .'
What was he leading up to?
'Well, from Siam to Cambodia, all along the Royal Way from Dangrek to Angkor, there are large temples – and these have been located and described in the Inventory. But there must be others, still unknown even today . . . We go to some small temple in Cambodia, pick up a few statues and sell them in America. This will keep us going for two or three years . . .'[1]

And so the Malrauxs' Indo-Chinese adventure began – a mixture of École du Louvre lecture, café chat, idiotic gamble and put-up job. This Cambodia did not erupt into the Auteuil drawing-room quite by chance however. For André and Clara it was a familiar 'elsewhere'. Clara tells how her father, on the day he died – she was fourteen at the time – had promised her that she would see Angkor, and she had continued to believe it.

The couple had often visited a room in the Musée du Trocadéro that contained more or less authenticated works of art and other objects belonging to the Khmer civilisation. Then there was the Musée Guimet, where André had made friends with the curator, Joseph Hackin, a very fine scholar. Hackin enjoyed the company of this eloquent, impassioned young man. They would spend hours together talking over this or that ingenious idea that Malraux had picked up from a lecture at the École des langues orientales, perhaps, or from a conversation with some visitor passing through Paris.

The most remarkable of these visitors was André Salmony, who was working in the museum in Cologne. He had been sent by some mutual friend or other (Kahnweiler perhaps) and arrived at the Malrauxs', six months earlier, with an enormous briefcase under his arm. He informed the young couple (he was little more than thirty himself) that he was planning an exhibition of comparative art which, for once, would not confine itself to the masterpieces of Greek or Gothic culture, but would place side by side the most varied, most astonishing examples of different civilisations. A highly original notion at the time!

'He then took out a bundle of photographs, which he proceeded to handle with the skill of a cashier, spreading them out on the table, placing them side by side according to some subtle law of affinity,' Clara Malraux recalls.[2] 'It was the first time I'd seen a Thai sculpture. Then a marriage was formed before my eyes of a Han head and a Roman head. Deeply moved, we stood before these to us new affinities and wondered whether the will that had given rise to these works was directed at the same area of feeling, or whether, on the contrary, their kinship was purely formal. Salmony went away again, leaving behind some of these precious photographs, but leaving, within us, too, the intuition of a new way of seeing the world.'

About the same time, the ballet of the Court of Phnom Penh gave a few performances at the Paris Opéra. The splendid delicacy of the gestures, the sounds and the costumes enchanted the Malrauxs, who expressed their appreciation all the more vociferously in view of the general public's obvious unresponsiveness to these silky wonders. Thus, very slowly, there germinated within them the legend of the countries of the Theravada and the stones of Angkor. They read Pierre Loti and became entranced by his rich, highly coloured style; they poured over the Inventory of the École française d'Extrême-Orient.

André had not lost his skill at unearthing obscure texts in bookshop and library, and he soon came up with two articles that were to nourish and confirm his intuitions. The first, 'The Art of Indravarman', had appeared in 1919 in the *Bulletin de l'École française d'Extrême-Orient*. Its author, Henri Parmentier, was regarded at the time as one of the two or three leading experts on Khmer art. This short study stressed the originality of the works produced during the reign of this sovereign, that is, between the pre-classical period (seventh century) and that of Angkor (eleventh century). He instanced as an example of this refined art the little temple of Banteaï-Sre, which had been located and described by Lieutenant Marek in 1914, then by Demazure, and which Parmentier himself had studied on the spot in 1916. He praised it for its beauty and deplored its state of decrepitude.

Three years later, the *Revue archéologique*, in an article entitled 'Trésors mal gardés', revealed that the Fogg Museum at Harvard had just acquired a very fine head of the Buddha, a marvel of Khmer art, and concluded that 'given the vast quantity of Khmer sculpture and the difficulty of reaching the ruins of Angkor, one may accept without too much bad grace the emigration of these few specimens. But these losses must not become too numerous. *Caveant consules . . .*'[3]

This was just the sort of thing to fire Malraux's imagination: an abandoned temple containing wonderful works of art and losses that would still be accepted by the authorities 'without too much bad grace'. All these arguments, taken together, provided him with solid grounds for his project. His mind was made up. Moreover, the *caveant consules* advice called for immediate action. There was talk of new regulations, of a decree issued by the Governor-General of Indo-China on 21 August 1923 setting up a new commission of inquiry for the protection of the Khmer remains. Why wait until these works were placed under the explicit protection of the law?

André Malraux set out on a double quest: he needed some official mission that would 'cover' him in relation to the authorities and he also needed a potential buyer. He was very well

aware that the two things were incompatible and that, provided
with an official mission, it would be all the more reprehensible
to cash his finds (or his loot). But the two approaches remained
sufficiently vague in his mind (and in fact) to be capable of
being combined without hypocrisy or cynicism.

How objections were raised and then dismissed, how he
worked out his plans and how they materialised, is described in
some detail in *La Voie royale*, a novel in which two men, Perken,
the adventurer, and Claude Vannec, a young archaeologist,
attempt to discover and bring back for sale some wonders of
the Thai forest: they fight a savage tribe, the Stiengs, and
Perken, wounded by poisoned arrows, dies in a dream-like
mood of irony and despair.

This book is certainly not an autobiography (Claude is Malraux, but Perken is not Clara . . .), but the autobiographical
element is all the more evident today in that the romantic figure
of the grandfather has been authenticated in the *Antimémoires*.
The conversation on the ship to Indo-China between Claude
and Perken is very telling. Perhaps a few lines from it should be
quoted here:

> *Claude:* In the jungle between Laos and the sea, there are
> quite a number of temples Europeans know nothing about
> . . .
> *Perken:* Cassirer of Berlin paid five thousand marks for the
> two Buddhas Damrong gave me. But, as for looking for old
> sculpture . . .
> *Claude:* The Royal Way, the road that linked up Angkor and
> the lakes with the Menam river-basin . . . If you follow, by
> compass, the lines of the old road, you're bound to come on
> temples. Supposing Europe became covered with a dense
> forest, wouldn't it be absurd to imagine you could travel
> from Marseilles to Cologne by way of the Rhône and the
> Rhine, without coming across ruined churches? . . .
> *Perken:* The French administration, you know, hasn't much
> liking for . . .
> *Claude:* I've been sent here on a mission . . . Oh, unpaid, of
> course. Our ministries are obliging enough when it costs
> them nothing . . .

Perken: I know the ways of the French Administration. You don't belong to it, and they'll put every obstacle in your path. Still that's not the real danger . . . Let's talk money instead . . .

Claude: A small bas-relief, almost any statue, will fetch thirty thousand francs or so . . . A single bas-relief, if it's first-class, a dancing-girl for instance, sells for a couple of hundred thousand francs at least . . .

Perken: And you're sure of selling them?

Claude: Dead sure. I know the biggest dealers in London and Paris. And it's easy to fix up a public sale.

Perken: Easy perhaps, but a longish job, eh?

Claude: There's nothing to prevent your selling directly . . .

Perken: What's the idea behind this expedition?

Claude: I might reply – it would be the truth – that I have hardly any money left . . . A poor man can't choose his enemies. I mistrust the small change of revolt . . .[4]

The final touch put Malraux's personal seal on this imaginary conversation of lived experience and words spoken. Did the idea of a 'public sale' come as an ingenious and belated attempt at justification? Maybe not. But the vaguest part of this affair is still the story of the official mission. Clara writes: 'We obtained a commission, letters of recommendation, and confirmation of the fact that we had to inform the authorities of the results of our work.'[5] This was the least they might expect, in view of the mission's semi-official character. Clara adds that 'close inspection showed that all our official commission really authorized us us to do was to requisition some buffalo carts and their drivers.'[6]

In view of the fact that the *raison d'être* of this 'mission' was to make money, the Malrauxs made contact, probably through Kahnweiler, with 'correspondents' likely to be interested in 'a batch of Khmer statues'. A correspondence was begun with American and German dealers that provided evidence against them at their trial at Phnom Penh. The judgement of the Saigon court produced a correspondence between Kahnweiler and 'a M. Pach', which indicated that Kahnweiler had warned Malraux that it was illegal to export works of art from Indo-China.

Well-intentioned biographers allege that this exchange of letters concerned the collection of the Siamese Prince Damrong[7] that Malraux was supposed to be buying for a New York collector.[8] But Clara Malraux scoffs at this notion. The author of *Lunes en papier* had gone to Indo-China not as a middle-man, but as a 'conqueror'.

In any case, Malraux's plans and the permission that he had obtained to carry them out were much commented upon in the little world of arts and letters in which the couple moved. In a letter to Kahnweiler, Max Jacob spoke ironically of 'Malraux's mission': 'At last he will find his way to the East. He will become an orientalist and end up with a chair at the Collège de France, like Claudel. He's made for a professorial chair.'[9]

Quite clearly, we cannot reduce this enterprise of the Malrauxs, in 1923, to a looting operation intended to 'refloat' a couple of unlucky gamblers. The bait of financial gain was certainly an element in the affair – which is denied neither by Clara nor by Louis Chevasson, their companion. But when interpreting human actions, we must always be careful not to aim too low – especially, if we are dealing with a man who was to write *La Condition humaine* and command the *España* squadron.

But in refusing to aim too low, would we not be overshooting the mark in attributing to the adventure of 1923 an essentially aesthetic objective, the certainty of opening up for art a new, a renewed way, the discovery of a marginal, but important area, that of a transitional time and place between the Khmer and Siamese arts, between the nobility of the first and the prettiness of the second? Yes, probably. With all his string-pulling, Malraux was playing for high stakes in a game of audacity and ingenuity – and one can hardly fail to agree with Clara, who speaks of the whole affair with a nice mixture of romantic emotion and pugnacious simplicity, that 'the way we behaved in those youthful years was not without its grandeur: I shall lay claim to it with pride until the day of my death . . .'[10]

They threw themselves into their preparations, revisited the Musée Guimet, bought a dozen compass saws to cut the bas-reliefs they dreamt of, an automatic portable electric light, tropical clothes and tickets (first-class, says Clara, with a surprising naïvety on the part of these already confirmed globetrotters), but, more significant, they were not return tickets. They were leaving with their boats almost literally burned behind them.

They left one evening from the Gare de Lyon. Clara wept in the taxi. It was already the end of a life – and, possibly, the beginning of another – a real break with a family that had been shocked, but not irretrievably so, by the Florence adventure and their unlucky speculations. They arranged to meet the faithful Chevasson at Saigon – he was to leave two weeks later. The Malrauxs were going first to Siam, where they hoped to make a safe deal. André would then go to Hanoi to contact the officials of the École française d'Extrême-Orient. They would then make for Phnom Penh and the adventure would begin.

It was early October 1923: the rainy season, which would have prevented the transport of stone blocks through the jungle, was coming to an end. At Marseilles it was still warm. The ship on which they embarked, on 13 October, was called the *Angkor*.

4 *The forest*

THE 'French' Indo-China where the Malrauxs were to land late in 1923 was made up of four 'protectorates' (under indirect rule) and one 'colony' in the strict sense (under direct rule), Cochin-China, whose capital was Saigon. But in fact the three 'Annamese' (or Vietnamese, as they were later to be called) countries, Cochin-China, Annam and Tonkin, together with the two Buddhist kingdoms of the west, Cambodia and Laos, came under the jurisdiction of a governor-general, possessing wide-ranging powers, who resided at Hanoi (Tonkin). Annam did have an emperor and Cambodia and Laos kings, but they were mere puppets in the hands of the French administration.

The most important city, from the economic point of view and in terms of population, was Saigon, which then had about 200,000 inhabitants. The standard of living was higher in Cochin-China: the country was rich in resources and its inhabitants capable of rapid development. But the Annamese population – to a lesser degree the Catholic minority, which was defended by its priests and bishops – was ruthlessly exploited by the Europeans, who were free to conduct affairs more or less as they wished.

Cochin-China was the first to come under French rule, sixty years earlier. It was still a backward country, but less so than Cambodia, where for fifty years the French coloniser had been content to maintain order with the apparent approval of the native monarchy. Whereas a nationalist movement began to appear in the three 'Annamese' countries (Tonkin, Annam,

Cochin-China), Cambodia and Laos seemed to be sunk in resignation and a sort of peace, or sleep.

Malraux's voyage lasted twenty-nine days. The *Angkor* was not a very fast ship. But the voyage was not so much time wasted for André and Clara. Indo-China began at Marseilles: what they found on board ship was already colonial society, with its stratifications and taboos, its flabby racialism and embittered snobberies. Contact between it and them was not, and could not have been, easy. The circles that frequented the review *Action*, the *NRF* and the O'Steen bar did not prepare them for a world of conservative, suspicious civil servants: these men were not all stupid or corrupt, but their system of values had nothing in common with the Malrauxs'.

All the same, these conflicts had not yet assumed a political dimension. Malraux played the game as far as his 'mission' was concerned. The taste for order – one of his most marked characteristics – had not yet been affected by the rancour, the indignation and the lack of justice that were to determine the first of his public commitments, the following year, at Saigon. At Port Said, the sight of the statue of de Lesseps seemed to arouse in him feelings closer to those of the empire builders than to the redressers of wrongs.

At Djibouti, however, the colonial condition began to arouse in him a sort of disturbed rejection. Clara does not seem entirely aware of this in her *Mémoires*. 'This time,' she says, somewhat discreetly, 'it was elsewhere – another world. A square with earthen beehives touching one another: they housed human beings. In one of them, when night had fallen, beautiful and naked girls danced for us. At first it was only those we had paid; then, drawn in by the rhythm, the girls who were standing there in their dresses, watching, took off their clothes and joined in the dancing . . .'[1] The memory of this evening for 'broad-minded' tourists in search of the 'real thing' in African folk dancing was to provide Malraux with the background for the meeting between Perken and Vannec in the Somali brothel at the beginning of *La Voie royale*.

Owing to a fire in the *Angkor*'s bunkers, they arrived in Singapore two days late. As a result, they missed the connection that was to take them to Siam, where they hoped to buy works of art. Had they got there they might have been spared the risks that awaited them in Cambodia. Clara Malraux recalls with a touch of irony the project of buying the collection of a Prince Damrong, invented, she suggests, expressly for the purposes of the trial. A stay in Bangkok had been planned however. The fire on the *Angkor* decided otherwise and turned them towards adventure.

They put into Saigon just long enough to discover the shop-keepers of the rue Catinat, the sticky pleasures of rum and soda at the Pointe des Blagueurs and the charms of the tamarind trees and the orange-red coral trees. They had to set off again, this time for the École française d'Extrême-Orient, at Hanoi, where André Malraux was received by the acting director, Léonard Aurousseau, a Sinologist who knew very little about Khmer archeology, but who was perceptive enough to realise how improvised and incomplete was the knowledge of the young *chargé de mission*.

A strangely convincing echo of this interview is to be found in the conversation between Ramèges and Vannec in *La Voie royale*.[2] It has been said that this novel is not autobiographical. But too much about the young archeologist Claude Vannec – the references to the shipowner grandfather, his horror of spiders, the project of discovering the Royal Way linking Angkor and the temples of the Middle Mekong and the Menam, the difficulties involved in cutting away the bas-reliefs, his differences with the colonial administration – is reminiscent of André Malraux for us to overlook the workings of memory here. The incident of the conversation between Ramèges and Vannec is excellently done and we will return to it.

In any case, Vannec's views are pure Malraux: 'For museums are places where the works of an earlier epoch which have developed into myths lie sleeping – surviving on the historical plane alone – waiting for the day when artists will wake them to an active existence . . .' One can almost hear the minister of 1962. Whether or not he actually said this, André Malraux creates an authentic picture of Vannec and, through him, of Ramèges-Aurousseau:

'Let's hear about your projects, Monsieur Vannec. You intend, if I'm not mistaken, to explore the region lying along the line of the ancient Royal Road of the Khmers? . . . I may as well tell you at once that all that track . . . is quite obliterated over long stretches, and near the Dang-Rek range disappears completely . . . It is my duty, my official duty, to warn you of the risks you will have to run. You are doubtless aware that two of the leaders of official exploring parties, Henri Maître and Odend'hal, were murdered there. And yet our unfortunate countrymen knew that part of the country very well . . . You will be given supply warrants which will enable you – on application to the local Deputy Resident, needless to say – to procure native carts and cartmen for the transport of your kit. Fortunately, an expedition like yours travels comparatively light.'

'Do you call stones light objects?'

'It has been decided – to prevent any repetition of the regrettable incidents of last year – that all objects of whatever nature shall be left *in situ* . . . where they are. A report will be drawn up about them. After perusing it, the Head of our Archeological Department will, if necessary, proceed . . .'

'From what you've told me, it doesn't seem likely that the Head of your Archeological Department will venture into the regions I propose to explore.'

'Well, it's a special case. We shall look into it.'

'And, what's more, supposing he's willing to risk his neck there, I'd like to know why I should go pioneering just for his benefit.'

'You'd rather do it for your own, eh?'

'In the last twenty years your official parties haven't once touched that region. No doubt they'd better things to do. Personally, I know the risks involved – and I want to run them without official control.'

'But not without official assistance, I think?'

These few sentences say all there is to say. The misunderstanding is created and dissipated; the trial opened and the defendant's plea virtually made. The themes of profit, risk and aid are clearly stated. If the conversation was written after the event – after the two trials – it is all the richer for it. They provide a first sketch of Malraux's thesis and of the ingenuousness of his theories (the risks incurred give one the right to profit) and convey the counter-thesis of Ramèges-Aurousseau (such a mission must be disinterested). If the official texts had not been enough to exclude any idea of gain, of appropriation by the finder, the official aid implied by the commission granted in Paris, verified and confirmed in Hanoi, made it even more unacceptable.

All the interference, the abuse, the troubles to which the Malrauxs were later to be subjected do nothing to diminish the impregnable position adopted by the authorities. Malraux could not play the cards of legality and of adventure at one and the same time, and he was intelligent enough to understand the extent of the warning he was given. The following passages of *La Voie royale* show clearly enough that the young man knew from that moment that he was throwing himself into a trap, set by himself and himself alone – hence his attempt to incriminate, not Vannec, but Ramèges:

> He's behaving like a company director building up reserves . . . He may even think that if the men he sent out there are dead, they died just that his colleagues might carry on their jobs . . . If in his heart of hearts, he is defending a group interest, he'll turn nasty, that's sure.

Aurousseau, with whom André Malraux was then on good enough terms personally to accompany him on a visit to a fortune-teller in Hanoi, described in the *Antimémoires*, had for him both the right and the spirit of the contract constituted by the commission. Furthermore, Vannec juggled the documentation: it was then much less than twenty years – in fact, hardly seven – since Parmentier had recognised the temple of Banteaï-Sre, after Marek had found it and Demazure had visited it in 1914. It is obvious enough that the 'risks' on which Malraux prides himself so much in the person of Claude Vannec are those taken by the heroes of *La Voie royale*, and not the infinitely more modest ones of the Malrauxs' brief incursion into the jungle.

And the warnings were to multiply. Two weeks later, after

another brief visit to Saigon, where they met up with Louis Chevasson, there they were – side by side with Henri Parmentier himself, with his 'white goatee, rather gay Bohemian beard' and his flowery language, praising to Clara her husband's knowledge and 'disinterestedness'[3]! – sailing up the Mekong and the Tonle-Sap to Siem-Reap. From there, they travelled by car to the Angkor complex. Over this exquisite township, with its waters running through the norias, there reigned at this time a delegate called Crémazy, who, it appears, handed him a letter from the Director of the French Institute, who felt it 'incumbent' on him, 'with a view to enabling you to keep the persons who may accompany you under proper surveillance' (!), to bring to his notice the order of the Governor-General, dated 1908, which declares that 'all ancient edifices, whether already located or hereafter to be discovered, situate within the provinces of Siem-Reap, Battambang and Sisophon,[4] shall be deemed to be monuments of public interest'.[5]

This fresh warning (one wonders whether it was actually expressed as such) would have put an end to any enterprise that was intended to remain within the law. Was the text in question in fact based on law? Could one classify in so few words so complex and disparate a collection of objects? Walter Langlois quotes from a letter that Édouard Daladier, then Minister for the Colonies, had sent to the National Assembly with a view to replacing with new legislation a regulation that 'does not correspond in a satisfactory way to the aim intended and . . . is, in any case, vitiated by flagrant illegality'.[6] In any event, a new order for the protection of the Khmer antiquities had been issued a few weeks earlier, in October 1923. From a legal point of view, Malraux was trapped. Whether it was the Rubicon or the Gordian knot – the precedent is of little account – he either had to try his luck against the law or give up. He tried it.

Does risk justify anything? The risk is not the same for Claude Vannec and Perken on the one hand and for André and Clara Malraux on the other. The tragic confrontation with the Stiengs in *La Voie royale* is the heroic version of a difficult thirty-mile excursion through the jungle carried out, with courage, energy and patience, by three young tourist-aesthetes whose enterprise would be less likely to arouse admiration today.

For those of us who travelled the same path twenty-two years later, when the almost invisible track of 1923 had become a roadway fit for a jeep, the enterprise seems to have had something vaguely adventurous about it, especially for Clara . . . If Malraux had nothing more than this incident to his credit, his claim to the noble title of adventurer would not pass undisputed. In short, they set out, as Clara charmingly puts it, 'to put works of art that were being threatened by the jungle back into circulation . . .'[7] They were accompanied by a young guide called Xa – as in *La Voie royale* – and who, as in the novel, had been accused before them as a thief.

Wearing sun helmets and duck suits, with water-bottles and cameras slung round their necks, they set off on horseback. Their animals were so small that André's feet touched the ground. Behind them came four covered carts, drawn by buffaloes. Xa, the interpreter-guide, and a dozen coolies accompanied them. In the stone of her ring, Clara carried a white powder: even to this day, she doesn't know whether it was cyanide of potassium (O Human Condition!) or bicarbonate of soda! An image, in little, of the adventure that was about to begin . . .

Where were they going? Right up to the last moment they were not quite certain of the existence of the small temple of Banteaï-Sre, mentioned in one of Parmentier's articles four years earlier. Was it still standing? Had it not already been dismantled by peasants, who had a very natural tendency to make use of these fine, dislocated blocks as hearth-stones? They remembered the descriptions given first by Henri Parmentier,[8] then by Goloubew and Finot:[9]

'In the middle of the jungle . . . On the right bank of the Sturm Thom, a tributary of the Siem-Reap, three kilometres north-north-west of the Phnom Dei . . . is a sandstone monument whose small size is offset by the remarkable perfection of its execution and the extraordinary delicacy and interest of the carving . . .'

One of these pieces, indeed, was already known to them: this was a statue of Siva brought back in 1914 by Marek to the museum at Phnom Penh. An ambiguous precedent . . . What was left of the ruined temple since the visits of Marek, Demazure and Parmentier? They moved on towards Banteaï-Sre, following more or less the course of the Sturm Thom. To cover the twenty-five miles or so that, they were told, lay between them and it, they would need about two days.

We have two versions of this brief trek through the jungle: Clara's and André's in *La Voie royale*. The 'fictional' description is a fine piece of writing:

> Claude was growing aware of the essential oneness of the forest and had given up trying to distinguish living beings from their setting, life that moves from life that oozes; some unknown power assimilated the trees with the fungoid growths upon them, and quickened the restless movements of all the rudimentary creatures darting to and fro upon a soil like marsh-scum amid the streaming vegetation of a planet in the making. Here what act of man had any meaning, what human will but spent its staying power? Here everything frayed out, grew soft and flabby, tended to melt away into its surroundings which, loathsome yet fascinating as a cretin's eyes, worked on the nerves with the same obscene power of attraction as the spiders hanging there between the branches, from which at first it had cost him such an effort to avert his gaze.[10]

Malraux felt this horror of spiders as strongly as Claude (Clara notes that he has always had an almost pathological loathing for them: 'He even saw them in his dreams and then he would cry out . . .'). In her *Mémoires*, she provides an authentication of the novel, completed since in a television interview given by André Malraux himself in 1972.[11] At one stage in their trek, he remembers, a cloud of butterflies rose up from the small caravan, which they had covered with a white powder, leaving them, in the heart of the green forest, like Pierrots . . .

Here is Clara's version:

> Was the forest growing thicker? Was it really turning into this greenish vat where the sun could never penetrate? . . . There was something rotting all around us. The lianas were no longer the only danger now, for there was also this thick reddish earth in which the horses stuck. There were the mosquitoes too, a curtain of furious insects that went with

us, a curtain that we pushed through and that closed again all around, before us and behind . . . Sometimes the path disappeared. My companion sat well on his horse. His mind was wholly fixed upon the carrying out of the plan that had brought us here and he was sure of its success, therefore he suffered less than I did from exertion in air so thick that you could feel it filling your mouth and then going down your throat.[12]

A lot of words for a two-day excursion into a forest. Spiders, mosquitoes, coolies? All right, a safari, so what? But we must remember the period, the youth of these people, their inexperience, the uncertainty (the madness . . .) of the enterprise, and agree that the atmosphere was certainly one of adventure, if not of heroic deeds. The air of mystery, moreover, was deepened by the fact that after thirty hours of travelling no one had heard about any temple. But one old man thought he remembered a track that used to lead to a pile of stones . . . This time they had to cut their way through the undergrowth with machetes. And so after six hours of this, they were nearing their goal. This is how Clara describes the moment:

> The old man stopped, his machete held high: there was an open doorway in the bush, a doorway opening on to a little square courtyard with its paving all heaved up. At the far end, partly fallen, but with two of its walls still standing firm, a pink, carved, decorated temple, a forest Trianon upon which the splashes of moss looked like ornaments – a wonder that we were not the first to see but that we were no doubt the first to gaze upon in this way, breathless at the sight of its graceful dignity, lovelier than all the temples we had seen hitherto, at all events more moving in its forsaken state than all the raked and swept Angkors . . .[13]

This delightful 'forest Trianon' was the same one that I visited, restored, standing proudly erect in its own cleared space, twenty-three years later. Did Clara really see this exquisite masterpiece or rather what the narrator of *La Voie royale* describes in more sober terms as:

> A chaos of fallen stones, some lying flat, but most of them

upended; it looked like a mason's yard invaded by the jungle.
Here were lengths of wall in slabs of purple sandstone, some
carved and others plain, all plumed with pendant ferns.
Some bore a red patina, the aftermath of fire. Facing him he
saw some bas-reliefs of the best period, marked by Indian
influences . . . but very beautiful work; they were grouped
round an old shrine, half hidden behind a breastwork of
fallen stones . . . Beyond the bas-reliefs were the remains of
three towers razed to within six feet of the ground. Their
mutilated stumps stuck out of such an overwhelming mass
of rubble that all the vegetation round them was stunted;
they seemed socketed in the débris like candles in their
sticks . . .[14]

For realism, I think we would turn this time to the novelist's
version. What we know from the photograph of the state of
Banteaï-Sre in 1923–4 is closer to André's than to Clara's
description.

Since the stone carvings embedded in the walls were far
better preserved than those of the blocks lying on the ground,
they now had to set about detaching their 'property'. Their
saws broke, as described in *La Voie royale*. Picks, cleavers,
levers and ropes were more effective. It took Malraux and
Chevasson two days – the guide and the coolies stood fearfully
to one side and Clara stood 'sentry duty' – to detach seven
stones forming four great blocks decorated with very fine bas-
reliefs (which I saw in 1945, replaced *in situ*, as the late M.
Aurousseau put it).

> Carved on two faces, the corner-stones represented two
> dancing-girls . . .
> 'How much d'you think it's worth?' Perken asked . . .
> 'Hard to say. Over five thousand francs anyhow.'[15]

(The francs of that time were worth much the same as those
of today.)
They hoisted up the stone blocks, piled them carefully into
the carts and returned to the track, to arrive once more at the
Sturm Thom, the hills, the spiders and the mosquitoes. Twenty
hours of sweaty, exhausting riding brought them at last to the

tall towers of Angkor. At their feet lay the bungalow where questions were sure to be asked. Four carts, twelve coolies for less than six days in the forest? Could anyone seriously doubt that Crémazy had them under surveillance and that the contents of the carts would not be reported?

Clara, André and Chevasson had no sooner left the quay at Siem-Reap, two days later, on a boat ballasted with over a ton of stone from Banteaï-Sre, than the director of the bungalow, Debyser, had given Crémazy all the necessary details concerning a cargo addressed to the firm of Berthot and Charrière, of Saigon, which to all appearances consisted of archeological items protected by a Khmer royal edict. The information was verified at one of the boat's stops by one of the Angkor archeologists, M. Groslier.[16] And as the boat sailed gently towards Phnom Penh, an arrest-warrant was being drawn up by the authorities of the Protectorate.

They anchored at nightfall on 24 December, in full view of the scarlet and gold curved roofs of the royal palace, at the point where the Mekong joins the Tonle-Sap. Having decided not to debark until the next day, they slept in their cabins. A little after midnight, they were awoken by three inspectors from the Sûreté, the French Criminal Department:

'Follow us.' 'Where to?' 'The hold. We want to check your baggage.' We followed. Standing there by our camphor-wood chests they had the air of customs men . . . 'Are these chests yours?' 'The chests, yes. And what is more they are booked in our name. But when we left Siem-Reap they were empty.' 'I see. Well, open them.'[17]

A classic scene. Even Clara did not manage to show surprise.

5 *The magistrates*

NEITHER André Malraux nor Louis Chevasson was gaoled, yet both, together with Clara, were found guilty a week later. The Malrauxs settled in at the Hôtel Manolis, a Greco-Cambodian establishment of doubtful charm, but then the best that Phnom Penh had to offer. They remained there four months.

They were forbidden to leave the city, even for a walk. So they read obsessively – whatever they could lay their hands on. The municipal library was particularly well stocked with memoirs, letters, sociological or geographical studies of the region, etc. They recited poetry at each other for days on end. And they would act out their scenes of cops and robbers. Sometimes, in the hotel restaurant, amidst the army officers and tax-inspectors in dinner jackets and their ladies in long evening gowns, they would be seized by a sudden desire to dance: they noticed that these honest folk tended to avoid them. One day, M. Manolis, the manager of the hotel, handed them a bill. They had had no money since Fernand Malraux's last cheque at the end of the first month. Now, after robbery, they were going to compound their offence by bilking. The future certainly looked gloomy.

Clara had an idea: she would commit suicide. Not for real, of course. She would swallow a tube and a half of gardenal and André would arrive on the scene, quite by chance, ten minutes later and save her. She would be taken out on a stretcher to the hospital. Her husband would join her and settle in with her. In this way, they'd get free board and lodging. These trials brought them closer together and revived their awareness of the realities of the place. Once outside the society of civil servants and tourists, they talked with the nurses, the hospital staff and the doctors. They became aware of certain realities. As each day passed, they came closer to the truth of the colonial condition. It was there, in the suffocating heat of the hospital at Phnom Penh, from April to June 1924, that they began to become aware of what was to form the basis of their first political commitment.

The suicide attempt was not enough for Clara. Though occupied with translating *The Psychoanalytical Diary of a Little Girl,* which she had brought back from Berlin two years earlier, she could think only of escape, of returning home. She was hurt by the endless silence of her family, whereas André regularly received letters from his parents. She went on hunger strike. After four or five days, she weighed a mere eighty pounds. In her semi-coma, she heard André whisper: 'Don't lose heart: I'll certainly end up by being Gabriele d'Annunzio!'[1]

But Clara did not owe her freedom to any such novelettish wire-pulling. The examining magistrate informed her that 'a wife is required to follow her husband everywhere', so her presence on the scene of the pillage was not a punishable offence . . . She would return to France and organise the defence of her two companions. The police had completed their inquiries. The trial would begin in two weeks. 'They have no important evidence,' André told her. 'I shall be on the boat before you reach France.'[2]

The time for her departure arrived: she, little more than a skeleton, shivering with malaria, hollow-eyed, and he, 'his complexion . . . disagreeably close to the colour of mustard'. They didn't know what to say to one another, she lying on her stretcher and he standing beside her. 'But when the ambulance drove off I saw him with his sun helmet, his semi-stiff collar, his white duck clothes, standing there in the middle of the road with his arms hanging loose at his sides, standing there cut off from the others, an orphan.'[3] The first phase of André Malraux's first Indo-Chinese adventure had come to an end. It was now the turn of the magistrates – and the journalists.

The affair first came to the attention of the public on 5 January 1924, in a fairly well-informed article in the *Écho du Cambodge*.[4]

Three days later, under the significant headline, 'Vandales et pilleurs de ruines', a Saigon daily, *L'Impartial*, served up the same news, accompanying it with indignant comments by its editor, Henry de Lachevrotière. This man, whose own reputation was far from unblemished, professed his virtue all the more forcefully in that the governor of Cochin-China, his principal backer, had suggested the line he should take. Both these characters were to turn up later.

The police investigation of the affair lasted over six months. The examining magistrate, M. Bartet, who, at the outset, had given proof of his goodwill by refusing to take the suspects into custody, on the grounds that to do so would be out of keeping with the needs of the investigation or the gravity of the offence, took the trouble to obtain an expert opinion on the damage done to the temple. Naturally it was Henri Parmentier, later to become a friend of the Malrauxs, who, assisted by Victor Goloubew, provided this opinion.

The two archeologists were joined, at the end of January, by Louis Finot, director of the École française d'Extrême-Orient, who, seeing the report, decided first to clear the ground around Banteaï-Sre, then to organise an *anastylosis* – in other words, a systematic dismantling of the monument, stone by stone, with a view to its reconstruction. This was an indirect homage to the plunderer André Malraux, whose enterprise had, after all, proved useful to the preservation of masterpieces.

The investigation that Bartet then set in motion was in no way prejudicial to Louis Chevasson, who was praised for his 'modesty' and 'good behaviour'. But the file on 'Malraux, Georges-André' produced by the Paris police was well calculated, in the atmosphere of a French colony of the 1920s, to have an adverse effect on the chances of the accused. Feverish literary activity, familiarity with *avant-garde* artistic circles (coupled, of course, with the words 'Bolshevism' or 'anarchism'), familiarity with German-Jewish *émigrés*, marriage to a Jewess of Prussian origin, friendship with Georges Gabory (the author of *L'Éloge de Landru*) – everything conspired to make of Malraux, Georges-André, the archetype of the asocial intellectual, the amoral adventurer, the stateless, embittered dilettante.

The trial of André Malraux and Louis Chevasson, accused of

'despoiling monuments' and of 'misappropriation of fragments of bas-reliefs stolen from the temple of Banteai-Sre, of the Angkor complex', opened at last before the Phnom Penh *tribunal correctionnel* at 7.30 am on 16 July 1924. It was to take up three hearings, spread over two days. It attracted a large public, mainly on account of the strangeness of the affair and the personality of the principal defendant.

The proceedings were presided over by a magistrate called Jodin, who seemed more concerned with what attitude to adopt and with his own witticisms than with the truth to be uncovered. The state prosecution was in the hands of Procurator Giordani. André Malraux's counsel was Maître de Parcevaux and Louis Chevasson's Maître Dufond. The heat was stifling.

Malraux made the stronger impression on observers as ill-disposed towards him as the special correspondent of *L'Impartial* of Saigon: 'He is a tall, thin, pale young man, with a hairless face illuminated by a pair of extremely lively eyes . . . He speaks with great facility and defends himself with an acerbity that reveals unquestionable qualities of energy and tenacity . . . He has been able to defend his positions with surprising energy, refuting the investigation on every point.'[5] While the correspondent of *L'Écho du Cambodge* wrote that the defendant gave 'a veritable archeology lecture'.

This display of talent worked both for and against him. For him, in that it showed that he was not the mere adventurer-crook described in certain police reports, and proved that he really was the semi-professional archeologist he claimed to be. But his brilliance and self-confidence not only revealed him as the true inspiration of the enterprise, but prejudiced the magistrates – judge and public prosecutor – against him and reduced the defence's chances of pleading attenuating circumstances on the grounds of the defendant's youth and inexperience.

The statements made by the two principal witnesses did not help him. The delegate at Siem-Reap, Crémazy, attacked them quite ruthlessly, making use, furthermore, of police information that had not been brought to the knowledge of the defence. The man with the carts made full use of the fact that warnings from Paris and Hanoi about the visitors had increased since their arrival – which is why they had been carefully watched and unmasked without difficulty.

Henri Parmentier was less harsh. It must not be forgotten that he had rediscovered and studied Banteaï-Sre seven years before the travellers of 1923; that he had produced a serious description of the site, and that it was on the basis of his work that Malraux had launched his own expedition; that he had then welcomed the newcomers to Angkor in the most friendly way – only to discover later that the temple of which he was in a sense the godfather had been cut up into sections and put into packing cases by these young people . . . However, judging by the reports of his statement published in *L'Impartial* on 21 July 1924,[6] it does not seem as if he was in any way vindictive in his attitude towards them. His thesis, according to which the temple was in ruins – which explained the length of time it took the École française d'Extrême-Orient to classify it – went in favour of the defendants. Furthermore, in his conclusion, he praised the aesthetic discernment of these 'young amateurs'.

One of André Malraux's interventions concerned the business of buying the collection of the Siamese Prince Damrong for an antique dealer. This project, as I have mentioned, was supposed to be the main purpose of the trip. What could be more natural than to act as a middle-man between two collectors? The expedition to Siem-Reap was merely an injudicious sideline to the main business in hand.

Walter Langlois, a conscientious researcher, says that Damrong was 'a former member of the king's cabinet and a longstanding collaborator of the École française d'Extrême-Orient'.[7] Malraux, says Langlois, was supposed to go to Bangkok after his expedition to Siem-Reap, whereas according to Clara they were supposed to call in at Bangkok before, and this had been postponed on account of a fire in the ship's bunker. In any case, the whole affair is confused, largely because André Malraux's own intentions were as changeable as his statements.

As to Malraux's behaviour in court, we cannot do better than turn to the account of Garine's trial in *Les Conquérants*.[8] This account is as autobiographical as the description of Claude Vannec's dealings with the administration. In it we see Malraux–Garine – accused of complicity in an abortion case – dreaming his way through the proceedings, unable to believe that all this was happening to him. What was he guilty of? What do these fools want with him, with their confused evidence, their jargon and their robes? What kind of a nightmare was this? And why was he in it anyway? The absurd was there, right there, and it was no use trying to oppose, when, physically, one could do nothing about it.

On 17 July, the second and last day of the trial, the indictment was first read out: the affair was made to look like a forest hold-up. M. Giordani had quite obviously no talent for either archeology, psychology, or, indeed, anything to do with the Malraux case. Then came the counsels' speeches. Maître de Parcevaux, André Malraux's counsel, expended a great deal of effort to prove, quite simply, that no offence had been committed, since the temple in question was not a classified monument. Furthermore, what authority was entitled to issue such a decree, to ensure the protection of monuments, and to institute proceedings? The French government? The king of Cambodia? The École française d'Extrême-Orient?

On 21 July, Maître Jodin passed judgement: three years imprisonment and five years prohibition from entering certain areas for André Malraux; and for Louis Chevasson, eighteen months imprisonment. The accused had, of course, to surrender the bas-reliefs.

I cannot resist quoting a few particularly picturesque passages from this indictment, a masterly mixture of local colour and pedantry:

> Whereas in the case in point . . . the accused intended to commit an act not of sterile, but of fruitful vandalism, and whereas the damage that they committed to the prejudice of art and archeological science constituted acts that were merely preparatory to the offence of the theft . . . a veritable act of burglary . . . Whereas . . . the said Malraux attributed, as he himself admits, an aim of archeological commercialism to the voyage that he carried out in the Far East, with the title of *chargé de mission* . . . was in contact with dealers of ultra-Rhenish nationality [!!!] trafficking in works of archeological value, in exchange for promises of liberality worthy

of a Roland Bonaparte [???], succeeded in camouflaging this vulgar robbery under the appearances of an 'official mission' . . .

The scandalous severity of the sentence, combined with the brutal, offhand manner of the magistrate and the strong impression of entrapment that hung over the whole affair gave Malraux the profound feeling of being the object of injustice, at the hands of men who represented a false, traditionalist world, the natural opponents of youth, talent and imagination.

The condemned men appealed, of course, to the court in Saigon, which was due to meet in two months. This time, they took their defence more seriously: they were lucky enough to obtain the services of two of the best-known members of the colony's bar, Maîtres Béziat and Gallois-Montbrun. But most of the press was already poisoning the atmosphere that surrounded them. On 22 July, Lachevrotière, the publisher of *L'Impartial*, whose special correspondent at Phnom Penh had provided an unfavourable, but relatively objective account of the trial, fired the first shots by publishing the photographs of the dismembered bas-reliefs[9] and demanding exemplary punishment for the 'vandals', while admitting that 'whole consignments of Buddhas were descending the Mekong to enrich certain collections – if not for cultivated local amateurs'.

A furious Malraux rushed to the offices of *L'Impartial*, where Lachevrotière kept him waiting, then pulled the rug from under his feet by offering to allow him to express his own point of view in an interview. Impatient to be heard, and flattered by the opportunity of playing the star, even at this price, Malraux agreed. On 16 September, *L'Impartial* published a version of the interview under the heading, 'The affair of the Angkor statues'.

André Malraux has not always been well advised in his relations with the press. He came off particularly badly that day. The journalist, who had come not perhaps with the worst intentions, was won over to some extent by Malraux's charm – he described him as having 'eyes that burn brightly, then become veiled with melancholy'. Malraux told how he had taken only 'a few truncated bas-reliefs' from a 'pile of stone no more than four feet high', and that his arrest was 'due to a misunderstanding'. The situation of his father, whom he presented as 'a legendary figure on the Paris Bourse' and the managing director of 'one of the largest international oil companies', may have given the impression that he had come on a commercial mission; his wife's origins may have aroused a certain amount of mistrust as to the real purposes of the voyage. A finer collection of imprudences, impudence, boastfulness and contradiction it would be difficult to find.

The interview left a rather bad impression. But Malraux was fortunate in that Lachevrotière, not content with placing the accused in an unfavourable light and with making the best of the opportunity offered, acted according to character and tried to blacken Malraux's name beyond all credibility. In Malraux's reply, he asked Lachevrotière what he would have thought of a newspaper that had treated him in a similar way during his trial on charges of blackmail and corruption, eight years earlier. In polemics, the crudest arguments are often the best. The virtuous publisher of *L'Impartial* feigned indignation, then remained silent until the opening of the appeal hearings.

As in Claudel's play *Le Soulier de satin*, the action of the 'Malraux affair' was played out over two continents. While André, during the endless rainy weeks of the monsoon, was plumbing the depths of human baseness, Clara, in a Parisian summer, was appreciating the generosity of a legion of friends, colleagues and supporters.

Clara tells with great feeling and frankness of the tribulations of her journey from Saigon to Marseilles, and on to Paris: her brief affair with a French diplomat on board ship; the friendship first forged during the voyage with Paul Monin, a Saigon barrister who was to play an important role in the life of both André and herself, helping them to resolve this conflict of interests, administrative regulations and personalities in a wide-ranging political debate that culminated in *Les Conquérants* and *La Condition humaine*; the landing at Marseilles, where she found a telegram awaiting her from her father-in-law, saying that he could not be there to meet her and that he was expecting her at Orléans; the discovery of the truth from a former chambermaid who received her in the (rather dubious) hotel she kept at

Montmartre, and informed her of the three-year prison sentence, the news of which, not to mention the vicious comments to *Le Matin* and *Le Journal*, was splashed all over the Paris newspapers and came to the young woman like a bolt from the blue; and, finally, the reunion with her family.

The word 'divorce' cropped up at once. 'Never at any price,' Clara replied. 'You aren't going to stay married to this bum, this common criminal?' said her elder brother. 'Certainly I am, and more so than ever.' Her mother was crying: 'The fellow has always lied! . . . He hasn't even got his *bac*! . . . His father isn't a director of anything at all . . . He's never worked since you were married . . .' And there was the sagging face, the inert form, the whitened hair of Mme Goldschmidt, very naturally upset by the police investigations carried out among her naturalised family and friends with all the insensitivity usual in such a situation. And she suffered deeply from the snubs offered her by friends, tradespeople and neighbours. Then there was the family plot to have her put away in a 'rest home', which she was tricked into entering on the pretext of accompanying her exhausted mother, and her escape . . .[10]

The first allies she tried to recruit were André Breton, and his wife, whom she won over after arriving at their apartment at dawn and proceeding to draw a portrait of André innocently languishing in prison and describing their adventure as that of a Rimbaud who happened to prefer archeology to trade. She then saw her father-in-law, who, once Clara had sworn that André was 'innocent', threw in his lot with the common cause. And she visited André's mother, in the tiny apartment she had rented near the Gare Montparnasse after the sale of the grocery business at Bondy. The affection she received from Mme Malraux – who insisted that Clara should join her, her mother and her sister in their two-room flat – deeply moved Clara.

The next day, assisted by Fernand Malraux, Marcel Arland and Paul Monin, who had postponed his return to Saigon in order to help her, Clara launched the idea that was to alter the course of the whole affair: why not ask a collective of well-known writers to stand surety for André's literary talent, for the promise that he had shown and for his irreplaceability in the world of letters?

Max Jacob offered his support to the 'Malraux clan'.[11] François Mauriac, who was bound to Malraux by no previous fellow-feeling, and who was under no kind of moral obligation to him, rallied to the cause. André Breton moved from friendly sympathy to active support. On 16 August, he published an article entitled 'For André Malraux' in *Les Nouvelles littéraires*. On 6 September 1924, *Les Nouvelles littéraires* published the text of the following petition, together with some impressive signatures:

> The undersigned, deeply concerned at the sentence which has been passed on André Malraux, trust in the consideration with which the law customarily regards all those who help to increase our country's intellectual heritage. They wish to vouch for the intelligence and the real literary worth of this writer whose youth and whose already published works give rise to the highest expectations. They would profoundly deplore the loss resulting from the application of a penalty that would prevent André Malraux from accomplishing what we can all rightfully expect from him.

It was signed by most of the well-known writers of the time, including André Gide, François Mauriac, Pierre Mac Orlan, Jean Paulhan, André Maurois, Max Jacob and Louis Aragon. Malraux could come before the Saigon judges with the best possible pledges of his standing as an artist.

On 8 October, at 8 am, André Malraux and Louis Chevasson appeared before their new judges; the court was presided over by M. Gaudin, a judge of appeal, with a fair reputation for integrity.

The president of the court opened the hearing with a long, meticulous account of the facts, which led to brief objections by the counsel, Maîtres Béziat and Gallois-Montbrun, and with a reading of the documents in proof, which, this time, were known to the defence. The afternoon was devoted to the Public Prosecutor's charge, which was extremely long, detailed and well supported. Describing Malraux as 'vain' and 'a liar', the Procurator demanded, for Chevasson, confirmation of the sentence passed on him on 21 July and, for Malraux, in addition to the sentence passed by the Phnom Penh tribunal, an extension of the ban on entering certain areas and the withdrawal of his civic rights.

A tall, well-built, strong-featured man, possessed of a resounding voice, Maître Béziat[12] stressed that the question was not only whether the acts committed were against the law, but also which law. Cambodian law? The building in question was situated in a territory attached to Cambodia only by an order issued by the Governor-General of Indo-China, which itself had been confirmed by a decree of the President of the Republic only eight years later – that is, outside the legal period of delay. This region could not, therefore, be legally regarded as Cambodian territory. While as far as French law was concerned, these stones could only be regarded as abandoned.

How, declared Maître Béziat, could one speak of the untouchable character of this monument? It would be if it had been classified. But M. Parmentier had gone there in 1916 and carried out a very thorough study of these ruins. Why, then, had he not initiated proceedings for their classification? And the barrister reminded his listeners that many others had done what Malraux was now being charged for doing: 'How many people have taken from the ruins of Angkor artistic riches of far greater value?' And then came the conclusion: 'If my client is condemned for the slip that he has made, then, in the past, we should also have condemned those admirals, prominent residents and other mandarins of equal importance for the depredations that they committed against these same monuments'.[13]

The court's decision came on 28 October, and very largely corroborated the conclusions of the defence: Malraux was given a one-year suspended sentence, with no prohibition from entering certain areas, and Chevasson an eight-month suspended sentence. The court ordered the restoration of the bas-reliefs to their original site. A brief quotation from the judge's summing-up reveals the changes that the affair had undergone in the interval between the two trials:

> Considering that after acquiring genuine artistic knowledge . . . the young writer Georges-André Malraux . . . decided to come to Indo-China, attracted by the marvels of the Angkor temples and of Khmer art . . .

Considering that Malraux and Chevasson took away bas-reliefs that they had removed . . . and that this was a fraudulent act . . .

Considering that the two defendants are very young, and that the information provided about them is not of a detrimental character . . . etc.

André Malraux was still not satisfied. He was determined to proceed to the Supreme Court of Appeal, where, he was convinced, he would be given repossession of the bas-reliefs from Banteaï-Sre on the grounds that he was their 'inventor'. Six years later, in an interview with André Rousseaux, he declared that the sculptures 'are sequestrated in the museum at Phnom Penh . . . The Supreme Court of Appeal has quashed the sentences: but we still haven't got a final judgement on the matter.'[14]

In fact, Malraux was doubly in error: the bas-reliefs had been replaced at Banteaï-Sre where they can still be seen today; the Supreme Court of Appeal had decided to quash the Saigon judgement, because 'it makes no mention of the publicity given to a hearing devoted to the examination'. A trifle. The condemned men did not get reparation on the main question: the Supreme Court of Appeal in no way upheld the true grounds for the appeal, although a magistrate as celebrated as Procurator-General Mornet, who was the Procurator of the Pétain trial, had declared, so some people say, that both judgements, that of Saigon and that of Phnom Penh, had been made 'in contempt of all justice'.[15]

On 1 November 1924, André Malraux and Louis Chevasson embarked for Marseilles on the cargo-ship *Chantilly*. Humiliated, smarting from the wounds inflicted on them, shaking the dust of this accursed land from their feet? Not in the least. When asked recently about the scars left on them by this affair, Louis Chevasson replied: 'For me, it was the best time of my life. It was a great adventure, we took risks, we faced up to our enemies. The judicial procedure seemed to us more absurd and aberrant than cruel: we were often seized by uncontrollable fits of laughter! We never lived as intensely as then!'

Apart from the irony of the situation, which delighted him

as a lover of Alfred Jarry, Malraux discovered in this first Indo-Chinese adventure reasons for a new struggle. What he had first sought, he had not obtained. But far more important than a few stones and the means 'to live quietly' for three or four years, he brought back with him sympathies, convictions, a sense of urgency and the means of living anything but quietly for far longer than three or four years. Whether or not he was spurred by rancour, by a desire for revenge, he had discovered a cause to defend, and to defend dangerously.

Since the conversations in the hospital at Phnom Penh, he had had others that did not concern Khmer art and legal proceedings. He had met Paul Monin, who had returned from Paris, and, through him, the leaders of the movement for the liberation of the Annamese (as the Vietnamese were then called). He was as attracted by these protesters as he was repelled by the upholders of the colonial order (civil servants, judges, journalists). He had discovered something that he was later to call fraternity.

On the eve of their departure for France, André Malraux and Louis Chevasson, 'symbols of colonial injustice' and 'friends of the Annamese', had been the guests of honour at a banquet organised by Paul Monin. Thus this archeologico-judicial misadventure, which might have left them with nothing but bitter memories, concluded on a note of triumph. Rejected and condemned by official society, Malraux was welcomed by a counter-society of which for a quarter of a century he was to become a very active ally.

Despite the ordeals he had undergone – or perhaps because of them – André Malraux had decided, with Monin, to return to Indo-China before he had even left Saigon. He and Monin were agreed in thinking that the 'natives' could no longer be defended solely in the law courts and that a newspaper should be devoted to this task. And they would publish it together. Thus Malraux was leaving not only to put some fresh air between M. de Lachevrotière and himself, to repair his health and to return to his wife and family, but above all to raise the funds for such an enterprise and, in the first instance, a team of collaborators.

His reunion with Clara was marked by the ardent ambiguity

that imbued all their relations. On 29 October she had received a brief telegram: 'One year with suspended sentence.' Three weeks later, she was at Marseilles, on the quayside. He smiled, then asked, very quickly: 'But what have you been doing, messing around with my mother?' He was annoyed to know that his family secrets had been revealed, believing that they were still secrets. Then: 'In a month or six weeks you and I are setting off again for Saigon . . . The Annamese need an independent newspaper. Monin and I are going to edit it.' He then gave her the present he had brought back for her – a small packet of Indian hemp ('a wonderful music starts to play and words give rise to coloured images. You can guide the show that goes on inside your head. I'll help you by reading poetry aloud'). She took the drug and began to hallucinate. In the midst of 'this removal from my own being', she talked to André of her affair on board ship. 'I saw a man sitting on the foot of the bed, weeping.'[16] This was, inverted by the personality of the narrator, the scene of Kyo and May in *La Condition humaine*. 'If you had not saved my life, I should leave you . . . To think that now this fellow imagines he has the right to despise you . . . I know what a man thinks of a woman he has had . . .'[17]

They spent a few days with Fernand Malraux, who was now convinced that his son had been the victim of a political intrigue directed against a generous soul who held the colonial order in contempt. A noble simplification! This made it all the easier for André to ask his father for more help. 'I will not accept defeat,' he said. According to Clara, her father-in-law's pride was the equal of her husband's. The stock exchange was then having a little boom. 'When you reach Singapore,' said Fernand Malraux, 'you will find fifty thousand francs waiting for you in the bank. You must shift for yourselves to get there. What's more, I should like to make it quite plain that you must not expect any other sum from me. Anyone can make a mess of things once, but if you do it twice you no longer deserve to be helped.'[18]

A few days later – two days, in fact, before their departure – André received a letter by special delivery from the publisher Bernard Grasset, summoning him to his office. Grasset was offering him a contract for three books on the basis of a letter from François Mauriac, the firm's star author. Grasset persuaded André Malraux to accept an advance of three thousand francs, adding: 'And if you can manage it, don't be too long sending us a book. Think of the wonderful publicity that all these writers have given you!'[19] A clever man – a combination, valuable in a publisher, of flair, business sense and generosity.

Before embarking, the Malrauxs called at Saint-Benoît-sur-Loire to see André's old friend Max Jacob, who wrote to friends that Malraux had offered him a lecture tour in China for a good fat sum! The old man didn't believe him, of course, and was rather surprised that in recounting his stay in Asia Malraux had made no mention of 'prisons, revolutions, ransom, famine . . .'[20] Max would not have long to wait!

PART III

THE CHALLENGE

====

6 A French colony in 1925

ANDRÉ MALRAUX'S first Indo-Chinese adventure (1923–4) centred on the admirable pile of pink sandstone hidden in the dark depths of the forest known as Banteaï-Sre. The second (1924–5) was marked by the personality of one man, Paul Monin. In his varied, tumultuous life, Malraux was to meet the most brilliant and most famous men of his time, from Picasso to Trotsky, from Gide to Mao Tse-tung, from Eisenstein to de Gaulle. But perhaps he never met a purer spirit.

Paul Monin came from an upper-middle-class family in Lyons. At the outbreak of war, aged eighteen, he signed on for the army and was several times wounded. When finally invalided out of the forces, he returned home only to find an alien, half-ruined family awaiting him. As soon as he had recovered from his latest injuries – he had been very seriously wounded in the head – he decided, for reasons that still remain unclear, to make a new life for himself in Indo-China. So, in 1917, accompanied by his wife and new-born son, he set sail for the East. He rapidly made a reputation for himself at the Saigon bar, initially for his professional ability (he was a brilliant public speaker), and later for his political views. In a society so riddled with conservatism, a racism tempered by paternalism and a generally repressive attitude, he immediately expressed his friendship with the 'natives', then known as Annamese.

Was he a Marxist revolutionary? Not in the least. Certainly Paul Monin had incited the seamen registered for service in the navy to strike in 1922 and, on occasion, waved the red flag. But there was nothing of the social agitator about him. He had one concern only: justice. For him, the colonial problem was not a matter of class, structures or ideology, but of respect for human beings. If he had an ideology it was that of the French Revolution.

Clara Malraux had met him during her return journey, in July 1924, and immediately struck up a friendship. He was a man of great personal charm, with a face the colour of ochre, a low forehead and finely-chiselled features. His warm, generous nature made him at once a devoted supporter of the cause she defended. He provided her with copious advice and useful addresses. On his return to Saigon, he met André Malraux. It was the day before the appeal trial was to open and, as Clara had predicted, they immediately became friends. Both men were enemies of injustice, populist 'aristocrats', swashbucklers of the barricades. And yet how different they were in many ways!

The one, a lawyer for whom there existed causes, men and principles, but no intellectual, suspicious of theories, a man of action rather than an ideologist; the other, a writer, bristling with ideas, an intellectual through and through, a manipulator of concepts, drunk with art and knowledge; the one eminently a man of the collectivity, the other hyper-individualistic. But they had in common a loàthing for injustice, more moral in origin in the case of Monin and perhaps more aesthetic for Malraux, and contempt for a society based on compromise, conformism and exclusiveness, as well as for racism and the bureaucracy of fools.

In the third volume of her memoirs, *Les Combats et les Jeux*, Clara Malraux describes Monin with great subtlety:

> A Frenchman giving what had been given to him, he had no wish to be a leader of men of other races: but around 1925, a crucial time no doubt, he was one of the first to establish new relations with them . . .
>
> Did he know that the values of these men were not his, which was precisely what had made our temporary domination possible? I don't think so.[1]

Today André Malraux speaks of Paul Monin with rather condescending fondness. But he stresses the almost exaggerated sense of justice, the disinterestedness, the eloquence and courage of the man who, from the floor of the court, dared to fling this remark in the face of a magistrate: 'In my time, Monsieur le Président, the ermine [that tops the robes of French magistrates] was always white!' Yet Malraux refuses to admit that Monin played a decisive role in his development.[2] Clara declares that in the building of this 'barricade' that they attempted to set up against colonial society 'our collaborator played an infinitely greater role than we did'. It was not Monin who wrote *Les Conquérants*, and in the history of ideas, if not in the revolution of our day, it is *Les Conquérants* that counts, and not the work of Maître Monin, barrister and politician. But without Monin, *Les Conquérants* would probably be quite unimaginable.

In February 1925, the Malrauxs arrived back safely in Saigon. Monin was waiting for them on the quay. After being welcomed back by their friend and ally, they settled in, like everybody else, at the Hôtel Continental, at the very centre of European activity, between the municipal theatre, the central market and the rue Catinat. Nearby, in the rue Pellerin, were Maître Monin's chambers. As we know, their first concern was the founding of a newspaper. But before they could do this they needed to know where they stood, for whom and against whom they were supposed to be fighting, and the nature of the régime they wished to overthrow.

Clenched in the grip of governor-generals like Martial Merlin, who had succeeded the intelligent and (more or less) liberal Albert Sarraut, Saigon was an odd combination of self-satisfied torpor and fear. Before the world crisis affected the rubber market, business went on its usual way, watched over by an administration that was often competent enough, but which had no other mission than the preservation of the status quo. Fortunes were amassed in a clammy world of crumpled banknotes and import–export deals.

Yet the prosperity, largely based on the systematic exploitation, backed by military might, of an extraordinarily proud and sensitive people, was tainted by fear – a fear that grew stronger each day. Deprived of virtually all civic rights, electors (in Cochin-China only) in the proportion of one in a thousand, victims of the gradual seizure of the land, excluded from almost every sector of economic development, denied almost every right of self-expression, the seventeen million Annamese, divided up between the semi-protectorate of Tonkin, the protectorate of Annam and the colony of Cochin-China, were sub-human beings, objects, fit only to become coolies on the plantations and paddy fields, or minor civil servants with a small share in the administration of Cambodia and Laos to keep them quiet.

But the system was beginning to crack up. Since the beginning of the century, the nationalist leader Pham Boi Chau had (from abroad) been calling on his fellow-countrymen to revolt. After presenting the demands of the Indo-Chinese at the Peace Conference in 1919, Nguyen Ai Quoc, later to be known as Ho Chi Minh, had joined the ranks of the newly-formed French Communist Party in 1920 and gathered around him a number of workers and students living in France. One of his mentors, Phan Chu Trinh, condemned to death, then later pardoned, was preparing to return to Indo-China.

The revolution of October 1917 had begun the radical re-examination of the bourgeois world, and above all of the colonial system that provided its basis. The nearest big city to Indo-China, Canton, had become the capital of the Chinese revolution, and it was there that the grand alliance was to be formed between the left wing of the Kuomintang and the young Chinese Communist Party. It was under the influence of their Chinese comrades that young Annamese exiles had formed the *Thanh-Nien* around Ho Chi Minh, who had recently arrived back from France, via Moscow. It was in Canton, in 1924, that a young Tonkinese nationalist had tried to assassinate the Governor-General, Merlin, who was on a visit to China.

This Saigon of mushrooming prosperity, Pernod with ice, peaceful smoking and feverish speculation was being undermined from within by the growing awareness of the young Annamese of the intolerable conditions to which they were subjected, and from the outside by the rise of Asian nationalism and the, still discreet, but none the less effective, support given them by the Soviet Union and the Communist International. This, then, was the ground on which Monin and Malraux hoped to act.

Clara describes the situation very well: 'All around us, a land of paddy fields, which remained greener than our fields, more open too, crossed by canals, divided up by dykes; a city crammed together in humid heat. Around us, men whose voices, even when they shout, seem to emanate from the silence.'³

This country must first be seen, beyond the opulent, humid city that tapped it and sent its resources off to Paris. In April, Monin took the Malrauxs to Phan-Thiet, in South Annam, a small town famous for the manufacture of *nuoc-mam*, the fish pickle that is the national condiment. Fifteen years earlier, Ho Chi Minh had been a schoolteacher there. A friend of Paul Monin, Monnier, owned a garage there. They arrived in the middle of a plague epidemic and were forced to take refuge in the mountains near Lang-Bian, but not before Monin pointed out to the Malrauxs several even more striking cases of exploitation in this microcosm of the colonial system.

On the plateaux surrounding the pleasant summer resort of Dalat, they met coolies fleeing from the recruiters who had taken them by force to the hevea plantations, to those beautiful red fields where they would suffer and die. Bound by three-year contracts that subjected them to slave labour that did not always ensure their subsistence, constantly in debt, knowing that they themselves would be forced to pay for their return journey to Tonkin, 'they expected to have their skeleton-like bodies buried in the winding-sheets they had brought with them at first: for here one can be naked and alive, but not naked and dead.'⁴

In this way they got to know the people for whom they were fighting and what they were fighting for. Not only did they make physical contact with the colonial condition, they were also made to experience the arbitrary rule of colonial power. Because he had collected funds to buy an aeroplane as a present for the Kuomintang on the occasion of the death of Sun Yat-sen (22 March), a Chinese businessman called Kang was apprehended and held under arrest (the euphemism used was 'placed under surveillance'). It took all the determination and eloquence of Paul Monin throughout April 1925 to get him freed. This followed closely on the affair in which a group of large

European firms had tried and, thanks largely to Monin, failed to gain a monopoly of the port of Saigon, ruining in the process a great many Chinese and Annamese tradespeople. It was on this double success that the new paper, *L'Indochine*, was to be launched.

But the terrain was no less dangerous for that. It was decided to send André Malraux to Hanoi – in an attempt to obtain the neutrality, if not the support, of the Governor-General – and Clara to Singapore, where she was to acquire rights to publish large extracts from the excellent newspapers in the British colony. André had no more success than he had had eighteen months earlier with the École française d'Extrême-Orient. He saw a cabinet attaché, who informed him that no obstacle would be placed in the way of a French-language daily newspaper, but that there could be no question of authorizing a paper in *Quoc ngu*, the national language (the letters of which had been Romanised for three centuries). An organ in this language would obviously have a much greater effect than a paper published in French, which could only reach a tiny élite.

In the 1920s, press legislation was extremely strict in Indo-China. The decree of 30 December 1898 laid it down that permission had first to be obtained for 'any publication in the Annamese language, in Chinese, or any other foreign language', not only in the colony of Cochin-China, but also in the protectorates. The reference to 'any other foreign language' could hardly fail to disturb a 'native' of Saigon. Here was a country where 'native' was synonymous with 'foreign'.

Before they could come to grips with the censors and other representatives of the colonial power, Monin and Malraux had to ensure the financing of their paper. They found most of their backers among the enlightened Annamese bourgeoisie, and more particularly in the Chinese community of Cholon, which generally supported the Kuomintang, and for whom any progress in the emancipation of a neighbouring people was a promise of future support for the cause of Chinese liberation. One evening, the Malrauxs and Monin were invited to Cholon to celebrate the presentation to the organisers of *L'Indochine* of sums of money collected by the Chinese communities throughout the colony:

At the table, a single white woman, a single woman, myself, and two white men, Monin and André; we were used to the situation by now. It was an important meeting – which did not stop anyone getting up to smoke a few pipes on a wooden platform behind us . . . We drank and proposed toasts. The first was a vote of thanks to Monin for his interventions and for the friendly gestures he had made towards the [Chinese] Republic . . .

Before the meal came to an end . . . Monin got to his feet and spoke of his attachment to the Chinese cause. It was in the interests of the French to fill the vacuum left by the departure of the British; the French democratic tradition brought with it the possibility of economic expansion that would benefit all countries and not just a few greedy colonists. He spoke of the directives that formed the basis of Sun Yat-sen's policy and to which his successors remained faithful: government of the people, by the people and for the people . . .

My companion stood up. Several times he pushed back the lock of hair that fell over his forehead, then raised his index finger . . . 'We are going to start a newspaper together . . . We are going to struggle side by side . . . It would be wrong to think that our views are identical. What has brought us together, what unites us, are the enemies we have in common.'[5]

This fraternal evening spent with these Chinese, so close and yet so different, seems to have had a profound effect on André Malraux. Clara, whose every word, at such moments, reveals both insight and observation, goes on:

After the Kuomintang banquet, André became aware for the first time that a body of men was not the sum of the individuals that composed it, but a new element that went beyond them. This justified the interest shown to human beings none of whom in himself would have seemed worthy of attention.

In the country we had left, we had been beaten, forced into submission . . . At what moment did we decide that we had endured this submission long enough, that we would now change roles, and that it was now our turn to act upon the world, to leave our mark upon it? From the moment, I suppose, that our dreams of reversing the situation no longer seemed so absurd. Once the dice were thrown, we acquired an insatiable taste for our own game. As every moment passed, I watched my companion become more and more what he did.[6]

7 A fighting newspaper

THEY decided at first to call the newspaper they were going to
start *L'Indochine*. It was a title that had nothing provocative, or
even, at first sight, political about it, but it had the advantage
of situating the enterprise well and truly in Asia, without limit-
ing it to Saigon or even Cochin-China: they also wanted to
reach the élites of Hué, Hanoi and Phnom Penh. They found
offices, at 12 rue Taberd, not far from Monin's chambers in the
rue Pellerin, and set about forming their team.

In the Saigon of 1925, indigenous journalism was represented
by a handful of gifted Annamese intellectuals: Nguyen Phan
Long, a novelist of refined sensibility and a liberal politician who,
on a day of great emotion, solemnly conferred on Paul Monin
the title of 'Annamese citizen', and who, twenty years later, was
to become the ephemeral leader of one of the phantom governments of the semi-independent Baodaiist Vietnam within the
French Union; his colleague Bui Quang Chieu, who shared
with him the editorship of *La Tribune indigène* and the leadership of the Constitutionalist Party, and who, through weakness
of character, did even less than Long to serve the movement of
national liberation; Nguyen An Ninh, the best of them, who
had made the independent satirical paper, *La Cloche Fêlée*,
courageous enough in its criticism to be prohibited for some
months prior to the appearance of *L'Indochine*. It was to him
that the Governor of Cochin-China addressed the now famous
words: 'If you want to train intellectuals, go to Moscow! The
seed you wish to sow in this country will never sprout!'

The 'journalism' of Saigon also consisted of a few papers in the hands of the administration or business circles – all of extremely poor quality. First among these was *L'Impartial*, some of whose attacks on Malraux have already been quoted. The invariably aggressive tone of the editorials of its publisher, Henry de Lachevrotière, reminds one irresistibly of Lenin's description of the press as 'the watchdogs of the bourgeoisie'.

The only newspaper of value was *L'Écho annamite*, published in French by 'natives'. It was there that *L'Indochine* found its most reliable, competent and faithful collaborator, Dejean de la Batie. Son of an Annamese woman and a high-ranking French diplomat who, having recognised him as his son, gave him a good education, he had chosen to devote himself, as he put it, to 'the defence of the race to which I owe my mother'. To certain of his Annamese friends who reproached him with leaving *L'Écho* for a newspaper founded by Frenchmen, he replied: 'the name of Monin is in itself sufficient guarantee of the pro-Annamese tendencies of *L'Indochine*,' and added that he had felt obliged to respond to the appeal of men who had 'approached the Annamese with outstretched arms and open hearts' and who, furthermore, had placed 'powerful forces' at the service of their just cause. A true professional, resolute militant, and faithful friend, who showed that he could resist pressure and the threats directed at his family, Dejean de la Batie was, with Monin, Clara and André Malraux, one of the cornerstones of *L'Indochine*.

They were joined by two young Annamese intellectuals, Hin and Vinh, and later by Nguyen Pho, whom everyone first suspected of being in the pay of the police, but who, after the departure of Dejean and the Malrauxs, became the able manager of the paper (under the new title, *L'Indochine enchaînée*). Hin, a native of the Hué region, the son of a Mandarin family, was all contained violence, ready to explode at any minute. He became Malraux's model for Hong in *Les Conquérants* and, later, for Chen in *La Condition humaine*.

This trio, who were joined on occasion for long nocturnal discussions in Monin's drawing-room by Nguyen Phan Long, Nguyen An Ninh, and later their older comrade, the celebrated Phan Chu Trinh, who had returned from France in the autumn, opened for the Malrauxs the doors of the true Indo-China.

Absent from such discussions, of course, was their real leader, Pham Boi Chau, who was first exiled, then imprisoned, and Ho Chi Minh, at this time in Canton training cadres who would later relegate such talk to the museum. But it was an Indo-China enlarged to the dimensions of Asia that they were discovering through their Kuomintang friends from Cholon, Dong Thuan and Dang Dai. Clara saw in these stocky, fearless men the Jews of a diaspora already close to a great return home. It was there, under the great fan blades turning slowly on Monin's ceiling, that the themes of *La Tentation de l'Occident* and even of *La Condition humaine* were developed.

Clara began to smoke, but not André. As we have seen, he had already smoked hashish, but as his wife remarked opium requires 'more passivity than he possessed'.[1] With Monin they both went for long nocturnal walks around Bien Hoa which (before it became an important American airbase in 1960) was, according to Clara, the local red-light district. She describes the two men 'wearing suits which, if they had not been of linen, would have been suitable for a turn along the Avenue du Bois: André, with his neck squeezed into a tie, Monin, wearing a bow-tie, each carrying an ebony cane, which he flourished stylishly'.[2] On other evenings, the two friends met for fencing practice in readiness for a confrontation with their 'friend' Lachevrotière, with whom Monin had fought a duel the previous year. This life of revolutionary dandies, defenders of the weak, the orphans and the outcasts, must have delighted Malraux.

A mordant description of the man that Malraux was at this time is provided by a friend of Clara's, a nonchalant adventurer of the Saigon streets. In 1925, he says, André Malraux was 'a very humorous guy. He did not take himself seriously – even less any of that rotten gang who were plundering the country . . . With his cauliflower ears, pointed chin, huge eyes, which they really were, with the pupils set high up . . . He hated people who took themselves seriously. He thought such people were the cause of all the evil in the world . . .'[3]

L'Indochine made its appearance on 17 June 1925. The first three issues were distributed free of charge. Forty-six issues followed before the paper was finally strangled. *L'Indochine* saw itself from the outset as a 'free organ, open to all, unconnected with any banks or commercial groups, in which polemicists will write with acerbity and the moderates with moderation'.[4] In fact, the 'moderates' were reduced to Dejean, who could only bite when he deliberately set out to do so, and Clara, who had acquired the rights of reproducing the English-language press of Singapore – especially the *Singapore Free Press* – and passed them off, in all innocence, as the work of *L'Indochine*'s 'special correspondents'.

Looked at today, *L'Indochine* has a very old-fashioned air about it, with its naïve layout and thick type. But something of the brilliance of its writing survives. Monin and Malraux wanted to found a campaigning newspaper. Almost every day, the front page carried an editorial written by one or other of them against some powerful figure in the régime – Cognacq, the Governor of Cochin-China, or Darles, his frightful deputy, who was known as 'the butcher of Thai-Nguyen'.

In the second issue, Malraux wrote an attack on the Governor, Cognacq. This former doctor had helped to found the Medical College at Hanoi and had been regarded, for a time, as a liberal. He had been on good terms with the 'Young Annam' move-ment (which Malraux and Monin were now trying to revitalise) and had arrived in Saigon with a reputation for honest dealing. Either power had gone to his head, or he had become the tool of Darles, a civil servant who had made a name for himself for his almost sadistic taste for repression – whatever the reason, he ruled over Cochin-China with sanctimonious brutality and complete absence of scruple.

Malraux launched fearless attacks on the Governor, who was trying to depress sales of the newspaper by threatening sub-scribers and discouraging buyers. Malraux nicknamed him 'Monsieur Je-menottes' [*menottes* are handcuffs] and answered the threats directed against *L'Indochine* with other threats: 'A gesture to be expected from a *valet de chambre*, but quite un-worthy of a Governor! . . . You have tried to run everything single-handed. This was a plausible theory, but one that you alone approved. The people's representatives are now clearly in opposition to the policy of your friends. In France, these silent demonstrations may well be noted.'

But the Governor had already found cavaliers to defend his outraged virtue. Those 'common enemies' on whom André Malraux depended to weld together his alliance with very different men and forces were to reveal their strength and their hatred. Their attack was to bear on three fronts: Monin's 'Bolshevism', André Malraux's legal past and the authenticity of the information published by *L'Indochine*. What these people could not stomach was the explosion of talent, daring, non-conformism and disinterest – yes, this time 'disinterest' does apply to Malraux – in this little world reeking of clammy, profitable servility.

The first number of *L'Indochine* opened with an interview with the scientist Paul Painlevé, new head of the French government, by Jean Bouchor. It was stated that the views contained in the interview had been expressed some weeks before the accession of Painlevé to the premiership, but not how the interview had been obtained. Painlevé said some highly interesting things. First, that 'the Indo-Chinese population should have a consultative voice in matters relating to the colony'. Then, that 'since education is the best means of assimilating the races,' the Annamese should 'have access to our education, at all levels'. Finally, that 'the French and native press ought to be free'. Today, such views seem mild or paternalistic, but in Saigon the effect was like so many lashes.

Lachevrotière set out, not to refute the new premier's ideas, but to throw doubt on the authenticity of the interview. *L'Indochine* replied by pointing out that since this number of the paper had not yet reached Paris, the prime minister could hardly have expressed a valid opinion on the matter. The paper would obtain confirmation of his statements without delay and meanwhile it would exhibit to the public the manuscript of Jean Bouchor's article. The 'interview' does appear to have been made up of statements made by Painlevé and no doubt represented his views. But quite clearly he had no desire, just after his accession to the premiership, to avail himself of the services of an opposition newspaper to make an attack on the colonial administration.

André Malraux was not a man to confine himself to a quarrel regarding the authenticity of sources. He launched a virulent and witty attack on his old adversary. Malraux had certainly succeeded in unearthing some highly unsavoury details from Lachevrotière's past, the most telling perhaps being his reply to the charge of blackmail laid against him in the Saigon court. He begged the judges to take no account of such accusations on the grounds that, as he put it, 'I was only doing my job as a police informer! . . .'

One can see the level, the colour, the smell of the bog in which the Malrauxs and Monin were struggling. But there were times, no doubt, when André Malraux could hardly conceal the feelings of triumph with which he launched his attacks: he was too avid a reader of *Bouvard et Pécuchet* and *The Possessed* not to find some perverse pleasure in human stupidity and baseness. Some years later, André Gide was to express surprise that there were no fools in Malraux's novels – to which Malraux replied that there were quite enough to be found in life. But it is surprising that *La Condition humaine* and *Les Noyers de l'Altenburg* contain no characters like Lachevrotière, except in the form of some single contemptible action on the part of a Clappique, a sadistic gesture by Nicolaieff in *Les Conquérants*, or the pessimistic malice of Mollberg in *Les Noyers de l'Altenburg*.

It is surprising too that despite this concert of insults they had the leisure to live at the Hôtel Continental, in the midst of Saigon, passing every day, on the terrace of the hotel, in front of the theatre, beside the church, at the harbour front, insulters and insulted. How was this possible? 'European' Saigon was so small then. What a den of wild cats it must have been!

Mediocrity though he might be, Governor Cognacq represented, by virtue of his office and the power that went with it, a more worthy adversary for these duellists. After Malraux's first article he had summoned the young man to the palace, hoping either to detach him from Monin by some favour, or to intimidate him. The visitor replied with nothing but sarcasm and proceeded to publish extracts from the conversation that merely revealed (or confirmed) the Governor's baseness and stupidity. And the struggle began, not on the level of personal wrangling, as with Lachevrotière and his ilk, but on the main subject of dispute: a system of government founded on police terror,

Malraux at four years old.

A family snap taken on
holiday at Dieppe,
with Malraux, age eight,
in the foreground.

Malraux with Clara,
his first wife.

As a hussar in Strasbourg.

Malraux with Louis Chevasson,
above as joint editors of *Aldes,*
right as amateur archeologists in
a Saigon pagoda, between the two
trials (autumn 1924).

Malraux in 1926.

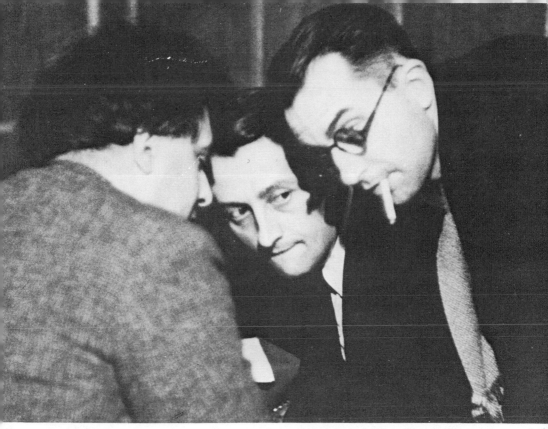

Malraux *above*, with Ilya Ehrenburg and Paul Nizan, and
below speaking at the International Writers' Congress in
Paris in 1936. Gide is on his left.

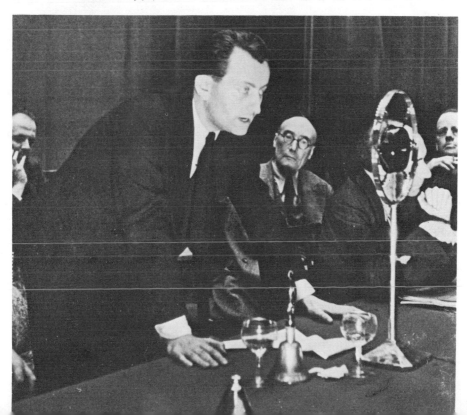

In the Allier, at the Chevassons', in September 1942, at the
time of the first contacts with the British networks.

The Minister with Emmanuel d'Astier.

Malraux and de Gaulle.

On the eve of his departure for Bangladesh, March 1973.

favouritism, corruption and racial discrimination. On this level, the somewhat confused, incurably provincial and exotic aspects of *L'Indochine* – one cannot wallow in mud and not get dirty – were more than made up by the courage, the relevance, the efficacity of the campaigns promulgated by the newspaper. It became essential for the authorities that *L'Indochine* be crushed.

The first of the campaigns launched by Monin and Malraux succeeded in stopping the operation of the 'Khanh-Hoi property company', which had been formed some years before with a view to 'developing the port of Saigon-Cholon' and to gaining control over the harbour traffic and the management of the warehouses. The managing director of the company was no less a person than one of the Governor's most faithful civil servants, the 'inspector of political affairs', Eutrope, while the prime mover of the enterprise was the president of the Chamber of Agriculture, Labaste, also a close colleague of Dr Cognacq. As published in *L'Indochine*, the contract laid all the obligations on the municipality and none on the company. The affair consisted of getting a formidable monopolistic operation financed by the municipality of Saigon (and ruining, in the process, innumerable small businesses).

L'Indochine's second campaign was still more daring and salutary, for it concerned the Annamese peasantry, the prime victims of the system of exploitation. On 10 July, the editors of *L'Indochine* were visited by five peasants clad in the shiny black *kai-ao*. 'We are peasants from Camau,' they said, 'and we have come to demand justice . . .' And on 11 July 1925, *L'Indochine* revealed that the auctioning off of a very large area of land, recently reclaimed for cultivation, in the Camau region, in the far south of Cochin-China, famed for the fertility of its rice-fields, had been rigged. Furthermore, behind the 'consortium' that was planning to rob the peasants of most of their land (at a ridiculously low price, fixed by the authorities) was no less a person than Governor Cognacq himself. 'Before the peasants left the offices of *L'Indochine*, Monin said: "We'll go as far as the courts. And we'll have reliable interpreters, which is unusual enough here." He smiled, his upper lip curling back a little to the right. Seeing him smile, the Annamese were already almost reassured, ready to dismiss an enemy who was more vulnerable than they imagined.'[5]

Letters confirming Monin's revelations flooded into the offices of *L'Indochine* from other peasants threatened with dispossession and even from French rice-growers sickened by the manoeuvre. Malraux appealed directly to Governor-General Monguillot to put a stop to this shameful operation. The day before the day fixed for the 'auction', Dr Cognacq made it known that two of the provisions of the procedure, the two most irregular ones, had been annulled. Thus the auction could take place without incident – and with no glaring profiteering.

But Monin and Malraux could not be content with making their paper a satirical goad. They aimed higher and claimed to be formulating something like a government programme. At this time, neither of them was in favour of a radical liberation of the colonies. While, from his exile in Japan, Pham Boi Cho was pleading for the end of foreign rule in Vietnam and, since joining the Third International in December 1920, Nguyen Ai Quoc – Ho Chi Minh – had been working out an action programme in which reformism within the colonial context would be gradually excluded, Monin and Malraux remained advocates of an egalitarian assimilation in the best Jacobin tradition, not simply because they believed it to be more possible, but from conviction.

Their plea was basically for a recognition of the demand expressed by Phan Chu Trinh in the columns of *L'Indochine* on 29 June 1925: 'Let us be given the same law as the French and we will want nothing better than to live under the protection of France. French law for all!' When one of the leaders of the Annamese intelligentsia, who ten years earlier had been inspired by Ho Chi Minh, was talking like that, why should Frenchmen like Monin and Malraux have been more extreme in their demands than this national hero?

Cognacq's principle remained the basis of cultural policy: any literate person was a potential revolutionary. Hence the mediocrity of secondary education (Albert Sarraut had had to rage and storm before a lycée was established at Saigon). Hanoi University, the only one in Indo-China, which had a mere thousand places for a population of twenty million, did not offer degrees equivalent to those of the universities in metropolitan France. 'Health officers', not fully qualified doctors, were produced. This made it extremely difficult for young people to go to France to complete their studies: furthermore, the dossier that they had to compile if they wished to do so was totally dependent on the goodwill of the police authorities – that is, on their family's record for good conduct. Newspapers like *Le Courrier saigonnais* openly congratulated themselves on this procedure: 'in this way the authorities bar the way of anti-France'. By blocking the way to France!

Malraux and Monin fought valiantly to denounce this state of affairs, just as they pleaded for the emendation of a naturalisation policy that today would be regarded as alienating, but which was then one of the aims of an intelligentsia eager for equality and rights and indignant about what Nguyen An Ninh, in *La Cloche Fêlée*, called the 'constipation' of naturalisation (thirty-one cases in 1924!). Monin was able to prove that naturalisation was easy enough to come by – it simply cost the applicant 3000 piastres!

So Monin, with his newly acquired title of 'honourable citizen of the Annamese nation', and his friend Malraux, 'a victim of arbitrary colonial rule', considered that the time had come to resuscitate a movement known as Young Annam, which had had some success in the immediate post-war years, especially in Hanoi, but which had then become embroiled in intrigues with the colonial authorities and fallen into decline. Owing to his propensity for 'writing up' events, Malraux later presented himself, in various interviews and letters, as the leader of the Young Annam party. This organisation seems never to have grown much beyond the staff of *L'Indochine* and a few friends. Apart from Malraux and Monin, the main organiser of the party was Nguyen Pho, an attractive, complex young intellectual from Tonkin; as we have seen, he was already being regarded by his colleagues as a police informer. This situation did little to encourage a feeling of collective confidence.

Young Annam left practically no mark on the country: no literature, no hostile press coverage, no accounts of any meetings – and the police took little notice of it. Neither Walter

Langlois, in his excellent essay *L'Aventure indochinoise d'André Malraux*, nor Clara, in *Les Combats et les Jeux*, makes any more than a passing reference to it. As journalists, Monin and Malraux had a profound impact, but as militants they seem to have passed unnoticed, except as partners of more important figures in the struggle for Annamese reawakening.

When, at the end of September 1925, Phan Chu Trinh was able to return to Saigon, accompanied by Nguyen An Ninh, Dejean de la Batie and Clara were the only members of the group to meet them on the quay and take part in the moving reunion that followed. Neither Monin nor Malraux was there: a strange absence on the part of men who claimed to be galvanising the 'energies' of the Vietnamese people. Was it, as Clara rather maliciously suggests, that the Annamese were not prepared to choose as their leader 'the revolutionary, half-conquistador, half-civil servant, who, crook in hand, was leading his sheep, with a combination of severity and gentleness, towards adulthood . . . Reality has mocked our legends: the Asian leaders are Asians . . .' These few, rather simple, but telling words explode the whole assumption on which, for all its generosity of heart and mind, the idea of Young Annam – and the myth of *Les Conquérants* – was based.

Although Young Annam did not expand as its creators had hoped, *L'Indochine* continued to fight valiantly in a struggle whose outcome became clear by the end of July. Pressure, threats, blackmail: sellers, distributors and buyers were ordered to boycott the paper of 'the Bolshevik Monin and the adventurer Malraux'.

One scene, among others, described by Clara Malraux throws a curious light on this small, enclosed world and on the future works of André Malraux.

> Hin stood like a squat pillar in the middle of the drawing-room. He wasn't even looking at us. He knew what he wanted to do. In his place, a European would have been pacing up and down to steady his nerves. Hin probably felt no tension whatsoever: he had made up his mind to kill Governor Cognacq . . .

The acting Governor-General, Montguillot, was expected at

Saigon. Some procession or ceremony would enable Hin to carry out his action: as a press photographer he would be able to get close to his victim and shoot. The whole editorial team of *L'Indochine* were gathered round him, fearful, hostile or incredulous:

'You'll miss.'

'I'm a good shot . . .'

I could see nothing but Hin, his short legs apart, his hair raised in a crest in the middle of his cranium, his dark, large-grained skin. I thought he was right. I also thought that if he carried out this gesture it would be the end of any hopes for that country.

Monin then spoke:

'You'll be arrested, Hin.'

'And condemned to death,' Hin replied, like a character out of a Malraux novel.

I took my eyes off Hin for a moment and saw Dejean shrug his shoulders.

'It's not on,' he said.

'I shall do it,' said Hin, 'because it has to be done. He's nothing but a wild beast. Because of him, the fields are taken from the *nha-ques*. There must be a change.'

'It won't change just because you kill him. And if there is a change, it'll be for the worse. It'll give them an excuse at last to treat us as enemies.'

'The important thing is to attract attention to ourselves,' said Hin.

. . . In any case, for them, our patriots are never anything more than pirates or murderers.'

'It's a question of being effective murderers . . .'

'. . . You've no organisation behind you that could use the disorder that would follow to carry on the struggle.'

'Organisation, organisation . . .' repeated Hin. Then, becoming suddenly angry, he shouted: 'I don't care. I don't care. I don't care.'

Just near the door, he stopped and looked round at us. He was no longer sure whether we were friends or enemies. Without particularly intending to, our eyes met. I know what

he was thinking: 'We'll free ourselves of you without you.'
I knew he was right.[6]

Monin was then called away to the telephone: he was told
that Montguillot had cancelled the visit he was supposed to
make to Saigon.

The Hong of *Les Conquérants* and the Chen of *La Condition
humaine* were to carry their plan right through, but the characters have already taken shape.

The cancellation of Montguillot's visit to Saigon got the little
Indochine group off the hook – but only for a while. The paper
could not now be saved even by an apparently crucial decision
of the French government: the appointment as Governor-
General of Indo-China of a man whose name struck terror into
the camp of Monin's enemies, Alexandre Varenne, a Socialist
deputy and vice-president of the lower house. A Socialist
governor! On 31 July, in *L'Indochine*, Monin gave a warm welcome to this 'friend of liberty', this 'enemy of arbitrary rule',
whose appointment would lead to 'many valuable reforms'.

It was too late. Since 20 June, Monin and Malraux had not
ceased protesting against the pressure exerted by an administration that 'summons Annamese who happened to be guilty of
subscribing to *L'Indochine* and scolds them roundly for doing
so,' and which 'denigrates' those who write for the paper. They
threatened to bring the matter to the attention of parliament.[7]
But Cognacq proved the stronger. He informed *L'Indochine*'s
printer, a Eurasian called Louis Minh, who had courageously
agreed to work for the so-called 'Bolsheviks', that if he per-
sisted he would get no more orders. And that wouldn't be all:
he would have a typographers' strike on his hands, for example.

On 14 August, Minh warned the publishers of *L'Indochine*
that he would have to stop working for them. Monin tried to
knock on other doors. He soon realised that Cognacq had fore-
seen this and had already issued warnings to all the other
printers in Saigon. *L'Indochine* was killed.[8]

On the day before they were silenced, on this same 14 August
1925, André Malraux had published, in the last number of the
doomed paper, what may be regarded as his manifesto on the
colonial question for the 1920s. It is a fine piece of writing that

shows Malraux to be already a moralist and a master of political prose – although he certainly does not emerge from it as a revolutionary:

Our policy in Cochin-China and Annam is very simple at the present time: it says that the Annamese have no reason to come to France, and it involves immediately a coalition, *against us*, of the best minds and the most vital forces in Annam. It would seem that the political idiocies of sectional interests and money are applying themselves with unusual determination to destroying what we have been able to do, and to reawakening in this old land, soon with memories of a great past, the muffled echoes of six hundred revolts . . .

Travelling through Annam, from the mouth of the Red River to the Mekong delta, one notices one thing above all: the name of every illustrious city is that of a revolt. Its most moving plains bear the names of battles. The tomb of Le-Loi lies in ruins, but the songs that exalt the sombre grandeur of his life of courage and adventure live still upon the lips of every woman and in the memories of every fisherman. At Quang-Ngai, Thanh-Hoa, Vinh, reserves of energy of which there is so great a need in the Far East are waiting to see realised the new understanding that we have promised them . . .

Paul Monin, the Malrauxs, Dejean de la Batie and their friends did not consider themselves beaten. Were they thinking, as Clara suggests,[9] of seizing the offices of *L'Impartial*, whose insults had been redoubled by their silence, in order to prolong the appearance of their paper? Had they done so, the style of May 1968 would have found a distant precursor. If we are to believe what Paul Morand says in his *Papiers d'identité*, André was thinking of leaving for Canton, where, since the end of May, a general strike had been called, as in Hong Kong. But his visit to China was to be a short one. It was obvious that *L'Indochine* could find no printer in the colony. But the paper now had a press at its disposal – all it needed to resume publication was a set of type. This commodity was unobtainable in

Indo-China. However, they had been told that it might be found in Hong Kong, where the British authorities were less restrictive and reactionary than the French of Hanoi and Saigon. In short, the paper sent Clara and André Malraux to Hong Kong to obtain the type necessary for relaunching *L'Indochine* under the nose of Dr Cognacq.

On the deck of the ship that was carrying them to Hong Kong, Clara was told by a phlegmatic Englishman that the captain had just sent a telegram informing the British authorities that 'the reddest Bolshevik of all Annam' was on board.[10] The news travelled fast: with the result that when the ship arrived in the harbour, paralysed by the general strike, they were the only passengers whose luggage the coolies would carry!

Luck was with them. The day after their arrival they read in an advertisement in one of the colony's newspapers that the Jesuits were modernising the equipment of their paper and wished to sell their old type. So they set off to climb the Peak, resigning themselves (half-laughingly, half-ashamed) to being carried there by coolies. They were given a cordial welcome by the Jesuits. The whole matter was settled very simply. The material was not at all expensive. Some of the type would not be available until the following week, but the good fathers promised to dispatch the remainder themselves.

Mission accomplished.

Tourists once more, they were now free to sample the hospitality of their British hosts. They discovered the ambiguous charms of Macao, melting into the enormous crowd – followed the whole time by diligent little spies, who became less and less discreet as time went on and who, in the end, actually offered their services as guides.

On arrival in Saigon, the cases of type were confiscated on the pretext that certain dispatching formalities had been omitted. M. Cognacq was persistent. But a week later the type sent by the Jesuits themselves arrived, with ecclesiastical punctuality – and this enabled preparations for the reappearance of the paper to go ahead.

But, meanwhile, let us look again at these 'four or five days of false holiday' spent by André and Clara in Hong Kong. Until 1931, it was all the author of *Les Conquérants* was to know of China. These few hours, wandering aimlessly from the top of the rock to the stinking back streets of Kowloon, from the fish markets of Victoria to the 'curio' shops of Sing Wong Street, were to give birth to the fascinating inventions of *La Tentation de l'Occident* and the evocations of *Les Conquérants*.

8 L'Indochine enchaînée

SO BEGAN the career of *L'Indochine enchaînée*. It was to prove even more brief than that of *L'Indochine*: from the beginning of November 1925 to the end of February 1926, theoretically appearing twice weekly, with interruptions due mainly to the caprices of the printing press. In all, twenty-three issues were published – the last five, in January and February, after the Malrauxs' departure. It was a strange paper, but a very fine one, with all its irregularities and misprints, its technical clumsiness and lack of order, its thick paper and its dropped characters. ('Wooden characters, just like in the sixteenth century!' cried Malraux joyfully.) This newspaper, bearing the scars of its persecution, is one of the most moving testimonies that remain to the courage and obstinacy of Malraux's life and work.

These characters, bought from the English-speaking Jesuits of Hong Kong, had none of the accents that are needed in French. At first, the result was deplorable. But on the third night, *L'Indochine* received a strange visit, described by André Malraux in the preface to *Indochine S.O.S.*:

> When you came to see me, the action of the government had finally put an end to the only revolutionary newspaper in Indo-China and the peasants of Baclieu were reduced to pacified silence . . . You took out of your pocket a handkerchief tied as a purse, with the corners sticking up like rabbits' ears . . .
> 'They're just "e"s . . . "E"s with acute accents, grave accents and circumflexes . . . Tomorrow many workers will

do as I have done; and we'll bring all the accents we can.'

You opened the handkerchief, emptied out on to a press stone the tangled type and set them out with the end of your printer's finger without further comment. You had taken them from the presses of government newspapers, and you knew that if you were caught you'd be tried, not as a revolutionary, but as a thief. When they were all in line, like the pawns of a chess-set, all you said was: 'If I'm caught, tell the Europeans what we have done, so that they know what is going on here.'

In fact, it was Clara who received a group of five men, at night, on the terrace of Monin's villa, where she was staying in the absence of the two 'bosses'. Her account is more sober:

> Their hands rummaged under their long tunics and took out a tiny parcel. Before offering them to me in their joined, open palms, in the usual manner, they made the deep bows due to those one respects, the *lai* that they had refused to perform before government employees. Very rapidly their nimble hands untied the corners of their handkerchief-parcels to present the object of their offering: printing characters stolen from their place of work . . . I would like to have expressed our gratitude, our desire to work with them, but I was alone and did not speak Annamese. I bowed to them, in turn, hands joined, like the *qua-ninh* Chinese . . .[1]

L'Indochine, enchaînée but not quite gagged, was ready to welcome Varenne: Monin and Malraux wished to give the arrival of a Socialist governor its full significance. They were, to say the least, disappointed. Varenne – who, in any case, had been expelled from the Socialist Party a month after his appointment for accepting this pro-consular post – was not one of those strange Socialists enamoured of colonial wars who proliferated under the French Fourth Republic. He was a well-intentioned man, but, as often happens in such cases, he would not rest until he had made people forget his original label.

Monin had prophesied that the arrival in Saigon of 'the Socialist Varenne [was to] mark the inevitable hour of retribution'. The day after the new Governor-General's arrival, Monin and Malraux published an 'open letter' in which they wrote: 'Governor Cognacq has done as much damage to this country as a war.' But the two rebels tried in vain to contact Varenne. And it was with sorrow at first, then anger, that they heard him declare to the colony that he intended to concern himself first, not with 'Annamese reforms', but with 'social reforms' and, where abuses were concerned, it would be better 'to forget the past'. This led to the cry of indignation published in the last November number of *L'Indochine enchaînée*: 'Socialist yesterday, conservative today . . . Yet another conversation under the sign of the piastre!'

'If this freedom that is so dear to the hearts of the Annamese was granted them immediately,' the Governor-General stated, 'and if they abused that freedom and sowed discord in the country by the extremism of their ideas, it would not be long before a wave of reaction swept everything away . . .' (In other words, reaction now in order to prevent reaction in the future!) Ten days after his arrival in Saigon, Monin wrote: 'Never has a governor-general taken so little time to discredit himself!' For Monin and Malraux, who did so much to appeal to the democratic instincts of metropolitan France against the colonial régime, the pusillanimity of this metropolitan democrat, and a Socialist at that, was like a contradiction of all they stood for.

The collapse of Monin's and Malraux's last hopes seems to have exacerbated still more their hatred of the system. In an extremely violent article entitled 'In praise of Torture', Malraux relates that a policeman had beaten a suspect to the point of maiming him in order to extort money. He concluded that this 'torturer and informer' had every chance of being elected President of the Colonial Council for his good work!

One last cause was to mobilise the talents, courage and vitality of the two friends – and bring Malraux back to Phnom Penh. This was what came to be known as 'the Bardez affair'. Bardez, an administrator in Cambodia, was given the job of collecting a new tax on the rice harvest. He was met with resistance, of a passive kind at first, from the village of Krang-Leou. He seized one of the peasants as a hostage in order to force the others to pay up, but having succeeded refused to release the man. The ensuing argument ended – for Cambodian gentleness can suddenly be transformed into violence – in Bardez and his guards being lynched. The authorities soon had a riot on their hands. Troops arrived on the scene and seized three hundred suspects. The affair had to be examined and tried, but it was entrusted not to a magistrate but to a high-ranking civil servant. Malraux saw an opportunity of unmasking both an odious tax system and a legal system based on 'government information', of which the year before he himself had been the victim. He dashed to Phnom Penh and became a passionately involved observer.

The Bardez trial involved a whole series of legal abuses of a kind known only too well to Malraux: the obvious partiality of the judge, the constant intervention of political civil servants, an attempt to poison the defence counsel, Maître Gallet (who claimed that 'the crime of Krang-Leou was committed by the whole of Cambodia', for it was the result of 'general discontent'), refusal to allow defence witnesses. When the hearings were over, Malraux took his revenge by publishing the following comment in *L'Indochine enchaînée*:

> It cannot be repeated too often that before being applied in the colonies the various laws should be thoroughly revised. I would like to see, for example, a law that would be based on the following principles:
>   1 Every defendant to have his head cut off;
>   2 He will then be defended by a barrister;
>   3 The barrister to have his head cut off;
>   4 And so on . . .

But *L'Indochine enchaînée*, in turn, collapsed. Clara and André had spent the last of their money. Their room at the Hôtel Continental had not been paid for months. They were still being served with a few meals under the reproving eye of the cashier, but how long would this go on? Clara tells us: 'André remembered the contract with Bernard Grasset . . . He wrote to the publisher, mentioned a book he was working on. At the end of November, he said to me: "There's nothing left for me now but to write." There could have been worse ways out of the situation it seemed to me. Living in Saigon was becoming as unpleasant for me as living in Phnom Penh had been.'[2]

By early December 1925, they were thinking of nothing but leaving. But they were not to do so before yet another dramatic incident occurred: an attempt was made on the life of Paul Monin by an Annamese (almost certainly in the pay of the police). Monin was awoken one night to find his mosquito net pulled open by a man brandishing a razor. It was Chen again, the Chen of *La Condition humaine* . . . In the last December issue of *L'Indochine enchaînée*, which appeared just as they were embarking – their Chinese friends had lent them, without any security, the money for two return tickets – André Malraux took his 'leave' of Indo-China. He justified his retreat thus: 'We must appeal to the French people through speeches, through public meetings, through the press and through pamphlets. We must get the working masses to sign petitions in favour of the Annamese cause . . . This is why I am leaving for France.'

They left on 30 December 1925, embittered and disillusioned. The fine friendships forged in the rue Taberd and the rue Pellerin had become less close. Was it, perhaps, because failure embitters those who set out to do something? Or was it a simple matter of money or precedence? Or disagreements on tactics or policy? Paul Monin, who a year before had welcomed them with open arms, did not even see them off at the harbour. Only two Chinese friends from Cholon, Dong Than and Dang Dai, accompanied them to the ship. As they made their farewells, they handed Clara a tin of lychees, depicting prophetically, two young dancers dressed in red.

The twenty-four-year-old man who returned to France in January 1926, almost chased out of Indo-China, cut off from his friends, his hopes dashed, once again financially ruined, his health impaired, was passionately involved with this continent of Asia that he was only just beginning to know, and possessed of a strength, an acuity, a stylistic mastery in his writing that went well beyond the talents and gifts of the young traveller of 1923.

On the deck of the ship that took him and his wife from Singapore to Colombo, from Suez to Port Said, he wrote the letters to Marcel Arland that were later to become *La Tentation de l'Occident*: a work in which he tried to compare oriental man's relation to the world – of which he had caught a glimpse in his encounters with his Chinese friends in Cholon, in his visits to the peasants of the Ha-Tinh, in the Phnom Penh trial in which fifty Khmer peasants struggled in the grips of colonial justice, in the evenings spent with Nguyen Pho or 'Hin-the-rebel' — with the ambitions, wants and capacities of Western man.

9 Asia: the dream and the reality

JANUARY 1926: with the ship that steered its course from Cap Saint-Jacques towards Singapore, Asia receded into the background. What Malraux had seen of it, what he took back with him – what they both took back with them – were the marks of a double adventure in Indo-China, one dubiously, the other nobly intentioned, but both ending in 'failure'. The stones of Banteaï-Sre were still in Cambodia and the vices of the colonial system were as oppressive as ever.

They had brought back nothing, nothing had changed, except themselves. They were no longer the fickle adventurers of 1923. They had acquired an experience of Asia that was broader, deeper, more painfully earned than that of most Europeans, and although it was limited to Annamese Saigon and Chinese Cholon represented nevertheless one of the essential points of confrontation between Asia and Europe. They had been more than observers; they had been actors in a conflict between a continent just beginning to wrench itself from an age-old impotence and a West in a state of permanent cultural aggression.

At the beginning of 1926 their experience of Asia was confined to Saigon, Cholon, Phnom Penh, a few visits to Hanoi, Central Annam and the Mekong delta, and the brief journey to Hong Kong. It is quite a lot if one considers the atmosphere of passion, intensity and conflict in which those two years were experienced. It is much less compared with the 'pathetic trimmings' that André Malraux allowed to be created around his life and even helped to sustain. Was it a matter of fraud, a practical joke, an elaborately conceived piece of pseudo-history or an oriental tall story? Or are we in the world of Chateaubriand and his imaginary conversation with George Washington?

It is true that the legend of an André Malraux fighting for the Chinese Revolution, hero of the Canton revolt of 1925 (and even of the Shanghai uprising of 1927) dies hard, and that he himself helped to create it. Such serious authors as Walter Langlois, Janine Mossuz and André Vandegans, over-impressed perhaps by semi-confidences, pregnant silences, subtle allusions, a certain self-assurance and incidents described in dazzlingly 'authentic' detail, have added to the legend. Professor Georges Pompidou went further than anyone along the road of 'mythification': he gives as four years (1923–7) the length of Malraux's stay in Asia, during which he 'fought at the side first of Chiang Kai-shek, then of the Communists'.[1]

As soon as he had returned from Indo-China Malraux dropped hints here and there that he had gone to China not simply as a tourist, nor even as a journalist, and that *Les Conquérants,* on which he was still working, was based partially at least on experience. To over-inquisitive interviewers, he would refuse to give any details at all, which was regarded as normal enough in view of the 'responsibilities' he had assumed. While those who said: 'You who fought in China . . .' were not corrected.

For most of the writers and politicians of the time, Malraux was 'the-man-who-has-been-to-China' and fought there. Was this because of what he said, or what he did not say? During the summer of 1928, just after the publication of *Les Conquérants* in the *NRF,* a Berlin review, *Die Europäische Revue,* published a German translation of the novel by Max Clauss, with the subtitle, *Ein Tagebuch Der Kämpfe um Kanton 1925* (*Journal of the Struggles in Canton*), thus giving the impression that the book was an account of actual events experienced by the author.

The biographical note on the cover of the book – which could only have been provided by Malraux himself – reads: 'Born in Paris. Carried out an archeological mission in Cambodia and Siam on behalf of the Ministry of the Colonies (1923). Leading member of the Young Annam Party (1924).

Kuomintang commissar for Cochin-China, then for Indo-China (1924–25). Delegate for propaganda in the leadership of the nationalist movement at Canton under Borodin (1925).'[2]

Malraux was to go a little further, five years later, in a letter to Edmund Wilson, the famous American critic, dated 2 October 1933, in which he describes himself as 'Kuomintang commissar first in Indo-China, then in Canton'.[3] Meanwhile, the novelist-commissar has risen in the world. The letter is all the more regrettable in that it is addressed to a man of the highest authority, who at the time believed the legend, and at a time when Malraux was no longer the young author recovering from the wounds inflicted on him in Asia, but the already famous author of *La Condition humaine*.

Yet André Malraux was no longer using deceit in a systematic way in order to sustain his legend. The dates spoke for themselves, and could be checked by anyone who took the trouble to do so. Those of his public activities in Saigon in 1925, of his return to Paris, at the beginning of 1926, of his contacts with Grasset and with the *NRF*, all give the lie to Malraux's 'Cantonese' period. The myth proved stronger, however. For half a century, Malraux preferred to allow himself to be accused of the worst kind of deception, rather than clear up the whole matter. Thus Trotsky could accuse him in 1937 of having 'worked for the Comintern-Kuomintang' and of having been 'partly responsible for the crushing of the Chinese revolution',[4] and Roger Garaudy could blame him for 'the reckless, even provocative insurrection in Canton, which led to the massacre of the workers'.[5]

Yet when he met some specialist in Asian affairs, some well-known traveller, Malraux became modest, attentive, self-effacing, confining himself, on the subject of China, to asking questions. In 1928, Pierre Naville[6] asked Malraux to lunch, in order to introduce him to one of the most celebrated representatives of the Comintern in Asia, the Dutchman Sneevliet, alias Maring, the only European co-founder of the Chinese Communist Party, later to become a Trotskyist. Naville was astonished to see Malraux, then basking in the glory of his Chinese legend, quite content to listen to Sneevliet and to ask him about this or that development in the Chinese revolution, without contributing any views of his own to the conversation. For a former lieutenant of Borodin (and for Malraux!) this was certainly self-effacement. Indeed, Sneevliet seems to have gained the impression from this meeting that the young writer had little but the vaguest notions about the Chinese revolution, even for a mere observer.[7]

Another thing. When, in the *NRF* for April 1929, Bernard Groethuysen reviewed *Les Conquérants* and discussed the problem of the 'historical novel', he made no reference whatever to any actual participation on the part of Malraux in the events on which the novel was based. This is important, because Groethuysen was a close friend of Malraux, one of those whom Malraux most respected, one of those to whom he *owed* the truth. Groethuysen's silence here is therefore all the more illuminating.

And yet – and this is what matters – there are the intuitions of *La Tentation de l'Occident*, the powerful evocations of Canton – the streets of Shameen, the feverish atmosphere of the political meetings, the sultry nights – in *Les Conquérants* and five or six admirably truthful scenes in *La Condition humaine*.

The additional experience André Malraux was to acquire with Clara, in 1931, during the only journey to continental China that he made before his ministerial visit in 1965, could not have amounted to very much. In a letter to the Japanese writer Akira Muraki, he even denied having visited Shanghai before writing *La Condition humaine*,[8] which proves that he can err by understatement as well as by exaggeration . . .

It must be admitted that Malraux the writer was not trying to deceive his public or even to put it on the wrong track. This China, inhabited by foreigners, whose revolution would be carried out by Russians, natives of the Baltic states, Germans, Swiss and Franco-Japanese, is presented as having a fictional, not a documentary truth. And that is why perhaps it seems so accurate. The world, he said later, is beginning to resemble my books. This is not quite so in the case of China. But it is true that his visions re-create a world that is as true as the true one, and that the Asia of his dreams arouses emotions almost as strong as a real Asia.

It would be a mistake, in his case, to ignore the part played by experience. His two great Asian novels are in no sense 'reportage', since the author was closely involved in none of the events described. (*La Voie royale* is, of course, another matter – this novel, despite the 'pathetic trimmings' so dear to Chateaubriand, is often inspired by actual experience, as we have seen.) But *Les Conquérants* and *La Condition humaine* are based on a real historical situation, the attempt of the founders of *L'Indochine* to support, even to guide, the Annamese nationalist movement in the direction of social liberation.

Like Borodin, like Garine in *Les Conquérants*, like Kyo and Katow in *La Condition humaine*, 'guiding' the Chinese masses towards the containment of their collective freedom within the confines of the Comintern, Monin and Malraux had acted *on* the Indo-Chinese terrain and peoples. The texture and themes of the two novels are considerably illuminated by a study of the Indo-Chinese activity of the two leading spirits of Young Annam, a stillborn, limited, ineffective movement, but one that provided Malraux with an imaginative nucleus and base. For him, the Indo-Chinese adventure was the negative from which he made the enlargement of *Les Conquérants* and even of *La Condition humaine*.

Of all the characters of Malraux's 'Asian' novels, the only ones that are taken directly from life are the two terrorists, Hong and Chen, both based on Hin, the journalist on *L'Indochine*, so vividly described by Clara, who planned to assassinate the Governor of Cochin-China. Certain characteristics of Cheng Dai or Rebecci, in *Les Conquérants* might be traced to the Malrauxs' companions at Cholon. And the odd idea of making Kyo, the leader of the Shanghai insurrection, a Eurasian may have been suggested by the personality of the half-caste Dejean de la Batie, one of the co-founders of *L'Indochine*. What matters is not so much details of this kind, but rather a general atmosphere, involving a dialogue between different societies and civilisations, the possibility of better relations based on real fraternity, for which Monin was for so long the symbol.

The man who had led the Malrauxs into the second Indo-China adventure left Saigon, shortly after their own departure for Paris, and went to Canton. At a somewhat more modest level, it was he who had experienced something like Garine's

adventure. We know nothing of the relations between the two
publishers of *L'Indochine* in the years 1926 and 1927. Did Monin
write to Malraux ? If he did, his letters could have been the most
valuable source for *Les Conquérants*. André Malraux remembers
no such communication.

We do know that Paul Monin returned to Saigon in 1927 and
died there at the end of the year from a fever contracted during
a hunting expedition across the Moi plateaux. This great lawyer
died poor, leaving a wife, herself seriously ill, and a son, Willy,
who had become a journalist. Paul Monin's Saigon friends
managed to persuade his widow that he should be buried on
Vietnamese soil.

A great imagination would not need more than this experience, this individual, these friendships to provide the basis for
literary creation. What Malraux had acquired at Phnom Penh,
Saigon, Hanoi and Hong Kong were atmospheres, smells, acute
moments of fraternity, tension or hate, experienced with an
intensity that the cities of Asia, the police and courts, the newspapers and Chambers of Commerce of Indo-China revealed
more sharply than their European counterparts.

Could he extrapolate a China in turmoil from this Indo-China
in disarray ? Could he reconstruct Canton and Shanghai from
Saigon and Cholon, Chiang Kai-shek's torturers from those of
Dr Cognacq, the traffickers of the Bund from those of the rue
Catinat, the massive uprisings of China from the social disturbances of the Mekong delta or Saigon harbour, the strategists
of Canton from the comrades of Young Annam ? Yes, since that
is precisely what he did, with irrefutable force – for us, if not
for Chinese readers themselves.

The Asia that Malraux brought back with him was not the
sleeping giant of the Chinese revolution. It was the angry young
Indo-China, suffering and victimised, in which, in a minor key,
were to be found all the intrigues and movements that led to the
disturbances of 1945. When he left Saigon, Ho Chi Minh, who
was still called Nguyen Ai Quoc, had just spent over a year as
the International's delegate at Canton, where he worked with
Borodin; even more important, he had founded the *Thanh-
Nien*, the youth movement that was to become the nucleus of
the Vietminh.

In Indo-China tendencies and forces were emerging that were to lead, four years later, to the two explosions of Yen Bay and Nghe-An, the first a *putsch* at the instigation of the nationalists, the second a peasant uprising at that of the Communists. Meanwhile, at Cholon and in the Chinese communities, imperceptible splits were occurring within the Kuomintang parallel with those which, at the time of the Northern Expedition, from Canton to Peking, were to alter the whole course of the Chinese revolution.

In 1967, during an interview on Italian Radio, Malraux was asked about his experiences in Asia. 'Be careful,' he said, 'Malraux's Asia at that time was not China, it was Indo-China . . .' Such a straight, categorical answer was rare enough, but he went on to draw a somewhat astonishing parallel between Young Annam and the Vietminh, between his own former political position and that of Ho Chi Minh, which, in his view, was then much more moderate than it later became – an assertion that simply cannot be sustained.

But in either case, fact or fiction, there is an element of conscious risk, of adventure, of courage. There is an Asia experienced that is merely a fragment of that imagined Asia from which, within a period of seven years, were to spring *La Tentation de l'Occident, Les Conquérants* and *La Condition humaine.* At the source of this imaginative torrent was a very pure spring, the dangers incurred and the compassion experienced by an insecure, warm-hearted young man whose defiance of authority was to become transformed, by often tortuous ways, into a genuine sense of fraternity.

On the boat that took them once again from Saigon to Marseilles, in January 1926, Clara and André were sitting side by side among the reproduction furniture of the second-class saloon. There, surrounded by yelling children, yet isolated within himself, André Malraux looked out on to the gangway. Clara writes:

> Had we wished disaster upon ourselves? In that Indo-China that was destroying and enriching us – a disaster that drove us back to a fundamental questioning of all our

assumptions. There we were once again, almost defeated, sailing on in search of new discoveries . . .

We really had confronted men and events. We had been formed by the consequences of our actions and we were returning to Europe in possession of a language that was no longer quite that of others . . . The man to whom I had entrusted myself was trying at last, with his own weapons, to master the world which so far had resisted him and on which, through writing, he would impose his vision . . .[9]

Book 2

====

FRATERNITY

PART I

THE POWER OF THE PEN

10 *Homecoming*

HE HAD gone away half-formed and divided, led more by his rejections and his daydreams than by his own real desires; he had gone more to acquire than to conquer. He returned more self-assured, more conscious of his revolt; his character had been forged in his struggles, he was already Malraux, in outline.

The wanderer had become a rebel, still given to a certain aestheticism, of course, still tending to the pedantic – as *La Tentation de l'Occident* shows – but much of the fustian has been swept away. He had not yet found a cause to serve, nor did he quite have the art to serve that cause well. But there was now a tension within him, a fever far more powerful than the bookish hot-house dandyism of the early years.

He had known a man worthy of respect, devoted to total struggle; he had faced adversaries of invincible stupidity; he had laid bare the mindless cruelty that lay beneath the surface of colonialism. He had left the libraries and confronted life.

The France of February 1926 was a more divided nation than the France he had left in 1923. The government based on the left-wing coalition that emerged from the 1924 elections stumbled on from failure to failure; its only success was in forcing the retirement of the President of the Republic, Alexandre Millerand, a former Socialist, whose authoritarianism almost brought parliamentary democracy to a standstill, and replacing him by the inoffensive Gaston Doumergue. But the budgetary deficit and inflation grew worse from day to day. The ninth Briand government went the same way as those of Painlevé and

Herriot. The majority felt compelled to appeal to unpopular men like Caillaux.

In July, with the return of Édouard Herriot to the premiership, the situation reached the bottom of the curve: the pound was valued at 243 francs, the dollar at 50. Panic swept the country, and the terrified Left agreed to the recall of the man who embodied everything it hated, who symbolised the coalition of power, public order and money, the man who was trusted by the banks and the small savers, the hope of the 'patriotic party' – Raymond Poincaré.

The climate of the France of 1926 was epitomised in the defeat of this flabby Left and the 'restoration' of the party of moral, monetary and colonial order – a party that triumphed with the resolution of the first serious crisis encountered by the French 'imperial' system. In Morocco in May 1926, Abd-el-Krim submitted to the French power of Rabat (it was not forgotten that six months earlier Monin and Malraux had opposed the sending of Annamese troops to Morocco to reinforce Marshal Pétain's forces of repression). The monarchist Action Française was triumphant.

But other forces and other enthusiasms were also attracting attention. The Young Communists, under the adventurous leadership of Jacques Doriot (who turned fascist ten years later and became a pro-Nazi chief in 1940–5), were becoming more and more active. Meanwhile the Surrealist movement was proving to be more than a mere fad of a few cultured noncomformists and misfits. Abandoning the extravagant anarchism of its early days, the group led by Breton, Aragon and Éluard was moving closer to Communism, and became associated with the Marxists of the Clarté group. It still refused to allow itself to be subjected to the discipline of any revolutionary party, but on 1 March 1926 *La Révolution surréaliste* stressed 'the broad measure of agreement that exists between the Communists and our movement', and the explosive activity of that movement was to become more organised and more politically orientated.

Malraux returned from Indo-China convulsed with anger at the caricature of bourgeois society represented by the colonial world of Saigon, at the cruel, narrow-minded outlook of *L'Impartial,* Dr Cognacq and the Phnom Penh court. From every point of view, he seemed ready to join the ranks of the Surrealists, like him, children of Rimbaud and Nietzsche. And yet he never allied himself with Breton, who had bravely supported him at the time of the Saigon trial.

What was it, then, that made the Surrealists such anathema to Malraux? Half a century later, he suggested that the distance between them was due mainly to the fact that he had been away in Indo-China during the movement's early activity.[1] This is hardly adequate as an explanation. According to Marcel Arland,[2] it was rather Breton's authoritarian style that prevented Malraux from joining the group. In a more general way, one might say that the young rebel of Saigon was too well aware of his own revolt, of an independence won at the cost of severe personal trials, to follow a movement created and shaped by others. It was not until his discovery of the International that he found a church large enough for his pride and his aspirations towards active fraternity – however temporary his association proved to be.

He was a man of dreams, subject to hallucinations, something of a wizard, a devotee of Rimbaud, a lover, like the Surrealists, of Lautréamont, Jarry and Corbière. He already idolised the great irrationalists, Nietzsche and Dostoevsky, but he was unreceptive to the appeals of the unconscious as launched by the writers of the Manifesto and Breton, the 'pope'.

Clara describes very wittily the meeting of the two sacred monsters, Breton and Malraux, in January 1925:

> I can still see Breton and Malraux opposite one another, the first with that rather heavy intensity that emanated from him and the second full of high-strung eagerness. When he arrived he had an ebony stick without ferrule that he had bought in Singapore; it was very long, and as he swung it it gave him a great air, but with time, for the very reason that it had no ferrule, it wore away, and it was not far from coming down to the dimensions of a cigarette holder. The session did not last long; it ended with a plan for another meeting, which was to take place a few days later, still at the rue Fontaine. When we rang the bell on the appointed day no one came. 'I'm sure they are there,' said my companion. 'I

heard them.' I did not believe him; yet it was he who was right: we received a letter informing us that since the Surrealists were in the midst of an automatic writing séance they thought that we could not fail to be a disturbing element – which was not so far wrong, either.

Our relations stayed at that point for years.[3]

They never really improved.

In fact, it was Aragon, even more than Breton, who aroused Malraux's antipathy. And even when, after the adoption of common positions in the years 1935–9, and after the struggles of the Resistance, Aragon praised Malraux in splendid if somewhat glacial terms, Malraux did not relent. However, in 1966, on the occasion of a projected exhibition of Soviet art presented by Aragon, and which came under the purview of Malraux as Minister of Culture, Claude Gallimard, their common publisher, managed to bring them together in his office, on neutral territory. The witness was not disappointed. As he left, Malraux remarked: 'What did you think of our performance?'[4]

When I asked Aragon, six years later, about his relationship with Malraux, he refused to reply. Why? 'I like him too much – while my [communist] friends don't like him enough . . .'[5] Malraux himself was content to maintain a touchy silence on the matter.

A later incident, which was highly significant at the time, did much to arouse André Malraux's instinctive hostility towards the 'group'. At the beginning of 1929, the review *Variétés* devoted a special number to Surrealism. Between good pieces by Éluard and Queneau was slipped a provocative article by André Thirion denouncing Malraux in the vilest terms: '. . . the swindler Malraux . . . who . . . will continue his dirty work by following *Les Conquérants* with a fictionalised life of Colonel Lawrence, is now regarded as a revolutionary!'

Malraux replied to the editor of *Variétés*, Van Hecke, who was very close to the Surrealists: 'A certain M. Thirion, in a rather dim-witted way, informs your readers (who probably couldn't care less) that I intend writing a life of Colonel Lawrence. Not so. I am writing two lives in verse of the colonel: the first in Alexandrines, the second in octosyllabics.

And if M. Thirion bothers me any more, I'll do another, in verses of one foot.'[6]

So Malraux's return to Paris in 1926 was first marked by a rejection of the movement to which the more recent episodes in his life, and even perhaps his whole life, would seem to have brought him closer. But it was towards a much more conformist world that he turned: namely, the publishing firm that Bernard Grasset ran with something approaching genius.

This was not, as we know, a chance encounter. As early as 1924, the publisher of the rue des Saints-Pères had opened his doors to the Cambodian 'criminal' and detected the powerful personality that was emerging in this hunted young man. Should this miracle of enlightened self-interest be attributed solely to Bernard Grasset's proverbial flair? No. The two men had been brought together by another, François Mauriac, who in 1924 had signed the writers' appeal in favour of the condemned Malraux and written a warm letter of encouragement to Clara.

In any case, since it was Grasset who had given him a contract and an advance at that difficult time in his life, it was naturally to him that André Malraux turned when, in February 1926, he was looking for a publisher for a hundred or so manuscript pages that he wanted to call *La Tentation de l'Occident*. Bernard Grasset was commercially-minded enough to regret that 'his' author should present him with this austere piece of writing, rather than the novel inspired by his Cambodian adventure, which he was still writing. But Malraux was especially attached to this philosophical work and Grasset had the wit to give in. The novel would arrive all in due course, all the more mature, all the more finished for the delay. This generous-minded young man must be allowed to express himself. The sap was there. If he thought he was Nietzsche, then let him try and write a *Zarathustra*. If he was a genius, we'd all see before long. The time of talent would come later.

Before leaving Saigon, Malraux had promised his friends to lead a campaign in Paris against the colonial régime. He did not keep his promise – at least until 1933. Instead of the expected political meetings and revolutionary speeches, he devoted his time to literary activity, mainly concerned, it is true, with Asia and East-West relations, but hardly calculated to overthrow the colonial order.

In four texts, published in 1926 and 1927, André Malraux contrasted with brilliance and ingenuity the individualistic activism of Europeans and the oriental sense of collective harmony: a book, *La Tentation de l'Occident*, extracts from which had appeared in April in the *NRF*; an interview entitled 'André Malraux and the East', published in *Les Nouvelles littéraires*; an article in the *NRF* on Massis' *Défense de l'Occident*; a short article on 'European Youth'. These pieces constituted a sort of corpus of thinking that revealed a real intellectual acuity, an already brilliant handling of ideas and a respect, very rare at the time, for the values of Confucian society. But there was nothing here that measured up to the expectations of the young Annamese and Chinese friends that André and Clara Malraux had left at Saigon and Cholon.

La Tentation de l'Occident was published by Bernard Grasset in July 1926. Read again today, this essay, written in the form of an exchange of letters between the young Chinese Ling, appalled by the neurotic will to govern and efficiency of the West, and his French contemporary A.D., fascinated by the wisdom of the East, reveals the defects as well as the qualities of its author. It displays with provocative naïvety (the author was twenty-four) the virtuosity of a clever student abroad, a thirsty consumer of ideas that are accepted as self-evident before being assimilated and verified, but it also contains amid all the solemn rhetoric some extremely penetrating insights.

Ling writes (pp. 81–2):

> I too have walked in your incomparable gardens, where the statues of kings or gods mingle their long shadows at sundown. Their extended hands seem to be offering you a past heavy with memories and glorious deeds. Your heart wishes to discern in the union of these slowly lengthening shadows some long-awaited law. Ah! what lament would be worthy of a race which, in order to rediscover its highest thoughts, can only call upon these faithless dead. Despite its real power, the European evening is feeble and empty, empty as the soul of a conqueror. Of all man's vainest, most tragic

gestures none has ever seemed to me more vain and more tragic than that by which you are forever questioning your illustrious shades, O race doomed to power, O desperate race . . .

And A. D. (pp. 158–60):

In order to destroy God, and having destroyed him, the European spirit has annihilated whatever might stand in man's way . . . There is, of course, a higher faith: the faith that is declared by all the village crosses, and those same crosses that stand over our dead. That faith is love, and it brings peace. I shall never accept it; I shall not demean myself to ask it for the peace for which my weakness cries out. Europe, great cemetery inhabited only by dead conquerors, whose melancholy becomes still deeper as it adorns itself with their illustrious names, you leave around me nothing but an empty horizon and the mirror brought by despair, old master of solitude . . .

The spirit of Chateaubriand looms over these pages. In 1926 they attracted the attention of the literary augurs. Albert Thibaudet, the most influential critic of the day, deigned to comment on this work by an unknown young man: its author was, he said, 'less profound than Keyserling', but 'he had a sense of poetry, of synthesis, of the Chinese ideogram' that was reminiscent of Claudel and Saint-Jean Perse, and his 'active, muscular pessimism' was not without savour.[7]

This was a good début, and it brought André Malraux to the attention of the journalists. *Les Nouvelles littéraires* asked for his views on East-West relations. Ours, he replied, is 'a closed civilization, lacking in spiritual purpose: it forces us into action. Its values are established on a world dependent on facts . . . The notion of man that we have inherited from Christianity was based on an exalted awareness of our fundamental disorder. Such a disorder does not exist for the Oriental . . .'[8]

He could have found no better occasion to develop his plea for Asian harmony than in replying to Henri Massis' *Défense de l'Occident*. This pamphlet by one of the leading spokesmen of nationalistic conservatism was a denunciation of the disturbing

aggression to be found in Asia, which, for him, included both
Bolshevism and otherworldliness. Curiously enough, Malraux's
reply was above all on the factual level: you feel threatened by
the progress of the Kuomintang in Asia? If that's all you're
worried about, forget it.

11 Conqueror and farfelu[1]

AT THE beginning of March 1928, the first of five sections of a novel entitled *Les Conquérants* appeared in *La Nouvelle Revue française*. Between a visit to his engraver, the negotiation of a contract with his printer and the final preparation of two *farfelu* texts for the reviews *900* and *Commerce* ('Écrit pour un ours en peluche' and 'Voyage aux îles fortunées'), Malraux found the time and energy to write his second Indo-Chinese adventure – a considerably magnified version of the anti-colonial struggle in which he had been involved.

There is no indication – either from him, Clara, his publisher, or any of his friends at the time – of the way in which he developed his account of the great 1925 strike at Canton and Hong Kong, or of the creative processes that enabled him, side by side with a Borodin that scarcely differed from his original and a Hong-the-terrorist modelled on a Saigon journalist, to shape the powerful yet imaginary figure of Garine.

He had four kinds of material at his disposal: his own memories of Indo-China (the Phnom Penh and Saigon trials, the foundation of Young Annam, discussions with Monin, experiences with the police and the colonial authorities); notes taken during his brief visit to Hong Kong with Clara in August 1925; contemporary press cuttings and the accounts of Paul Monin, who had been living in Canton and took part in the uprising. Out of these disparate elements a strong, coherent book was born. It tells the story of Garine, a Swiss-born adventurer who inspires the revolutionary strike of 1925 in Canton, together with Borodin, the envoy of Moscow. Devoid of any ideology except that of revolt against bourgeois society, Garine combines his sparkling intellectual gifts and ferocious audacity with the managerial technique of Borodin. The novel, astutely linked with real facts and people (like Borodin himself), ends with the departure for Europe of a fatally ill Garine.

Les Conquérants was published in five issues of the *NRF* (March–July 1928) and in book form by Grasset at the end of the summer. The effect produced by this violent work was in direct proportion to its own violence, and one can only applaud the perspicacity shown by a press that half a century later strikes one as being so very conservative.

The pundit Paul Souday, writing in *Le Temps*, had reservations about the book: he disliked 'the excessive use of concrete detail', but acknowledged the author's 'sense of movement and drama', while in *La Presse* an enthusiastic Waldemar George declared that it was 'more than a new form of art', it was 'a new vision', and in *Les Nouvelles littéraires* the great novelist-diplomat Paul Morand gave a friendly welcome to 'this very fine book, which combines the sense of detail of a thirteenth-century chronicle and the technical, exhaustive dryness of a modern police report'.

The most impressive comment came from Emmanuel Berl, one of the most famous liberal essayists of the time, who was to become a close friend of Malraux. In his *Mort de la pensée bourgeoise*, published in the spring of 1929, he wrote:

> I regard *Les Conquérants* as an event of the greatest importance in contemporary moral history. I am astonished that this fact has been so little recognized, that so much of the discussion about the book has been of an aesthetic nature when it so obviously concerns something that goes well beyond the aesthetic. For me, Garine is a new type of man. His very existence resolves a number of problems and difficulties. It poses new ones, too. The bourgeois who are seduced by Malraux's art will understand tomorrow, if they do not understand today, the danger that Malraux involves them in, and they will soon cease to read his book for the information on China, for the descriptions, for an account of events or for its psychological insight . . .[2]

This was rubbing salt into the wound. The more prudent had begun to realise that these picturesque characters were set in motion by an individual who felt a great deal of anger. However, this did not preclude wordly success, or certain evasions, or the use of historical licence.

On 8 June 1929 (at a time when the review *Bifur*, which was in fact close to the Surrealists, published an addition by Malraux to the portrait of Borodin, the Bolshevist agent, that stressed the 'Roman' aspects of the character), an organisation of the liberal left, the Union pour la Vérité, founded at the time of the Dreyfus affair, organised a public discussion on *Les Conquérants* at the Salle des Sociétés Savantes. The novelist's own contribution[3] is worth quoting at some length for the light it throws on the work itself and on the author's moral and political attitudes at the time, and because it foreshadows in a very powerful way the Malraux of the 1930s:

> . . . The passions that drive the novelist concern not so much the artistic value of his work as the violence of the feelings that he arouses, whether intentionally or not. For me, Garine is certainly a hero (in the sense in which hero can be differentiated from character). It is clear that he embodies a particular view of life; and I think that the extent to which my opponents attack the book is not due to the extent to which they feel the book is more or less well written.
>
> The facts described in this book have been challenged in writing. There is not a single point in *Les Conquérants* that can be defended on real, historical grounds. But to the extent that a character is invented, he always acts with a psychological truth that is bound up with real, historical events . . .

After describing *Les Conquérants* not as an 'apology for revolution', but as 'the story of an alliance between the Bolshevik, for whom the bourgeoisie is a social reality inevitably doomed to be superseded in the course of history', and Garine, for whom the bourgeoisie represents 'a certain human attitude', Malraux identifies himself with Garine:

> . . . we must speak of Garine's trial; this element is extremely important. I am little inclined to the view that

psychological events have no importance in the lives of revolutionary leaders; on the contrary, I believe that they are of great importance. I think it would be very difficult not to find a fundamental opposition between the revolutionary leader and society in the period preceding his action. But I believe that this opposition often springs from the revolutionary character of the man who becomes a leader . . .

He does not know how the Revolution will turn out, but he knows where he will go when he has taken a particular decision. He couldn't care less about the earthly paradise. I cannot lay too much stress on what I have called the mythology of ends. He doesn't have to define the Revolution: he makes it.

When Saint-Just set out on his course of action, he was not yet a republican; and Lenin did not expect the Revolution to produce the NEP. The revolutionary is not a man with a ready-made ideal; he is a man who wants to demand and get the most he can for his people, for those I called just now his brothers-in-arms.

The fundamental question for Garine is not so much how one can take part in a revolution as how one can escape what is called the absurd. The whole of *Les Conquérants* is a perpetual demand, and indeed I have insisted on the following formula: escape from this idea of the absurd by fleeing into the human. Of course, it might be said that there are other ways of fleeing. In no sense, do I claim to answer this objection. I am simply saying that Garine, in so far as he has escaped the absurdity that is the most tragic thing that faces a man, has set an example . . .

. . . It is not a matter of being right or wrong, but a matter of knowing whether the example provided by Garine acts effectively as ethical creation. Either it acts on the men who read it, or it doesn't. If it doesn't, *Les Conquérants* raises no questions; but if it does, I am not arguing with my opponents; I will argue with their children.[3]

With all its accumulated sense of tragedy, adventurous shortcuts, pseudo-Marxist approximations and doctrinaire insolence imitated from Saint-Just, this is one of the finest, and at any rate the clearest speeches ever made by Malraux. The themes of efficacity and male fraternity of *L'Espoir* are already to be found here.

But he is not yet the man of a single passion, a single cause, obsessed with his own act and his act alone, that was so to astonish Ehrenburg in Spain. He is still in two minds, anxious to attract as well as to defy. No sooner had *Les Conquérants* appeared than he published, under the Gallimard imprint, and as if to pay his share on entering the great firm as director of Department of the arts, *Royaume farfelu*. In this story, Malraux gave full expression to the vein of fantasy which, ever since *Lunes en papier*, had run side by side with his realistic vein.

One might well be surprised to see a resurgence of this earlier mode, with its tone of decorative evasion, its brittle light-heartedness, its gaiety masking despair, in a literary career that was already, with *Les Conquérants*, moving in such a definite direction. But one should not underestimate Malraux's *farfelu* side, the acuteness of the pessimism expressed in those cere-monies and festivals performed in the shadow of death.[5] The *Royaume farfelu* is the kingdom of the grimace, of non-being, of fate, of the irremediable. This highly decorated prose is a funeral chant. One may dislike this art of tinsel and gossamer, these pavanes for dead infantas. But they, too, with their greenish light and their smell of decay, belong to Malraux's world.

Royaume farfelu is important for the date of its publication, which makes it the antithesis of the voluntarist and, it must be admitted, fraternal *Les Conquérants*. It is important, too, because it marks André Malraux's entry into the firm of Gallimard – that is to say, into the only publishing house that then had, with Gide, Valéry and Paulhan, the subtle mandarin of the staff, an aesthetic, a leadership, structures, and which offered its authors a certain style of life.

Malraux was certainly no stranger to Gaston Gallimard, hav-ing published regularly in the *NRF*, the house review, since 1922. He was often to be seen on the firm's premises. But did Bernard Grasset allow this young genius, whom he had helped in 1924 and launched on the public in 1928, to desert him so easily for his imposing rival? Gaston Gallimard assures us that he did, because Grasset was not possessive and preferred the pleasures of discovering new talent to the management of a career. It seems that Grasset even offered him a sort of association in which he would act as talent scout, leaving the publishing and distribution to Gallimard.

So, in short, André Malraux was appointed art editor by Gaston Gallimard, who does not remember the event as being particularly dramatic; the ensuing forty-four years of collaboration with one of the most striking personalities of the century left no painful trace in his memory. He remembers only two dramatic episodes – both, indeed, connected with Trotsky: when, in 1929, Malraux claimed to have organised an expedition (with, in particular, his colleagues of the *NRF!*) to rescue the founder of the Red Army from internment at Alma-Ata; then, in 1945, when he threatened to leave the firm after a very cruel comment by Maurice Merleau-Ponty on the relations between Malraux and Trotsky appeared in *Les Temps modernes*, then published by Gallimard.[6]

Malraux, who had brought with him to Gallimard's his Indo-China fellow-traveller, Louis Chevasson, did not have very clearly defined functions. He was stuck up in a small office under the roof that he called 'the cabinet of Dr Caligari', and had no fixed timetable. In fact, he worked very hard there – at least when he was in Paris and not off on some journey with Clara to the Pamirs, to Persia or to Japan. He showed no particular genius as an editor of art books: the works he produced on Leonardo and Vermeer were not the finest examples of art book publishing in France and the exhibitions he organised at the Gallimard offices from 1931 – on the Buddhist sculpture of the Pamirs or on the works of Fautrier, for example – aroused little more than curiosity.

The strange thing about Malraux's role as a discoverer of new talent was that it was most successful in the field of Anglo-American literature, whereas he himself hardly spoke any English. It was he who introduced D. H. Lawrence, Faulkner and Dashiell Hammett to the Gallimard list and even devoted two of his most famous prefaces to the first two. He found nothing comparable in German, Russian or Spanish, all of which cultures were much more familiar to him than English.

How could a writer so obsessed by action and images not be a passionate cinemagoer? He had been ever since his childhood at Bondy. In 1922, with Ivan Goll, he had tried his hand at distributing German films in France. On returning to Europe, he discovered the new Soviet cinema of the 1920s – it was a revelation. Early in 1927, a 'private' showing of *Battleship Potemkin* had aroused enormous enthusiasm, but the censor had forbidden the public showing of the film on the grounds that it was 'revolutionary propaganda'. *La Revue européenne* asked for the views of a hundred writers and well-known members of the entertainment industry. Malraux launched a violent attack on the ban, referring in particular to the problem of the cinema industry in France:

> In a country that has no censorship of the press, the censorship of the cinema would be a mere absurdity were it not a defence in the hands of a small number of companies that I do not need to name. These companies don't care a fig for the increase in professional value that artists may obtain from the showing of such a film. We can only hope that your initiative may force them to disclose their behaviour.[7]

A man may be defined by his friends and acquaintances. In the late 1920s, at Gallimard's, he came to know, sometimes on terms of friendship, some of the most remarkable men of his time. Setting aside Marcel Arland – already an old friend – and two men about whom we shall have more to say later, André Gide and Bernard Groethuysen, he was closest to Paul Valéry, Roger Martin du Gard, Louis Guilloux, Pierre Drieu la Rochelle and Emmanuel Berl. If he did not become as close a friend of Claudel, whom he ranked as an artist above all the others, it was because the poet-diplomat was not often in France.

What attracted him in Valéry was his brilliant intellect – and his unequalled capacity for scorn. At the high point of a discussion on Erasmus, Valéry was heard to say, in his thin, suburban voice: 'And, anyway, who cares?' His anti-historicism irritated Malraux, a devotee of Michelet and an unlucky candidate for Marxist knowledge. He also hated Valéry's idea of the death of civilisations, which, he said, Valéry had 'pinched from Spengler'.

But he was entranced by Valéry's freedom of thought and haughty coldness. Yet none of these companions was as dear to him as Drieu la Rochelle, the only one who could unreservedly be called his friend, despite the most fundamental disagreements – the one tempted by Communism, the other fascinated by fascism.

Malraux had met him towards the end of 1927. He described Drieu, then very little known, as 'dominating the group with his presence'.[8] Very quickly they recognised a common intellectual interest. Both regarded themselves as Nietzscheans, passionately concerned with lucid action, with 'dreams that had their feet on the ground'. When *Les Conquérants* appeared, Drieu was entranced. Berl described him reading Malraux's book 'slapping his thighs and repeating over and over again: "Ah! the little rascal! Ah! the little rascal!" '[9] The tall, bald young man with the vague stare and the easy flow of speech and the dazzling author of *Les Conquérants* agreed at once on the need for an active pessimism, resistant to ideologies and devoted equally to action and lucidity. In December 1930, just prior to the publication of *La Voie royale*, Drieu gave the *NRF* a long article entitled 'Malraux, l'homme nouveau'. It turned out to be the best piece so far devoted to him:

> Like most Frenchmen, Malraux lacks invention. But his imagination is aroused by facts. One has the feeling that he can hardly go beyond the facts that he himself has known. The adventures described in his books have the stark, truthful quality of a direct transposition from reality.[10] But through a brief, rapid series of events, Malraux's art brings out in striking relief the postulates of his intellectual temperament. The events form a single line and treading this line is a single character, a hero. This hero is not Malraux, but the mythical figuration of his own self, more sublime and more concrete than himself. In this Malraux possesses the most vital faculty of the poet and novelist.

For sixteen years they were to maintain a friendship that remained strangely unaffected by the historical upheavals in which they were both plunged and which, from 1933 onwards, were to throw them into opposed camps, Drieu trying to find a new cause in fascism and Malraux fellow-travelling with a Communism that was essentially quite alien to him. Drieu, who referred to himself as Malraux's 'brother in Nietzsche and Dostoevsky',[11] once taunted Malraux with being 'no more a Marxist than Stalin'. Despite the fact that Drieu had described Malraux as a 'Soviet agent' in 1936, their correspondence continued uninterrupted, even during the Occupation (when one of them was an outlaw and the other among the outlawers) and the Liberation (when their roles were reversed). Right up to his suicide, Drieu referred to Malraux as one of his two or three last remaining friends.

It was while travelling abroad in 1930[12] that André Malraux learnt of the death of his father, whose rapidly deteriorating health had driven him to suicide. Since André's return from Indo-China relations between them had become good once again. André often visited his father at his apartment in the rue de Lubeck and Clara, who was very fond of this simple, often simplistic, man who had given her such unstinting support during the Saigon trial, did much to bring father and son together.

André Malraux's legendary reserve as regards his private life makes it impossible to estimate the effect that his father's tragic death had on him. However friendly their relations may have been, father and son did not have a great deal to say to one another. Skirting round the subject in an interview in 1967, André Malraux said: 'I had a great deal of admiration for my father: he was a tank officer, which I found very romantic . . .'[13] However, in Malraux's subsequent books (*La Condition humaine*, *Le Temps du Mépris*) the theme of the father suddenly replaces that of the superior companion (Garine and the narrator, Perken and Claude). This cannot be mere coincidence.

What cannot be doubted is that suicide, as an emergency exit, and also as an affirmation of supreme freedom, was to obsess Malraux more and more. At the beginning of the *Antimémoires*, he refers to his father's true suicide and his grandfather's false suicide. His friends Eddy du Perron and Drieu la Rochelle were to choose the same death. It was not enough that this life should be lived out under the shadow of the irremediable: it was also necessary that this irremediable should appear

to him from the domain of choice, and that death could assume
for him the form of will.

André and Clara always had a passion for travelling. A certain
kind of travelling, of course, in which they discovered forms,
stones, men. They would decide to set off again and they would
set off, without giving much thought as to how or where they
would end up. There was a certain 'Orient-Express' snobbery
about this attitude, a desire to remain faithful to one's own
personality. It was not for nothing that they became the
martyrs of archaeological tourism!

In 1929, then, they set out for a somewhat vague East that
gradually took shape: they found themselves in the Soviet
Union, at Odessa, Batum and Baku, where nothing and nobody
could tell them how they could go any further. Clara stood on
the platform yelling out in German: 'Is there a train for Tiflis?'
Theirs was already a 'hippy' form of travelling that the as yet
undeveloped Intourist organisation could still tolerate. They
were dazzled by Persia. They made the usual expedition to
Isfahan, and no country, no civilisation was to enchant them
more, except India – at least as far as he was concerned.

They came back the following year, in 1931. The whole
journey had taken nearly a year: it was their first world tour.
As in 1923, André had been entrusted with a mission, but this
time by a friendly power, the firm of Gallimard. He was to
bring back material for an exhibition that he had long dreamt
of organising, in which the Greek and Buddhist civilisations
would stand side by side. This time they set out with a plan, a
map and money. They stayed for a long time in Persia, discovered the Pamirs, Afghanistan, crossed the Khyber Pass into
India and stayed in New Delhi, already laden with objects for
their exhibition. They then moved on to Calcutta, saw Singapore again, and arrived at last in continental China – Canton,
Shanghai, Peking . . .

André Malraux is suspected of finding the real Canton insuf-
ficiently like the Canton of *Les Conquérants*. He took a few notes
in Shanghai. *La Condition humaine* was already gestating, but he
wanted it to be a metaphysical novel and the city itself was no
more important to the book than St Petersburg was to *Crime*

and Punishment. They left China and moved on to Manchuria, Japan, Vancouver, San Francisco, New York . . . There, they finally ran out of the money allowed them by their publisher. The 'Greco-Buddhist' statues were getting heavy and André did not like to be stingy. At New York they informed Gaston Gallimard of their distress and, until another cheque arrived, they were reduced for the next ten days to visiting Manhattan on foot.

Between the second visit to Persia and this world tour, Malraux had finally published *La Voie royale* – a heroic version of the Indo-China adventure of 1923–4. The press was very favourable again. Prior to reading in the December number of the *NRF* the enthusiastic study by Drieu la Rochelle quoted from above, Malraux was able to savour in *L'Action française* one of those highly coloured, juicy, sonorous homages that the extreme right polemist but penetrating critic Léon Daudet handed out: 'In these dishonourable times of spiritual sloth . . . Malraux paints with his pen . . . with a fearless, dangerous talent . . . incisive yet languid, at once sombre and luminous like some *chiaroscuro* painting . . . Certain pages are reminiscent of one of Rembrandt's visions . . .'

The publication of *La Voie royale* could not fail to stir the embers of the 'affair'. This occurred on the occasion of an interview given by Malraux to André Rousseaux, a well-known critic of the time, published in *Candide*. With admirable frankness, spiced with a few provocative lies, the novelist admitted that Vannec's story *was* his own and trotted out the old, somewhat specious legal arguments (the danger involved, the non-appropriation of the stones, the absence of any 'classification') to justify the enterprise. Rousseaux pretended to be disappointed:

M. Malraux resumes his defence . . . Before long, I shall hear myself saying that the bas-reliefs were *res nullius*, that they have been sequestered, and that he still lays claim to them. Alas, what pitiful concessions to bourgeois order! . . . I break off the interview, I flee. I leave M. Malraux deeply disappointed. I had thought, for a moment, that I was encountering pure anarchy, and I admired, in spite of myself,

its lucid, gloomy despair, its horrible, sublime beauty. I now
fear that there is no such thing as pure anarchy, except perhaps in M. Malraux's books . . .[14]

Thus ill-treated by some magazines, Malraux was not tempted
to resume any journalistic job, even when his friend Berl
launched *Marianne*, a potential rival to the right-wing magazines
Candide and *Gringoire*, that would be, if not actually 'left-wing',
at least open to leftist opinion and hostile to the creeping
influence of fascism.

For this reason, and because *Marianne* was published by
Gallimard, Berl had high expectations of Malraux. In fact,
although articles by Giraudoux, Morand, Saint-Exupéry and
Giono appeared regularly in *Marianne*, Malraux wrote only five
times in as many years for the review. But his contributions
were always important ones – on Indo-China, on Trotsky, on
Fascism, for example. We shall come back to these.

It was at the editorial offices of *Marianne*, where he called
from time to time to pit himself against Berl, to try out an idea
on him, to sharpen his wit – and also for the sheer love of print
and a layout to be redesigned – that André Malraux met a tall,
very beautiful girl, with a clear complexion, grey-green eyes
and liberated manners. She was called Josette Clotis and was to
play an important role in his life some years later. For the time
being, she was preparing publication for a very likeable little
novel, *Le Temps vert*, to which her charm and gaiety added some
merit. She was to become one of the most faithful and most
active contributors to *Marianne*.

12 *The paths of glory*

ANDRÉ MALRAUX at thirty. Let us take a look at him. Never was he to be more instinct with life, never was the brilliance of his intellect to be more in evidence – and never was he less involved in the more petty activities of the literary world. Those who knew him then, around 1932, before the world-wide success of *La Condition humaine* and the obligations of the political struggle had altered (by enlarging) his image, remember him as an exceptionally brilliant personality. Thus Monique Saint-Clair (Mme Van Rysselberghe, André Gide's best woman friend, the 'petite dame'):

> After a long absence in Persia, we were able to take him out in the car. No sooner had we shaken hands and put his suitcase in the boot than he exclaimed: 'In Persia, divinity' . . . It takes a long time to know anything more of Malraux than his intelligence, which seems to occupy all the available room. When he says 'I' it is rather his public personality that is speaking. His private personality is always in the background. To allude to it at all would be to break the rules. A simple 'How are you, Malraux' is almost always bordering on indiscretion . . .[1]

In 1933 Manès Sperber, arriving in Paris as a German political refugee, went to see Malraux. He was no sooner sitting on the sofa than Malraux exclaimed, with passionate concern: 'But explain to me why the fascist régimes don't produce art worthy of the name?'[2] Sperber remembers the meeting as if it had been an encounter with Saint-Just . . .

Of course, certain people had reservations. The liberal-minded bourgeois Alfred Fabre-Luce also saw him in late August 1932:

> People were very attracted by Malraux's enthusiasm, his eloquence, his nervous energy. His forelock kept falling over his eye and he would throw it back in a movement that revealed a noble brow and actually drew attention to it. He pretended to read in women's hands what he had observed of them. I have always seen him exercising the profession of magician in some form or other . . .[3]

And there is the wonderful portrait by Maurice Sachs, in that superb fresco of Paris in the Thirties, *Le Sabbat*:

> The person who most left his mark at the *NRF* was André Malraux. If people were dazzled by him, it was with good reason: an intelligence unequalled in its vivacity and agility, a fine voice, a warm and persuasive way of speaking, an admirable face that was beginning to be rather spoilt by all the tics that he seemed unable to rid himself of, elegance in everything: in his walk, in his dress, in the gestures of his very beautiful hands; on top of all this, qualities of understanding, attentiveness, curiosity, and considerable generosity. And yet there was a touch of the charlatan about him! . . . He could not see things properly because he believed that unless one is everything, one is nothing . . . Yet one did not get to know him without becoming fond of so courageous, so coldly heroic a person, passionate, yet with almost as much impartiality as can be found in passion, accessible to pity, obliging, the friend of suffering mankind, yet not very human, too rational, sometimes dreamy, never mediocre and, when all is said and done, pretty *farfelu*. He never took me seriously and, I don't know how, but that made me see the lighter side of his seriousness, the superficial aspect of his knowledge, but also the beautiful and lovable qualities of his personality. A great man, but doing his best to seem greater.[4]

A great man? Others still saw him as a retarded adolescent, especially certain visitors to the apartment in which Clara had

set up home, at 44 rue du Bac, a few steps away from the NRF.
She held sway in the (rather modest) drawing-room. He had
arranged a study for himself in the entrance hall – there was
nowhere else. He sat there, facing the door, like a hunted
animal expecting attack. His behaviour with his wife could still
have a touch of timidity about it. But their marriage was beginning to show signs of wear. The birth of Florence, in 1933,
merely consolidated for a time what had been a sometimes
admirable relationship.

André Malraux prowled around Marxism – but to no avail.
His thinking had centred in turn on Pascal and Nietzsche and
had always been haunted by Dostoevsky. He was unable either
to find himself in the world or to discover a meaning in the
world. He believed that effective action was the only response
to the absurd worthy of man. Did not Garine and Perken owe
their defeat merely to the fact of their failure? The time had
come to create heroes whom defeat would not render absurd
because they would have experienced a new brotherhood.

André Malraux was thirty years old. He wrote *La Condition
humaine*.

In order to write what, for him, was to be a Dostoevskian novel,
worthy of the Karamazovs, whom he regarded, together with
T. E. Lawrence, as the 'fifth gospel', he shut himself away for
a time in the Chevreuse valley, in the house of an excellent
specialist in things Asiatic, his friend Eddy du Perron, with
whom he seems to have discussed the themes of the book and
to whom, in fact, it was dedicated.

La Condition humaine tells the story of a group of revolutionaries implicated in the Shanghai uprising of April 1927, that
was crushed by Chiang Kai-shek's troops. Three figures on
their side dominate the action: Kyo, son of a Japanese mother
and of a French intellectual (old Gisors, whose wisdom and
scepticism permeate the book); Katow, Russian militant, the
perfect comrade, with a touch of Tolstoyan serenity; Chen, the
terrorist, the only Chinese character of the team. Two other
powerful personalities, Ferral, the French imperialist banker, in
love with the gorgeous and ironic Valerie, and Clappique, the
Shakespearian fool, move through a story full of murders,

violence and torture, which reaches its climax with the famous scene of Kyo and Katow, arrested by Chiang's police and waiting for their terrible ordeal – thrown into the scalding boiler of a locomotive. Both have cyanide pills: Kyo swallows his own and dies, while Katow, seeing two frightened young prisoners, offers them this way of escaping suffering, and goes unflinchingly to an agonizing death . . . The most celebrated pages ever written by Malraux.

Why did Malraux choose this particularly complex episode in the Chinese revolution, and these cosmopolitan characters? Malraux, who once described it as 'reportage', never wrote a book more based on imagination. He brought back few notes from his trip to China the year before. He used press cuttings and a few notes taken by his friend the reporter Georges Manue, whom he had urged so much to follow the rise of the Kuomintang and the subsequent crisis in the movement.

The central character, Kyo, can hardly be based, despite what has been said to this effect, on Chou En-lai, who was then practically unknown to him. Only Chou's role as head of the Shanghai workers' movement in the first months of 1927 bears out such an assumption, whereas neither in temperament nor in political thinking can he be identified with Malraux's hero. The real model may have been a young Japanese writer who, in Paris, in 1922, had been a friend of Ho Chi Minh (then Nguyen Ai Quoc), and later of Malraux: he was called Kyo Komatsu.[5]

The character of Ferral was based on one of the brothers of Philippe Berthelot, the famous diplomat, who had also worked in banking in China in the 1920s, while much of Clappique, including his picturesque diction and verbal mannerisms, was taken from René Guetta, a journalist then working on *Marianne*. More important, Chen appeared earlier in a less subtle form as Hong in *Les Conquérants*: both characters were inspired by young Hin, the friend of the Malrauxs in Saigon, who had been so set on killing the governor. As for old Gisors, it is possible that certain features were taken from Gide. Malraux had just lost his father and become a father in turn. For the first time, his heroes were given family ties that play a role in the action.

The title derives explicitly from Pascal, who describes man's fate as a fate of prisoners in chains, awaiting their ordeal. But

Malraux has remarked on several occasions that what inspired the choice of title was a feeling of the impossibility of communication – characteristic of men's condition – that had been revealed to him, as Kyo relates, when he realised that man hears others with his ears, but hears himself with his throat: two systems of communication that involve two types of exchange, two truths – a falsified, absurd relationship. For Pascal, the condition of men is that of being condemned to death; for Malraux it is that of being imprisoned and aphasic.

However, in a letter written at the time to a young eighteen-year-old called Gaëtan Picon[6] who had just published a study of the book in a small review, *La Hune*, Malraux wrote: 'The framework is not fundamental, of course. The essence of the book is what you call the Pascalian element.'

Completed at the end of 1932, the book first appeared in six instalments in the *NRF*, from January to June 1933. It disconcerted a good many readers, beginning with André Gide, who observed in his *Journal* on 10 April 1933: 'I have re-read from beginning to end *La Condition humaine*. This book, which, in serial form, seemed to me excessively involved, disheartening because of its richness and almost incomprehensible because of its complexity . . . seems to me as I re-read it altogether, utterly clear, ordered in its confusion, admirably intelligent, and, despite that . . . deeply embedded in life, involved, and panting with a sometimes unbearable anguish.'[7]

The book was an outstanding success. Among hundreds of reviews, let us single out one, perhaps the most interesting of all – for the Malraux of that time – written by Ilya Ehrenburg and published in May 1933 in *Izvestia*: 'André Malraux's new novel is enjoying a well-deserved success. In the bookshop windows one can see the covers of its 25th impression and in the newspapers and reviews critics are still writing enthusiastic articles about the book.' However, the Soviet writer objected that 'it is not a book about either a revolution or an adventure, but a private journal, transcriptions of earlier discussions, a radioscopy of the author fragmented into several different heroes . . .' But, Ehrenburg observes:

Malraux's weakness lies elsewhere. His characters are alive

and we suffer with them, we suffer because they suffer, but there is nothing that makes us feel the need for such a life and such suffering. Isolated in the world in which they live, these heroes seem like hot-headed romantics. The revolution experienced by a great country becomes the story of a group of conspirators. These conspirators know how to die heroically, but from the first pages of the novel, it is clear that they must die. They reason to an enormous extent . . . Certainly, they spend a lot of time distributing guns, but it is hard to say what these guns are to be used for . . . When the revolution is defeated, it is not the defeat of a class, or even the defeat of a party, it is the effect of a fatality that hangs over the half-caste Kyo or the Russian Katow . . .

On 1 December 1933, *La Condition humaine* was unanimously awarded the Prix Goncourt. In its statement, the jury commented that in giving the prize it was acknowledging not only this particular book, but all three of Malraux's 'Asian' novels – *Les Conquérants* and *La Voie royale*, as well as *La Condition humaine*. But the triumph was not all plain sailing.

André Malraux had been desperately anxious to get the prize. He had persuaded Gaston Gallimard to launch an orchestrated campaign in his favour. It was thought that Malraux's great advocate would be Jean Ajalbert, a now forgotten realistic novelist, who had already voted for him when *La Voie royale* was being considered. To make sure of his loyalty, they got themselves invited to dinner by Ajalbert, a *bon vivant* who liked nothing better than receiving praise at his own table. Gaston Gallimard, who did not care for rich food, was nearly sick. André Malraux himself was too anxious to please to risk an allusion to his favourite restaurant.

With Ajalbert won over, it remained to convince Roland Dorgelès, author of a popular description of Indo-China, *La Route Mandarine*, who was indignant that someone who had been convicted of theft could be rewarded with a prize. 'I saw him, with my own eyes, between two policemen at Phnom Penh.' To which, apparently, Ajalbert replied: 'What! How dare you bring such arguments here! If I had seen him at the other end of the world, a French writer between two policemen, I'd have pushed the policemen away and stood beside him!'

Over and above this rather shabby wheeling and dealing and the fame that suddenly overtook him, what he – and Clara with him – most enjoyed was the warm and perceptive encouragement of the best critics of the time. The review by Ramon Fernandez in *Marianne* seems to sum up the general attitude:

> M. André Malraux marks a turning-point in French literature. This literature was hovering between analysis and action, as between two opposite poles. M. André Malraux has corrected this error by showing that a well-chosen action, if carried through to its full conclusion, is the best touchstone of moral truth.
>
> Seen from the inside, M. Malraux's work may be seen as a renewal of the concept of tragic will, or, rather, as a tragical critique of will. Will in all its forms, and above all the willed rejection of the world as it is, makes man a hero. But at a certain stage in our development, in our own time indeed, maturity and lucidity are eroding this will from the inside. We can see the vanity, the illusion of our will. Yet if we continue to act, a new sense of tragedy will be born from the very excess of our energy and from the coexistence of our stubbornness and our lucidity. In other words, the tragic wall, M. Malraux's marble wall, is no longer outside, but within the souls of his characters. The result is quite striking: the lucid Prometheus loses none of his strength. On the contrary, his strength is increased by a discreet, but implacable scepticism that serves, as it were, to purify it. In M. Malraux's work, the will begins where it usually ends: after the liquidation of illusions and beliefs . . .[8]

It was in the midst of this vociferous triumph that André Malraux learnt of his mother's death. He always showed the greatest discretion where his family life was concerned, but in the case of his mother this was carried to still further lengths – and many of his friends have remarked on the fact.

From adolescence onwards, his relations with her were not of the easiest. We have seen how badly he reacted when he learnt of the intimacy that had grown up between his wife and his mother. What we are faced with here is one of the least discernible corners of André Malraux's life and moral attitude. All these works and not a single mother – except, fleetingly, in a story, *Le Temps du Mépris*, which he has practically disowned.

At the moment when fame was his, at the age of thirty-two, André Malraux was an orphan.

13 *Interlude over the desert*

ON 23 March 1934, *Le Journal* published the following dispatch:
'The airman Corniglion-Molinier, his mechanic Maillard and
one passenger[1] landed at 11.50 am at Orly airport . . . The aviators
were returning from a trip to Arabia . . .' Thus the most naïve
publicity stunt of André Malraux, then at the height of his
fame, was presented by one of the three great Paris daily
newspapers!

'These lands of legend attract eccentrics,' Malraux writes in
the *Antimémoires*,[2] thus determined to situate his flight to the
fallacious ruins of the capital of the Queen of Sheba in the
atmosphere that this obsessional word evokes for him – an
atmosphere of nocturnal unconsciousness and misty fatality, an
impalpable cloud of spiders and butterflies: destiny, antiwill.

He had just received the Prix Goncourt. He was therefore
rich and famous. When he was about to give in to such tempta-
tions, Rimbaud set out for Abyssinia and T. E. Lawrence
(about whom he thought a great deal at this time) suddenly
broke with literature and sank into the anonymous life of a
soldier. It would be asking too much of André Malraux to
expect him to become a Zouave at Oran or a sapper at Chateau-
roux. But why not put this new-found glory to the test, by
playing double or quits with it on the very same terrain as the
hero of *Seven Pillars of Wisdom* and the poet of *Les Illuminations*.

Then there was the demon of action, there was the somewhat
sticky atmosphere that surrounded him in Paris since he had
been awarded the prize, and there were other dangers – the
Nazis had been in power in Germany for a year and the extreme

right presented a similar threat in France. At the approach of 'times of trouble', which were to involve a long mobilisation, a struggle which Malraux was to evade less than anyone, why not have a last fling? 'When I come back from a job that has been dangerous in some way, I feel entirely a man again,' Malraux confided to his friend Nino Frank.[3]

He had just been received at the French Geographical Society by the great explorer Charcot, who mentioned the recollections of an unusual man called Arnaud, a nineteenth-century explorer of the Yemen, who, in 1843, was supposed to have discovered the capital of Balkis, the Queen of Sheba, beloved of Solomon. Malraux rushed to the records of the Geographical Society, just as he had done ten years before to the archeological studies of the Khmers in the École française d'Extrême-Orient. There he discovered a marvellous character, Joseph Arnaud, a Provençal pharmacist and amateur Arabist, who, with little more than a few candles and a hermaphrodite donkey, had crossed the southern Arabian desert and seen Mareb before going blind, drawing the plans of the city in the sand for the benefit of the French consul, Fresnel, and going off to die a pauper in Algeria. These were the tracks, Malraux decided, that he must follow.

Following the traces left by Arnaud, his donkey and Aetius's Roman legions, there were also the ghosts of Rimbaud and T. E. Lawrence, and the echoes of a book that had haunted his childhood, Flaubert's *La Tentation de Saint-Antoine*. From his schooldays in Bondy, he had had a passion for Flaubert, for sumptuous word masonry, constellated prose. He had felt more drawn to Queen Balkis (or Makeda) after hearing the accounts of a storyteller in a marketplace in Isfahan and of a strange German traveller he had met near Bushire.

So it was there that he must go. But how? With Arnaud and his donkey in mind, he first thought of doing the journey on foot, armed only with a few words of Persian picked up during a few lectures at the École des langues orientales and three brief visits to Isfahan. But, in any case, the Shiite faith of the mountain people of the Yemen did not teach them Persian[4] – and certainly not the Persian spoken by a Goncourt laureate.

He talked about his project to an acquaintance, Édouard Corniglion-Molinier, who, as an airman, naturally suggested that he should attempt an aerial exploration and offered to fly the plane himself. He had useful connections, he knew his job, the prospect of discovery amused him and fame attracted him. So Corniglion it was.

They needed a machine. The writer and the airman both knew Paul-Louis Weiler who, as managing director of Gnome-et-Rhône, had a good reconnaissance plane at his disposal, a Farman 190, which he generously lent to his two friends. As for money, André Malraux got most of it from *L'Intransigeant,* where he had friends. In any case, a report by a Goncourt prize-winner on one of the mysterious desert capitals is not something a great daily lets slip. Shortly before leaving, Malraux met the reporters from *L'Intransigeant* and remarked, offhandedly: 'There's a fifty-fifty chance I shan't come out of this alive.'[5]

They set off in the evening of 22 February, with a mechanic called Maillard, who had certainly exercised more skill and lavished more care on the technical preparation for the flight than Malraux had in the planning of the route: they first had to land at Cairo in order to get their first map, in English, of Yemen-Hadhramaut, and then again at Djibouti, where they learnt that this map did not agree with the one used by the airmen at the French base.

The brief stay in Cairo was interesting. Among other things, Malraux visited the Mariette Museum, which astonished him, and then spent a long evening in the company of a group of fascinated young Egyptian intellectuals. One of them, Georges Henein, then a Surrealist, remembers the meeting very vividly: 'He talked to us for hours of St Paul. As recent readers of *La Condition humaine* we expected more up-to-date allusions: it was a long time before we realised that he was referring to Stalin...' Before leaving him, they asked him what they should read. 'Trotsky's *History of the Russian Revolution* and *Le Canard enchaîné* ...'[6] And so the man who was setting out, in a trance, in search of the Queen of the Desert came, spoke and conquered.

The three men left Djibouti on 7 March 1934, unable to start their flight from Aden, which was closer to their objective, but where the British received them less warmly, since the RAF regarded the area over which they wished to fly as one of their own preserves. They could fly eleven to twelve hours without refuelling and they needed four or five hours to reach the Mareb area on the Aden parallel and the approximate meridian of Hodeida and Sana. In fact, the objective was very inaccurately located. After all, the expedition was supposed to be a 'discovery'. But given the plane's normal range and the amount of reserve fuel they had brought with them, they could not afford the luxury of much reconnaissance.

Corniglion sat in front at the controls, with Malraux and Maillard behind him. They were wearing flying gear, but had brought 'Arab' clothes with them in case a forced landing made them play at being Lawrences. *Royaume farfelu,* indeed! They had been flying – against the wind – for five hours. They had flown over Mocca and had just passed on their left a very beautiful, fortified city that could only be Sana. Soon they would have to choose between giving up or taking what might turn out to be a road of no return. The pilot, worried about the discrepancies between the two maps, handed Malraux his notebook, on which he had scribbled: 'I think we're off course.'[7] And the two men took to thinking over a sentence of Arnaud's: 'Leaving Mareb, I visited the ruins of ancient Sheba, which in general has nothing to show but mounds of earth . . .'[8]

Corniglion reduced altitude. And it was then that occurred what they both have called a 'discovery' and which Malraux was to describe in *L'Intransigeant* of 9 May 1934 in these words:

> To the right, in front of us, a huge, almost white patch was beginning to form into a beach of colossal pebbles in the middle of the desert. Was it a geological accident? A mistake? We kept repeating to ourselves that we must wait until we were closer; but already, deep down within us, we had recognised towers and we knew that it was the city.
>
> We arrived overhead, watching it grow like a hungry man eating.
>
> The shattered mind had to choose between a mass of oncoming dreams. And we followed both the Bible and legend: if this was the city of the queen, then it was contemporary with Solomon. Was this huge monument, this sort of Notre-Dame tower, beneath which a perspective of terraces tumbled down to the petrified skeleton of a river, the palace of

which the Prophet says in the Koran: 'I saw there a woman
governing men, seated on a magnificent throne; she and her
people worship the sun'?

. . . In another mass of stones is an almost Egyptian-
looking temple: trapezoidal towers, a vast slanting terrace,
propylaea. To the side, a stretch of wall a hundred and twenty
feet high. What was this wall? . . . Beyond the ruins are
innumerable Bedouin tents. Tiny flames appear over these
dark patches: we are being shot at.

. . . Between bits of wall scattered here and there have piled
up over the centuries the remains of all the cults of the
ancient world . . . City of magician queens, how good it is to
see you tear your fortune from the gods and to imagine still
from the odour of your sand something of the perfume of
the sacred substances! . . .

This surprising reporter then suddenly concludes on a more
familiar note:

A pity one can't land; a tiny people of blue and green
lizards are no doubt bringing a fitting end to one of the
world's most beautiful legends.

When, thirty-three years later, the journalist turned into the
autobiographer, the tone became more gentle, the sentences
lighter and something resembling retrospective modesty attenu-
ates the evocation of the miracle:

We could see the ground more and more clearly as we
flew lower, struggling with the view-finder as the plane
tilted over, like agitated waiters in a café juggling with their
trays. We were no longer over the desert, but over an abandoned oasis showing traces of cultivation; only to the right
did the ruins encroach on the desert. Those massive oval
ramparts, whose debris was clearly visible against the soil,
could they be temples? How to make a landing? To one
side lay the dunes, in which the plane would overturn; to
the other, a volcanic soil with rocks projecting from the
sand. Closer to the ruins, the ground was caved in everywhere. We flew still lower, and went on photographing.
The horse-shoe walls opened on empty space: the town,

built of sun-dried bricks like Nineveh, must have similarly reverted to the desert. We turned back to the main mass: an oval tower, more ramparts, cuboid buildings. Tiny flames flickered against the dark patches of Bedouin tents scattered outside the ruins. They must be firing at us. On the other side of the walls we began to make out the mysterious traces of things whose purpose we could not fathom. That flat H on the tower overlooking the ruins, what did it represent? Part of an observatory? The terrace of a hanging garden? They were still common in the high Yemen, these gardens of Semiramis now reduced to humble kitchen-gardens, but covered with dream-grass, the hemp of the Old Man of the Mountain . . . A pity it was impossible to land![9]

And three pages later, almost as if he had not noticed, he adds that 'almost nothing' remains of Sheba. The truth can be good sometimes . . .

On the evening of 7 March 1934 they made a rather adventurous landing at Obock. The next day, from Djibouti, they sent off the following telegram to *L'Intransigeant*: '*Have discovered legendary capital Queen of Sheba stop twenty towers or temples still standing stop at the northern boundary of the Rub El Khali stop have taken photographs for L'Intransigeant stop greetings Corniglion – Malraux.*'

Between these hours of autosuggestive fever and the time at which the *Antimémoires* were written, the whole business was cut down to size.

The seven articles published by the Parisian daily, beginning on 3 May 1934 at the top of the front page, beneath thick, eye-catching headlines and accompanied by photo-montages that look rather like naïve forgeries, but which caused a sensation at the time, now seem like a huge practical joke.

Indeed, it was not long before the seriousness of the 'discovery' was being called into question – and in the most irritating way for André Malraux. On 6 April, in *Le Temps*, there appeared a letter from an explorer called Beneyton, who not only cast serious doubt that 'the ruins over which M. Malraux has flown' were 'the legendary Mareb discovered by Halévy in 1870', but even suggested that the aerial archeologists must have confused it either with Tehanna (a neighbouring site along the coast), or with Temma ('which I myself discovered in 1911'), or even with Mocca . . . Which was tantamount to accusing Malraux and his companion of ignorance, naïvety or lying.

Malraux reacted very strongly to the form of the attack, but more prudently as far as the substance of the charge was concerned. Four days later, on 10 April, the editor of *Le Temps* published a reply in which Malraux admitted that 'the town we flew over is not Mareb, which was discovered in 1843' and added that 'if, like anyone else, we run the risk of making a mistake when identifying a town that we have seen, our contradictors run the risk of making an even graver mistake in identifying a town that they haven't seen at all . . . We are well aware how unsure any identification that is not based on epigraphy can be. But what we saw were ruins five times larger than any so far found in southern Arabia, and the only ones still standing . . .'

André Malraux concluded: 'We twice flew over Mocca, which is five hundred kilometres from the town in question. We never mentioned Tehanna, which is indeed on the coast, but Rubat el-Khali, which is far inland . . . There is no question of our confusing a town of the Sheba confederation with Mocca, any more than the Acropolis in Athens with the Champs-Élysées.'

Thirty-three years later, neither the word 'discovery', nor the idea behind it can stand up to examination. Not a single specialist of the southern Arabian world takes either the touched-up photographs or the fantastic reportage seriously. Although the aerial expedition over Hadhramaut involved greater danger than the crossing of the Khmer forest in 1923, the stones of Banteaï-Sre certainly had greater reality.

In a book entitled *Missions très spéciales*, Edmond Petit, himself an airman, tried to discover the truth about the expedition of 7 March 1934. He quotes the views of several specialists in the Yemenite civilisation, in particular Jacqueline Pirenne. This expert Arabist suggested that what Malraux wanted to see and describe as Mareb, the supposed capital of the Queen of Sheba, is an oasis formed by a number of different sites, some inhabited, others in ruins: Duraïb Kharib, Ashil-Rumm, etc. But she didn't rule out Mareb. In fact, in 1952, an American archeological mission really did discover Mareb – and it turned out to be not too dissimilar from what Malraux thought he had seen!

Malraux had risked his life for a biblical queen – and her descendant, the heir of Menelik and Emperor of Ethiopia, let it be known that he would be glad to receive him. So he set off in the direction of Addis Ababa, where the Negus was still awaiting Mussolini's centurions. For André Malraux, hitherto on bad terms with established authority, this was the first of a long series of dialogues with the world's leaders. He describes Haile Selassie with refreshing simplicity:

> Here is the Negus in the royal guébi. He is seated on a Galeries Lafayette sofa in front of his toga-clad dignitaries. While the interpreter calls Corniglion-Molinier Monsieur de la Molinière because the Negus with the sad smile had received some Junkers two days earlier, the roar of the lions of Judah can be heard through the windows. For centuries, their cages have lined the great avenue of the palace of the emperors of Ethiopia, who number the queens of Sheba among their legendary ancestors . . .[10]

But if he speaks of the Negus in a pedestrian style, Malraux triumphs when it comes to describing the return journey, giving us the famous account of the cyclone, followed by the return to life, which he included in the novel he published the following year, *Le Temps du Mépris* (as if to add a little warmth to this somewhat dry account), and which he took up again, with little alteration, in the *Antimémoires*.

One can hardly refrain from quoting a few sentences from it. First because it is a very fine piece of writing, in which the Malraux of *L'Espoir*, the mature, self-confident Malraux, replaces the pasticheur of Flaubert; and, secondly, because these moments – those of 'the meeting with the cosmos' and of 'the coming back to earth' – are those that have left a particularly deep impression on the man. They mark the threshold of his second life, that in which, to use the terms of the key-text that he was to publish a few months later, 'difference' gave way to 'fraternity'.

We had set off from Tripolitania for Algiers, though the weather forecast was not promising . . . [The tone of the *Aeneid*, with a dash of Saint-Exupéry.] We struck cloud, and after a long smooth stretch where the map showed scarcely a hillock, vertical crests, still snow-covered, suddenly loomed up against a continually darkening sky. It was the Aurès [the mountains located south-east of Algeria].

We were at least seventy miles off course, plunging into an immense cloud, not calmer or stiller at this height, but poised like an animal ready to pounce, compact, alive and murderous. Its flanks advanced towards the aircraft as if it were hollowing out at its centre, and in the immense, slow deliberation of its movements it seemed to be girding itself not for an animal combat but for some inexorable cataclysm. The brownish-yellow outlines of its frayed flanks, like a glimpse of headlands in a foggy sea, merged into an unending grey, seemingly boundless because cut off from the earth: for the dark cotton-wool of cloud had now slid beneath the plane, hurling me into the realm of the sky, itself occluded by the same leaden mass. I felt as if I had escaped from gravity, as if I were suspended somewhere between the worlds, grappling with the cloud in a primitive combat, while below me the earth continued on its course, which I would never cross again . . .

At the centre of the cyclone, the plane was turning full circle, making level turns around itself . . .

Corniglion was clenched to the controls, at the highest pitch of concentration; but his face was a new face . . . the face of childhood . . . I realised that I was trembling, not in my hands (I was still holding the window) but in my left shoulder. I scarcely had time to wonder whether the plane was back on an even keel when Corniglion pushed the stick forward and cut off the engine.

I knew this manoeuvre: lose height, take advantage of the force of gravity to burst through the storm and try to pull out again close to the ground . . .

3000
2800
2700 (I felt my eyes bursting out of my head, in

their frantic fear of suddenly seeing the mountain . . .)
1650
1500

12. . Not horizontal and straight ahead as I expected, but far off at an angle. I hesitated before the unreality of this forty-five-degree horizon (the plane had been falling at a tilt) but already everything in me had recognised it, and Corniglion was struggling to right the aircraft. The earth was still far off beyond this sea of obscene cloud, of floccules of dust and hair, that had already closed round us again, and then opened up once more; and suddenly, three hundred feet below us, a leaden landscape loomed up through the last shreds of mist, black splinters of sharp hills around a pallid lake which spread its tentacles out into the valley and reflected the sullen sky with a geological calm.

The battered aircraft crawled under the storm, 150 feet above the peaks . . . At last I took my hand away from the window, and remembered that my life-line was long . . . an immense peacefulness seemed to bathe the new-found earth, the fields and the vineyards, the houses, the trees and their sleeping birds.[11]

This 'coming back to earth' took place on the airport at Bône (where, as in a Chaplin film, they were praised for their 'performance', being mistaken for some other airmen).

For André Malraux, wandering through the streets of the town, it was first of all:

. . . an enormous red hand which was the glove-maker's sign in those days. The earth was peopled with hands, and perhaps they might have been able to live by themselves, without men. I could not recognise the shops, this furrier's window with a little white dog trotting between the dead skins, sitting down, then setting off again: a living being, with long hair and clumsy movements, which was not a man. An animal. I had forgotten animals. This dog was strolling around quite calmly in the shadow of death, whose fading rumble still reverberated inside me: I found it hard to sober up from the intoxication of the void.[12]

This flight, which so rightly haunted Malraux, turns up again in an article entitled 'L'homme et le moteur', published in the *Gnome-et-Rhone Journal*[13] before the series of reports in *L'Intransigeant*. But here the tone is far more sober than in any other of the versions of this adventure:

> The plane . . . is certainly the mechanism by which courage can be analysed most lucidly. We have been too much in the habit of regarding courage as an instinct: one might as well say that there is no way of analysing love other than as an instinct . . . I think courage is a destruction of ideas . . . When the storm forces the plane to nosedive and we suddenly see land vertically, there is something within us that says that this is not the plane falling, but the earth that has gone mad.

The machine certainly inspires him in a way that stones never did. He is now ready for the road that he will take at the side of those citizens and devotees of the technological age, the Communists. In this new age, as one of the characters in *La Condition humaine* puts it, 'the factory . . . the church of the catacombs [will become] the cathedral [where we will see] instead of gods, human strength struggling with the earth'.

While those who still wish to dream of Sheba, Queen Balkis and the despair of Solomon can always go back to the accounts of Joseph Arnaud, donkey-driver, chemist, a teller of tales with burnt-out eyes – but eyes that have seen.

PART II

FELLOW-TRAVELLER

14 Commitment on the side of the Communists

'ANDRÉ MALRAUX will not go the way of the Gisors.' Thus Ehrenburg concluded his article of May 1933 on *La Condition humaine*: for him, Malraux had chosen revolution against an aestheticising idealism and flight into artificial paradises, to which Ehrenburg, for once a rather heavy-handed Marxist, reduces the character of Kyo's father. It is ironical that if, in 1933, André Malraux was moving in a direction calculated to satisfy for a time Ilya Ehrenburg and his friends, it was due largely to the influence of someone who is supposed to have partially inspired the character of old Gisors, Bernard Groethuysen.

When dealing with as powerfully imaginative a work as *La Condition humaine,* we must certainly not exaggerate the role of 'keys'. When, in June 1972, I asked André Malraux whether or not Groethuysen was the model for Gisors (and for old Alvéar in *L'Espoir*), he replied: 'These characters are too pathetic to reflect him completely. There was nothing pathetic about him. He was too wise.'

Bernard Groethuysen? The name is hardly known today, even in Paris. But between 1930 and 1950 this man, at the helm of the *NRF*, played an essential role, for at least a generation, in introducing France to Kafka, German philosophy and Russian literature. If, among the living, Malraux had a master, it was this German-Dutch philosopher with the face of a Socrates and the manners of a mujik, a Marxist in spirit and a disciple of St Augustine.

Malraux first met him when he joined the *NRF* in 1928. He

came very rapidly under the influence of this ex-professor of sociology at Berlin University (where he had worked with Max Weber), a Marxist so totally disinterested that he would willingly have spent his life rewriting (or writing) works signed by others. Which, in fact, is what he did.

'Grout,' as everyone called him, was the son of a Dutchman, a doctor (who went mad) and a Russian woman. At twenty, he fell in love with France. He joined the *NRF* after the 1914–18 war as a specialist in foreign literature and became the friend of André Gide and Jean Paulhan, who wrote an admirable article about him after his death in 1946.[1]

Paulhan, who lived for years in a studio next to Groethuysen's, in the rue Campagne-Première, described him, 'his green eyes sunk deep under his scarcely visible eyebrows . . . cuttle-fish eyes with sinuous eyelids', sitting in the nude, reading aloud with him *Chéri-Bibi* [a popular serial about convicts breaking out of jail], or stretching a sheet over a hole in his ceiling to keep the rain off his bed. He spent hours arguing with a neighbour, a prostitute by night and a painter by day, or with his concierge, a former policeman who was involved in tracking down deserters in 1917 – so successfully in this case that he actually persuaded him to join the Communist Party. He did the same for André Gide, whose *Retour d'URSS*, in 1936, came as a great blow to him. His friendship for Gide survived, but he declared, in all seriousness: 'In a classless society, there will be no room for the Gides of this world.'

For fifteen years, Groethuysen played an essential role in André Malraux's intellectual life. His Marxist faith, his deep sense of irony, his knowledge of the German and Russian minds, his sense of universality, his belief in a certain idea of man shaped – sometimes by negation – Malraux's vision and thinking in the 1930s. Without Groethuysen it is difficult to imagine Malraux's revolutionary commitment between 1934 and 1939, his silence on the subject of the Moscow trials and the Soviet-German pact of 1939 and his persistent loyalty to the *USSR* until the end of the war.

One cannot fail to note, with a sort of perplexity, that Malraux's sensational break with his former fellow-travellers (his speech at the congress of the National Liberation Movement in

January 1945) preceded by only a few months Bernard Groethuysen's death, in Luxembourg, on 27 September 1946. A
quarter of a century later, Malraux spoke of his old friend in
these terms:

> Of all the men I have met, it was he who established with
> the greatest certainty the idea of intellectual genius. But he
> attached no importance to what he wrote. He was the only
> case I have known of oral genius. I met him one day with
> Heidegger and a few *farfelus*: he was head and shoulders
> above everyone else! He was like Socrates to Plato . . . He is
> perhaps the man I have most admired. When he was there,
> we just buzzed around him like bees . . .[2]

Almost up to the moment when Adolf Hitler was installed in
the Chancellory of the Third Reich, André Malraux was not
really a 'committed' writer. Despite 'Grout' and men who had
less hold over him, but whom he respected or saw regularly –
from Romain Rolland to Ehrenburg – he remained a rebel
rather than a revolutionary. When, in October 1930, a contributor to *Monde*, the review edited by Henri Barbusse, questioned him about the role of the writer, he replied that his duty
was '*to express the tragic feeling of solitude*'.

Just prior to the publication of *Les Conquérants*, however, he
stated quite explicitly, in the course of a meeting of the 'Union
pour la vérité' on 8 June 1929, that this novel was not 'an
apologia for revolution'; what he had done was to formulate
the reasons that justify the alliance between an incorrigible
individualist like Garine and the Bolshevik organisation. This
sounds very like a plea for fellow-travelling.

The following year, he published *La Voie royale*, in which he
seems to be appealing for the praise that Drieu la Rochelle
heaped on him in his *NRF* article:[3] 'Malraux sees the condition
of man from the point of view of the individual' – though also
emphasising the extent to which the friendship between his
heroes broadens and warms the individualism of these adventurers. From *Les Conquérants* to *La Voie royale*, or rather from
his political struggles at Monin's side in Saigon to the corridors
of the *NRF*, it is difficult to say that Malraux had been moving

towards revolutionary fraternity. And when he met Malraux for the first time, in 1932, Ehrenburg noted: 'André Gide was then sixty, André Malraux was about thirty, but they both seemed to me, by turns, adolescents who had not yet tasted grief, and old men poisoned not by alcohol or nicotine, but by book-addiction.'⁴

On 30 January 1933, the Nazis seized power in Berlin. It is a date that cuts through the interwar years like a hatchet blow – in fact, the active opponents of the hatchet were already being decapitated in the Third Reich. The vague terrors of *Le Royaume farfelu* were replaced by an all too close, all too every-day horror. The 'temps du mépris' – the title of one of his forthcoming books – had begun. Malraux-the-ambiguous, like, at the same time, de Gaulle-the-even-more-ambiguous, did not err. The 'times of trouble' had come and required a different kind of behaviour.

Seven weeks after Hitler's advent to power, on 21 March 1933, the 'Association des écrivains et artistes révolutionnaires' (AEAR), an organisation created a year earlier and manipulated by Paul Vaillant-Couturier, leading journalist of the French Communist Party and Maurice Thorez, then a young Com-munist leader who showed great interest in cultural matters, called a meeting at the hall of the Grand Orient de France, in the rue Cadet. André Gide was in the chair. Comparing 'the Nazis' enormous effort to crush the German people' with 'cer-tain painful abuses' being practised in the Soviet Union, he declared: 'Why and how I have come to approve the one and reprove the other is because in the terrorism being practised in Germany I see a revival of a most deplorable, a most detestable past. While in the establishment of Soviet society, I see a future of unlimited promise.'⁵

André Malraux was there too. He had joined the AEAR in December 1932,⁶ but it was the first time he had expressed himself in so militant a group, in one where people addressed one another as 'Comrade'. Ehrenburg has left this description of the evening: 'Malraux talked intelligently. His features were constantly twisted by a nervous tic. Suddenly he stopped, raised his fist and yelled: "If there's to be a war, our place is in the ranks of the Red Army!" '⁷

Was he so unintelligible? Some fine-sounding phrases can be extracted from the text of his speech, later published in a pamphlet entitled *Ceux qui ont choisi*:

> For ten years fascism has spread its great black wings over Europe . . . Soon there will be action, blood for blood . . . First we owe it to ourselves to perform a concrete action to help the German writers who have paid us the tribute of trusting us! Those who are being persecuted in Germany are being so not because they are Marxists, but because they have retained a sense of dignity. German fascism has shown us that we are confronted by war. We must do our utmost to make sure that it does not take place: but those we are dealing with are deaf, we know that they are not listening! To threats, let us reply with threats, and let us know that we can turn to Moscow, to the Red Army!

The resolution passed at the end of this extremely militant meeting was in keeping with the phrases declaimed from the platform: it denounced 'French imperialism, the accomplice of Hitler, as Thiers was the accomplice of Bismarck' and condemned the Treaty of Versailles in the same terms as the Nazi terror: here was André Malraux travelling along other paths than archeological tourism, the drug adventure and aesthetic individualism. He never actually joined the Communist Party, as we know. But he did become a militant of sorts.

This was also the time when *La Condition humaine* was beginning to appear in the *NRF* (January–June 1933). It took less effort to associate this book with the revolutionary trend than in the case of *Les Conquérants*. From Garine to Kyo, from Borodin to Katow, and even from Hong to Chen, the author's development towards a more coherent and more positive vision of revolution is clear. The anarchistic adventurism that coloured the first book is replaced by a 'leftism' in which Trotskyist tendencies can be (and were) detected. The cosmopolitanism is always strongly felt, the pessimism is, from a Marxist standpoint, open to criticism and the Communist reader might well be puzzled by all the metaphysical questioning. But, essentially, the book is about revolution.

The publication of *La Condition humaine* coincided with the appearance of *Commune*, the review of the 'Association des écrivains et artistes révolutionnaires' with which Malraux had become associated. In its first issue (July 1933), *Commune* gave a warm reception to *La Condition humaine*. While having 'certain reservations as to the role attributed by Malraux to the Third International', Jean Audart[8] compared the novel with other novels about revolution, such as Pilniak's *Naked Army*, and observed that Malraux 'is not content with mere facts to the exclusion of the individual will'. He has shown that 'a social novel cannot ignore the personal dramas of individuals' and 'realises this union of the psychological and the social in a particularly concrete way'.

Ambiguous in his attitude to Marxism, but clearly committed to the struggle against fascism, Malraux was to become even more closely allied with the militant left in this decisive year of 1933 in the area of anticolonialism. We have seen how far he seemed to have moved away from his Indo-Chinese allies of 1925, scarcely touching on the subject again, even when the account of Claude's adventures in *La Voie royale* gave him the opportunity of doing so. Of course, the book was to have had a sequel, entitled *Les Puissances du désert*, in which Claud Vannec, too, might have confronted the colonial powers on other matters than the ownership of works of art. But there was no shortage of colonial crises. The year 1930, which also saw the publication of *La Voie royale*, had seen two serious and bloody uprisings in Indo-China, at Yen Bay and Nghe An. These had been described by such well-known journalists as Louis Roubaud. A writer bearing a name almost identical with that of Malraux's former comrade, Paul Monet, published an implacable book on the colonisation of Indo-China, *Les Jauniers*. Malraux still kept his peace.

Suddenly, on 11 October 1933, under the simple title 'S.O.S.', *Marianne* published an article by André Malraux whose violence seemed to be proportionate to its author's long silence. Malraux based this scorching condemnation solely on the official minutes of two trials that had just ended, the first with the acquittal by the court of Hanoi of five legionnaires who, in May 1931, had massacred several political prisoners with repugnant cruelty, the second with death sentences on a number of Annamese Communists by the Saigon court:

> Lest any doubt should remain as to my position, I wish it to be understood that, having lived in Indo-China, I cannot conceive of a courageous Annamese being anything other than a revolutionary. But it is not my intention here to expand on my own views; I wish simply to reveal the threat presented by a stupid régime and ask who accepts it. Fascism is a doctrine that one either approves or combats; stupidity is not such a doctrine.
>
> We claim allegiance to the doctrine of democracy. But we must have at least a minimum of logic. If one is the strongest, one can spend one's time hitting people; it's a matter of taste. But one should do it with one's bare hands, not with the Declaration of the Rights of Man . . .
>
> The logic of the democratic position would be to take up once more what was achieved by the Revolution and naturalise the natives *en masse*. The creation of a 'French democratic empire' of a hundred million inhabitants is a bold hypothesis. But it is less bold than Bolshevism – or fascism . . .
>
> Whenever the natives spit on one of their fellow-countrymen because he has betrayed them, he is awarded the Legion of Honour to hide his disgrace. But he mustn't be surprised if the peasants – nineteen out of twenty of the population – turn Communist. Every Communist movement that fails arouses a fascist response, but every fascist movement that fails arouses a Communist response too. This is reasonable enough. But what is now taking place is not at all reasonable: a madman is shooting down passers-by, shouting 'I am Order' . . .
>
> The word Communism can mean anything . . . Under its shadow Stupidity charges around Indo-China like a mad bull . . . Any desire for revolt is labelled 'Communism' – and it sounds good on electoral platforms. Let us sleep in peace . . .
>
> But be careful: in the end, the real Communists will begin to realise that it is not very effective to shout at meetings that the proletariat will not tolerate much longer what the

proletariat tolerates so well; that at this very moment, like a
sinister echo of the speech, the condemned men are being
shot; that these vain revolts, these raids by natives armed
with cudgels against the Legion's machine-guns, are good
only for getting the best Annamese militants killed. They
will give up revolt and begin to organise in secret, for cutting off people's heads is not a lasting way of preventing
them from using them. Even with a scythe.[9]

And they will wait for war to break out in Europe.

Young men, those of you under forty, you know that war
is here. Europe carries war within her, as any living body
carries death; you may die from it, you will not die without
being in it. However hard you shut your eyes, the whole
world is shouting it in your ears. You who know, because
you have heard it shouting and moaning beside you throughout your adolescence, how difficult it is to kill and to die
even when one's conscience is clear – at a time when, whatever your position, the very meaning of your life is at stake,
it is perhaps these men that you will be sent out to fight. You
in whose shadow wars prowl like crouching witches, whispering, 'You will be dead', another . . . is being prepared for
you.

For, nationalists, communists, liberals, there is one thing
you all know: in the end, a country can get tired of anything
– even of being killed for nothing.

Malraux is not a timid writer. Yet he has seldom expressed
anger with such force and splendour. Two years later, the
echoes of it can still be heard in a preface to Andrée Viollis'
Indochine S.O.S., which borrows the title of Malraux's *Marianne*
article.[10] The second text is less powerful, less vibrant, but it
poses very well the political problem of colonisation:

> The game of the colonial enterprises and the administra-
> tion that is dependent on them is to claim for the action that
> they exert over the natives the rigour that the state ought to
> exert over them, and which they prevent it from doing so . . .
> Those who, in reply to Andrée Viollis' questions, claim to
> see a just basis for colonisation, forget that the missionary
> with his leper-hospital is beneficial only to the extent that he

is not used as a justification for the drug-peddler. And that it is easy for the Annamese to reply: when the French build roads or bridges in Indo-China, let them be paid for doing so, as they are paid when they manage engineering projects in Siam or Persia; and let them then spend the money they've earned as they wish. For if those who work are also to be given *political* power, in addition to their pay, then soviets must be set up in France, from the specialist to the workers.[11]

For Malraux, it was no longer enough to link the colonial question and the social question: would decolonisation reduce to nothing the arguments of Marxism in a developed economy? He had already resumed the antifascist debate on the terrain where it now appeared as a matter of urgency: in Europe.

Ever since he had been awarded the Goncourt Prize, André Malraux had taken every opportunity that was offered him to use his new-found fame to influence public opinion and to warn it against the Nazi menace. On 20 December 1933, in an interview in *Marianne,* he denounced the preparatory manoeuvres being made for a conflict in which the Soviet Union would be opposed to a Franco–German coalition. Certainly, he said,

> public opinion is not very enthusiastic about the prospect of war. But it can be made to be. Let us take a look at this operation. The spokesmen of the steel-lords are in favour of an understanding with Hitler. The world oil combines, Royal and Standard, and the banks with which they are linked, are overtly favourable to Hitler and overtly antagonistic to Russia. *Le Matin* at the moment makes interesting reading. But no matter. What is happening is very curious indeed: on the one hand, there is a powerful group of economic interests preparing in the near (oil) or more distant (steel) future for war against Russia; on the other hand, there are the 'left-wing' political forces, for which I can feel little enthusiasm but which are quite obviously the only substantial opposition to this war . . .

Wouldn't it be difficult to get the French and the Germans to fight side by side? Yes. But these things can be arranged. It must first be done via Germany. Poland on the one hand and Russia on the other . . . But could such an operation be carried out without the establishment of fascism in France?

I don't believe that fascism can prosper in France. It's always a mistake to confuse fascism and authority . . . When a class is in danger, you get fascism. When the nation is in danger, you get Jacobinism. And the Frenchman, who is more threatened in his nation than in his class, will be Jacobin, not fascist.

I do not believe in some 'political biology' that enables us to predict the future development of the fevers at work in Europe and the world. War does not break out because the most favourable circumstances are at work. No. When one reads that the state of Europe today resembles the state of Europe in 1914, it is not wrong; but it is wrong to conclude from this that a war 'like 1914' will result from it . . . When so many forecasts can be made, there remains only the will. I say: whatever the circumstances, I will not participate in a war against Russia.[12]

As always with the political Malraux there is a mixture of penetrating views and adventurous approximations. But we have to agree that six years before Munich, and seven before the Vichy régime, Malraux was more clear-sighted than most. A curious remark too, for a militant, that reference to 'left-wing political forces, for which I can feel little enthusiasm, but . . .' Before long, he would have the chance to make up for it.

15 A congress in Moscow

THE opportunity arrived. The following summer (1934) a writers' congress was to take place in Moscow. At Ilya Ehrenburg's Paris flat, Malraux met Konstantin Fedin, who spoke to him of the condition of writers in the USSR and of the importance of the congress, which its organisers wished to be more 'open' than the congress at Kharkov where, in November 1930, the group of 'proletarian writers' (the 'Rabcors') had tried to exclude all those who would not comply with their discipline – the first manifestation of what was to become 'Zhdanovism'. In short, Malraux was invited to the Moscow Congress, together with Aragon, Paul Nizan and Wladimir Pozner – all members of the French Communist Party – and Jean-Richard Bloch, who was later to become one.

He was further encouraged to go by the fact that a Soviet organisation, the 'Mezrabpomfilm', was planning to make a film of *La Condition humaine*, under the direction either of Joris Ivens or Dovzhenko, the great director of *Earth*. Furthermore, if we are to believe Ehrenburg[1] and the interview that Malraux himself gave to the *Literaturnaia Gazeta,* he was working at the time on a novel about oil and wished to go to Baku (which he had already visited briefly with Clara in 1929).

At the end of May, Ehrenburg and he set off together, by sea, on board the *Dzerzhinsky*, via London and Leningrad, where they arrived on 14 June, welcomed by a delegation including Alexis Tolstoy and Paul Nizan.

André Malraux had been preceded in Moscow by the publication of an article by Paul Nizan in the *Literaturnaia Gazeta* for

12 June. 'Malraux is not a revolutionary writer,' he wrote. 'He is one of those young writers in the public eye who, emerging from the bourgeois class, condemn that class to a natural death and rally to the support of the proletariat. But this alliance contains personal reasons quite unconnected with the revolutionary cause.'[2]

Later, on 16 June, Malraux defined his own position in an interview published in the same review:

> Aversion for imperialist war and personal knowledge of the 'rights' of the 'enlightened' French bourgeoisie in Indo-China were, in fact, the deep reasons that have made me a revolutionary writer. But I am not a pacifist! . . . If war breaks out, and I think it will be Japan that starts it, I will be the first to work for the formation of a foreign legion and, in its ranks, gun in hand, I will defend the Soviet Union, the country of freedom.[3]

Ehrenburg has described the astonishing atmosphere in which, for two weeks, in the Hall of Columns of the Palace of Trade Unions, the congress took place dominated by the moustachioed face and gravelly voice of Maxim Gorky. Gorky presided beneath the gigantic, fraternal portraits of Shakespeare, Molière, Cervantes, Balzac, Pushkin, Gogol and Tolstoy, flanked by a veteran of the Paris Commune, Gustave Isnard. Before 25,000 devotees, Gorky spoke. He was followed by Zhdanov, who recalled Stalin's view that writers are 'the engineers of souls'. While Ehrenburg, then regarded as the Soviet expert on Western literature, proclaimed its 'irremediable decadence'.

A debate got under way between the supporters of the 'Broad Front' open to alliances with certain bourgeois elements, led by J. R. Bloch, and the chief spokesman of the 'Narrow Front', Karl Radek. In order not to have to choose between them, Aragon confined himself to lyrical flights in praise of Rimbaud and Cézanne.

Then Malraux appeared. With Théodor Plievier and J. R. Bloch, he was the only non-Communist placed on an equal footing with the 'big names' of the congress.

You have been hailed so often that you must be tired of replying. If we were not attached to the Soviet Union, we would not be here . . . It will be said of you: 'In spite of every obstacle, through civil war and famine, for the first time in thousands of years, they put their trust in men!'

[Here the speech deviated somewhat.] Does the image presented to us by Soviet literature really express the USSR? As far as external facts are concerned, yes. From the point of view of ethics and psychology, no. The trust you place in everyone, you do not always place in your writers . . . If writers are the engineers of souls, do not forget that the highest function of an engineer is to invent! Art is not a submission, but a conquest . . . a conquest almost always over the unconscious, very often over logic. Marxism is the consciousness of the social, of culture, the consciousness of the psychological.

To the bourgeoisie that said the *individual*, Communism will reply *man* . . . that is, more consciousness . . . The rejection of the psychological in art leads to the most absurd individualism . . . it signifies concretely that he who is supposed to have thought most about his life keeps it to himself, instead of transmitting it to others . . . The works you admire most, those of Maxim Gorky, have never ceased to present the kind of psychological or poetic discovery that I am arguing for here.

You are bringing to birth here the civilisation from which Shakespeares emerge. Do not let them be smothered beneath photographs, however fine they may be! The world expects of you not only the image of what you are, but also of what is beyond you, and which soon you alone will be capable of giving it![4]

This strange, bold speech, in which, under the very noses of the Soviet establishment, *Marxism* was opposed to *culture*, Stalin implicitly accused of knowing less about poetry than metallurgy, Socialist realism reduced to the level of photography and suspected of being the instrument of 'submission', was not received with unmixed feelings.

Karl Radek, Lenin's old companion, replied:

Our mass public does not know Malraux. Extracts of his work have been published in the review *International Literature,* which only reaches a small number of readers here . . . Malraux is a brilliant writer. He is recognised as such by our enemies. One has only to read the article by the Academician François Mauriac in the organ of the French bosses, *L'Écho de Paris* . . . As for Comrade Malraux's fear that one day some new Shakespeare will be smothered in our cradle, this merely proves his lack of confidence in those who will take care of the infant in this cradle. Let this Shakespeare be born! – and I'm certain such a Shakespeare will be born – and we will take care of him . . . At the times in which the Shakespeares of the past lived, culture was nourished by a very small section of society . . . By bringing culture to tens of millions of men, our culture gives us a hundred times more chances of finding Shakespeares.[5]

Radek, according to Ehrenburg, was rather intimidated by Malraux's tics. He became very concerned about them, feeling convinced that it was a sign of Malraux's displeasure, when the discussion began to go against him. Ehrenburg tried in vain to persuade him that this was not at all true when Malraux's face continued to twitch during the next speech, by Nikulin! 'I must say something else about Comrade Malraux. One of his sentences has given rise to many different interpretations: "Let all those who place political passions above the love of truth abstain from reading my book *La Condition humaine*. It is not for them!" . . . Does this mean that he bows to the dead, without thinking of the living . . . "The truth of this world is death," wrote Malraux. "The truth of this world is life!" we say!'

Malraux asked to speak again and leapt up to the platform: 'If I thought that politics was beneath literature, I would not be leading, with André Gide, the campaign for the defence of Comrade Dimitrov in France, I would not go to Berlin, with a commission from the Comintern to defend Comrade Dimitrov; indeed, I wouldn't be here!'

He was applauded. But a shadow remained. It is not certain whether it was entirely dispersed by André Malraux's replies to the questions put to him by *Pravda* on 'the most interesting aspects of the Congress', published on 3 September 1934. Speaking of Socialist realism, the visitor declared:

An established society languishes after romanticism, while a new world, in the process of being formed, languishes after realism. This is precisely why such a realism is inevitably so vast; the building of socialism is the measure of its power . . . The speed of change in the USSR is transforming a type in a few years. As a result, not only will new types emerge, I think, but a new species of types: the types of a society in the process of being formed. I believe that Marx's principal idea of man is the following: man must be defined by what he does, not what he thinks. This shows us the way Communist art should follow; indeed, this idea was implicit in many of the delegates' speeches during the Congress.[6]

This stay in the USSR was studded with incidents that were to mark out very clearly the frontiers between the visitor and his hosts. Many years later, André Malraux was to describe with astonishing vividness a party in Gorky's *dacha*, attended by J. R. Bloch, Aragon, Anderson Nexö, Plievier, Becher and a refugee from the Nazi camps called Bredel.

We had reached the *zakuski* when we heard footsteps, those of a man wearing boots. The conversation stopped: it was Stalin, looking like a benevolent police officer. He asked me if there was anything interesting happening in Paris at the moment. I said there was a film of Laurel and Hardy and started to imitate a trick with crossed fingers that Stan Laurel had made famous – everyone left the cinema trying to do it . . . Stalin sat down, surrounded by his bodyguards. As I ate, I had a feeling I'd lost my passport, that it was no longer in my breast pocket. A rather unpleasant feeling to have in Moscow, eh! I leant forward to look for it under the table . . . And what did I see? Stalin, Molotov and *tutti quanti* twisting their fingers under the tablecloth, trying to imitate Stan Laurel . . .[7]

André Malraux is a novelist, it must be remembered. Clara much less so. She tells how during a reception at which Leonov, seized by an attack of almost Dostoevskian self accusation, had called himself a 'Soviet barbarian' and an 'upstart', André raised his glass to 'a great absentee, Leo Davidovich Trotsky . . .'

The most valuable and most enjoyable hours of this visit to the USSR were those he spent with Sergei Eisenstein. The project of making a film of *La Condition humaine*, which had first been offered to Ivens or Dovzhenko, had in turn attracted Eisenstein, and he was working on a screenplay. Malraux was delighted. The opportunity of working with the creator of *Battleship Potemkin*! The great theatrical director Meyerhold worked with them. He hoped to make an adaptation of the novel for the stage. We do not know why these plans came to nothing. Perhaps because of Malraux's political attitude at the Congress and during his stay. Perhaps because of Eisenstein's . . .

In short, the visit was a very lively one, in which Malraux met a wide range of people. Though he was treated as a famous guest rather than as a comrade, as an artist rather than a militant, he was given ample opportunity to express himself, both in public and in the press – opportunities that he was not slow to grasp. It was certainly as a 'fellow-traveller' that he saw himself, an antifascist, but non-Marxist, revolutionary. As such he was regarded by his hosts, admired, with reservations, and used extensively.

But the congress was not quite over as far as he was concerned. Two months after his return, on 23 November 1934, a meeting was organised in Paris to consider the implications of the Moscow Congress. André Gide, Paul Vaillant-Couturier and Andrée Viollis, the great anticolonialist reporter, were on the platform. Malraux spoke, without notes. On the relations between Marxism and Soviet literature, he remarked: 'To claim that an art can ever be the application of a doctrine never corresponds to reality . . . Between the two are living men!'

Touching on the problem of the artist's 'freedom', as seen from the point of view of bourgeois freedom, he began by affirming that 'the bourgeoisie has never expressed itself directly' and that:

> For over sixty years, as far as the great works of art of the West are concerned, it has no longer been a question of depicting a world, but of expressing through images the

development of a personal problem . . . A separation has
occurred between those who are in harmony with their
civilisation and those who are not . . . There is only one
artist among us who, if he were in this hall now, could say,
as any Soviet artist in Moscow can say: 'You know me and
admire me each in your own way.' And that is Chaplin.
Agreement among men before a work of art can only be
found in the West in the field of comedy, and we rediscover
a real communion only in laughing at ourselves!

. . . In the Soviet civilisation, the first important fact is the
weakening of the artist as an object of interest in his own
eyes; the world seems to him more interesting than himself
because there the world is being discovered!

. . . A great deal has been said about the mistrust that
developing Russian society has been forced to have for man.
But we must be careful here: this mistrust affects only the
individual! . . . Soviet society can create a humanism, the
fundamental attitude of man to the society that he has
accepted . . . in which the important thing will no longer
be the particularity of each man, but his density, and in
which he will defend not what separates him from other
men, but what enables him to rejoin them beyond themselves . . .[8]

16 Thaelmann and Dimitrov

ON HIS return from the USSR in the autumn of 1934, Malraux seemed more attracted by the comradeship he had experienced among his Soviet hosts than repelled by the police violence and the neo-bourgeois conformisms of Stalinist society. What did he know at that time of the fate of Osip Mandelstam (arrested three months earlier) or of Victor Serge? We can only suppose, in the absence of proof to the contrary, that he knew nothing.

In any case, it was with redoubled enthusiasm that he threw himself into the campaign then being arranged by the external organisers of the Third International. Chief among these in Paris was the astonishing Willi Münzenberg, a German exile who was the inspiration and the manipulator of various movements such as the 'Amsterdam-Pleyel', so called after two congresses held in Holland in 1932 and in Paris in 1933, on the basis of an antifascist pacifism inspired by the beliefs of Romain Rolland. For three years prior to the 1935 Congress of the International, which was to adopt it officially, the strategy of the 'Broad Front' already had its disciples and militants (but what a strange strategy – to preach peace, while denouncing its mortal enemy!). It is to Münzenberg that the success of the campaigns for Thaelmann and Dimitrov – masterpieces of propaganda at a time that was the golden age of this shady art – must be attributed.

In fact, Malraux did not await the arrival of the apparatchikis from the 'grey house' – as he always called the headquarters of the Comintern – to throw himself into the struggle for those two famous enemies of Nazism, Ernst Thaelmann, the General

Secretary of the German Communist Party, and the Bulgarian George Dimitrov, the secretary of the Third International. Both men had fallen into the hands of the Gestapo, Thaelmann on 3 March 1933 and Dimitrov on 27 February, after the Reichstag fire, for which the Nazis had decided to blame him: at the time, Dimitrov was carrying out in Germany, the most dangerous of all terrains, a mission that Jules Humbert-Droz, then his colleague at the Comintern, termed 'of secondary importance'. It is possible that Stalin, who had accused him of 'right-wing deviation', wished to compromise Dimitrov, and even get rid of him.[1]

The trial of Dimitrov and his three companions Tanev, Popov and Torgler opened on 21 September 1933 before the 'Supreme Court of Empire' at Leipzig. Playing the objective observer, Goering himself arrived on the scene in an attempt to impress the defendants. Malraux immediately made known his support for the defence cause – in particular, at the 'counter-trials' set up in London and Paris by Münzenberg. Dimitrov was acquitted at the end of December, but remained in custody. A committee for his release was set up by Malraux and Gide.

At the beginning of 1934, the idea arose of asking for an interview with Hitler with a view to obtaining Dimitrov's release – despite the acquittal, he was still being held in Moabit prison, near Berlin. Gide agreed to go with Malraux. They set off on 4 January 1934. This journey remains one of the least-known episodes in Malraux's career. However, we do know that Hitler refused to see the two writers – which was only to be expected. Who did they see in Berlin? In the course of a conversation in February 1972, André Malraux told me of a meeting with Goebbels, which, I must admit, sounded less than entirely authentic.

'What you seek here is justice,' the Nazi Minister for Propaganda is supposed to have said to his two visitors, but what interests us, here, is something else: German justice!' Gide, it appears, was flabbergasted and could only murmur, 'What a pity!' Malraux himself, for once, does not say what his reply was. He is content to wonder, even today, at the astonishing inconsequence of people who, having mounted the Reichstag fire and implicating in it one of their most formidable enemies,

Dimitrov ('as innocent of the main charge, as such, as he was guilty of *all the rest* . . .' says Malraux), try him in an almost regular fashion, with benefit of international publicity, and then find themselves faced with an acquittal . . . Whether or not it can be attributed to the efforts of Gide and Malraux, Dimitrov was freed towards the end of February 1934. Malraux now wonders whether the acquittal and release of Dimitrov indicate that at this time (1934) 'Hitler and Stalin were already entering into collusion'.[2] It is an interesting hypothesis, for it involves a quite different level than that of deals between secret services, which as we now know, were – and are – common currency.

The campaign for the release of Thaelmann proceeded along parallel lines with the Dimitrov campaign. It had begun in November 1933 with a meeting presided over by Gide and Malraux. This led to the setting up of the international committee for the release of imprisoned German antifascists, or the Thaelmann Committee. Malraux, who rarely quotes his contemporaries, takes up Barbusse's phrases, 'Thaelmann has a red mind as one has red blood! . . . We must win Thaelmann like a victory!'[3]

On 9 May 1934 – the very day on which *L'Intransigeant* published the last instalment of his report of the 'discovery' of the capital of the Queen of Sheba, André Malraux presided with André Gide over a pro-Thaelmann meeting in protest against the creation by Hitler of a 'people's court' to pass rapid judgement, against which there would be no appeal, on antifascists.[4] Two weeks later, he also took part in a 'national antifascist rally' at the Cirque d'Hiver, in Paris. And the campaign for the release of the German Communist leader continued unceasingly throughout 1935.

Julien Segnaire, who was to become one of his closest lieutenants in Spain, tells how he met Malraux for the first time at a pro-Thaelmann meeting in Brussels in 1934. He spoke, yet again, of the Red Army, and for these young Belgian Communists he was the archangel of the Revolution.

His pleas for the release of the German Communists, especially the speech he made on 23 December 1935 at the Salle Wagram, in Paris, for the second anniversary of Dimitrov's acquittal, made use, if not of direct experience, at least of infor-

mation he had received from the German comrades to whom
he was to dedicate *Le Temps du Mépris*. He had just met an
émigré, sent to Paris by the Third International to take charge of
the 'Institute for the Study of Fascism' (INFA), who was to play
an important role in his life and become one of his closest
friends: Manès Sperber.

Another important organiser in the Institute was Arthur
Koestler, who describes his first visit to Malraux thus:

> As a fervent admirer of Malraux's, I was overwhelmed by
> the occasion, but went on bravely about the great prospects
> of INFA, and its even greater need for donations. Malraux
> listened in silence, occasionally uttering one of his charac-
> teristic, awe-inspiring sniffs, which sound like the cry of a
> wounded jungle beast and are followed by a slap of his palm
> against his nose . . . When I had had my say, Malraux
> stopped, advanced towards me threateningly, until I had my
> back against the garden wall, and said:
>
> *'Oui, oui, mon cher, mais que pensez-vous de l'apocalypse?'*
>
> With that he gave me five hundred francs, and wished me
> good luck.[5]

It was in the context of the Thaelmann campaign that one of
the most justly famous, and most illuminating texts of André
Malraux's career must be placed. This was the preface to *Le
Temps du Mépris*, the novella which Malraux dedicated in 1935
'To the German comrades, who have thought fit to pass on to
me what they have suffered and how they have held firm'. It
was in this preface that Malraux really emerged as a revolutionary writer.

Malraux was not exactly the type of writer who works 'to
order'. The freedom of his imagination, the high regard in
which he held his art, the economic independence he had enjoyed since the publication of three successful novels – nothing
could persuade him to sign anything that he had not intended
to write.

Yet, towards the end of 1934, in order to expose the scandal
of Nazism, to bear witness to the horror of the repression and
the concentration camps, André Malraux wrote a book that
came to him perhaps less spontaneously than any of the others.

Furthermore, we know that he was planning at the time a novel 'about oil', which he dropped for *Le Temps du Mépris*. With the help of Sperber and Gustav Regler, of information received direct from Germany, of what he heard from Bredel, an escapee from the Nazi prisons, whom he had met in Moscow, and of the brief notes he had brought back with him from his short visit to Berlin in January 1934, he constructed the story of Kassner, an imprisoned German Communist leader, who is freed by a comrade assuming his identity.

Did he write this text at the request of Willi Münzenberg or some other representative from one of the antifascist organisations he presided over or ran, such as the Thaelmann Committee? It is difficult to say at this late stage. What is true is that whether *Le Temps du Mépris* was a work 'to order' or spontaneous, it is the least successful of the works of his maturity. Thirty years later, in conversation with Roger Stéphane, he even referred to it as a *navet*, a 'dud'.[6]

It is strange that a novelist who found such powerful inspiration in horror, torture and death, and who had at his disposal far more precise information about the sufferings of the left-wing German militants than he had had about those of the Shanghai workers, should have failed to convey completely either the scandal of the concentration camps or the obsessive life of the prison cell. Berlin, fascism, the bestiality of the repression in Europe were close at hand – and it is as if his book made them further away than the Canton tortures and Katow's cyanide.

But this laborious novella, which concludes dramatically with the account of the cyclone and the 'return to earth', transposed from the Algerian Aurès to the Carpathians, followed by a strangely domestic 'finale', in which a mother and her child appear for a moment, is preceded by a preface that is to Malraux what *J'accuse* was to Zola: the turning-point at which the artist threw himself into the arena.

Of course, Malraux had long been, for four or five years, a 'left-wing' writer, linked with a number of Communist-inspired organisations. But with these six short pages, he declared himself, openly, as a fraternal combatant. A passing mood of fidelity? It is easy to see it in this way thirty-seven

years later. At the beginning of 1935, at the approach of a tor-
ment that looked like being worse than the one from which
Kassner came back to life in his zinc aeroplane, it was a manifesto heavily laced with risks for its author.

We will quote from this basic text only the last paragraph.
Here André Malraux seems to reject thirty-five years of his life
in favour of the collectivity into which he is entering: 'It is hard
being a man. But it is no more difficult to become one by
deepening one's communion with others than by cultivating
one's difference – and the first nourishes with at least as much
force as the second that which makes a man a man, that by
which he goes beyond himself, creates, invents or conceives of
himself.'

We have arrived at the period of virile fraternity: not in
order to dominate the Stiengs, as in *La Voie royale*, or to give
meaning to one's own death, as in *Les Conquérants*, or to abolish
existential anxiety as in *La Condition humaine* – but because the
collectivity of men to which one is bound is threatened at the
deepest level.

The Communists – those at least who dared at the time to use
their intelligence – understood it aright. Although *L'Humanité*
published an article by a man named Garmy that was stupid
enough to criticise Malraux for his choice of subject (for 'there
is no need to reach the heart of China or Hitler's prisons to
discover proletarian action'), Aragon, ignoring for once any
other ground than the political, wrote in *Commune*[7] that the
Communist in *Le Temps du Mépris* had a different truth from the
heroes of Malraux's earlier novels, while Nizan, in *Vendredi*,[8]
declared that this latest book opened the way to 'a responsible
literature'. In the USSR, a critic writing in *International Literature*,
V. L. Omitrevski, declared that André Malraux had 'found his
truth in Communism'.[9]

Le Temps du Mépris marked a turning-point not only in
Malraux's political biography, but also in his life as a man and
as a writer, with the appearance of a child in the final pages of
this essentially adult work. The reference here is biographical:
Kassner, returning home, mentions those 'furry fish' that belonged to the fantasy world shared by André and Clara. In
March 1933, they had had a daughter, whom they called

Florence, in memory of all that the city had meant for them. But their marriage was threatened for all that.

Nino Frank describes them during the rainy summer of 1935, in the Nièvre, going to eat crayfish at Pouilly and battling with the little 5 hp Rosengart that Clara had just bought: 'She had her own way of driving, accompanied by sardonic remarks from her partner,' but the little car stopped on the hillsides 'so often that we had to get out and help it on its way, us laughing, Malraux patient and polite as always with Clara, but with a certain irritation written on his face, all the more understandable in that she, who always sat regally at the steering-wheel, blamed the Rosengart's hardships on him.'[10]

17 The maestro of the Mutualité

HOWEVER, they arrived home safe and sound, for that summer André found time to organise the International Congress of Writers, which assembled at the Mutualité[1] an extraordinary band of European intellectuals horrified by the prospect of Nazism – even those who were already alerted to Stalin's own brand of terror. It was the congress of 'those for whom the advent of fascism was a personal insult' – as Maxim Gorky wrote in a telegram apologising for his absence.

There, too, the Soviet influence was exercised without restraint. In his memoirs, Ehrenburg does not conceal his own part in the organisation, often playing the role of mediator between the various left-wing tendencies – liberal, Marxist, Christian, Surrealist, traditionalist or humanitarian – even succeeding in not opposing the participation of the Trotskyists. This was the heyday of the 'Broad Front' strategy, and the participation of such liberals as Huxley, Forster, Benda, Martin du Gard or Sforza was warmly welcomed by the high command, which consisted of Ehrenburg, Malraux, Moussinac, J. R. Bloch, Aragon and Louis Guilloux.

Finally, on 21 June 1935, André Gide sat down at the big table set up on the platform of the Mutualité. It was stiflingly hot and, Forster, Benda and Heinrich Mann excepted, they took off their jackets, as in a Renoir film. Vaillant-Couturier wore a smart summer suit and a loosely knotted bow-tie. Seven discussions were scheduled, to be spread over five days. Of the expected speakers, there was already one notable absentee; the young Surrealist poet, recently converted to Communism, René

Crevel, who chose to commit suicide just as the congress was about to open. A motion of homage was passed that many found too discreet.

The general theme of discussion was 'the defence of culture against fascism'. The question of 'cultural heritage' would be presented, in particular, by Forster, Brecht and Benda; Waldo Frank, Aragon and Huxley would speak on 'the writer in society'; Gide, Musil, Max Brod and Malraux on 'the individual'; Barbusse, Nizan, Ramon Sender on 'Humanism'; Chamson, Guéhenno, Tristan Tzara on 'nation and culture'; Sforza, Heinrich Mann, Gustav Regler on 'the creation and dignity of thought . . .' Finally, 'the defence of culture' would be left to Alexis Tolstoy, Gide, Barbusse, Alfred Döblin and Malraux – who, the day before, had spoken on 'questions of organisation'. Strangely enough, this programme was adhered to for the most part.

We are now at the peak of Malraux's political career (in the 'professional' sense of the word). Flanked by Gide, Aragon and Ehrenburg, but dominating them because he alone among them could speak equally well in the manner of Forster or Regler, Koltzov or Sforza; with a mixture of cynicism and lyricism, he manipulated this European parliament of fellow-travellers, militants and upper-middle-class humanists thrown together by Hitler in an alliance that terrified most of them.

On the first day, Gide had used all his chilly genius to forge a synthesis between national cultures and internationalism, between individualism and a sense of community, then, on the second day, paid homage to the 'plebeian' genius exemplified by Rousseau and Diderot and maintained that 'lies' had some part to play in the idea of 'civilisation'.[2]

Malraux spoke on the themes already outlined in his preface to *Le Temps du Mépris* (which was now in the bookshops): 'Communism restores to man his fertility', 'to be a man is to reduce as much as possible the comic side of his existence'. These formulas, which were to reappear again and again in Malraux's work, were thrown out there at a disconcerted, often sympathetic, sometimes irritated audience. He certainly held that audience when proposing his answer to a question posed by Gide and Benda: 'Is a communion now possible between us intellectuals and the people?' – 'Yes, such a communion with the people is possible, not in its nature, but in its *finality*, in its *revolutionary will*.' And being unable to refrain from playing the prophet of will against destiny, he concluded with a sort of cry: 'Whatever its consequences, the next war will no doubt mean the end of Europe . . . Yet it is up to us to maintain and strengthen the will of western man.'[3]

Two incidents broadened the scope of these confrontations. On the evening of the second day, 22 June, the session devoted to 'the individual' was scheduled. It gave an opportunity to the opponents of the Stalinist system to ask certain embarrassing questions. Henri Poulaille, representing the 'populists', and André Breton, representing the Surrealists, had asked to join the congress in order to present the question of repression in the USSR and, in particular, of the fate of an imprisoned writer like Victor Serge. Ehrenburg and Aragon so arranged matters that they were refused. But when Malraux took the chair at the meeting, he could not – under pressure from Gide and others – refuse to allow friends of Victor Serge in the audience, in particular Magdeleine Paz Marx, the Italian Socialist Gaetano Salvemini and the former Belgian Communist Charles Plisnier, an opportunity of expressing their views.

Vaillant-Couturier and Aragon jumped to their feet and tried to silence the contradictors, but to no avail. Magdeleine Paz managed to express the protests of those for whom their participation in the antifascist struggle did not make them forget the crimes committed against Socialists in 'the fatherland of Socialism'. Claiming to reply for the Soviet delegation, Mikhail Koltzov assured the audience that Serge 'had been involved in the plot that ended in the assassination of Kirov',[4] and Nicolai Tikhonov shouted out: 'We do not know this character . . . but he's an embittered counter-revolutionary that the Soviet police have prevented from doing further harm!' In fact, Tikhonov knew Victor Serge only too well, since Serge was his translator. 'How could he forget the hymn to courage of his admirable epic ballads, which I had translated into French?' Serge asked in his *Mémoires d'un révolutionnaire*. On the third day, Malraux and Gide decided to take steps to get Soviet letters represented by artists more worthy of them. Was this as a result of Tikhonov's sinister attitude to Serge, or simply because, in the absence of Gorky, the Soviet delegation seemed intellectually unworthy of the country of Lenin?

André Malraux describes this instructive episode thus:

> Gide and I went to the Soviet embassy to demand, in view of the importance of the Congress, that the French proletariat might be given the opportunity of hailing the artists that it most admired, namely Pasternak and Babel. (Obviously, the French workers didn't give a damn for them! . . .). The ambassador cabled at once to Moscow.
>
> The next morning the telephone rang at Pasternak's home . . . His girl friend ran to answer it. 'Who? The Kremlin?' Pale with fear, she went back to him, crouching at the bottom of the bed, and handed him the receiver. A flabbergasted Pasternak heard: 'Stalin orders you to go at once and buy western clothes and take the train tonight for Paris. The day after tomorrow, you'll give a speech on the subject of Soviet culture.' Pasternak preferred first to fall back into a feverish sleep, in which he dreamed of Chekists and forced labour. He then set out to do some shopping and arrived in Paris wearing an incredible rabbi's frock-coat and a sort of Mao-type cap, which hardly helped him to pass unnoticed on the boulevards . . . Fortunately, we were the same height. Pasternak had a strange kind of beauty. In Russia, it was said that he resembled both an Arab and his horse.
>
> At the Congress, he stood up on the platform and declaimed a very fine poem, of which I read the translation; the whole hall rose to its feet to applaud . . . He then made his speech, which amounted to this: 'Talk politics? Futile, futile . . . Politics? Go to country, my friends, go to country, pick flowers in fields . . .' This was Stalin's delegate! [5]

According to another version, that published by *Commune*, Pasternak's speech was somewhat more substantial, but just as charming: 'Poetry will always be in the grass. It is and will always remain the organic function of a happy being, reforging all the felicity of language, clenched in the native heart . . . The more happy men there are, the easier it will be to be a poet!'

We don't know how Isaac Babel got from Moscow to Paris,

but we do know that this exuberant, spontaneous, witty character delighted the solemn audience at the Mutualité, turning the platform into a stage and recounting a few stories that showed that in spite of everything the spirit of modernity was transforming the Soviet Union. 'Thus, when a young peasant friend of mine who had become an airman got his comrades to fly in formation over his village on his wedding day, I call that a victory of the new man.' (Five years later, as we know, Isaac Babel was shot.)

It fell to Malraux to bring the Congress to a close, on 29 June. He was tired, tense, more tic-ridden than ever, and the Serge incident had done nothing to clear the air. Yet those who were there remember it very vividly. When Malraux spoke, people listened:

> This Congress was held in the worst possible conditions – especially financial conditions. But judging by the anger it has aroused, we know that this Congress has really taken place. We have made it possible for those who have been deprived of the right to speak to do so and for a solidarity to express itself. It is of the nature of fascism to be in the nation, ours to be in the world! Our aim was the defence of culture. But this Congress has shown that a work of art is dead when deprived of love, that works of art need us to come alive again, they need our love, our will . . . for the heritage is not passed on, it is conquered! . . .
>
> Soviet comrades, what we expect of your civilization, which has preserved its old faces in blood, typhus and famine, is that thanks to you their new face will be revealed . . . Innumerable differences play beneath our common will, but this will is *there*. It imposes on the faces of the past their new metamorphosis. For every work becomes a symbol, a sign, all art is a possibility of reincarnation . . . Each of us must recreate in his own field, through his own research, on behalf of all those who are in search of themselves, open the eyes of all the blind statues and turn hopes into acts of will, revolts into revolutions, the age-old suffering of mankind into human consciousness![6]

All the themes are to be found there – and not only those of the 'revolutionary' phase of 1933–9, but those of the 'aesthete' period of the 1950s, of the struggle for the transformation of pain into hope and experience into consciousness, and also the most central theme of all, that of metamorphosis. Malraux is there, at the intersection of the tragic romanticism of *La Condition humaine* and the lyrical realism of *L'Espoir*, the Malraux of 1935, the man of all possibilities, of all directions, committed to a strategy, almost a prisoner of it, yet at the same time wildly free in imagination and dream, in harmony with others and more than ever himself.

The striking thing about this career as a vehement fellow-traveller (vehemence is a quality of fellow-travellers, who need to be forgiven for their 'difference' and their refusal of discipline) is that it never, or almost never, took place within the framework of national politics. 'It is our nature to be in the world,' declared the orator in the Mutualité. True enough. But what was happening in France in the second half of the 1930s provided as many reasons to mobilise a revolutionary artist as elsewhere.

But it so happens that Malraux, so ardently engaged in struggles on behalf of the Chinese (*La Condition humaine*), the Vietnamese (the long *Marianne* article, the preface to Andrée Viollis' book), the Germans and Bulgarians, and, later, the Spanish, was practically absent from all the discussions concerning, in the first place, the French people. When, the day before 6 February 1934 – which showed, to all who wished to see, that a tendency of a fascist type existed in France – a 'Committee of Vigilance of Antifascist intellectuals' was formed under the triple presidency of the Socialist anthropologist Paul Rivet, the radical philosopher Alain and the Communist physicist, Langevin (a triumvirate that prefigured the Popular Front), and on 5 March this committee launched 'an appeal to the workers' signed in a few days by several thousand writers and artists, Malraux's name was not to be found on it. Was he too busy at the time discovering the remains of Balkis, Queen of Sheba?

Yet this silence was not simply due to some incident of his adventurous, many-faceted career. During the whole of this period, so rich in opportunities for action, during these 'times of trouble', stretching from 1934 to the dislocation of the Popular Front and the outbreak of war, Malraux is hardly to be seen on any platforms except those relating to Spain – except, that is, on 14 July 1935, when he took part in a meeting beside Daladier and Thorez, Rivet and Langevin.[7]

It is as if, like the tragic poet of the French classical tradition, André Malraux considered worthy of his genius only a subject which, if not distant in time, was ennobled by distance in space. (Something of this attitude can be found in the 'third-worldism' of the left in the 1960s, which preferred to do battle for the Palestinians or the Vietnamese than for the French proletariat – an attitude that would be more understandable on the part of some Middle Eastern colonel than of the long-winded bureaucracy of some organisation of the European left . . .)

It might be said that Malraux did not believe in the future of fascism in France: his interview of December 1933 in *Marianne* seems to support this view. But since then what had happened in France could be called a revision of this diagnosis. 'Francism', the most obvious of fascist organisations, was grotesque; Déat, a former Socialist turned pro-Nazi, still ambiguous; the nationalist Croix-de-Feu a bourgeois stronghold. But a combination of antiparliamentarian feeling, a yearning for order, economic uncertainty, a certain 'war-veteran' mentality and corruption in political circles meant that French political life was already heavy with something that was to burst in 1940.

Was the bold and perspicacious Malraux lacking in perspicacity here? Or even in civic courage? It would be difficult to regard as a 'flight' a commitment with those who, in Europe, were then being subjected to the most furious attacks of fascism! In any case, it was more exciting being a revolutionary d'Annunzio than laboriously trying to unite forces and people that the habits of a lifetime had made dull, touchy and jealous – the people who, for one brief, magnificent summer, were to constitute the Popular Front.

If we put the question in this way, is it not like asking Malraux why he is Malraux, or criticising Byron for not taking up the struggle in the Lancashire cotton-mills, rather than setting out for Greece? There is no end, and probably no point, to discussion on the matter. There are infantry and there are cavalry. Nomads and stay-at-homes. Poets and prose-writers. But perhaps we should look for other, more serious motives for this peripheral strategy: motives more worthy of a man of indomitable courage and one who was often more lucid than his more flamboyant attitudes would lead one to believe.

If Malraux avoided the platforms of the Popular Front it was probably because what was to be heard from them was too ambiguous. He had gone along with the 'Amsterdam-Pleyel' movement when it was a question of getting Thaelmann or Dimitrov released from Hitler's jails. Not when pious sophists tried to reconcile pacifism and resistance to Nazism. For a man like Malraux, much more than for most of his friends, an armed, violent, military confrontation with the Nazis and their accomplices had been inevitable since 1933. Several of Malraux's statements quoted above testify to this.

So Malraux could not bring himself to associate with a whole current of thinking, of an essentially anti-militaristic kind, that was incapable of distinguishing between the great 'Kriegspiel' of 1914 and the monstrous, biological, fundamental threat of Nazism. A plot can be denounced, but a flood has to be fought. Malraux was to fight on the grounds where the flood first appeared.

When Malraux reappeared in public, during the Popular Front period, it was on the subject of Ethiopia – the Spanish Civil War had not yet broken out. On 4 November 1935, the International Association of Writers for the Defence of Culture, created at the June Congress, held a meeting at the Mutualité in defence of Ethiopia, which had been invaded a month earlier by fascist Italy. Mussolini was defended by a group of sixty-four French intellectuals led by Henri Massis, who attacked 'the powers of disorder and anarchy . . .' concerned to defend 'savages' in the name of 'obscure interests'.

Malraux's reply, published six months later in an article in *Crapouillot* devoted to colonial problems, is extremely virulent:

> . . . Reactionary intellectuals, you speak of 'a few savage tribes combining together for obscure interests'. Certainly those who are pushed around by interests here are the

Ethiopians! They'll be wanting to go and civilize the Italians next! . . .

In fact, colonization is not as simple as it first seems. One usually takes an Asian or African country at the time of its conquest and compares it with what it later became. But it is not a question of comparing the Cochin-China of Napoleon III with the Cochin-China of today, but Indo-China and Siam, Morocco and Turkey, Baluchistan and Persia. Not to speak of a country which, around 1860, it seems, had an imperative need of being civilized: Japan . . .

It is clear that, even in terms of your own ideology, what you call becoming civilized is simply becoming European-ized. We needn't argue about that. But which countries are becoming Europeanized most quickly today? Precisely those that you do not control. The Muslim women of Morocco, Tunisia and India are still veiled. Persian women are scarcely veiled at all. Turkish women not at all. Which is the only country in which a mandarin class still exists? It is not China, or Japan, but Annam . . .

. . . When Marco Polo found in China a city of over a million inhabitants, he did not think so highly of Venice. In the sixteenth century what was the French court compared with those of the kings of Persia or the emperors of China and Japan? Paris was still a confusion of alleys when the Persian architects were marking out the great avenues of Isfahan with four rows of trees and planning a royal square as large as the Place de la Concorde. Even Versailles is a pretty small piece of work compared with the Forbidden City in Peking.

But in a hundred years all this had changed. Why? Because the West had discovered that the most effective function of intelligence was not to conquer men, but to conquer things.

No civilization, white, black or yellow, began with the warrior; it began when the legislator or priest set about civilizing the warrior; it began when argument prevailed over the deed. All civilization involved awareness and respect for others . . . It is precisely at the point when Abyssinia asks for specialists that she is sent cannon. If she wins the battle, she will be neither more nor less Europeanized than if she loses it. Killing off a mass of people first is one way of getting them into hospitals: I don't know that it's the best. Ah! what paradises the colonies would be if the West were to build hospitals for all those it has killed and gardens for all those it has deported!

In those years, all his blows – whether against colonialism, fascism or capitalism – had their effect. The author of *Le Temps du Mépris* was an exemplary fellow-traveller. This is clear enough from the hatred borne him by the spokesmen of the extreme right. This brief portrait by that master of hatred, Lucien Rebatet, leading columnist of the fascist *Je suis partout*, is a good example. Referring to the 'rabble' of the Popular Front, he says: 'And never absent, with his sex maniac's face twitching with tics, is his lordship André Malraux, a sort of Bolshevist, quite unreadable sub-Barrès, who nevertheless arouses the admiration of Saint-Germain-des-Prés, even among certain right-wing dupes, thanks to a certain erethism of vocabulary and a hermetic way of recounting Chinese events wrapped up in a mass of adjectives.'[8]

The friendship felt for him by one who was equally exemplary, but as a militant, Paul Nizan, is no less significant. The references to Malraux to be found in the letters and articles published by Nizan during those years (in *Intellectuel communiste*,[9] for example) are full of warmth and trust. One of these is also amusing. Towards the end of the summer of 1935, Nizan had to put off a lunch date with Malraux. He was going to the post office to send a telegram to his friend apologising for the change of plan. The postal clerk read the name of the recipient and said: 'Malraux? Professor Malraux? So you must be Paul Nizan . . .'

Fraternity was expressed in many different forms – even postal ones. For Malraux, it was to take on a more powerful expression in Spain. But before we follow him there, let us account for his relations with three characters without whom there would have been neither artist, adventurer, nor the strange revolutionary that was to find fulfilment there.

THREE MEN

18 Gide

GIDE entered Malraux's life about 1922, preceded by a *brioche*, and left it bit by bit, not with a bang, but a melancholy murmur. Malraux has several times described his first encounter with Gide, who had arranged to meet him in front of the Vieux-Colombier theatre. 'He held the sphere of the *brioche* in his mouth and was surmounted by the whole *brioche* . . . To shake hands, he snatched the *brioche* from his mouth and held out his hand . . .'

There was always something obscure, something incongruous about their relationship. Why was Gide, who of all those older friends, from 1923 to 1951, was most bound up with his public life and at whose side he had fought more political struggles than with anyone, less of a friend than Drieu la Rochelle, who was divided from him by so much, or less of a master than Bernard Groethuysen, who was above all separated from him by his allegiance to Marxism?

Between Malraux and Gide there was always an essential difference of attitude towards history and art, the two fields most dear to Malraux. 'What distinguished us from our mentors, at twenty, was the presence of history . . .' The sentence from Malraux I quoted on the first page of this book was aimed above all at André Gide. Twenty-five years earlier, Malraux complained to Gaëtan Picon that Gide preferred *Anna Karenina* to *War and Peace*. A significant choice.

But André Malraux and André Gide also had quite different attitudes in the aesthetic field. Malraux summed up this difference thus: 'I have always been more interested in creation than in perfection. Hence my constant disagreement with André Gide . . .'[1] This did not, however, prevent them from sharing a common enthusiasm for Dostoevsky, Nietzsche and Baudelaire. Nor did it prevent the establishment of a fascinating and creative friendship that grew and flourished over a period of thirty years – a friendship as strange, perhaps, as that between T. E. Lawrence and George Bernard Shaw. Dissimilar and disagreeing, the man of 'difference' and the man of 'fraternity' travelled boldly along the same road, from the *NRF* to the antifascist committees. It is a road that we must follow if we are to understand André Malraux.

The young Malraux, as we have seen, recognised Gide as one of his first mentors – after Apollinaire and Max Jacob. He was just twenty when he wrote and published in *Action* his 'Aspects d'André Gide', which might be seen more as a sort of declaration of allegiance than an act of homage:

> To strive towards some uncertain end in full consciousness of one's own value and of the possibility of increasing it is the manifestation of all intelligence and all true faith . . . Gide, who is not a saint, teaches love . . . He is a director of conscience . . . Whereas Barrès is content simply to give advice, Gide has shown the struggle that exists between our desires and our dignity, between our aspirations and our will to dominate them that I will call internal disorder. Fortunately, the greatest living French writer, one of the most important men alive today . . . has revealed to half of what are called 'the young' what an intellectual conscience is.[2]

A year later, in the review *Le Disque vert*, Malraux pursued and expanded his paean of praise for Gide. Under the title of 'Ménalque', he addressed the creator through the hero of *L'Immoraliste* – explicitly preferring the former to the latter:

> To tell the truth, you have no influence; you have action – which is nobler. But the indifference that you seem to possess for those whom you have guided and the advice you give them to leave you are the expressions of a refined form of lying. You leave those whom, for a time, you have guided – true! But not in the way they think. And you smile, know-

ing how fatuous it is to believe oneself free . . . For you leave
them as the bowls-player leaves the bowl that he has just
thrown. But the bowl has this advantage over your disciples:
it does not believe itself to be free. It gives me pleasure,
Ménalque, to imagine you, with your 'pirate's face', as a
bowls-player observing Machiavellianly – for you are de-
moniacal, don't forget – the bowls that you have thrown
change direction . . .[3]

We have a third study of André Gide by André Malraux,
written twelve years later: a review in the *NRF* of *Les Nouvelles
Nourritures*. It is, of course, the most interesting of the three,
because the author's critical intelligence has had time to mature,
as has also his knowledge of Gide and his work. But one can
also sense in this piece a greater independence from the older
writer. The theme chosen by Malraux as an approach to Gide's
essay-poem is one that most fascinated him: the relation in a
writer's work between telling the truth and strictly imaginary
creation.

Observing that what strikes him most in Gide's work, as in
that of Montaigne, Pascal and most of the great French nove-
lists, is the 'tone of voice', he declares that 'the world of the
modern artist is that of his affirmation', which, in the case of
Gide, 'rests on others': 'Zarathustra cares little for the anonymous mass of his disciples . . . Ménalque needs Michel or
Nathanaël.' It is at this point that Malraux poses the problem of
the relation between the *Journal* and the creative work. What
separates the first *Nourritures* from the second, he says, is not so
much the adhesion to Communism as the enterprise of the
Journal, which, like that of Jules Renard, becomes an 'obsession'
and, in the end, sucks in most of the writer's creative faculties –
the writer being 'forced to prefer . . . the real to fiction'. In
Malraux's view, this fruitful weight of the *Journal* succeeded in
redirecting the trajectory of the oeuvre 'from Racine towards
Stendhal'. And he concludes:

> Gide's strength as artist and as moralist stems from the
> fact that the is always *justifying* something. This is the case
> with almost all the modern writers who exert a moral influ-
> ence. The reader pays in admiration to the artist what the

artist gives back in justification. This book will justify
many of those who wish to think intelligently about their
generosity.

The admiration is still there, with a touch of critical cor-
diality. But the distance is obvious. Certainly, for Malraux, to
pass 'from Racine to Stendhal' is an improvement. But the
parallel with Jules Renard, following the brief allusion to Pascal
and Nietzsche, by way of counter-examples, is a little disdainful.
'Uncle Gide', as Malraux was then in the habit of calling him, is
shown respect, but more out of friendship than enthusiasm –
especially if one takes into account the close ties that bound the
two writers together at this time, both as literary advisers of the
firm of Gallimard and as leaders of antifascist organisations.
When one remembers that the subject of the article is not only
the 'prince of letters', the sublime mandarin of the rue Sébastien-
Bottin, but also the moral leader of the European left, one may
well find the tone somewhat reserved. Since becoming his
'comrade', Malraux seems to have moved away from Gide
aesthetically.

All those years the aesthetic exchanges between the two
writers were close and constant. And not only within the *NRF*
and the group that it stood for. One of their mutual friends was
Julien Green, who had begun to publish some of his best novels,
such as *Adrienne Mesurat*. Yet the two Andrés used to meet at
Green's with Emmanuel Berl and Jacques Schiffrin, founder of
the much admired collection of classics, '*La Pléiade*, at Gal-
limards'. In his *Journal*, Green describes a lunch that brought
them all together in May 1929:

> Eroticism came up as a subject for discussion. Malraux
> spoke brilliantly, and maintained that eroticism appears in
> full force in those countries, only, where the conception of
> sin is to be found . . . A short time later Gide, on being asked
> by Malraux for a definition of the Christian, looked at us and
> said: 'I feel pretty sure that I'm going to be ploughed.' But
> Malraux persisted: 'But you have touched on the question
> in your *Montaigne*.' 'Oh!' Gide replied, 'I touched on it, I
> touch on everything!'[4]

How can one better suggest the intellectual ascendancy that this twenty-eight-year-old Malraux exerted on the illustrious avatar of Goethe that Gide then seemed to be? On another occasion, they were discussing how little the contemporary novel dealt with contemporary events. As one of Green's guests was objecting that after all Balzac wrote novels in 1845 that took place in 1820, Malraux cut in, 'Don't let us speak of Balzac!' And everyone seemed to agree . . .[5] In his own *Journal*, Gide remembers his own reactions in the course of the same exchange of views: '. . . despite the extraordinary eloquence of Berl and Malraux . . . I tried to take part in it, but had the greatest difficulty merely following them and seizing their thoughts . . .'[6]

On many other occasions in his *Journal*, Gide expresses this feeling of inferiority, or at least of slowness, that the brilliant Malraux tended to give him:

As with Valéry, André Malraux's great strength lies in caring very little whether he winds, or tires, or 'drops by the wayside' whoever is listening and who has hardly any other anxiety (when I am the one listening) but to seem to be following, rather than to follow really. This is why any conversation with those two friends remains, for me at least, somewhat mortifying, and I come away rather crushed than exalted.[7]

In March 1933 the period of companionship began: Gide and Malraux were associated in the campaign against Nazism – which, for them, took the specific form of a journey to Berlin to get Dimitrov released from prison. On the platforms of the Mutualité and the Salle Wagram, a suburban cinema or a provincial theatre, one could see side by side the illustrious mandarin with the slit eyes, the prelate's hands and the frosty voice, and the pale young man with the forelock, the thundering phrases and the incisive gestures. Gide would look at Malraux, a sort of smile of jubilation breaking over the dry lips. When his turn to speak came, Gide would speak briefly, apologetically: 'Excuse my being brief . . . I am too anxious to hear our Comrade Malraux!'

Yet it would be wrong to see their relationship as that of a wild adolescent and an old man carried away by the younger man's enthusiasm. Gide had his place, which was an important one – more important than we can possibly realise forty years later. In 1933, it was he who published, in *Marianne*, the key text on fascism. And the day after 6 February 1934, Ramon Fernandez heard a worker remark: 'We ought to get guns and march into the rich districts! . . . With someone at our head, a leader, a man . . . Someone like Gide!'[8]

Yet what did they think, as they looked at one another, in front of the crowd of surprised militants and gawping sceptics? What did Gide, who frequently cast himself in the role of Socrates, think of this Alcibiades with the raised fist? And Malraux of this 'uncle', who was a piece of Gisors, something of Clappique and more the Alvear of *L'Espoir* that he was already carrying within him, the image of that acceptance of death against which he pitted his life?

Fellow-travellers they may have been – but they were travelling on different sides of the road. The one a defrocked cardinal in search of a church, where he could meditate and be with others, echoing with hymns and the murmur of exquisite confessions; and the other, the preacher of an abstract and conquering fraternity, an apostle Paul leading a crusade. With or without collusive winks and muffled laughter, their joint expedition to the countries of the revolution lasted three years. It came to an abrupt end in 1936: Gide's fervour, already sorely tried, finally collapsed in contact with the bitter realities of Soviet life, at the very moment when, in Spain, Malraux's enthusiasm, fed on real danger and effective action, reached its height.

Between the old man getting out of an adventure into which, despite his misgivings, he had thrown himself with all the enthusiasm he could muster, and the young man finding his own truth in action and a long-sought fraternity, the break was to take an almost comic form. It did not entirely put an end to their friendship however.

There is something strange about the exact symmetry of their progress: it was in the summer of 1936, with the smoke of history in their nostrils, that their political trajectories collided. They were two tragic characters whose destinies were acted out on the most tragic stages of their time – for Gide in the Soviet Union and for Malraux in Spain. The two 'returns' coincide exactly, on 3 September 1936, and are mentioned on the same page of the *Journal*.⁹ In counterpoint with his own 'dreadful confusion', the traveller returning home from the Soviet Union in the company of his friends, Schiffrin and Guilloux (secretary of the 1935 Paris Congress), evokes the burning hope of the fighting man from Spain:

> Yesterday, I saw Malraux. He has just arrived from Madrid, to which he returns in two days . . . He doesn't seem to me too tired. His face is less marked by nervous tics than ordinarily, even, and his hands are not too feverish. He talks with that extraordinary volubility that often makes him so hard for me to follow. He depicts their situation, which he would consider desperate if the enemy forces were not so divided. He hopes to gather together the governmental forces; now he has the power to do so. His intention, as soon as he gets back, is to organize the attack on Oviedo.

Let us overlook the delusional aspect of these confidences and the 'power' that Malraux seems to be attributing to himself, and note that Gide, cut to the quick as he then was, relates these events with sympathy and continues to place himself in spirit in the struggle experienced and described by his friend. A few pages later, he refers warmly to one of his young friends joining the International Brigades, at the instigation of a young woman who has had 'an excellent influence over him'.¹⁰

Their refound friendship was to remain unbroken either by the separation of the war, their divergent attitudes to the defeat (Gide's temporary resignation, Malraux's astonishment . . .), or the first upheavals of the occupation.

They met again, shortly after Malraux's escape, at the beginning of 1941, on the Côte d'Azur, between Nice and Menton, totally absorbed by literature and art. In an article published in 1945, Gide evoked the atmosphere of these meetings:

> I remember his sudden agitation, at Cap-d'Ail, where I had gone to spend a few delightful days with him, when the morning papers reported the news of an uprising in Persia. His work – *La Lutte avec l'ange*, from which, the night before, he had read me large chunks of the first draft – immediately

became of secondary importance. 'And to think I might have been there!' He did not actually say this, he had no need to: this dogged obsession was only too evident in his gaze, in his features, which tensed at once, in the quivering of his entire being . . .[11]

Nevertheless, clouds still crossed their sky. It was the period at which Gide confided to a mutual woman friend: 'I give him confidences, and he pays me back with anecdotes . . .' This observation throws a great deal of light on their relationship. One day Sartre and Simone de Beauvoir arrived in Paris. They called on Gide and told him of their intention of seeing Malraux too. 'I wish you a *good* Malraux,' were 'Uncle' Gide's parting words.

At the Liberation, 'Colonel Berger' and Gide resumed their meetings. When a new weekly, called *Terre des Hommes*, appeared, one of the first articles it published was an article on Malraux by Gide. This emotional piece is reminiscent in many ways of the young man's 1921 essay on the author of *Les Nourritures terrestres*:

> Malraux is ready for anything and anyone, always receptive, I would have said permeable, if I had not also known how resistant he is to anything that might influence his decision or undermine his will. He acts at once. He assumes responsibility and compromises himself. Wherever a just cause has need of a defender, or wherever some fine combat is taking place, he is there in the breach. He offers himself and devotes himself to it unstintingly, with a mixture of valour and despair . . . Above all, he is an adventurer . . . I am no more surprised today to see him assuming important government functions than I was earlier to see him an army chief, an airman, a film director or a revolutionary leader. In fact, I can least imagine him at a desk . . . His genius nags him: 'What!' he must say to himself, 'while I write, I might be living, acting . . .' and soon becomes disgusted with this absence of danger . . .

In 1967, just as the *Antimémoires* had appeared, Roger Stéphane asked Malraux in the course of a television interview:

'Did Gide play an important role in your personal life?' 'Not very,' Malraux replied. 'We knew each other over a long period of time, but in fact, there was something very odd about our admiration for Gide . . . We admired him for what he might produce . . . We all expected another *Faux-Monnayeurs*. Well, there never was another *Faux-Monnayeurs* . . .'

And, a little later, Malraux added, comparing Gide with Roger Martin du Gard: 'Gide always struck me as being a worker of the pen, as others are workers of the sword or the machine-gun . . .' Is it fair thus to belittle the traveller to the Congo, the man who went to Berlin to argue with the Nazis, the speaker at antifascist meetings, when one is oneself not only a 'worker of the machine-gun', but also so attentive to the workings of one's 'pen'?

These mutual criticisms, which hung over their friendship like a cloud, can be found through a third party in a page of the *Journal*. In a preface that he had just written (in 1936) for a book by his brother Claude, Pierre Naville complained that, prior to his 'conversion', Gide had not allowed himself to be influenced by the great events of his time (the same charge as Malraux's 'absent from history'). Gide's reply – to Malraux *via* Naville – is as follows:

> If the great literary works of the time of Louis XIII and Louis XIV showed a reflection of the Fronde, if we heard in them an echo of the Royal Tithe, perhaps Pierre Naville would have more consideration for them; but they would have lost that superior serenity which has made them last. As for me, I hold, quite on the contrary, that when social preoccupations began to clutter my head and heart, I wrote nothing more that matters. It is not fair to say that I remained insensitive to such questions: but my position in regard to them was the only one that an artist must reasonably take and which he must strive to maintain. As for Christ's 'judge not', I understand it as an artist *too*.[12]

This was written at the time of *L'Espoir*. The contradiction could not be more total. Twenty-five years later, Malraux wrote in his *Antimémoires*:

When Gide was seventy, people wrote that he was the greatest French writer . . . He described to me a visit from Bernard Lazare, who was determined to engage in the furious struggle that was to become the Dreyfus affair: 'He terrified me: this was a man who put something above literature . . .' The Purgatory of Gide owes much to the fact that history did not exist for him . . .[13]

19 T. E. Lawrence

TO GAËTAN PICON, who wrote of Malraux that 'Lawrence's life fascinated his', he retorted: 'It does not fascinate me, it intrigues me to the highest degree. The life of T. E. Lawrence constitutes a powerful accusation, it is not exemplary and has no wish to be.'[1]

Exemplary or not, the character of Colonel Lawrence was for the young Malraux one of those myth-makers on which his imagination fed and which brought to life his demon for action. And he sometimes spoke of Lawrence as 'Nietzsche become Zarathustra'. In the *Antimémoires*, we read that the fame of Mayrena (a Dutch adventurer who became 'king of the Sedangs'), which was at its height in 1870, but declined after his death in 1890, had been revived by the fame of Lawrence – which began to spread in France in 1925.[2] He had already noted this key-sentence from Lawrence: 'Day-dreamers are dangerous men, for they can play out their dream with their eyes open and make it possible.'[3]

In fact, Lawrence's name hardly appears in Malraux's writings until 1929. This does not mean, however, that the young writer was not already haunted by the man of the desert. The hostility towards the British Empire that is expressed in *Les Conquérants* is limited to British policy in China. So the 'intelligence service' side of 'T.E.L.' would not, it seems, be antipathetic to the young French writer, who very early dreamt of 'the legend of Lawrence . . . the dazzling legend of a Queen of Sheba army, with its Arab partisans deployed beneath flying banners among the jerboas of the desert, and imaginary battles in the defiles of rose-red Petra'.[4]

About 1929, then, a 'crystallisation' occurred. When, about 1933, Malraux took up his pen to plead the cause of the Annamese, and again, in 1936, that of all colonised peoples, he must have thought of 'T.E.L.''s appeals for the emancipation of the Arabs. To each his cause. (To each, too, his refusal. Lawrence's refusal is more selective, and is directed only briefly at British strategy. His pro-Arabism is strongly tainted with hostility to French domination, much less so with regard to domination from London – of which he was, except for short periods, an intelligent executant. He hailed Churchill as a saviour and accepted enthusiastically the neocolonial formulas of 1922, doing much to get them accepted. It is true that Malraux was hardly more critical of the de Gaulle of the 1950s.)

In 1934, the departure for Mareb and the flight over the Sheban sites remind one irresistibly of Lawrence. The comparison becomes explicit in the *Antimémoires* where Malraux remarks, in his account of the 1934 adventure, written during his journey to Asia in 1965: 'Our steamship is now heading for Aden, whence Rimbaud set out for Abyssinia; and it has just come from Jedda, whence T. E. Lawrence took off into the Arabian desert.'[5]

The force of an obsession is not to be measured by its degree of truth, but by its power to create material. If the legend of Washington had not been so strong, Chateaubriand would have taken care not to invent his visit to the general-president. Is the meeting between Malraux and Lawrence equally mythical? Does the account that Malraux gives of this meeting from time to time express a dream, a wish, a yearning, rather than a fact? This is how he described it during an interview given to *L'Express* after the publication of the *Antimémoires*:

I met Lawrence once. Only once, in the bar of some big hotel in Paris, I forget which one.[6] We weren't on an equal footing, you know. He already had under his belt the *Seven Pillars*, his collaboration with Churchill during the Peace Conference, his break with the world and that halo of mystery that the Intelligence Service gave him. Of course, the real mystery was not to be found there. I had my suspicions, but I couldn't be sure at the time. I was a young

French writer with just the Prix Goncourt under my belt. That was little enough. He was extraordinarily elegant. With an elegance of today, not of his own time. A roll-neck sweater, for example, a kind of nonchalance and distance.

I find it difficult to remember what we talked about. All I remember is that he had a passion for engines – motor-cycle and boat engines. It was a relatively short time before his death. Did he really want to die? I have often asked myself the question and never come up with an answer.[7]

At this point, Malraux goes on to repeat a strange story, which he has recounted on a number of occasions, notably in an interview with Roger Stéphane – and which seems to reveal more fidelity to Lawrence than to historical fact:

But there is one story that should be cleared up. When he was killed on his motor-bike, it certainly seems that he was carrying a dispatch to some post or other. Now I have been told that it was a very strange document. The text ran: 'Say no to Hitler.' No to what? And who was saying 'no'? In any case, the laconic tone is certainly Lawrentian.[8]

We have no record of Malraux's reactions to the death of T. E. Lawrence on 13 May 1935. At the time, he was in the thick of his fellow-travelling campaigns. But when he volunteered as a private in the tank corps in 1939, did he not give some thought to the precedent of T. E. Lawrence, who abandoned his rank of colonel and his fame as a kingmaker for the humble position first of an air mechanic, then of a tank mechanic, after his break with the authorities in 1922? In any case, the character obsessed him more and more – and this obsession increased when, with the coming of defeat, the last bastion of freedom against the Nazis was that tiny band of RAF fighters that disputed the sky with Goering's bombers. The last liberal heroes of the West, as Malraux said of Lawrence. And from 1942, the contacts he made with various British agents parachuted into France could not fail to bring him closer to the type of noble adventurers produced by the English public schools, of which T. E. Lawrence remains the archetype.

In 1942, André Malraux was working on two books – side by

side with his work on art. The first was *La Lutte avec l'ange*, of which, as we know, there remains only the first part of *Les Noyers de l'Altenburg*. The second was a study of Lawrence, of which he kept only the first chapter, published in 1946. But the first book, of which the principal thread consists of the adventures of Vincent Berger, is almost as clearly inspired by Lawrence as the second.

This Alsatian intellectual who, as a teacher in Constantinople, takes up in 1909 the cause of pan-Turanism,[9] joins Enver Pasha, sets out on a mission across Afghanistan and the depths of Asia to reunite the lands of Turan, and finally realises the vanity of his enterprise – how can we fail to see a model for him in Feisal's adviser? There is the same attitude of mind, the same behaviour, the same fanaticism, the same despair.

It is a curious thing, but when, twenty-five years later, Malraux took up this text in order to rework it into the *Antimémoires*, the presence of Lawrence seemed to have been diminished, in favour of a more Pascalian or Nietzschean questioning of human destiny in general.

Of the book entirely devoted to T. E. Lawrence, on which he was working at the same time, only a short essay, entitled *N'était-ce donc que cela?*,[10] has survived. Had Malraux ever written so voluminous a book? He declared as much to Janine Mossuz,[11] adding that he had 'destroyed' it. Gaëtan Picon, visiting Malraux in Corrèze in the spring of 1943, saw the manuscript devoted to T. E. Lawrence lying on his host's table: it was a thick pile of paper. In any case, it is stated at the end of this short essay that it was an extract from *Le Démon de l'absolu*, a forthcoming work. Whether or not it is a fragment or a whole work, this text is extremely disconcerting.

N'était-ce donc que cela? (Is that all it amounted to, then?) is the conclusion that Lawrence attributed to his reader, at the end of a meditation on his life and work at the moment when, in 1922, he was about to sink into anonymity and military slavery, and when he felt 'even more committed to this intellectual adventure than he had been to the Arab adventure' (writes Malraux), 'imprisoned with this book for his decisive fight with the angel'.[12]

'A book that is a little better than those written by so many retired army officers, containing some hysterical passages', the author of the *Seven Pillars* wrote to a friend, adding that he had wanted to write a work worthy of *The Brothers Karamazov* or *Zarathustra* and that it seemed to him that he was rereading 'the memoirs of a dynamiter' – written by 'a second-rate journalist'. Political failure was followed by artistic failure. Hence the conclusion: 'I do not forgive myself for not being an artist, because there is nothing nobler in the world.'

The strange thing is not that Lawrence, a masochist and so absurdly proud that humiliation was his natural state, should have written these cruel lines, but that Malraux, who loved and admired him, and who was similar to him in so many respects, should subscribe to them apparently without reservation. Nothing in this text offers the slightest corrective to Lawrence's despairingly selfcritical title. Nothing leads one to believe that the author of *La Lutte avec l'ange* challenges this admission of failure.

Was it because he himself had failed to give to his Vincent Berger the vigour of Garine or the strength of Manuel in *L'Espoir* – not to mention the great model that he shared with T. E. Lawrence, Dostoevsky – that he was so willing to echo this admission of failure? Or was it that, through a Lawrence defeated by circumstances, he could give expression to his own despair at the march of events? After all, the cause to which he had devoted the last seven years of his life, that of the antifascist struggle side by side with the Communists, had just received the frightful setbacks of the Moscow trials and the Nazi-Soviet pact. Yet *N'était-ce donc que cela?* does not conclude on a note of total despair. Malraux wishes to see it as an 'Ecce Homo', and what appears to him, beyond the artistic and political 'failure', are the religious, metaphysical dimensions of the character.

> . . . Lawrence, one of the most religious minds of his time, if by religious mind we mean one who feels at the depths of his soul the anguish of being a man, Lawrence . . . who called the *Karamazovs* a fifth gospel, did not write . . . fifty lines on Christianity . . . He seemed to be one of those whom the eternally crucified Jesus snatches from the ultimate solitude.

But he no more believed in the religion of his own people than he now believed in their civilization. There was in him an anti-Christian of the first order: he expected only from himself his own remission. He sought not appeasement, but victory, a conquered peace. 'Somewhere there is an absolute, that's the only thing that counts; and I haven't succeeded in finding it. Hence this pointless existence.'

And Malraux, as if to stress the identification, which becomes increasingly evident throughout this strange essay-confession, this auto-pamphlet, concludes:

> The absolute is the last appeal of the tragic man, the only effective one because it alone can burn away – if only with the man as a whole – the deepest feeling of dependence, the remorse at being oneself.[13]

Thus, at the very moment he appears to reject him, Malraux resumes his dialogue with Lawrence at the deepest level. He drags him with him from the world of Nietzsche to that of Pascal – as can be seen in many of the exchanges in *Les Noyers de l'Altenburg*.

On one point in particular a distinction must be drawn between Lawrence and Malraux, and that is in the confidence placed in action as a way of reaching the absolute.

In *N'était-ce donc que cela?*, Malraux writes:

> The instinct that leads the politician to the ministry, the minister to the role of leader, did not lead him to wish to direct Britain's colonial policy, but to transform once again into lucidity the confusion of what had until then been his destiny.[14]

Lawrence went even further in the renunciation of action:

> I saw stretching out before me a long prospect of responsibilities and commands that disgusted my contemplative nature. I thought it mean to take in this way the place of a man of action, for my scale of values was clearly opposed to that of men of action, and I despised their happiness . . .[15]

And again: 'Freedom could be exercised only by preferring

doing nothing to doing . . . For the clear-sighted, failure was the sole aim . . .'[16]

Malraux, too, of course, experienced such 'bouts of hopelessness' and renunciations of action. Garine expresses similar feelings, as do Perken, Chen and, above all, Alvear. But the overall tension of the stories and characters, and the behaviour of the squadron leader, the guerrilla, the militant, not to say the minister, witness in favour of action and even reveal a sometimes cynical sense of efficacity.

On the highest plane, it is expressed thus: 'Men united by hope and action reach domains that they would never reach alone.' On a quite different plane, here are two reflections: 'In 1946, it seemed to me that the men of the "system" were incapable of moving a chair. I didn't know what we'd do, but I knew we were capable of moving a chair.' And to someone who criticised him for being a member of a government that was waging the Algerian war, he retorted: 'Where has one a better chance of bringing the Algerian war to an end: at the Deux-Magots or the Hôtel Matignon?'[17]

During a conversation, in July 1972, in which I began to compare him with T. E. Lawrence, he interrupted me:

> Be careful. The difference between us is that Lawrence always told me that he was convinced that he would fail in whatever he undertook. While I have always believed that I would succeed in what I did! I act to win . . .[18]

Legend continues to link the two men with an almost compulsive force. In 1946, while writing a study of Lawrence,[19] Roger Stéphane went to London, where he arranged to meet a number of his friends. One of these was E. M. Forster who, says Stéphane, received him in cordial fashion: ' "Good morning, M. Malraux, how do you do?" I was quite taken aback, and reminded him that I had signed my letter with my own name. "Yes, yes," said Forster, "but I thought Malraux was your pen-name, because I knew he was interested in Lawrence and I didn't think two French writers could be interested in T.E. at the same time." '[20]

Lawrence faded. With de Gaulle, Malraux found the inspiring individual who could satisfy his hunger for history, his need for companionship and his aesthetic demands. The general put the colonel in the shade. References to Lawrence still occur here and there, in interviews like the one quoted above, or in a chapter of the *Antimémoires*.

During a visit to Oxford, where he went to receive an honorary doctorate, the friends with whom he was staying asked Malraux what he would like to see. 'The plaque on the door of Lawrence's room,' he answered. They looked all over Jesus College, where Lawrence had been an undergraduate. But no trace could be found of the great man, except a few photographs at All Souls', where he wrote part of the *Seven Pillars*. Decidedly, the insignia of fame do not take on the same form on both sides of the Channel.

T. E. Lawrence had admitted his 'passionate wish to be famous; and the horror he felt at being well known'.[21] Less histrionic perhaps, Malraux did not conceal his desire for fame. For the one, Sisyphus conceals himself behind his rock. The other makes the rock the base for his statue.

In the last resort, what really links them together, and what may account for Lawrence's influence over Malraux – after all, every influence begins with a similarity – is the fact that for both of them Nietzsche and Dostoevsky were major influences. The Nietzsche who appealed to them was above all the man for whom history is made up not of facts, but of myths. If Malraux had sought to subdue the demon that was in him and which drove him to transfigure into fiction whatever he touched, especially facts, to see the world only through the 'pathetic embellishments' that he imposed on it, Lawrence, the tragic imposter, would have deflected him from this virtuous effort better than anyone else.

How many lies go to make up the pillars of 'wisdom' of the one and the 'hope' of the other? Dreaming of shaping history, they do so by transfiguring it through words, more than through gestures – in this respect, hardly caricaturing the men who served them as models, Feisal and Churchill for the one, de Gaulle for the other. History or stories?

Then there is that 'demon of the absolute', which pursues them even more than the demon of imposture. The silence of God is much more evident in the case of the Englishman – all the more so in that he situates his enterprise in the very midst of the prophetic world, from Arabia to Palestine. Furthermore, Louis Massignon, a good judge, and someone who knew him well, described him as 'alien to any intussusception of the Mohammedan faith'. [22] While Lord Wavell, who fought side by side with him, speaks of him as a 'Catholic soldier'.[23]

And yet, and yet, the conclusion of Malraux's essay on 'T.E.L.' quoted above, leads us along a track where Claudel went too far perhaps in seeking Rimbaud. On the door of the chalet where he spent the last months of his life, T. E. Lawrence had written in Greek: 'What does it matter?' Malraux refers to this fact in the additional chapter of the *Antimémoires*. But he answers himself by quoting Dostoevsky and his chapter ends with these words: 'Every man is a reflection of Being.'

20 *Trotsky*

WHEN the Germans entered Paris in June 1940, Gaston Gallimard was careful, before leaving for the South, to burn several
papers that would have compromised his authors, and in particular one extraordinary document: the plan of an expedition to
Kazakhstan drawn up by André Malraux in 1929 with a view to
freeing Leo Trotsky, who had been deported to Alma-Ata on
Stalin's orders.

Malraux had put a lot of work into this fantastic project and
was planning to set up an association to collect the necessary
funds. Gaston Gallimard had had to intervene and throw all his
weight into persuading Malraux to give up an exploit more
suited to the Three Musketeers than to the history of the
revolution as revised by Stalin.

André Malraux was twenty-seven at the time. He was at one
with the mentality of the Garine he had made so powerfully in
his own image (with something of Lawrence added). Malraux
made no claim to making him even a remote reflection of
Trotsky, but in the contrasting characterisation of Garine and
Borodin, and especially on the few occasions when the two are
actually in conflict, there is a strong suggestion of the opposition between the 'Roman', managerial, bureaucratic Communist, of which Stalin was the model, and the 'conqueror'
Communist, of which Trotsky, the advocate of 'permanent
revolution', was the archetype. The link between this character
and some of the political actions of Leo Davidovich may be
unconscious, but it exists.

In a more general way, Malraux is already haunted by the

Red legend of October, the Winter Palace, the civil war, the mutinying sailors, the partisans and the 'Black Hundred'. When he wishes to sum up the twentieth century in an image, that of 'a lorry bristling with rifles',[1] he is thinking primarily of the birth of the Red Army, the patrols through a snow-covered Petrograd, the attempted coups engineered by the Kadets, an encircled Odessa, the crowds of Moscow workers. A magic figure presides over these violent images, with cap, pince-nez, goatee, upturned collar and dazzling eloquence, a sort of black eagle with powerful talons, Leo Davidovich Bronstein, alias Trotsky, People's Commissar for War and creator of the Red Army. What more romantic character could there be than that of the victor vanquished – more romantic than the reasoning, rational, persistent Lenin with his more earthbound eloquence. And a character who had the advantage over his illustrious elder of ending his days as a ghost of his former self pursued across the world by the agents of the very power he had helped to establish.

Malraux revered in Trotsky not only the builder of history. He also admired him for having taken, together with Lunacharsky, an active concern in the rights of the writer, even at the height of the civil war. This violent, intellectual strategist was certainly the hero of his dreams.

In short, Trotsky was the first – before, after Lawrence? – of those great living figures that take up in Malraux's eager imagination the roles of those revered ghosts Saint-Just, Rimbaud, Nietzsche and Ivan Karamazov. The legendary survivor of the most fabulous event of the century of which Malraux wanted to be a total participant, a myth-maker, an inventor of acts, an inspirer of gestures, he seized hold of the young man who had just written *Les Conquérants* and was already brooding on *La Condition humaine*.

The oddest thing is not that a young writer consumed with a yearning to make some epic act of defiance should be haunted by the survivor of the revolutionary heroes of October 1917 who was at the same time their historian. It is that the interest was mutual and that Trotsky showed great curiosity about this young writer who seemed to be playing at revolution rather than actually committed to it. After reading *Les Conquérants*,

Trotsky asked a friend about 'this young Malraux, who at least shows some will-power, unlike the heroes of Proust or Gide . . . Could he be won over for our cause? . . .'[2]

It took Trotsky over two years, however, to transform his questionings into criticisms. In April 1931 the *NRF* published an article on *Les Conquérants* by Leo Trotsky, which was later republished in *The Revolution Betrayed*. In it, Trotsky overtly links the revolutionary and the novelist, offering the latter the opportunity of an unhoped for debate, and gives to the brief imaginary account of an episode in the Canton uprising the almost authentic value of a chapter in the history of world revolution.

The dialogue between the two men is extraordinary on a number of counts. First, because Trotsky, the companion of Lenin, debates on equal terms with a little-known young writer whom he rather naïvely regarded as a protagonist of the Chinese revolution, and who responded with imperturbable aplomb to the arguments of this semi-fabulous personage. Again because the issue of the debate was a novel, based partly on fact, but the characters of which, Borodin and Gallen apart, were purely imaginary. The man of history replied to the man of fiction as if they were on the same level – though Trotsky, admittedly, encouraged Malraux to do so with disarming good grace.

Trotsky immediately places the book on a very high level:

> A dense, beautiful style, the precise eye of an artist, bold, original observation – everything combines to make this novel of exceptional importance. If I am speaking of it now, it is not because the book is full of talent, though this fact is far from negligible, but because it provides a source of political lessons of the greatest value. Do these lessons come from Malraux himself? No, they proceed from the narrative itself, unknown to the author, and they bear witness against him – to the honour of the observer and artist, but not of the revolutionary. However, we are right to appreciate Malraux also from this point of view: in his own name and above all in the name of Garine, his *alter ego*, the author does not grudge his judgements on the revolution . . .

Not for a moment does Trotsky doubt the veracity of the

narrator, who, for him has written not a novel but 'fictionalised history'. He praises Malraux's 'active sympathy . . . for insurgent China', though this sympathy is 'corroded by excessive individualism and aesthetic caprice', and his perception of 'revolutionary hatred' that 'would have been worthy of inclusion in an anthology of revolution if Malraux . . . had not introduced into his study a tiny note of blasé superiority . . .'

But what is above all important to Trotsky is the critique made in the book, 'unknown to the author', and which Malraux develops with relentless thoroughness, of the Chinese strategy of Stalin and the Comintern. For Trotsky – who is not above correcting the biography of Mikhail Borodin as provided by Malraux – the fault lies in the choice made by 'this small, foreign bureaucracy', in fief to Stalin and the Comintern (Borodin, Garine, Gallen, Klein, Gérard), in allying themselves with the right wing of the Kuomintang against the people, represented in the figure of Hong.

From the point of view of the history of Bolshevism and the development of Trotsky's ideas, this is a remarkable text, for it is imbued with a surprising degree of 'leftism', even for the advocate of 'permanent revolution'. Indeed, it is interesting to see the man who crushed the Kronstadt revolt praising such a prototype of the semi-anarchist terrorist as Hong.

Of course, Trotsky is not advocating the methods of terrorism. But he alleges that:

> . . . if Hong does not find his true way it is the fault of Borodin and Garine, who have placed the revolution at the mercy of bankers and merchants. Hong reflects the masses who are already stirring, but who are not yet fully awake. He tries with revolver and dagger to act *for* the masses paralysed by the agents of the Comintern. This is the unvarnished truth about the Chinese revolution.

> The dialogue between Borodin and Hong [cf. pp. 116–18 of the English edition] is the most terrible indictment of Borodin and his Muscovite superiors. Hong, as always, wants decisive action. He demands the punishment of the best known bourgeois. Borodin can only reply that one does not kill off those who pay up: 'Revolution . . . involves paying

an army.' These aphorisms contain all the elements of the noose in which the Chinese revolution was strangled . . . The army of revolution does not expect thanks: it makes people pay up.

Between . . . Canton and . . . Petrograd, there is this tragic difference: in China, Bolshevism, in fact, did not exist. Under the name of Trotskyism it was declared to be a counter-revolutionary doctrine and was persecuted by every form of calumny and repression. Where Kerensky had not succeeded in the days of July, Stalin succeeded ten years later in China . . .

And deploring that the author lacked 'a good inoculation of Marxism that . . . would have preserved him from a certain fatal contempt', Trotsky concludes:

> The book is entitled *Les Conquérants*. For the author, this titled has a double meaning where the Revolution wears the face of imperialism, that is, where it refers to the Russian Bolsheviks, or, more exactly, a certain fraction of them. The Conquerors? The Chinese rose up for a revolutionary insurrection, under the indisputable influence of the October coup d'état as example and under the flag of Bolshevism. But the 'Conquerors' conquered nothing. On the contrary, they handed over everything to the enemy. Although the Russian revolution provoked the Chinese revolution, the Russian epigones stifled it. Malraux does not make these deductions. He does not seem to think of them even. They stand out all the more clearly against the background of this remarkable book.

Fascinating as Trotsky's article is, Malraux's reply, delivered in the fearless tones of Saint-Just confronting Danton, is no less so. He wastes no space in paying homage to the great man who has done him the honour of challenging him, but counter-attacks at once and scores a point. In answer to Trotsky's rather severe comment that the author lacked 'a good inoculation of Marxism', Malraux points out that Borodin and the policy-makers of the International are Marxists and that neverthe-less . . .

And blending fiction and reality, aesthetic and historical problems with even more virtuosity than his opponents, he writes:

> When Trotsky adds that there is no affinity between the author and the Revolution, that 'the political lessons emerge from the book, unknown to me', I fear that he knows little of the conditions in which artistic creation takes place: revolutions don't make themselves, and neither do novels. This book is not a 'fictionalised history' of the Chinese revolution, because the main emphasis is laid on the relations between individuals and a single collective action. The documentation of *Les Conquérants* is open to the arguments advanced by Trotsky; but that alone. He finds that Garine is in error; but Stalin finds that Trotsky, in turn, is in error. When we read the poignant account of his fall in his *Life*, we forget that he is a Marxist, and perhaps he forgot it himself . . . Since Trotsky sees my characters as social symbols, we can now discuss essentials.

For Malraux, the essentials concern the 'possibilist' thesis based on the fact that in 1925–6, the Chinese Communist Party was incapable of doing anything unaided and that it owed its existence to its alliance with the Kuomintang. This is the thesis that was to be taken up again, word for word, by Vologin the bureaucratic Soviet envoy in Hankow, in *La Condition humaine*. Throughout his article, this young man of twenty-nine, who had never taken part in a single political struggle of any importance, sets out to teach Trotsky a lesson in political strategy. And, what's more, he does it . . . Not that his aruments are unanswerable, but they are powerful arguments – all the more so in that it is true that they are modelled on characters that he has himself modelled.

In this strange passage of arms it is the amateur who uses the weapons of the professional, leaving to the political leader the role of excitable idealist:

> The International had no choice . . . I said that its aim was to give the Chinese proletariat, as soon as possible, the class consciousness it needed to attempt a seizure of power; now

the strongest obstacle to class consciousness was society consciousness. Every Chinese militant was a member of one of the innumerable, so-called secret societies, the history of which is the history of China since 1911; the Kuomintang was the most powerful of these societies; *mutatis mutandis,* it is much more like our freemasonry than our radicalism. Before the fusion, Communist doctrine was that of an emerging society; afterwards, it became one of the doctrines of the largest society . . .

. . . In saying 'the Party first', Trotsky is defending a revolutionary principle whose value and primacy cannot be ignored . . . Indeed, I can only admire the heroic role, in the most realistic sense of the word, that Trotsky demands for the proletariat. But I must confront him with facts, and observe that a stronger Cheka (the Kuomintang controlled propaganda, not the secret services) might have been, from Hankow onwards, a possible solution.

And Malraux concludes:

By doing my characters the honour of regarding them as symbols, Trotsky takes them out of their temporal context. My defence is to replace them in it.[3]

Trotsky's reaction to this 'lesson' in Far Eastern Machiavellianism, given him by a man he assumed to be a true fighter, but who none the less was little more than a youth, was brief and dry: in *The Revolution Betrayed,* he wrote that he had asked for a good inoculation of Marxism for the young Malraux. Now, he didn't even hope for it . . . However, Malraux asked to meet Trotsky shortly after he settled in France, in July 1933, and Trotsky readily agreed.

Malraux had just finished *La Condition humaine,* which was appearing in the *Nouvelle Revue française.* In March, he had joined Gide in the antifascist campaign, within the Association of Revolutionary Writers and Artists. On leaving Turkey, Trotsky was allowed entry into France by the Herriot government. He was refused permission to reside in the Paris region, so he settled near Royan, in a villa in the little resort of Saint-Palais. It was there that Malraux, accompanied by a young Trotskyist militant, visited him on 26 July 1933. At the time, Clara was very concerned about the health of their daughter Florence and, to her great regret, could not go with him.

Malraux published an account of the meeting only nine months later in *Marianne*, soon after Trotsky had been expelled from France by the Doumergue government. It is a fine piece of writing, full of admiration for its subject:

. . . Gradually advancing in our headlights, behind a cautious young comrade carrying an electric torch, there appeared a pair of white shoes, white trousers, a pyjama top . . . The head remained hidden in the darkness of the night. I have seen faces that should express the extraordinary lives of their owners: yet almost invariably such faces are inexpressive. I awaited with something more than curiosity the mask that bore the marks of one of the last great destinies of the world and which stopped, dazzled, at the edge of the light.

As soon as that dazzling, bespectacled ghost materialised, I felt that all the strength of his features lay in the mouth, with the flat, firm, very finely drawn lips of an Asiatic statue. He laughed to put a comrade at ease, with a laugh of the head that was not in keeping with his voice – a laugh that revealed very small, very widely spaced teeth, extraordinarily young teeth in that delicate face with its fine head of white hair . . .

Trotsky did not speak his own language; but, even in French, the main characteristic of his voice is the total mastery over what he is saying – the absence of the emphasis by by which so many men suggest that they wish to convince another in order to convince themselves, the absence of any desire to attract. Despite the difficulty that some have in expressing themselves, superior men, almost without exception, possess that density, that mysterious centre of the mind that seems to proceed from firm beliefs, which goes well beyond them in every direction, and which comes from the habit of regarding thought as something to conquer and not to repeat. In the domain of the mind, this man had created his own world and lived in it. I remember the way he spoke of Pasternak:

'Almost all the young Russians follow him at the moment,
but I don't care for his work. I don't care very much for the
art of technicians, art for specialists.'

'For me,' I replied, 'art is primarily the highest or most
intense expression of a valid human experience.'

'I think that kind of art will be reborn throughout Europe
. . . In Russia, revolutionary literature hasn't produced much
as yet.'

'Isn't the true expression of Communist art, not literature,
but the cinema? There is a cinema before and after *Battleship
Potemkin*, before and after *Mother*.'

'Lenin thought that Communism would find artistic expression in the cinema. As for *Potemkin* and *Mother*, people
have talked to me quite a lot about them, as you have done.
But to tell you the truth, I've never seen these films. When
they were first shown, I was at the front. Later, other films
were shown, and when they were revived I was in exile . . .'

The visitor questioned him about 'the survival of individualism under Communism . . . as different from bourgeois
individualism as bourgeois individualism was from Christian
individualism'. To which Trotsky replied that, again, they
would have to go back to economics.

Christians were able to live in terms of eternal life and not
attach much importance to individualism because they were
very poor. The Communists of the Five Year Plan are in a
rather similar situation, for other reasons. In Russia, the
periods of the plans are necessarily unfavourable to any
individualism, even a Communist one . . .

And because the visitor pressed him further on this vital
point, he conceded:

A purely collective, a solely collective, ideology is irrecon-
cilable with the minimum of material freedom involved in
the modern world and Communism, in the short term. In
the very short term . . .

Malraux took his leave and the two men met again the next
day. They talked of Poland which, thirteen years before, had

sent French troops into battle against the Red Army, then of a possible conflict in Asia. What would the Soviets do against the Japanese? 'I think we'd fight on the Baikal,' said Trotsky – and Malraux noted that when he used that apparently surprising 'we', his face assumed an even more intense expression. But not when, referring to Stalin, he said 'the other' . . . And the 'Prophet Unarmed' began to prophesy. He said that the Americans, in search of new outlets, would 'seize China . . . And who will stop them? Europe will have enough on her hands . . . War with Japan will be inevitable.'

Later, they talked of many other things, of Lenin and of what he expected from Communism:

> 'A new man, certainly. For him, the perspectives of communism were endless.'

> He reflected again. I thought of what he had told me in the morning (about the permanence of some form of individualism) and, no doubt, he was thinking the same:

> 'But,' I said, 'it seems to me that you . . .'

> 'No, I think as he did really.'

> What was conveyed beneath his words, and what I thought I felt of the presence of Lenin in him was the wish to experiment, as soon as he found himself in a sphere in which Marxism no longer applied. In short, for him, the desire for knowledge led to action.

And then they spoke – Malraux spoke – of death. Trotsky went on:

> I think death is above all a matter of wear. On the one hand, there is the wearing out of the body and, on the other, the wearing out of the mind. If the two occurred simultaneously, death would be a simple enough matter . . . There would be no resistance. [Trotsky was sixty years old and seriously ill.]

At the moment of writing, that is to say, at a time when Trotsky was proscribed by a Communist régime that he had helped to establish and expelled by a French government that had emerged two months earlier out of a pre-fascist riot, André Malraux could not rest content with a mere interview or piece of reporting. At the end of the article, he compares his memories of Trotsky with the images of a film presented by the Communist Party that he had just seen showing a festive Moscow 'crushed by the gigantic portraits of Lenin and Stalin'. Addressing himself directly to the 'Old Man', Malraux acknowledges allegiance to his cause:

> How many among that crowd thought of you? A great many, certainly. Before the film, there were speeches demanding the release of Thaelmann; the speaker who dared to speak of you soon overcame, once the first moment of anxiety had passed, both bourgeois hostility and orthodox reserve: in this multitude that has silenced you, you live on like remorse . . . Against the government that is expelling you, all are with you: you are one of those outlaws that refuse to be turned into *émigrés*.
>
> In spite of everything that will be said, printed, shouted, the Russian revolution is for them one and indivisible, and something of the heroism that shook the Winter Palace disappears, humiliated, with your solitude . . .
>
> I know, Trotsky, that you expect of the implacable destiny of the world only its own triumph. May your clandestine shade, which for close on ten years had wandered from one exile to another, make the workers of France understand – and all those who are moved by that obscure desire for freedom, revealed clearly enough by the expulsions – that to unite in a concentration camp is to unite rather late in the day! There are too many Communist circles in which to be suspected of sympathy for you is as serious as being sympathetic to fascism. Your departure, and the insults of the newspapers, show clearly enough that the revolution is one . . .[4]

Was André Malraux then dreaming of a role as unifier? The day after 6 February 1934 he signed a statement demanding a 'United Front' that was disapproved of by the Communists. He made similar demands at various meetings organised against the expulsion of Trotsky. Two days after the publication of the *Marianne* article, he made a speech at a meeting organised by the Communist League (the left opposition) and the Socialist Party.

La Vérité, the official organ of the League, echoes Malraux's views:

> The speaker launched a rousing appeal for unity in the main task, revolution in France. 'We must understand that the revolution is one.' And returning to the expulsion of the leader of the Bolshevik–Leninists, he concluded amidst loud applause by demanding that 'one should cease to humiliate part of the revolutionary force that shook St Petersburg'.[5]

Two weeks earlier, Trotsky had shown his friendly feelings towards the young writer by taking up again, in the same periodical some of the arguments of his critical essay of 1931 in the *NRF*:

> The two novels of the French author Malraux, *Les Conquérants* and *La Condition humaine*, should be read with care. Although he seems unaware of political relations and consequences, the artist draws up here a crushing indictment of the policy of the Communist International in China and, through description and character, confirms in the most striking way everything that the left opposition had explained in theses and formulas . . .[6]

Throughout this period (1933–4), Malraux regarded himself, if not as a Trotskyist, at least as one of the Old Man's sympathisers. Perhaps not so much for Trotsky's ideas as for the myths that he embodied and the condition of Wandering Jew of the permanent Revolution that had been imposed on him. But his sympathy was strong enough to lead him to more senseless gestures than speaking at Paris meetings. We have already referred to the episode during the journey to the USSR in the summer of 1934, described by Clara Malraux in *Les Combats et les Jeux*,[7] when, in reply to a toast proposed by some official to the 'socialist fatherland', the guest of Maxim Gorky proposed the health of Leo Davidovich. Did Malraux really believe at the time that this bold gesture, which was received in 'icy silence', would be enough to get them, his wife and himself, 'locked up', as he had warned Clara? In any case, he made that gesture.

But the period of moral adhesion was not to last – even if the historical fascination remained intact. In Malraux's mind,

Trotsky is a great man, but he apparently carries no weight in the struggle against fascism, the only struggle that matters for Malraux. So he opts politically for the banishers against the banished. In April 1935, he begins the break by refusing to intervene in favour of a man who then claimed to be a Trotskyist, Victor Serge, deported by the Soviet authorities during the first great purge that followed the assassination of Kirov. In *La Vérité*, Trotsky noted this silence – not without bitterness.[8]

From then on, the gap continued to widen between the man who fought Stalinism strategically and the man who, for tactical reasons, accepted it. In Spain, the creator of the *España* squadron chose to 'play the game' with the Communists, who, according to him, were alone capable of stemming the fascist onslaught. He equipped his squadron – or allowed it to be equipped – with a Stalinist political commissar, and broke off all relations with the POUM (Workers' Party of Marxist Unification), whose primary objective was the one he held in 1934 – the unity of the revolution – but which the hatred of the agents of the Comintern pushed further and further towards Trotskyism. And he did nothing to condemn the witch-hunt of Trotskyists and anarchists that had been launched by the NKVD and the bosses of the International Brigades, or the bizarre procedure that culminated in the execution of Stalin's two closest lieutenants, Zinoviev and Kamenev.

So the break finally came – in dramatic fashion on Trotsky's part. In March 1937, while staying in the United States, where he was raising funds for the Spanish republicans, Malraux made various statements – in particular in an interview to the Mexican paper *El Nacional* – in favour of the USSR and its role in the antifascist struggle, contrasting it with the Blum government's policy of non-intervention. On 2 April, *La Lutte ouvrière*, the organ of the Internationalist Workers' Party (Trotskyist), published a harsh article, dictated by Trotsky,[9] entitled 'Concrete questions to M. Malraux'. A week later, the old Communist leader took up his pen himself to denounce the novelist-militant and the 'equivocal' character of his accusations against Léon Blum, then the Socialist French premier, bound up with the 'non-intervention' policy in Spain:

In all the questions concerning Spain, Stalin has followed and continues to follow a policy similar to that of Léon Blum . . . Must the responsibility for the policy that is being carried out in Moscow fall solely on Blum? However, Malraux's mission is not to clarify these questions. Like other diplomats, and especially 'unofficial' ones, Malraux says as little as possible about what most interests him.

New York is now the centre of the movement for the review of the Moscow trials. It is, let it be said in passing, the only means of preventing new judicial assassinations. It is not necessary to explain to what extent this movement is alarming the organisers of Moscow's amalgamations. They will go to any lengths to stop this movement. Malraux's visit is one way of trying to do this.

In 1926, Malraux was in China in the service of the Comintern-Kuomintang, and he is one of those who bear responsibility for the crushing of the Chinese revolution . . . Like André Gide, Malraux is a friend of the USSR. But there is an enormous difference between them, and not only in the scope of their talent. André Gide is an absolutely independent character who possesses great perspicacity and an intellectual honesty that enables him to call a thing by its true name . . .[10]

Unlike Gide, Malraux is organically incapable of moral independence. His novels are all drenched in heroism, but he himself is utterly lacking in this quality. He is a natural busybody. At New York, he is launching an appeal to forget everything except the Spanish revolution. Interest in the Spanish revolution, however, does not prevent Stalin from exterminating dozens of old revolutionaries. Malraux himself left Spain to carry out in the United States a campaign in defence of the judicial work of Stalin–Vishinsky. To which it should be added that the Comintern's Spanish policy reflects completely their fatal policy in China. That is the unvarnished truth.[11]

The violence of Trotsky's indictment can be explained. Some weeks earlier, in February 1937, during the second of the great Moscow trials, a Russian journalist, Vladimir Romm, declared that he had met Trotsky in Paris in July 1933 and received instructions from him for acts of sabotage in the USSR. Trotsky replied at once that he had not been in Paris in July 1933, but at Royan, where Malraux had paid a visit – which Malraux could confirm. Malraux remained silent, to the great fury of the 'Old Man', who communicated to the *New York Times* the contents of his article in *La Lutte ouvrière*.

Malraux's reply was as follows: 'M. Trotsky is so obsessed by whatever is of personal concern to him that if a man who has just fought for seven months in Spain declares that the first priority is help for the Spanish republic, then this declaration must, for M. Trotsky, conceal something else.'[12] A few days later, on the occasion of a dinner given in his honour by the newspaper *The Nation*, Malraux declared that 'just as the Inquisition did not affect the fundamental dignity of Christianity, so the Moscow trials have not diminished the fundamental dignity of Communism.'[13]

Thus the dialogue had become so embittered that Trotsky denounced Malraux as a Stalinist agent and Malraux was treating the revolutionary leader practically as a senile, obsessively egocentric war veteran. Even Trotsky's death did not bring the quarrel to an end. It is true that after the war (17 May 1947), André Malraux was to acknowledge his attachment to the creator of the Red Army when he confessed to the American journalist Cyrus Sulzberger that 'if there was a Trotskyist movement in France today which stood some chance of success, instead of the tiny handful of Trotskyites bickering with the Communists, I'd be a Trotskyite and not a Gaullist'.[14] (When, twenty-five years later, I reminded André Malraux of what he had said, he replied: 'C'est farfelu' (that's nonsense).

Yet Cyrus Sulzberger is not subject to hallucinations. Convinced that Malraux had said just that, he must have attributed all the more importance to the text of a letter from Victor Serge to Malraux that he quotes in the *New York Times* of 14 February 1948, in which Serge congratulates Malraux on the 'courageous and probably reasonable' position he had taken in joining the Gaullist RPF (Rassemblement du Peuple Français). And the American journalist added that Serge had been 'a great friend of Trotsky' – which might lead one to believe that if Trotsky had survived the icepick of Jackson–Mornard he would have joined de Gaulle's RPF . . .

On 9 March 1948, the great New York daily published a letter from Natalia Sedova, in which Trotsky's widow expressed indignation that Malraux 'after years of deliberate solidarity with Stalinism should assume the role of a Trotskyist sympathiser at the very moment he is allying himself with the centre of French reaction'. Recalling that it was in precisely the same *New York Times* that Malraux had presented the question of the Moscow trial as 'a personal quarrel between Trotsky and Stalin', and adding that, as de Gaulle's Minister of Information in 1945–6, Malraux had 'suppressed the French Trotskyist press', Natalia Sedova threw doubt on the friendship between Serge and Trotsky (which, in any case, had ceased long before Trotsky's death). She concluded: 'Let Malraux, and others, do what they will. They will not succeed in soiling Trotsky and the movement he founded.'[15]

Quoting this bitter text in an article for the review *Les Temps modernes*, Maurice Merleau-Ponty accompanied it with comment no less unflattering for Malraux, described as 'paranoiac', and as a man who, because of his 'ultra-subjectivism' and 'self-vertigo' (which enables him to confuse 'his' former quasi-Trotskyism with 'his' present Guallism), 'ceases to be a cause in politics' and 'becomes a thing, a tool'[16] (a plausible implication being 'of American imperialism').

This article, appearing in a review published, like the *NRF* by Gaston Gallimard, provoked the only crisis that ever occurred between Malraux and his publisher. Malraux threatened to break with the firm if Sartre's review continued to appear under its imprint. He even made pointed references to the ambiguous attitude of the *NRF* during the war. 'There are files that could be reopened,' he seems to have remarked. Gaston Gallimard gave in and *Les Temps modernes* moved to the other side of the rue de l'Université, to Julliard's. With the 'existentialists' out of the way, the 'Conqueror' now held the field – a procedure hardly worthy of a devotee of the 'liberal hero of the West' that he then saw himself to be.

Trotsky–Malraux . . . The story was not to end with this sorry settling of scores. At the time of the publication of the

Antimémoires, the author talked about contemporary history to Roger Stéphane on French television. In his book he had referred only in passing to Trotsky – whom he regarded 'with de Gaulle, Mao and Nehru, as the most remarkable man I have ever met'. But, he added, 'I will speak of him later.' When Stéphane tried to draw a parallel between Michelet and the author of the *History of the Russian Revolution*, Malraux objected: 'Trotsky is Michelet, minus the generosity. Trotsky did not welcome you with open arms . . . There was a deep and rather beautiful sense of fraternity in him, but not generosity.'[17]

And it was again before the television cameras, in a series entitled 'La légende du siècle' (1972) that Malraux referred most powerfully to Trotsky:

> He gave an overwhelming impression of genius. He spoke French very well and possessed a natural eloquence quite different from political eloquence. When you were with him, you were quite sure that you were in the presence of a very great mind. But there was an element of the unexpected too: one of the most surprising things about him was that his face was absolutely white. He had an extreme fair complexion and that sort of quiff you see on the photographs. He laughed quite a lot and he had the teeth of a child. As soon as he laughed, that rather odd eagle's face turned into a child's face.

After referring to the conflict between them in 1936–7 ('we fell out'), Malraux went on, in a way that revealed that he was still haunted by the great Communist leader:

> There was something of Victor Hugo, of the French Revolution in Trotsky's eloquence – the line of eloquence that stretches from Danton to Jaurès. A verbal eloquence that Lenin did not have. Trotsky was always convinced that whatever has been achieved the major problem was yet to be solved. This was the theory of 'permanent revolution', whereas Lenin practised the ladder theory: each step up was a victory. There was something of the squirrel hoarding his nuts about him. But when Trotsky had mounted three steps, he would say: 'And now we are confronted by the funda-

mental revolutionary problem.' The term prophet is certainly appropriate therefore . . . The great prophet is a preacher of the irrational.[18]

Speaking today, Malraux remains convinced that in the two great debates in which he and Trotsky took opposing stands, that concerning the Chinese revolution (should the Communists ally themselves with the Kuomintang, in order to increase their strength first, or try to exist separately at the risk of being crushed immediately?) and that of the Spanish Civil War (was the true struggle in Spain, at the side of the Stalinists, or in the Soviet Union, where the trials were unveiling the cruel face of Stalinism?), it was he who expressed the rational policy, and the 'Old Man' confusedly prophetic dreams.

But Franco won the battle, while the Soviet intervention in Spain gave Stalin an opportunity of liquidating anyone who did not directly serve his own power apparatus. As for China, the two theses both collapsed in favour of a third, that of the appeal to the proletarian peasantry, which the neo-Trotskyist Kyo, hero of *La Condition humaine*, merely glimpsed. (Did Trotsky sense the existence of what Mao discovered – the revolutionary forces smouldering in the countryside? His best biographer, Isaac Deutscher, implies that he did. Some Trotskyists believe he did. Most historians deny it.)

PART IV

SALUD

═══

21 The 'Coronel'

ANDRÉ MALRAUX was not totally unprepared when he landed in Spain, amid the tumult of war communiqués, hatred and contempt that marked the days of July 1936 and the opening pages of *L'Espoir*. For three months already, keeping aloof from the rather suburban enthusiasm aroused by the victory of the Popular Front at home, Malraux had been turning his eyes to a field of battle more appropriate to his romantic character.

Here was a theatre worthy of him, a country in which the emperor of the West walled himself up alive with a collection of clocks, where a slave poet reinvented chivalry, where furious priests created the word *guerrilla*, where Goya, with etchings nailed to the trees of the sierra, was the first to practise the disturbing art of political propaganda against the French invader. A country in which death is taken seriously. A world oddly symmetrical in his mind with that of Dostoevsky and Eisenstein, which continued to haunt him. ('Russia and Spain,' he has said, 'have this in common – spontaneous song.'¹)

The *Frente Popular* had triumphed in the elections of February 1936, three months before its French counterpart. But in Spain the Right did not take it lying down. Surprise attacks, wildcat strikes and assassinations succeeded one another, to the consternation of the moderates, Zamora, Azaña and Martinez Barrio. At the Congress of Intellectuals held in June 1935, José Bergamin, a Catholic antifascist close to the Communists, had asked the members of the International Committee (which was due to meet in July 1937) to come to Madrid. It was in response to Bergamin's invitation that André Malraux set out on 17 May 1936 for Spain, where, on 20 May, he was joined by two companions from the Association des écrivains, Henri Lenormand, a well-known dramatist of the time, and Jean Cassou, a Spanish specialist who had already gained a reputation for himself.[2]

Two days later, the three French writers attended a dinner given by their hosts after a meeting of the *Ateneo* circle, a favourite meeting-place of Madrid's democratic intellectuals. Eighteen months later, in an article in *Hora de España*, José Bergamin referred to the speech then made by André Malraux:

'For pleasure and for pain, such is the destiny of the artist, he who wrings his cries from himself. But it is the destiny of the world to choose the language of his cries.' It was with these words that André Malraux spoke to us shortly before our vital struggle began . . . This friend and writer who bound his destiny so strongly to ours also said: 'What men express by the word culture is contained in a single idea: transform destiny into consciousness. Revolution gives men only the possibility of their dignity. Each individual must transform this possibility into possession.'

Malraux went on to meet most of the liberal or progressive intellectuals – including Ramon Gomez de la Serna (whom he was to introduce briefly in *L'Espoir*), Rafael Alberti, Leon Felipe, Antonio Machado – and left-wing politicians like Largo Caballero, who was then known as 'the Spanish Lenin' and who, with the support of the socialist-revolutionary trade-union organisation, the UGT, seemed the arbiter of a pre-insurrectional situation. But when Malraux returned to Paris, it was neither the intellectual graces of the *Ateneo*, nor the rasping eloquence of Caballero that occupied his mind: to his friend Nino Frank he was full of his latest enthusiasm. He talked 'as of a revelation, of a new political tendency he had discovered, and which he thought was closest to the ideal one might have in politics: anarcho-syndicalism.'[3]

The Spanish fever did not incubate for long. On 17 July 1936, less than two months after André Malraux's return to Paris, a *pronunciamento*, which had been planned for several months by the leading generals of the Spanish army, Sanjurjo,

Mola, Goded and Franco, was launched. The Moroccan garrisons at Melilla and Tetuan revolted, and on 18 July a hundred and eighty-five generals out of a total of two hundred joined the dissidents.

The prime minister, Casarès Quiroga, minimised the affair, refused Largo Caballero the weapons he demanded for the trade unions, and resigned the next day. On 19 July, Martinez Barrio tried to negotiate with one of the leaders of the *putsch*, Mola, a freemason like himself. He was rebuffed and stepped down in favour of another moderate, José Giral, who decided to arm the people after announcing 'the dissolution of the army'. Despite these twists and turns of policy, the *movimiento* was, on the whole, a failure: of the larger cities, only Seville, Burgos and Saragossa followed; the navy, thanks to the crews and technicians, remained Republican. And the workers' organisations won the day in Madrid, Barcelona, Valencia and Malaga, and their autonomist allies controlled the Basque country. As such the *pronunciamento* had failed, not only because it did not enable the rebel generals to seize power in a few hours as they had hoped, but because it brought about the transformation of a political revolution into the very social revolution that they claimed to be preventing. The civil war had begun. It was to last thirty months.

André Malraux was on tenterhooks. His friend Édouard Corniglion-Molinier had announced on 19 July that he was going to Spain as a reporter on the Republican side, as Antoine de Saint-Exupéry had done for *Paris-Soir*. He could wait no longer, and on 21 July he took a seat in a plane bound for Madrid. He was going, he said, to make an on-the-spot report on behalf of the French democrats. But this 'report' was already, for him, a campaign. He was already assigning himself a major role in an event worthy of his epic imagination. Eleven years earlier, unknown, a week's stay in Hong Kong had been enough to make him a mythical leader of the Chinese revolution: could not ten days in Madrid in May, as a famous writer, open up to him a fine career as a Spanish revolutionary? What he said to his friend Alice Alley leaves one in no doubt. 'He already saw himself,' she says, 'as something like Governor of Spain!'

André and Clara landed at Madrid on 21 July.[4] Like most of André's friends, like Emmanuel Berl, for example, Clara was convinced that it was a lost cause, that their gesture was little more than an expression of sympathy. This was not André's view. They were met by their friend José Bergamin and the young writer Max Aub[5] who, thirty-three years later, still remembered Malraux's arrival as a dazzling apparition: 'He already lived up to his legend!'

Malraux, fist raised and the fraternal '*Salud*!' on his lips, scoured Madrid, then went on to Barcelona where, during the first days of hostilities, he collected the observations that were to provide material for several chapters of *L'Espoir*. At Barcelona airport, for example, he met a man storming around and bellowing for a plane to Madrid. He was the anarchist leader Durruti. Malraux offered to take him in his own plane and soon acquired great admiration for this fighter, on whom the 'Negus' of *L'Espoir* is partly based.

There is one thing he observed that is confirmed by almost everyone who was there: the fatal weakness of the Republican defence was their lack of air power. Half the fifty machines at the disposal of General Herrera, the (loyal) Commander-in-Chief of the airforce, were based in Morocco. They had landed on 19 July at Seville, unaware that the city was in the hands of the putschist general Queipo de Llano – who seized the planes and shot the pilots.

The Francoists did not yet possess the air power that Mussolini and Hitler were collecting for them. But on the ground they had such an advantage in armour that, failing an attack from the air, their columns would soon invest Madrid, either from the north, where Mola held Navarre and Old Castille, or from the south. Malraux returned to Paris in early August convinced that the fate of the Spanish Republic depended on the activity of a worthwhile airforce. He had connections in aviation circles – including Paul-Louis Weiler, who had lent him his aircraft for the Yemen escapade. And he had a friend in the government, Léo Lagrange, the young Socialist minister of 'Sport and Leisure' – perhaps the only member of the government, except Pierre Cot, the Air Minister, who was completely in favour of giving overt aid to the Madrid government.

Léon Blum himself was scarcely less so. But his two most influential ministers, both members of the Radical party (in the French meaning: that is, centre-left – more centre than left . . .) Yvon Delbos, the Foreign Minister, and Édouard Daladier, the Defence Minister, were strongly opposed to it. On 25 July, at a meeting of the Council of Ministers, they had put a stop to the first consignments of arms to cross the Pyrenees – with the support of Édouard Herriot, the sacred cow of French democracy, who was so totally anglophile that despite the underhand pro-Franco sympathies of Stanley Baldwin's Conservative government, he remained more receptive to injunctions from London than to the distress of his friends Azaña and Martinez Barrio.

On 8 August, the Blum cabinet signed the non-intervention pact, together with the U S S R, which was still hesitating to throw its weight into the balance, Great Britain ,which had originated the manœuvre, and the two Axis powers, Fascist Italy and Nazi Germany, which had signed the agreement only to violate it constantly and openly. Indeed, since March 1934, Mussolini had made an agreement with the representatives of the Spanish factions of the extreme right to provide military support in the event of a confrontation with 'the Communists'.

In a scene in *L'Espoir*, Malraux hinted that he had discovered, in questioning an Italian prisoner, that aircraft had left Italy for Morocco several days before the *pronunciamento*.[6] Non-intervention, especially during the first three months of the war, worked in favour of the rebels. Stalin, preoccupied at the time with the liquidation of his opponents (the third and last trial of Zinoviev and Kamenev, the so-called 'trial of the Sixteen', took place in August 1936), hesitated to help a régime in which the Communists still played only a minor role. He did not take part until October. Hitler, however, had already realised the lessons and advantages to be drawn from a training ground in which his experts could try out the effects of dive-bombing from the air covering attacks from waves of tanks, the bombing of open cities and radio propaganda against the enemy.

As for Mussolini, he had bet heavily on the Francoists and bound the future of his own régime to an enterprise that he had encouraged, as we have seen, long before it was put into action.

His power in the western Mediterranean could be unleashed and he regarded it as essential 'to steep the Italian temperament' in war after war. The Abyssinian expedition had just come to an end. Until the Savoia-Marchetti plane arrived, his Caproni would make it possible to organise an airlift that would mitigate the effects of the navy's defection. This would allow Queipo de Llano to make Seville the advance base of the operation, which would begin in Morocco. As for Salazar in Portugal, he was quite willing to do what he could behind the scenes to help the *movimiento*. It was, in fact, an international coalition, a 'Holy Alliance' of fascisms against an isolated Spanish Republic.

Planes for Spain? There were already a few in Toulouse. Under pressure from Pierre Cot and Léo Lagrange, Léon Blum agreed to turn a blind eye until the beginning of August: they would go where they were needed. But on 8 August the rule of non-intervention, which meant primarily an arms embargo, came into force. FAI and CNT[7] lorries could certainly be seen crossing the frontier at Behobie: I saw them myself. But they contained only small arms, clothes and food sent by the French Basques to their fellow Basques in Spain.

In Paris, Malraux was rushing around trying to get what was needed. ('The Byron of the age,' writes Hugh Thomas, 'acted as buyer on behalf of the Republican Government.')[8] One of his brothers-in-law had connections with the firm of Potez and acted as guide and adviser to one of Azaña's envoys, Corpus Barga, for a deal with the French Air Minister. In this way they obtained twenty aircraft, Potez 540s, which could fly with him to Spain before 8 August, soon followed by ten Bloch 200s. In the course of his next two visits to Paris, Malraux was to scrape together a few more planes for the war, in particular some Bréguets, 'bought at the flea market'.[9]

By 8 August he was at work at Barajas, the Madrid airport. He had got permission to form and command a squadron of foreign combatants that was to be known first as the *España*. The Spanish government generously granted him the rank of *coronel* on account of the efforts he had already made in the sphere of mobilisation and equipment. He was by no means indifferent to the honour and was certainly not averse to wear-

ing the insignia – however odd it may have seemed – complete
with flat cap and gold braid.

We will often refer to *L'Espoir* to describe Malraux's action
in Spain from the beginning of August 1936 to the end of
February 1937. All the indications are that once this mytho-
maniac was caught up in real actions he described them with
surprising fidelity. We shall come later to the diversity of
opinion on the effectiveness of what he did. However cautious
the Chinese precedent may make one, it would be wrong, I
think, to speak of a 'Spain of dream'. For seven months, his life
was inextricably bound up with Spain.

We must be careful not to attribute to Malraux all the actions
and all the views of Magnin, the character in *L'Espoir* who, as
leader of the squadron, represents him as far as his actual
activity is concerned – Garcia, Scali, Manuel and Hernandez are
in turn his intellectual and political mouthpieces. But the evidence of the most reliable witnesses and a reading of three or
four of the best histories of the Spanish Civil War confirm the
main outlines of the novel, as far as the life and activity of the
squadron are concerned. It is reportage of genius, certainly, and
as such refines reality. But reportage it is, and therefore a reflection of reality.

One would hesitate to say that Malraux, a very amateur airman, unsuited to piloting, with virtually no knowledge of
bombing or navigation who, indeed, was rather clumsy in his
movements, and who had a rather 'artistic' way of wearing his
tunic or even his helmet and the braided cap, could have been
an effective fighting man. But what is certain is that his incredible physical courage had a strong enough effect on his companions to ensure his real moral authority. And his ready flow
of words, his kindness and the sense of humour of which he is
(or at least was then) capable endeared him to pilots and
mechanics. Furthermore, of course, his fame as a writer, the
wide range of his contacts, the tokens of friendship that were
shown him by a number of the Spanish leaders, from Caballero
to Negrin, not to mention the Soviet ambassador Rozenberg
and such influential, semi-official figures as Ehrenburg and
Koltzov (the *Pravda* correspondent), conferred on him an aura
and authority that could not fail to impress his subordinates.

As to the relations between Malraux and the Communists who fought beside him, there is not only the evidence of some of those Communists, in particular Paul Nothomb (Julien Segnaire), whom Malraux took as the model for Attignies in *L'Espoir*,[10] but also the portrait of the protagonist in a story by the same Segnaire, *La Rançon*.[11]

In this story, two Communists, Cacerès, a member of the Central Committee of the Spanish Communist Party, and Grandel – a self-portrait of the author, like him a Communist militant who had come to Spain without the permission of his party's leadership (they were still awaiting a decision from Moscow), and an officer in the Belgian airforce – are talking about 'Réaux' (who is an extremely faithful portrait of Malraux). Cacerès tells Grandel that he is to be the Party's representative in the international squadron (which Segnaire himself was) and adds:

> 'Réaux, who commands it, is a friend and we're very glad to have him. But he's not one of us. Your job will be not so much to keep a watch on him as help him and prove to him that the Communists are the best in flying as in everything else. And I warn you he's not convinced of that yet . . .'
>
> 'They say he's ready to join the Party . . .'
>
> 'You've read his books! Action has brought him close to us and he's the reverse of a pure intellectual. He exposes himself to danger, he's always in the front line, he admires our efficiency, but the Party, you see, the Party . . . Anyway, we can't give him directives, so you'll have to convince him . . .'[12]

And was Malraux's participation in the fighting really effective? Undoubtedly so, and his physical courage, his desperate determination to make his presence felt, his fear of not sufficiently asserting his virility – all this lends credence to the view of those who saw him in action that he was a leader of men, apparently impervious to danger, both in Spain and in Alsace in 1944–5. To a reporter who, in an interview for *Le Magazine littéraire*, asked him whether Malraux really had taken part in the fighting against the Francoists, Segnaire replied:

It's strange that anyone should doubt it. I was with him

over Teruel when we had flak all around us. Malraux risked his life as much as any of the comrades. But his role was obviously more important, first because he had to command the squadron, and secondly because he had to supply it. If there were planes, it was thanks to him . . .

As for the fact that he was never wounded in Spain – apart from a few bruises he got in an accident in December 1936 – this does nothing to minimise the risk run or the responsibilities assumed.

And was that what Malraux 'had come to look for' in Spain? Perhaps we will find out in the course of this account of his activities there. We must first quote his annotation in the margin of Gaëtan Picon's book:[13] 'In fighting with the Spanish republicans and Communists, we were defending values that we regarded (that I still regard) as universal.' And we should add to that these words by Segnaire: 'What attracted Malraux to the Spanish war was the fact that he felt he could play a very important role in it with very small means. With a few men and aircraft, he could play a decisive role.'[14] For this revolutionary was an élitist, for whom action is all the more attractive when it is performed by a few knights of the Round Table.

In short, he was recognised as leader by a group of far from ordinary men and volunteers of very different types. Nicola Chiaromonte, the Italian writer to whom we owe a very fine text on 'Malraux and the demon of action', devotes no more than a short passage to Malraux's activity in the squadron, though Nenni says he took part in bombing missions.[15] But Segnaire, who joined the squadron at the end of August 1936, never actually met him in the squadron. Communists like Paul Nothomb, left-wing democrats like Viezzoli, Maréchal and Abel Guidez, and plain well-intentioned men like Lacloche and Spinelli fought for four months side by side with strangely assorted mercenaries and formed, until the crises that broke out in November, a sort of amalgam.

The squadron was formed at Barajas, the Madrid airport, then moved in turn to Alcala de Henarès, to Alcantarilla, not far from Albacete, and to La Señara, near Valencia. For two months, Malraux and his companions lived at the Hotel

Florida, on Madrid's Gran Via. Pietro Nenni, the Italian Socialist leader who went to fight in the International Brigades, has described the Malraux of that time and the atmosphere in which the 'internationals' lived in Madrid in the August of 1936:

> The Hotel Florida is a sort of Tower of Babel . . . It houses Malraux's airmen, journalists, the Republic's guests of honour and the band of adventurers that never fail to turn up at wars and revolutions. Malraux has organized a mercenary airforce that is giving incalculable service. Thin, almost frail, his fine face stamped with intelligence, Malraux throws himself wholly into what he is doing, like a real fighter.[16]

This Hotel Florida was an odd headquarters. Military secrecy had been established there and searches were often made. But in the restaurant, where journalists of any and every tendency had entry, there was a blackboard on which, I was told by someone who was there, Malraux or one of his adjutants would often outline the plans for the next day's operation.

'The Alcalà and the Puerta del Sol,' Nenni continues, 'are very lively up to 3 am. The cafés are full to bursting point . . . I sometimes go to a Basque restaurant with Malraux and his wife, Teresa Alberti and her husband, the poet of the militia, the Russian Koltzov, Soria, the Catholic intellectual Bergamin, Corpus Barga, etc. We talk excitedly about the day's events. We are like bows stretched by an invisible, yet present archer: the Revolution.'[17]

Georges Soria was the Madrid correspondent for the French Communist Party daily *L'Humanité*, and a whole group of left-wing papers, from *Ce Soir* to *Vendredi*. He remembers the Malraux of August 1936 in the warmest terms:

> His manner was then simple, direct and, once one had made contact, relatively easy. Tense as a spring, his forelock covering his eye, a fag-end in his mouth, full of vocal tics, dressed in a careless-elegant way, his everyday conversation consisted of a mass of images and brilliant ideas that literally fascinated the circle of people around him. He used this power with a sort of tyranny that one can easily forgive. In

the small, shifting international society formed by the writers who had gone to Madrid as an expression of their solidarity with the Spanish people, André Malraux occupied a very special place. Everyone admired him for facing dangers of aerial warfare for which he was in no way prepared. His legend grew as the battle for Madrid aroused people's consciences.

Before and after the formation of his international squadron, Malraux was to be seen everyday in the late afternoon in the lounge of the Hotel Florida, which has since disappeared. It was the time people met to discuss the latest news. Everyone told what he had seen at the front or in the city. The Russians, Ehrenburg and Koltzov, were there, the Chilean Pablo Neruda, the American John Dos Passos and the great Spanish poet Rafaël Alberti. It was the most brilliant literary salon of the period. I took part there in the most astonishing conversations I have ever heard.

Malraux spoke English and German badly, and neither Spanish, Italian, Russian, nor Chinese . . . How did he manage always to be at the centre of attention and to gather the most prestigious individuals around him? He spoke in French, in a language of great syntactical complexity and with a vocabulary that was never impoverished by a desire to be easily understood. For the French there, it was a feast. For the others . . .

I remember conversations between Malraux and Hemingway in which 'Ernie', staring at his glass and obviously 'turned off', was waiting resignedly for Malraux to finish his breathless improvisations in order to get a word in edgewise. The two men respected, but hardly liked one another. 'Ernie' tended rather to seek the company of simple, quiet people and hated theorizing about politics or literature. Without malicious intentions, he called Malraux 'Comrade Malreux' – a bad pun [on *'malheureux'*, unhappy] that expressed his aversion for this type of intellectualism.[18]

Mikhail Koltzov's *Journal* is studded with references to André Malraux and to the role he was then playing. Here are two examples:

August 18: A lot of people to be seen at the airport, especially soldiers. André comes and goes – tired, thin, irritable – he hasn't slept for several nights; he's constantly being called from one place to another. The command of the squadron is carried out standing, in hasty conversations.

August 19: France, crazy country, what are you waiting for? The Germans have already appeared at Irun and San Sebastian. Bismarck's threat to 'apply the Spanish mustard plaster to the back of France's neck' is now being carried out. You have no Maginot Line here. Two dozen crackpots, the adventure-seekers of André's squadron, without passports, flying second-hand aircraft, have taken to the air to defend you, France . . .

There is nothing to prove that Malraux was consciously aiming at the defence of his own country, as Koltzov suggests. Until very recently, everything Malraux has said has made it clear that he was engaged in an ideological, rather than a national struggle. 'Our enemy out there was fascism'[19] he has often repeated, and has never tried to present himself, even in his last Gaullist phase, as a prophetic strategist of a patriotic struggle on the Second Front. But objective reality confuses both projects.

Anyway, they were there to fight. And Malraux fought – with an immediate effect that has been recognised by all but the pro-Franco historians of the war. This is especially the case with the first serious engagement undertaken by his men, his planes and himself, and the one that was to remain their least challenged triumph – the Medellin operation, whose importance in the defence of Madrid is stressed by Pierre Broué and Émile Temime,[20] as well as by Hugh Thomas.[21]

When speaking of the *España* squadron (which, it should be said, was never part of the 'International Brigades', even though it recruited a number of volunteers from their ranks at Albacete from November onwards), one must remember, if not the actual figures, at least the proportions. Malraux and his men never had more than six planes in the air at any one time. They never had more than nine aircraft in working order: two or three Potezes, two or three Bréguets, two or three Douglases, one or two Blochs – all worthy enough aircraft for the time, a match for the Heinkels, if not for the Fiats and Savoia-Marchettis, but so unsuited for bombing missions that at first the bombs had to be thrown out of the windows and other openings . . .

These pitiful figures, and these 'impossible' combat conditions, do anything but diminish what was accomplished by three dozen truly heroic men – including those of whom Pietro Nenni wrote: 'These so-called mercenaries who risk their skins are admirable men.' This was soon apparent when Malraux was given the mission of cutting the route of General Yagüe's pro-Franco column which, by moving from Andalusia through Estremadura, was trying to join up, via Merida and Badajoz, with Mola's forces stationed in Old Castile and Galicia. This was an operation of major importance that might alter the outcome of the war – and alter it it did when it was carried out two months later.

Malraux recounts the incident in *L'Espoir*:

On the aerodrome six machines of the latest type had lined up for the start, and even the sweltering heat could not abate the general enthusiasm. A column of Moors engaged in the Estremadura offensive was marching from Merida on Medellin. A strong motorized force, it was believed to contain the pick of the fascist army. Staff headquarters had just sent through a telephone message to Sembrano and Magnin, informing them that Franco in person was commanding the column.[22]

Unarmed and officerless, the militia in the Estremadura was putting up a more or less forlorn resistance. A scratch force of field labourers, potboys, innkeepers, saddlers, and the like, some thousands of the most downtrodden folk in Spain were sallying forth from Medellin with shotguns to face the machine-guns of the African brigade.

Three Douglases and three multi-seaters armed with 1913 machine-guns occupied half the width of the aerodrome. (There were no fighters, all had been sent to the Sierra.) Round them stood Sembrano and his friend Vallado; the

Spanish Air Line pilots Magnin, Sibirsky, Darras, Karlitch, Gardet, Jaime, and Scali . . . The whole ground staff had turned out in force for the occasion.[23] Jaime was singing a Flamenco folksong.

The squadron took off and soared south-west in two V-shaped groups . . .

Darras could see the road in front studded with little red dots at regular intervals . . . They were too small to be cars, yet moving too mechanically to be men. It looked as if the roadway itself was in motion. Suddenly Darras understood. It was as if he had just acquired a gift of second sight: seeing things in his mind, not through his eyes. The road was a solid mass of lorries covered with drab tarpaulins, yellow with dust, and the red dots were the bonnets painted in red oxide; there had been no attempt at camouflage. Spanned by the silence of the far horizons round the three cities, the land lay bathed in tranquil light, threaded with roads that forked out like the imprint of some huge bird's talons. And amongst all those quiet ways, one road there was that throbbed and thundered – the road of fascism.

On both sides of the roadway bombs were exploding; twenty-pounders that spurted spearheads of red flame and veiled the fields in smoke. There was nothing to show that the fascist column had put on speed, except that the road was throbbing still more violently. . . . Suddenly one section of the road stopped vibrating. The column had halted. Unnoticed by Darras, a bomb had hit one of the lorries, slewing it across the road . . .

Seen from the plane, the lorries seemed stuck in the road like flies on a strip of flypaper.

From his vantage-point above, Scali saw them in imagination, buzzing up into the air, or darting aside across the fields . . .

More lorries were slithering down into the fields, their wheels in the air. Now they were no longer head-on to the sun, massive shadows trailed behind them, cast by the declining rays; like dead fish rising to the surface of a dynamited pool, they became visible only when derelict . . .

'A pretty kettle of fish for Franco!' Sembrano chuckled to

himself. Then, falling in line, he flew towards Medellin . . .

The account of the bombers' attack triggered off by the Junkers of the German fighter command that had suddenly emerged from the clouds keeps the same tone of documented lyricism:

> Gardet stood waiting in the forward turret, a rifle slung across his back. Too far to make himself heard by the crew, he was pointing towards the enemy planes, gesturing frantically with his left arm. Standing beside Darras, Magnin watched the Junkers looming larger and larger as if air were being pumped into them. Suddenly all on board realized that a plane can crash. Gardet spun round his turret and the planes swept past each other with a fantastically accelerated rattle, all their machine-guns drumming in the cockpits. Few shots – only those fired by the under-turret machine-guns – had touched the Internationals. The Junkers fell away behind; one of them began to come down, without, however, crashing. Steadily the distance was increasing, when all of a sudden a dozen shots zipped through the cockpit of Magnin's machine. Under fire from the rear guns of the Internationals the five Junkers turned back to their lines, while the sixth went floundering down across the fields.[24]

A dispatch sent out on 23 August to *Paris-Soir* by its correspondent Louis Delaprée, a journalist who, before being killed in December, sent back to his paper some of the finest reports ever to be written on the martyrdom of Madrid, described the same battle, seen from the ground:

> At Medellin, the massacre of the column was the work of the airforce . . . The airmen saw not men, but insects. The order was given to disperse them. They annihilated them . . . In the middle of the road, a lorry had stopped. The driver, his head slumped over the wheel, seemed to be asleep. But the cargo of this exhausted driver was no ordinary cargo, but twenty dead men hit by the same burst . . .[25]

To say, as Malraux's Garcia does in *L'Espoir*, that this bold operation was 'the first victory of the war' is to underestimate the operations in Catalonia and the progress of the Durruti column in Aragon, for example. But in any case the raid of the Internationals had contributed a great deal to saving Madrid[26] and to gaining time for 'organising the Apocalypse'. This incontestable feat of arms could hardly fail to exalt Malraux's spirits. It was a few days later that the astonishing meeting with André Gide took place in Paris, when Malraux claimed that he now had the 'power' to unify the revolutionary forces and to prepare for the offensive on Oviedo![27]

'Coronel' Malraux was to be confronted by other dangers – in particular, those that Mola summed up in a phrase that was to become famous, when speaking of a 'fifth column' of fascist partisans who, completing the action of the four columns attacking Madrid from the outside, were to take the capital from the inside.

How many disruptive, or enemy elements had infiltrated the squadron? In *L'Espoir*, Malraux speaks of three German officers – about whom Magnin has an argument with the Communist leader Enrique that creates a lasting rift between him and the line of the Spanish Communist Party. In any case, the boss of the *España* squadron found enough reasons to relieve himself of one of his German volunteers to imagine a similar step. Clara Malraux relates how André asked her ('since you speak German', as he put it) to inform this pilot of his suspicions. To confront a hulking great officer in a hotel lounge and tell him that he is thought to be a Nazi and that he'd better move on is no small task for a woman, even for Clara Malraux. But she did it.[28]

It was to be their last 'combined operation'. Clara had just had an affair (perhaps to bring André back to her) with one of the pilots in the squadron, and amused herself by getting herself driven around in the cars of the POUM, Andrès Nin's semi-Trotskyist organisation, which was the pet hate of all the orthodox Communists around Malraux. Nothing at the time could have put him in a more false position. He won. At the end of August, Clara returned to Paris – where, a few days later, André Gide (as we have seen) was to be the avid witness of the discord that reigned between them, and that led to a divorce.

The 'Coronel' soon had to face other problems than those of

his disintegrating marriage. Throughout September, at Toledo which they had recaptured the day after the *putsch*, the people's militias had beseiged the Alcazar, where those who were to be called the 'cadets' had taken refuge. In fact, nine-tenths of the defenders were members of the Civil Guard, and Colonel Moscardo, their chief, had taken with him nearly a hundred wives and children of left-wing militants as hostages.

Franco had held up Toledo as the symbol of fascist heroism. He would do anything to recapture the city. Malraux went to Toledo on several occasions only to find to his chagrin that the revolutionary 'Apocalypse' had not been organised there. For him, Toledo remained the caricatural symbol of the 'lyrical illusion', the horrible powerlessness of an unorganised mass. The Spanish people, disarmed, delivered more or less defence-less to foreign intervention, had thrown itself into a sort of crazy heroism. However, in the last week of September, at Toledo, this heroism began to show signs of wear.

More than anything else, this panic that burst and trickled like an abscess through the city helped to rally Malraux, for a time at least, under the harsh discipline of the Communists – a development symbolised in the character of Manuel in *L'Espoir*. It was also the moment at which Stalin finally decided to bring the support of 'the country of revolution' to the Spanish people's movement. On 7 October 1936 the Soviet govern-ment, which on 31 August had forbidden all export of arms, published a note denouncing 'the military assistance given to the rebels by certain countries' and declared that it was there-fore 'free of the commitments proceeding from the non-intervention agreement' – a logical enough attitude. Angry people wondered why the same attitude could not have been adopted by the French government.

At the level of the *España* squadron, this change of attitude is reflected in an increase in the influence of the now pre-ponderant Communist element. On 7 November at Alcala de Henarès, where it had been stationed for some days, the unit commanded by André Malraux celebrated the nineteenth anni-versary of the seizure of power by the Bolsheviks by giving a banquet to which were invited the Soviet pilots who had just arrived from the USSR. Toasts were exchanged.

Curiously enough (especially in view of the atmosphere of the time: Zinoviev had just been liquidated and Tukhachevsky was about to be), none of the visitors paid even nominal homage to Stalin. It was Paul Nothomb, the squadron's political commissar, who gave the first toast to the General Secretary of the Soviet Communist Party – adding, to the shocked surprise of the Spaniards present, that in intervening in Spain, the USSR was defending itself.[29]

Another consequence of the Soviets' coming on to the scene was the appearance, on the platform of a lorry bought and equipped by the Association of Revolutionary Writers, of Louis Aragon and his wife Elsa Triolet who, at the roadside and in public squares, harangued the combatants. From the vantage point of his plane, Malraux could not help regarding this lorry with what Aragon always considered to be a sardonic eye.

Stalin's decision involved an appeal on the part of the Third International to form those very 'brigades' that the Spanish Communist Party had been crying out for and which included hundreds of its own comrades who, for three months, had been trying unsuccessfully to take part in the fighting. And so, on 22 October, and despite the mistrust of the Socialist and Anarchist leaders, the formation of the 'International Brigades' was officially announced. These 'brigades' were directly inspired by the Comintern – ninety per cent of their officers were Marxists and their organisation was based on the famous 'fifth regiment' whose discipline and technical abilities were the pride of the Spanish Communist Party. It is hardly surprising, therefore, that they gave an immediate boost to the influence and prestige of the Communists. In July, the Spanish Communist Party had a membership of 35,000 (the Anarcho-Syndicalists had two million and the Socialist UGT over a million). By the end of the year, its membership had risen to 200,000.

For Malraux, the formation of the 'brigades' not only coincided with the realisation that the Communists were almost alone in being capable of 'organising the Apocolypse'; it occurred at a time when his relations with his 'mercenaries' were undergoing a critical phase. A description of this crisis, theatricalised and caricatured of course, is to be found in the admirable scene of *L'Espoir* in which Leclerc, the prototype of the 'mercenary', spits out before the journalist Nadal all the anger of a man who had fled before the enemy's counter-attack and who is ashamed that he no longer possesses the moral resources without which such total physical commitment is intolerable.

His face twisted in a leer and his back hunched, Leclerc was coming down the stairs. The grey hood had made its appearance again, with the wisps of black hair protruding from it. His smile was far from reassuring and his arms seemed longer than ever. Pointing to Nadal, a gunner from the *Pelican I* called to him. 'Here's a writer come to see us. Come and have a drink with your colleague.' Leclerc sat down.

'So you're a writer, too, little smartie! What's your line?'

'Short stories. What's yours?' Nadal asked.

'Oh, saga-novels. Been a poet, too. There's never been another airman poet who sold all his stuff like me . . . Only fifteen francs. Sold out every copy. *Icarus at the Wheel* it was called. Because of the poetry and the flying, see?'

'Are you writing just now?'

'Given it up. But I can make some pretty patterns with a machine-gun.' . . .

'Yes. This is the life! What the hell should I be doing if I'd stayed in Paris? Piloting a passenger bus as like as not – might as well run a bloomin' baby carriage! If you're a Red you don't stand a chance, you got to take what comes along. No, thank you! Over here a man's a man. Look at me now! I was at Talavera, I was. Ask anyone about it. The gasworks blazed like Christmas puddings. One in the eye for Franco. Me, Leclerc, I stopped Franco, and I ain't one to brag. Get me? And look at the mates there. Do they look the sort of blokes that'd go round job-hunting just to get the order of the boot? Not they!'[30]

'What prompted you to come here?' Nadal asked Leclerc, pencil in hand. 'Was it the revolution?'

Leclerc shot him a vicious glance from the corner of an eye.

'What the hell's that to do with you? . . . Anyhow everyone knows what I am; I'm a left-wing mercenary. And if I'm here it's because I've bloody well got guts. And I'm air minded, as they say. That's a man's job, flying; it ain't no job for lily-livered skunks, or weaklings, or – journalists! Every man to his own taste. Get me?'[31]

Attignies, an anxious witness, whispers: 'If Magnin doesn't squelch them soon, these fellows will infect the whole squadron, like dry rot.' Then suddenly Leclerc poses the question of the mercenaries' contracts:

'Me, I ain't one to make complaints. But all the same, say I'd been killed today – might have happened, you know – what would have become of my contract?' . . .

Usually the danger shared in common by volunteers and mercenaries brought them together more effectively than the business of the contracts estranged them. But tonight the patience of the volunteers was sorely tried . . .

'I'm fed to the teeth with machine-guns that are only fit for the shooting-gallery at a fair,' Leclerc shouted. 'Fed to the teeth. I've got hair on my chest, I have, and I'm going to act like a bull, not a god-damned stool pigeon. Get me?' . . .

'Salud!' Magnin called, waving his fist like a handkerchief in the air. Statue-like he stood on the threshold, his moustache on the near side, blown down by the wind.

He strode forward, amongst looks of hostility, relief, or feigned indifference, and stopped before Leclerc.

'So, you had your thermos with you?'[32]

'It's not true! I hadn't a thing to drink!' . . .

'Nothing? That was unwise,' Magnin said.

He preferred a drunken pilot to a demoralized one.

Leclerc hesitated, puzzled, groping for a way out. 'The Pelican's crew[33] will return to Albacete at once,' Magnin announced . . .

Leclerc marched up to Magnin . . . On his face was an expression of undiluted hatred . . .

'Magnin, I say . . . to you!'

The hairy fingers at the end of the long ape-like arms were quivering convulsedly. Magnin's eyebrows and moustache seemed to bristle up, his pupils grew curiously still.

'You'll leave tomorrow for France, all arrears paid. You will never again set foot in Spain. That's all.' . . .

Magnin walked to the door, swift, indifferent, with his light stoop . . . He opened the door and said some words as if addressing the high wind sweeping across the plaza of Alcala.

Six guards entered. They were armed.

'Forward, the crew,' Magnin shouted.

Determined to safeguard his precedence, Leclerc went out first.[34]

A stunned silence falls in the room. The squadron commander goes on:

'With the fascists at Carabanchel,[35] men who acted as the men who have just left us acted, are playing the part of counter-revolutionaries.

'They will all be in France tomorrow. From today on, we are incorporated with the Spanish Regular Air Force. Each one of you must procure a uniform for Monday. All contracts are cancelled from today. Darras is appointed chief mechanic, Gardet chief machine-gunner, Attignies civil commissar. Those who do not accept this arrangement will leave tomorrow.'[36]

This is a famous passage and it does not ring hollow. So ended, it seems, any attempt to amalgamate volunteers and mercenaries. And so the second life of the squadron began: the integration of the volunteers from the 'brigades'.

22 *The volunteers of Albacete*

ABOUT the middle of November Malraux and his men set out for Albacete, while the government of Largo Caballero left Madrid for Valencia, leaving the capital in the hands of a defence junta presided over by General Miaja that included only one member of the government: the Under-Secretary of State, Fernando Valera.[1]

Albacete is a small, dusty, pink town on the edge of La Mancha and eastern Andalusia, sufficiently near to Cartagena for the movement of volunteers and Soviet supplies sent from Odessa not to be too delayed. The man who reigned over the little town and its now cosmopolitan population was André Marty, a huge, choleric man, excessively suspicious, whose large, blue eyes always looked as if they were about to pop out of his head.

The enrolment of the volunteers gave rise to the strangest rites. They were gathered together each afternoon in the arena. There, in the middle of the 'ruedo', stood Marty and his adjutant Gayman. Marty glowered down at the crowd: 'What we need is discipline! Those who want to go and fight right away are criminals!' Then Gayman called the roll of the officers, non-commissioned officers, specialists, troopers, etc.[2] From December onwards, he was also to ask whether there were any pilots or mechanics for Malraux's squadron. Recruitment was neither rapid nor very fruitful. But the draft went on.

One would meet Malraux in the streets of Albacete, wearing the uniform of the Spanish Air Force, with its fur collar, his face pale and tense, a cigarette twisting and turning in the corner of his mouth. His problem was how to replace the mercenaries with international volunteers . . . In one of the convoys, at the beginning of November, were three mechanics: Maurice Thomas, Ollier and Galloni. Malraux collected them as they were leaving the square, took them off to the bar of his hotel and enrolled them. They were soon bound for Alcantarilla, the squadron's base: no more than a field with a few hangars, one of which served as a mess.[3]

Their relations with the Spanish authorities were not always of the smoothest. They were criticised for their lack of discipline and for their heavy losses. Relations became worse when Colonel Hidalgo de Cisneros, a Communist as sectarian as he was inexperienced, became chief of the Republican air force.

At the beginning of December, the *España* squadron moved its base once again – this time to Valencia, a city of long-standing Republican traditions, where the government and diplomatic services had set up their headquarters. Malraux and his companions, now all volunteers, equipped (more or less) with uniforms, with a kind of discipline, with their latest Potezes and Bréguets – four could still be in the air at the same time – settled into a very pleasant estate, one of those Levantine orange groves where the poverty of the peasants seems to be masked by the richness of the land. It was called 'La Señara' (hence Segnaire's pseudonym). Near these 'Shakespearian orchards', which evoked for Malraux lines like 'In such a night . . .'[4] stood the ramparts of Sagunto.

It was not there that the squadron carried out its most useful actions for the Republic: but it was there that Malraux crowned his search for fraternity. Before disbanding, three months later, the men he had gathered round him experienced several weeks of friendship that none of them has forgotten. There Malraux found true friends.

Was it to symbolize the human success that concealed for a time the military setbacks of the group, gradually dwindling in numbers and technically inferior to the Soviet crews and equipment that had arrived at Cartagena and Barcelona, and the much more serious defeats of the Republic? Julien Segnaire thought of re-naming the squadron after its leader. He obtained permission to do so from the Spanish ministry, which proved quite willing to allow this rather marginal unit to declare its specificity. One day, at 'La Señara', Malraux noticed a supply lorry approaching, on the sides of which, in huge letters, was written *Escadrille André Malraux*. However, this did nothing to halt the decline of the unit.

Ilya Ehrenburg describes the Malraux of Valencia thus:

> During the winter [1936–7] I often met André Malraux in Valencia: his squadron was stationed close to the city. He is a man who is always in the grip of a single absorbing passion. I knew him during the period of his infatuation with the East, then with Dostoevsky and Faulkner, then with the brotherhood of the workers and the revolution. In Valencia, he thought and spoke only about the bombing of Fascist positions and when I started to say something about literature, he twitched and fell silent.[5]

With or without the *Izvestia* correspondent, Malraux made frequent visits at this time to the Soviet ambassador Rozenberg. Was he trying to obtain new aircraft, or other means of action? Was it at one of these meetings that he proposed the idea for those companies of machine-gunners on motor-cycles that were to reinforce the '5th regiment', the spearhead of the Communist organisation in Spain? In any case, these meetings were highly mysterious and his chauffeur was forbidden to talk about them, even to his friends.

Among these friends, there was one, Raymond Maréchal (the Gardet of *L'Espoir*), who became increasingly important to him. This amazing daredevil – his forehead had been dented in a terrible accident, as a result of which he had been trepanned – possessed incomparable spirit and courage. He was in love with all women and ready to die any time for his friends.[6] Indeed, the reverse was also the case. One of their companions swears that on one mission, Maréchal had gone without his parachute and Malraux made him put on his own.

In the cafés of the old city of Valencia, filled with the mingled smell of oil, pimentos and red mullet, the *coronel*, his helmet cocked to one side and his collar turned up, smothered in a cloud of smoke, prophesied about the imminent war in Europe. Opposite sat the pallid Segnaire, nicknamed 'Siegfried', his wife Margot and the stentorian Maréchal.

One day, he took them to one of the very rare bullfights to take place in the 'red' zone during the civil war.[7] Another day, one of his officers offered to introduce him to a French journalist who wanted to interview him, even though he had written articles against the Republicans. 'Get rid of him,' Malraux hissed, 'or I'll have to shoot him . . .'

On Christmas Eve 1936, Malraux was ordered to attack Teruel and the Saragossa road with at least two planes. He had been sent a peasant from the region who had located the site of an enemy airstrip to be destroyed and who could act as guide. The operation was planned for 26 December. But the plane in which the *coronel* flew overturned after take-off. The plane was a wreck. Malraux himself was only slightly bruised. The other plane fulfilled its mission, bombed the camouflaged airstrip – but was pursued by enemy Heinkels and shot down in the sierra: its gunner was Raymond Maréchal.

The next day, they learned that of the occupants of the plane, one was dead, the Algerian Belaïdi, and four others, including Maréchal, were seriously wounded. Malraux set off at once to organise a rescue operation for his comrades shot down in a sector that may or may not be in the hands of the enemy.

In Malraux's novel, Magnin sets out for Linarès. The squadron commander, escorted by a crowd of devoted supporters, climbs up towards Valdelinarès, from where the wounded are being brought down, bearing the coffin on which the machine-gun of the Potez has been placed:

> The bulls came into view again opposite. The Spain of his youth – love, make-believe, and misery! Now Spain was that twisted machine-gun on an Arab's coffin and birds numbed with cold crying in the ravines . . .
> At each change-over, the new bearers abandoned their stiff walk as they took up the shafts with affectionate care, moving off again to the accompaniment of the grunts which tell of physical strain, as if anxious to mask the betrayal of

their emotions which their solicitude conveyed. Their attention concentrated on the stones which obstructed the path,
thinking only of the necessity not to jolt the stretchers, they
moved steadily forward, slowing up a little on the steeper
inclines. And the steady rhythm of their tread over the long
pain-fraught journey seemed to fill the vast ravine down
which the last cries came floating from the birds above, with
a solemn beat like a funeral drum. But it was not death which
haunted the mountains at that moment; it was triumphant
human will . . .

Gardet did not look at them; he was alive, but that was all.
From the battlements the crowd could make out the bulky
coffin behind him. Covered with a blanket up to his chin, and
with a bandage under his flying-helmet lying so flat that it
was impossible that there could be any nose beneath it, this
stretcher was the visible incarnation of the peasants' im-
memorial conception of war. And nobody had forced him to
fight. For a moment they hesitated; not knowing what to do,
but determined to make some gesture. Then, as at Valdelinarès, they silently raised their clenched fists.

It had begun to drizzle. The last stretchers, the peasants
from the mountains, and the last mule were advancing between the vast background of rocky landscape over which
dark rain clouds were massing, and the hundreds of peasants
standing motionless with raised fists. The women were weeping quietly, and the procession seemed to be fleeing from the
eerie silence of the mountains, its noise of clattering hooves
and clogs linking the everlasting clamour of the vultures
with the muffled sound of sobbing.[8]

The squadron was approaching its end. Madrid, it was true,
had been saved by the beginning of February 1937, the overall
positions had been stabilised, the Republic still had a chance of
surviving and the USSR was continuing the rescue operation it
had begun in October. But the very continuance of its deliveries
of aircraft meant that the *Escadrille André Malraux* was doomed
to extinction: their own somewhat picturesque, daredevil
methods were replaced by the discipline of a comrade Popov,
who, strangely enough, bore the pseudonym 'Douglas'.

In *L'Espoir* Malraux sums up the situation of the squadron at the beginning of February 1937 thus:

> For two months now the International air force had been fighting on the Mediterranean front: the Balearics, Andalusia, Teruel. The suicidal flights of the 'Pelican period' were a thing of the past. In the air twice a day, and spending quite a substantial proportion of their time in hospital, the squadron had supported the International Brigade all through the battle of Teruel; fighting, doing repairs, photographing the results of their bombing while they fought . . . During one engagement they had scored hits on Teruel station and the enemy headquarters despite the anti-aircraft batteries, and an enlarged photo of the explosion was pinned to the wall of their messroom . . .[9]

Elsewhere, an urgent task remained; Malaga had fallen, on that same 8 February 1937, into the hands of the pro-Franco forces. And while Arthur Koestler, then a Communist journalist, was surprised by attackers and thrown into a prison from which he thought he would never emerge alive,[10] a crowd of over a hundred thousand refugees poured out of the city, pursued by the machine-guns of the Italian fleet and fighter command. In an attempt to halt the massacre, the high command at Valencia asked Malraux for two or three of his planes to confront, if not the more rapid and better armed Fiat fighters, at least the lorries of the fascists, which were also taking part in the pursuit of the refugees. These unfortunate people had to be given a chance to reach Almeria, a hundred and fifty kilometres away to the north-east.

Malraux did not take part in this operation of 11 February 1937 – the last in which the squadron was to display its prowess. This is how Delperrie de Bayac, the historian of the 'brigades', describes the incident:

> The squadron . . . commanded by André Malraux carried out its last sorties in the Malaga sector. At the end of January and the beginning of February, its Potez 540s and Bloch 200s bombed Cadiz, Cadiz harbour, where the Italian fascist volunteers were landing . . . From 8 February, its

planes were protecting the exodus. Its last combat took place
on 11 February . . . Over Motril, the Potez 540 piloted by
Santès (in *L'Espoir* he is called Sembrano) and Segnaire
(Attignies) was attacked at about 10 am by about fifteen
Italian fighters. A burst of fire lashed the front of the
bomber . . . Santès was wounded in the right fore-arm; the
right engine stopped, the left engine burst into flames. One
of the gunners, Galloni had a bullet in his calf. He was
replaced by Maurice Thomas, the mechanic. Santès continued to pilot with his left hand. He tried to keep altitude.
Fortunately, the Potez 540 had a large bearing area, but it lost
altitude and soon he had to choose between the sea and the
mountains: Santès chose the sea . . .[11]

In the fictional version, Malraux describes another phase of
the action, the efforts of the rescuers, who had arrived in cars in
search of the wounded, harassed by the refugees:

An old man, all nerves and sinews, with the strongly
gnarled features peculiar to aged peasants, was calling for
help; he carried a child only a few months old in the crook of
his left arm. There were plenty of equally pitiful cases along
that road. But perhaps a young child appeals to human
sympathy more poignantly than anything else. The doctor
had the car stopped . . . It was impossible to take the peasant
inside. He settled himself down on a wing, still with the child
in his left arm; but he found nothing to hold on to. From his
place on the other wing Pol was able to clutch the door
handle with his right hand; his left hand he stretched across
to the peasant, who gripped it firmly. The driver was obliged
to sit bolt upright in his seat, as the two hands met in the
front of the windscreen.[12]

For Malraux in Spain, it was one of the last expressions of
fraternity. The attempt to rescue the refugees from Malaga is
regarded by most historians[13] as the last action carried out by
the squadron, which had been created seven months earlier at
Barajas.[14] In one of the final pages of *L'Espoir*, Magnin, in his
old Orion, flies over the Republican troops routing the Italian
regiment at Guadalajara.

With his planes scattered to all the winds of Spain, and his comrades scattered – but how worthfully! – in all its grave-yards, all that he lived for now was this incredible '*Orion*', furiously buffeted by the blizzard, and the ramshackle planes beside it tossing like dead leaves upon the gale.

Those clean-cut ranks of hooded figures below the seething cloudwrack were covering not only the Italian position of the previous day but the spirit of a bygone epoch. Magnin knew well what he was watching now as, like a crazy lift, the '*Orion*' jerked him up and down; it was the birth-pangs of war.[15]

The end of the guerrilla war (in the air and on the ground), the birth of the army and of the 'reconstituted air fleet', the death or injury of his best companions – Maréchal, Segnaire, Guidez, Lacloche – the destruction of the aircraft that he had patiently assembled, all these things helped to put an end to the adventure of the André Malraux squadron at the end of February 1937. Not that 'his' Spanish war was over: there remained the propaganda tours abroad, the congress of writers, the book that was germinating within him, the film that he was to make – these were all means by which the artist was to act for the cause that he defended, as an artist – at the level at which he was incomparable.

This, according to some people, is what he should have been doing all along.[16] This view finds support in a work by Colonel Ignacio Hidalgo de Cisneros, the head of the Republican air-force who, though a member of a noble family and a friend of the Social Democrat leader Indalecio Prieto, had joined the Spanish Communist Party.

I do not doubt that Malraux was in his own way a progressive, or that he tried in good faith to help us. Perhaps he aspired to playing in Spain a role similar to that of Lord Byron in Greece? I don't know, but what I can say is that although the support of Malraux, a writer of great renown, was useful to our cause, his contribution as squadron commander proved to be quite negative.

André Malraux did not have the faintest idea what an aeroplane was, and he did not realize, I think, that you cannot improvise an aircrew, especially in wartime. As for the men he gathered around him, I regret to have to disillusion those who saw them as romantic heroes, freedom fighters, whose gesture made up for the unspeakable behaviour of a government whose hypocrisy was equalled only by its wickedness. Of course, there were among them three or four antifascists who had come to Spain out of idealism, and who gave proof of undoubted heroism. The others were simply mercenaries, attracted by the money ... Malraux, who knew nothing of the problems of aviation, enjoyed no authority among them and one can well imagine what such people were capable of doing, when left to themselves. Far from being a help, they were a liability.

On several occasions, I demanded their disbandment, but the Spanish government was opposed to it, on the grounds that it would create a bad impression in France if we sent back men whom a clumsy propaganda presented as 'heroic defenders of freedom' . . .[17]

This view of Malraux is that of Franco's supporters. The pro-Franco historian I consulted[18] wasted no time in quoting the accusations made by Hidalgo de Cisneros, adding that: 'Malraux, who did not have the least regard for Spain or for the Spanish, simply made use of this war to gain publicity for himself' and that 'his book does not arouse the slightest interest in Spain'. It comes as no surprise that a supporter of General Franco should add a touch of contempt to Cisneros' indictment of Malraux. The fact that in order to express his hatred he had only to elaborate on a portrait drawn by a Communist does no honour to a man who commanded the planes entrusted, like those of Malraux, with the protection of the Spanish people.

In February 1937, the review *Hora de España*, which expressed the point of view of the antifascist intellectuals (Antonio Machado, Léon Felipe, Rafaël Alberti, Pablo Neruda, José Bergamin), published the following lines: 'André Malraux affirms a heroic will and puts his faith – with hope or despair – in manly fraternity . . . It is not only a formal imperative, a passion worthy of praise, but rather a sense of the ethical . . . It is the expression of a Europe of men worthy of the name, a

Europe that binds its fate to Spain's . . .' Thirty-six years later, in October 1973, in Moscow, where she has lived since the end of the Civil War, Dolores Ibarruri, 'La Pasionaria', said of Malraux: 'I respect him. He is my friend. Because he loves Spain and has done us great services.'

Those historians (Thomas, Broué and Temime, Delperrie de Bayac) who express neither pro-Franco views, nor those adopted, ten years later, by the Communists, write that as far as foreign aid was concerned 'the first example of a serious organization is that of the International Air Force set up by André Malraux. The *España* squadron was of enormous service, at least in the first months of the war, at a time when the government's bomber command was totally non-existent . . . The Internationals were the only ones to act with any effectiveness, as in the bombing of the Nationalist column from Medellin . . .'[19] To conclude, one might quote Malraux's own words: 'At least we gave the International Brigade time to arrive . . .'[20]

Having accomplished that, he got up, in February 1937, and spoke from the platform of the Mutualité. Yet again . . . but this time, it was not the laureate of the Prix Goncourt 'whose heart was on the left', the hypothetical adventurer in Asia, flanked by Gide and Benda. It was a combatant who had the blood of Franco's soldiers on his hands. And the bourgeoisie did not let him forget it. People no longer came to listen to the thrilling rhetoric of this chimerical fellow-traveller of exotic revolutions. The struggles of the *Frente Popular* were too close for comfort: the echoes of their battles could be heard across the Pyrenees. This time Malraux had transgressed the rules of the game. He was a man to be feared.

A striking impression of this fear, and of the hatred that it inspired in some people, and the anguish it gave rise to in others, has been left us by a man who was soon (after the massacre of Guernica, in April) to take great moral risks on the same side, and who was later to arouse as much hatred as Malraux himself. At the time François Mauriac was a contributer to *L'Écho de Paris*. It was in this paper, seven days after Franco's *pronunciamento*, that Raymond Cartier called on the Blum cabinet not to commit the 'crime against the nation' of delivering arms to the legal government of Spain (to which, however, France was linked by an agreement that gave France a monopoly in supplying equipment to the Spanish Army).

Mauriac was there, at the Mutualité, waiting for Malraux:

> Against a reddish background, the pale figure of Malraux was offered, hieratically, to the acclamations of the public. His forearm bent, his fist clenched, was he about to multiply himself and wheel round his own idol's head? India and China had left a curious mark on this Saint-Just . . . As soon as Malraux opened his mouth, his magnetism declined . . . One could sense the laborious preparation of the man-of-letters . . . As a future People's Commissar, Malraux's problem was to transpose the written style into the spoken style. Did he notice me at the back of the hall? Across this forest of clenched fists, he took up once again a dialogue that had been broken off many years earlier, when this bristling young predator, with his magnificent eye, landed on the edge of my table, under the lamp . . .
>
> Malraux's weak spot is his contempt for man – the idea that one can declaim anything and the bipeds will listen open-mouthed . . . There is something of the hustler in this audacious man, but a myopic hustler, lacking in antennae, who depends too much on our stupidity. As when he declared, for example . . . that General Queipo de Llano had ordered by radio the bombing of hospitals and ambulances 'to weaken the morale of the rabble'[21] . . . He cannot lie, it must be true . . . but he cannot please either, this Malraux, despite the wild acclamations . . . When the hero left the platform, the temperature of the hall dropped. The applause suddenly died down. Malraux returned to his solitude.[22]

23 'Life against Death'

AT THE beginning of March 1937, André Malraux set out for the United States at the invitation of several universities (Berkeley, Princeton, Harvard . . .), organisations of left-wing actors and directors in Hollywood and the then pro-Communist New York review *The Nation*, which was then being edited by his friend Louis Fisher, who was at the time involved in supplying the Republican forces (he had turned his room at the Hôtel Lutetia, boulevard Raspail, into a clearing-house for arms).

It was Malraux's second visit to the United States, but the first that he had made with Josette Clotis, with whom – after his break with Clara at the end of 1936 – he was now living. The warmth of the welcome he received almost everywhere owed much to the young woman's charm. Like Hemingway, he was already a legend – the writer with a machine-gun in his hand. But his political commitment was regarded by young American intellectuals, and by others, much more seriously than Hemingway's.

No sooner had Malraux landed in New York than he began to prophesy about the war. Some of his arguments still have a certain savour – like those he gave to a New York daily, *The World Telegram*, in March 1937:

> The most important problem is that of the peasants. Franco has made contradictory promises to the landowners and to the peasants. But when the harvest comes, the peasants will demand the right and the means to cultivate the land, and Franco, bound by his conservative allies, will have to

refuse them and will then lose the only support he has among
the people.

His most striking intervention in the United States was the
speech he made at New York during a dinner given in his and
Louis Fisher's honour by *The Nation* on 13 March 1937. Since
he spoke only a few words of English, he was subjected to the,
for him particularly irksome, demands of sentence-by-sentence
translation. But the speech is worth quoting from:

> Why do so many Spanish writers and artists support the
> legal government, why do so many foreign intellectuals
> stand today behind the barricades of Madrid, while the only
> great writer who at first sided with the fascists, Unamuno,
> died at Salamanca, disowned by them, alone and despairing?

He went on to describe the descent of the wounded in the
Teruel sierra (the first public sketch of the great scene in
L'Espoir), and told how that evening, on his return, the echoes
of the music played by a unit of Moors near the road on which
the squadron ambulance was passing had suggested to him that
something immense was taking place, something unprecedented
since the French Revolution: 'World civil war had broken out.'
He went on:

> What does fascism bring with it? The exaltation of essen-
> tial, irreducible, constant differences – such as race and nation
> . . . Of its very nature, fascism is static and particularist.
> Democracy and Communism differ on the question of the
> dictatorship of the proletariat, not on fundamental values . . .
> Our aim was to preserve or to recreate, not particular or
> static values, but values on a human scale – not the German
> or the Nordic, the Roman or the Italian, but simply man . . .
> Between a member of a kolkhoz and a soldier of the Red
> Army, there is no essential difference . . . Between a German
> commando and a German peasant, there is a difference of
> kind. The peasant lives in the capitalist system, the soldier
> outside this system. Authentically fascist communion exists
> only in the military order. That is why fascist civilisation
> leads to the total militarisation of the nation, just as fascist

art, if such exists, leads to the aestheticisation of war.

In the struggle against nature, in the exaltation of the conquest of things by man, resides one of the highest traditions of the West, from *Robinson Crusoe* to the Soviet cinema. Determined as we are to fight in the defence of our reasons for living, we refuse to consider this struggle as a fundamental value. We want a philosophy, political structures and a hope that leads to peace, not to war . . .[1]

Alfred Kazin has given an enthusiastic description of this speech: 'He spoke with such fire that his body itself seemed to be speaking the most glorious French . . . His rhythms were so compelling that the audience swayed to them.'[2]

At Hollywood, where he got off the plane clutching under his arm a book that he had just discovered during the flight, Dashiell Hammett's *The Maltese Falcon*[3] (which some years later he persuaded Gaston Gallimard to publish), he was given a cordial welcome by William Saroyan and Clifford Odets, Miriam Hopkins and Marlene Dietrich, and such Frenchmen as Robert Florey and even Maurice Chevalier. He spoke at the 'Mecca Temple Auditorium'. For a few days, he was a 'must'. Naturally, he came out with some very quotable remarks. When asked in a discussion why a man so much in the public eye as himself should go and risk his life in Spain, he replied in English: 'Because I do not like myself.'[4] He had come, among other things, to raise money for the Spanish hospitals – and got it. At San Francisco, he presided at a dinner to which Yehudi Menuhin had been invited. At Berkeley he was awaited impatiently by the translator of *La Condition humaine* and *Le Temps du Mépris*, Haakon Chevalier, who was the inspiration of several 'Red' organisations on the west coast.

This visit, which satisfied his love of fame and comradeship, was overshadowed by the reserve expressed in official circles. Although it was the period of Roosevelt's 'New Deal' and one would have thought that the cause of the Spanish Republic would be more kindly regarded by American ruling circles than by their British counterparts, for example,[5] when he went to Washington there was no official representative to receive him, and there was even some question of withdrawing his entry

visa, on the grounds that he was a revolutionary 'who threatened the security of the United States'.

These threats could not, in his case, have very serious consequences. But the legend created at this time was to have
unfortunate effects. In May 1953, the United States National
Security Commission published a report concerning Robert
Oppenheimer in which mention is made of 'admissions' made
by the great scientist on the subject of Malraux:

> Dr Oppenheimer then declared that in December 1953,
> while he was in Paris with Mrs Oppenheimer, he dined with
> Haakon Chevalier and his wife, and the next day he went
> with them to visit a certain Dr Malraux. According to Dr
> Oppenheimer, Dr Malraux made a speech, in 1938, during a
> meeting organised in California for aid to Spain, chaired by
> Chevalier.
>
> Dr Oppenheimer declared that since then Malraux had
> profoundly altered his political opinions, that he had become
> a fervent supporter of de Gaulle and his most intimate ad-
> viser, and that he had abandoned politics to devote himself
> to purely philosophical and literary work.

He made a brief visit to Canada, first to Toronto, then to
Montreal, where an old worker walked up to him and put his
gold watch in his hand. When asked why, he replied that he
had nothing more valuable to give the Spanish comrades . . .
Malraux returned to France in the middle of April.

Ce Soir, the Communist daily that Aragon had just founded,
gave widespread coverage to Malraux's visit to the United
States. 'André Malraux tells how he touched the heart of
America!' – this was the headline of a short interview given
to Edith Thomas:

> He now remembers the crowds that he had to convince,
> and that he did convince. To the Babbits of the foreign study
> circles, to the factory workers, to the peasants of Canada, to
> the stars of Hollywood, Malraux talked of Spain . . . When
> an entire country is littered with wounded, he said, no exist-
> ing medical service is adequate. When a wounded leg is
> treated after an X-ray examination, the leg becomes normal

again. Without an X-ray plate, the leg almost always remains shorter. When I set out for Valencia, there were no more X-ray plates.

When a man is wounded in the arm by bullets, his wounds are cleaned by placing a tent in each wound. With anaesthetics, there is hardly any problem. Without anaesthetics, the wound has to be reopened slowly every day. When I left they were nearly out of anaesthetics . . .

Then a man jumped on to the table, his back to the chimney, and shouted to the crowd: 'Well! Who's going to give the first dollars? You, Madam, you . . .' He pointed his finger at her and the woman gave money. Others followed . . .[6]

Between mid-April and early July 1937, between a lecture, a meeting and another visit to Spain to hand over to President Azaña the fruits of his American tour, Malraux worked at his book. He often carried around with him a few sheets of scribbled paper.

On 3 July he was in Valencia, where, the following day, the second International Congress of Writers was to take place. This fulfilled a wish expressed by José Bergamin at the end of the first congress, which had taken place two years earlier at the Mutualité. President Azaña received the participants and Alvarez del Vayo, Foreign Minister in the Negrin cabinet, which in May had replaced that of Largo Caballero, moved among the delegates.

The pro-Soviet 'line' increasingly gained support. Ehrenburg, Fadeyev and Alexis Tolstoy were the most important figures at the congress. Malraux, too, was very much in evidence, accompanied by Stephen Spender, Hemingway, Tristan Tzara, Nicolas Guillen, José Bergamin, Antonio Machado, Anna Seghers . . . In his *Memoirs*, Ehrenburg describes this congress as 'a travelling circus':[7] it opened at Valencia on 4 July, continued at Madrid on 6 July, then moved on to Barcelona and ended two weeks later in Paris, at the Théâtre de la Porte Saint-Martin.

The Soviet delegates had wanted to turn the Congress into a trial of André Gide – first because his *Retour d'URSS* was a thorn in their flesh, and secondly because they desperately needed something to divert attention from the international

scandal caused by the assassination of Andrès Nin, the leader of
the POUM (which the Russians called 'Hitlero-fascist', on account of its Trotskyist sympathies). Everyone knew that Nin
had been kidnapped and liquidated by the agents of the NKVD
in Spain. Very little was said about Nin on the platforms of the
'travelling circus', and a great deal more about Gide, that other
'Hitlero-fascist'.

In his speech in Madrid on 8 July José Bergamin, brandishing Gide's tiny pamphlet, cried: 'This book is insignificant in
itself, but the fact that it has appeared at the very moment
when the fascists are firing on Madrid lends it, for us, a tragic
significance . . . This book by Gide is not a criticism, but a
calumny . . .'[8]

Malraux remained silent.

Bergamin was more inspired when he spoke of his own
country. At Valencia, on 4 July, he set the tone of the first
session of the Congress: 'All Spanish literature is written with
the blood of the Spanish people. Lope de Vega wrote: "Blood
cries out the truth in dumb books." Today the same blood cries
out the truth through dumb victims . . .'[9] And on the stage of
the Théâtre de la Porte Saint-Martin, it was again Bergamin
who aroused the sympathy of a crowd that was obviously
already won over, when he cried: 'We are life against death.'[10]

'The outstanding figure of the congress was undoubtedly
André Malraux,' writes Spender. 'The congress was dominated
by his nervous sniff and tic.'[11] With Ilya Ehrenburg at his side,
Malraux very nearly got himself killed on the road between
Valencia and Madrid, when their car hit a lorry carrying muni-
tions. 'The catastrophe was only just avoided,' writes Koltzov.
This merely served to give him a bigger ovation when he
appeared on the platform at Madrid. A similar welcome was
given to Gustav Regler and Ludwig Renn, who had taken over
the command of their brigades. But was this ovation enough to
stifle what Malraux must have felt as tacit acceptance of a
shameful act, the silence that surrounded the assassination of
Andrès Nin? How could a writer who, at that very time, was
portraying those magnificent anarchist fighters Puig and the
Negus, and Socialists like Magnin and Scali, keep silent about
the liquidation of a revolutionary like the leader of the POUM?

These problems concerning the contradictory demands of action and purity, spontaneity and efficiency, the transformation of 'the lyrical illusion' into hope, the Apocalypse into victory, formed the web of Malraux's finest book. He wrote it in six months, between May and October, after his return from the United States, during the spring and summer of 1937, while around Brunete the Republican army, formed at last, was losing its best cadres, those whose trials and maturity are described in *L'Espoir*.

Historically, *L'Espoir* was written out of the prospects opened up by the victory of Guadalajara and by the formation of Juan Negrin's government, which amounted to a seizure of concrete responsibilities by the Communists – responsibilities that involved the elimination of revolutionary tendencies for which the war against Franco was meaningful only if accompanied at the same time by social revolution, and the exercise of politico-military power by those who gave absolute priority to the war effort. This strategy which, with the replacement of Caballero by Negrin, became the official line of the Republican régime, necessitated an alliance with the bourgeoisie, and therefore the protection of property, discipline in battle, the dissolution of the 'spontaneous' groups, and lastly an unconditional alliance with the USSR, the only power that had decided to support the Republic and was capable of doing so.

Malraux set out for Spain in July 1936 under the spell of Anarcho-syndicalism; he returned a year later to describe its practical defeat and to stress the need for party discipline. 'The whole question is whether we will succeed in transforming revolutionary fervour into revolutionary discipline', he declared in February 1937, at the meeting that had so strongly affected François Mauriac.

In Malraux's oeuvre, *L'Espoir* represents the triumph of objective truth over imagination, of 'doing' over 'being'. With *La Condition humaine,* he had wanted to create a new type of metaphysical novel in the image of *The Brothers Karamazov.* For many reasons, one of which was a new reading of Tolstoy in 1935 (after his visit to the USSR, where, he observed, the work of Tolstoy was more highly valued than that of Dostoevsky, who until then had haunted him more perhaps than any other writer), he wanted his book on Spain to be read in the light of *War and Peace*.

But there was another influence that had led him to give greater importance to objective reality: his growing admiration for a certain kind of journalism, which he had already expressed in his preface to Andrée Viollis' *Indochine S.O.S.* In *L'Espoir*, he uses extracts from the dispatches of another great journalist, Louis Delaprée, of *Paris Soir*. Many of the most moving scenes concerning the crushing of Madrid by Franco's planes were inspired by Delaprée's reports, or are taken directly from them.

Above all, perhaps, it was his own experience as politico-military organiser of the Apocalypse over a period of seven months that impelled him towards a greater dependence on objective reality. When writing about China, he had given as much importance to souls as to bodies. In Spain, the all too obvious presence of bodies and the demands of action deeply affected him and gave his narrative and his heroes the 'density' of which he had always dreamt.

I shall not try to unravel the thematic intricacies of *L'Espoir*. The central intrigue is that of Manuel, a young revolutionary musician who, to be more efficient for the sake of the revolution, for 'the organisation of Apocalypse' becomes a dedicated Communist and an attentive pupil of a colonel of the Guardia Civil, Ximenès, a Catholic but a trained soldier. Running parallel throughout the book are the stories of Garcia, head of Red intelligence, who is advocating organisation versus spontaneity; of Scali, the Italian airman, divided between his ideal of democracy and the demands of efficiency; of Alvear, the old aesthetician who loves revolution without illusion; of Guernico, the Catholic writer supporting the Reds; of Hernandez, the liberal officer shot by the Francoists.

Nor shall I dwell for long on the 'keys' of the book, fascinating as such an exercise would be. But one would dearly like to know how much there is of Malraux himself in Magnin,[12] and how much of Serre (the former boss of a French aviation company who served in Spain), and also how much of himself Malraux put into Garcia, who is usually his spokesman and whose dazzling style is closest to Malraux's own; how much of Segnaire in Attignies and how much of Maréchal in Gardet;

how much of Gustavo Duran, the musician, in Manuel, of Matthews (the *New York Times* correspondent) in Shade, of Ascaso, the anarchist leader, in Puig, of Miguel Martinez, the Mexican militant, in Enrique, of Colonel Escobar in Ximenès, of Koltzov and Nicola Chiaromonte in Scali, and José Bergamin in Guernico.

From the historical point of view, and from the point of view of the development of Malraux's political consciousness – of his consciousness simply – this many-faceted book, as prolific and rich as life itself, overflowing with aesthetic and human generosity, is stretched, centred, ordered around the story of Manuel, the combatant who, day after day, sacrifices all that he holds most dear as a man to revolutionary efficiency: 'Every step I've taken towards greater efficiency . . . has estranged me more and more from my fellow-men. Every day I'm getting a little less human.'

From this point of view, the key scene of the novel – because, for Malraux, all creation, from *La Condition humaine* to the *Antimémoires*, boils down sooner or later to a problem of communication – is that in which two soldiers in Manuel's brigade, accused of treason, grab him by the knees and beg for mercy. Because he has to choose, he thinks, between victory and pity, he says nothing. And one of the men looks up to him and says: 'Ah, so you've no voice, now, as far as we're concerned!'[13] Kyo was horrified that he could not hear others' voices by the same means as he heard his own. Manuel gets to the point of no longer wishing to hear his own.

This huge, intense book, passionate and true at once, this book, which by sheer strength inspires and by its brilliance overwhelms all those who claim, through reportage, to make truth more true than fact, is a book for combat. Some months after its publication, Malraux had his first meeting with Gaëtan Picon, who expressed astonishment at the lukewarm reception given to *L'Espoir* by the critics who had so enthusiastically welcomed *La Condition humaine*. Malraux, who himself rates this book above any he has written before the *Antimémoires*, replied: 'That's because to like *L'Espoir* you have to be on the left – I don't mean Communist . . .'

Yet it was the Communists and their sympathisers who

provided the first readers of *L'Espoir*, large extracts of which were published in *Ce Soir* from 3 November to 3 December 1937. Since Aragon was the editor of the paper it was probably he who wrote the (anonymous) introduction to the work, which appeared beneath a large photograph of Malraux:

> Today we begin publication of extracts from a new novel by André Malraux: *L'Espoir*. Ever since the events in Spain began, we know that this great writer, who was awarded the Prix Concourt in 1933 for *La Condition humaine*, wanted to defend his ideas in some active way and that he created and commanded a Republican air squadron. His new book was created out of this living experience and it expresses this experience with all the resources that the author of *Le Temps du Mépris* has at his command. Just as in the midst of war Barbusse's *Le Feu* gave voice to the ordinary soldier, so *L'Espoir* rises from the battlefields of Spain.[14]

L'Espoir appeared in the bookshops at the end of November 1937. Malraux's Spanish friends were taken aback. Most of them admired the book, but would have agreed with President Azaña when he said: 'Ah! these Frenchmen! Trust them to get an officer of the *Guardia Civil* to philosophise!' It is hardly surprising if they did not recognise themselves in these characters, apart, perhaps, from Guernico and the Negus, who, after all, had more in common with Malraux than with anyone else. It is easy to recognise in the streets a Mr Micawber. It is more difficult with a Captain Ahab.

In France, the right-wing critics were markedly hostile. On the left, the reception was generally favourable, sometimes naïvely enthusiastic. Right or left, two commentaries on *L'Espoir* particularly stand out. The first was the work of a writer who was separated from Malraux by many things, even though they were both heirs of Nietzsche and Barrès – Henry de Montherlant. In his *Cahiers* there is this, on *L'Espoir*, published only ten years later:

> Monstrous things have been said about this book: that it is mere journalism! . . . Attention is an important quality in Malraux. It is a rule that the beauty of descriptive art usually

derives from precision, that is, from attention. Did he take notes? Did he take notes at the very moment things happened?[15] That it displays an absence of literary qualities – in this he often reminds one of Tolstoy . . . The pages on the shootings (page 184) represents a peak in the art of writing . . . In Malraux intelligence and action are reconciled – a rare event.

The reception given to *L'Espoir*, which was not proportionate to its value, can be attributed to a wish to prevent Malraux from occupying too great a place. I suspected as much, and I have been confirmed in my suspicions.[16]

It was in the American Review *New Republic*, in August 1938, that Louis Aragon expressed his feelings about *L'Espoir*. I quote from this article all the more readily in that when I questioned Aragon in 1972 about Malraux, he referred me 'to a text published in 1938 about *L'Espoir* which says all there is to say':

L'Espoir is a fundamental book in which our highest ideals are confronted with the most pressing realities . . . It expresses our time, and of what other book could one say as much? Malraux's greatness lies not in the fact that he explains the Spanish war, but in the fact that he plunged into it. Since *La Condition humaine*, a profound change has come over Malraux. Public events no longer serve as a pretext or framework for his work: they bear him up. Malraux is a realist in the sense that he transcends reality . . . I have it from the author himself that *L'Espoir* is a totally new book in his oeuvre because 'for the first time', he told me, 'I had more material than I could use.'

Aragon then confronts Malraux with this formula taken from the first extract from *La Psychologie de l'art* to be published in *Verve*:[17] 'The material of art is not life but always another work of art.' Well? 'In that contradiction,' Aragon declares, 'I find the tragedy of modern man, the *ecce homo* of this time of wars and revolution. The man who risks his life for the Spanish people writes at the same time that the only people in the world worthy of being saved is the people of statues.'

'An article that says all there is to say,' said Aragon. It certainly says a great deal about André Malraux.

24 *Hopes unfulfilled*

ON 27 May 1938, under the title 'The return of André Malraux', *Ce Soir* published an interview with the author of *L'Espoir*, who had just returned once again from Valencia and Madrid:

'Spain?'

'I shall be speaking at the Mutualité tonight. Not now, please, I can't go on. I haven't slept for 78 hours ... I've just come back from the Madrid front. The Republican army has been formed at last. There is now revolutionary discipline; it is admirable. The Republic will win. The new government has decided to "make war".'

'Days of hope?'

'No, certainty.'

But Malraux was already less preoccupied with strategy than with a new passion: the cinema. Not that it had led him to abandon his companions in the struggle. The film that he was making had been suggested, according to Max Aub,[1] during his visit to the United States, where friends had led him to hope that a film by him, about the war, could be shown in 1800 cinemas, and profoundly shock American public opinion – it might even drag the United States out of its neutrality ... At the Congress of Writers held in July in Valencia, a number of Spanish leaders (Azaña? Negrin? Alvarez del Vayo?) had shown interest in this possibility of shaking international opinion. Malraux was assured of help.

Shortly after finishing his book, early in 1938, André Malraux began to prepare the film. His friend Édouard Corniglion-

Molinier would be a co-producer. He assembled a first-class team of technicians – with the cameraman Louis Page, the editor Boris Pesquine, the Spanish writer Max Aub for the scenario, and the fine critic Denis Marion as assistant. Like everyone in the squadron from November 1936 onwards, they were volunteers: they had to be if they were to run the risks involved in working in a city like Barcelona, constantly under attack from enemy bombers based in Majorca.

Was the cinema Malraux's latest craze? Yes and no. Yes, if one considers that he is a man who concentrates totally on whatever subject happens to hold his attention. In 1936–7 it was impossible to talk to him about anything other than the bombings – as Ehrenburg observed, not without irony. But lacking planes, lacking men, lacking perhaps a mission, he suddenly rediscovered an art that had always interested him and which, because no other art is so close to action, was to fascinate him.

At thirteen he was enthralled by Pierre Decourcelle's melo-drama *Les Deux Orphelines,* at sixteen by Chaplin, at twenty by *Doctor Caligari* and at twenty-five by von Stroheim's first films. In 1934, in Moscow, his most stimulating hours were those he spent with Eisenstein, even when they had to give up the film of *La Condition humaine* that the great director was thinking of making. And in 1936, he was an enthusiastic admirer of Abel Gance's *Napoleon*, which had continued to haunt him. He was more than a gifted amateur, as his reflections on 'The Psychology of the Cinema', written the following year, abundantly showed. He had always dreamt – for the past ten years, at least – of making films. Now he was making one.

He very soon decided not to try and adapt the whole of his book – the proportions, the diversity, the ambitions of which were not translatable into images, if for no other reason than the slenderness of the resources at their disposal. They would concentrate, therefore, on a few significant episodes: the recruitment among the people, the role of the 'fifth column', the attack launched on a cannon by a car, the bombing of an enemy airfield and scenes of fraternisation in the mountains.

The 'autonomous government' of Barcelona put at their disposal an apartment, two secretaries, one of the three studios in

the city and civilian extras – mostly recruited in the small
Catalan village near the airport of Prat de Llobregat – and
soldiers (about 2500 men for the two or three crowd scenes).

From the beginning, Malraux had rejected the title of the
novel as too broad in scope. He first thought of calling the film
Sang de Gauche[2] – the second subtitle of the second part of the
novel, which is a very fine title. They then decided on *Sierra de
Teruel*, which is not entirely accurate, for most of the scenes
take place elsewhere. In the end, after the war, they adopted
Espoir, which is an attenuation of the book's title, but which is
sufficiently close to it to serve as a bait to the public.

But the film that Malraux made was not entirely the film he
wanted to make. During a conversation – undated – with
Claude Mauriac,[3] Malraux describes the film he had dreamt of.
It was to open with the image of a bull whose bellowing was to
merge into that of an air-raid siren: but in Republican Spain,
says Malraux, there were no more bulls to be found (they were
eaten). The film was to continue with the image of herds of
cattle being pursued by Franco's army, which then throws itself
like a tide on to the Republican positions. Lastly, a group of
peasants were to fill the bell of the village church with dyna-
mite, put it on to a cart, and launch it at the enemy tanks . . .

In fact, Malraux wanted the film to be full of symbols and
metaphors, as charged with poetic and allegorical images as
Battleship Potemkin. It was not so much the slenderness of the
resources at his disposal as force of circumstances and his passionate involvement in the struggle that led him to make a
more direct, starker film. *Espoir* is not so much the work of an
illustrious disciple of Eisenstein as that of a brilliant precursor
of Rossellini.

Of the thirty-nine sequences that make up the scenario, only
twenty-eight were shot, and in conditions that give this unprecedented and inimitable film an incomparable value. Authors,
technicians and actors moved in turn from Barcelona to Prat de
Llobregat, then to Tarragona, to Cervera, to the village of
Collbato in the Montserrat Sierra – where the great final scene
of the descent of the wounded was shot – and lastly to France,
Villefranche-de-Rouergue, whose admirable cloister is so profoundly Spanish, and to the studios at Joinville.

Shooting began on 20 July 1938, shortly after the battle of the Ebro, which, after the early Republican successes, was to decide the fate of the war. Barcelona had been bombed for five months by the Italians. Two months later, it was Munich . . . It was a strange production, in which reality and fiction constantly intermingled. The July heat is heavy in Catalonia, and in the Calle de Santa Anna and at Prat, Malraux, in his white trousers and sandals, looked like a thin tennis player – beside him he had a pretty partner, with unruly hair, wearing a sleeveless linen dress, Josette Clotis.

There were plenty of incidents. One day, says Boris Pesquine, the fascist airforce turned the Montjuich studio 'into a real sieve: bomb splinters fell into the paint pots'.[4] Another day, the stuntmen engaged by the artists' trade union were supposed to take part in a scene in which a car drives straight at the enemy: 'You start the car, then you throw yourself on the ground!' 'Me? but I'm a ventriloquist!' The artists' trade union had sent the wrong men.

Louis Page, Denis Marion and Max Aub have told innumerable stories of the same kind – how, for example, in order to create the illusion that the old Potez that had been pieced together in the studio was flying through cloud, they used a spray gun to paint a 'sky', which was placed on a trolley and rolled behind the plane: when speeded up the scene makes one dizzy . . .

Lighting, make-up and film-stock came from France. The negative print was sent to a Paris laboratory to be developed. The chief cameraman, Louis Page, worked in the dark: a month went by before he could see the rushes. The sound equipment was very defective: the soundtrack had to be re-recorded in France. 'Every time there was an alert – and there was an alert at least once a day,' he says, 'the electric current was cut off at the power station and was switched on again only fifty minutes after the end of the alert . . . For a whole night, we worked on the top of Montjuich hill, the floods lighting up the sky over the town, itself subjected to the strictest blackout. Fortunately, it was one of the rare nights when the Italian planes did not come from the Balearic Islands.'[5] Page, too, has remembered some of his 'tricks': for example, at the beginning of the great sequence in the Teruel Sierra, when a plane had to be shown crashing into the mountain, the camera was placed in a cable-car that skimmed the rocks near Montserrat – the impression of impact was quite startling.[6]

The shooting of the film was not quite finished, when, in January 1938, the Francoist forces of General Yagüe laid siege to Barcelona. The whole team had to move out, even though several sequences had still to be shot. A few hours before the entry into the city of the Moorish advance guard, Malraux and his team piled into three cars and crossed the French frontier at Port-Bou.

The final scenes were shot in the studio at Joinville. Malraux improvised a new montage – which he had begun again and again – and the film was finished in July 1939. Three weeks later, a showing was organised at the Le Paris cinema on the Champs-Élysées for the Spanish premier Negrin, who had taken refuge in France. The following week a second showing took place in another cinema, where, without knowing one another, a large number of Malraux's friends were in the audience, notably Claude Mauriac and Roger Stéphane. The film made a great impression.

The producers had planned to put the film on general release in September. But the intervening weeks had seen the signing of the German–Soviet pact, the declaration of war, the banning of the French Communist Party, and the introduction of censorship. *Sierra de Teruel,* a revolutionary film, was forbidden by the government of Édouard Daladier, beside whom Malraux had once sat on the platforms of the Popular Front. It was only by mistake that the only existing copy of the film was not destroyed under the occupation. The German censors had a list which stated that the copy of the film was labelled under the name of Corniglion-Molinier. The one they destroyed was the second copy of another film produced by Corniglion, Carné's *Drôle de Drame* – of which, fortunately, there were other copies. Thus *Espoir* was able to survive thanks to Marcel Carné. At the Liberation, Édouard Corniglion-Molinier, now a Free French general, but still the film's producer and owner, sold it to a distributor who renamed it *Espoir*, cut a good third of the final scene and added a prologue by Maurice Schumann whose voice, that of the spokesman of BBC 'Free France', was then very popular.

The film that Malraux, recently demobilised, but still 'Coronel', showed in certain cinemas as 'a typically proletarian work',[7] was very successful. Three scenes were particularly overwhelming: the one in which two Red soldiers armed only with a machine-gun drove straight at a fascist cannon (in the novel, it is Puig the anarchist who does this), and as they crash a flight of birds fills the screen; the scene with the peasant José, who, from the air, cannot find his village in the Sierra – in the novel a magnificent scene which is made even finer in the film; and, lastly, the scene of the descent of the wounded companions of the *España* squadron down the mountain, the high point of both book and film.

Fragmented by the circumstances of its creation, severely affected by lack of resources, clumsy, episodic, sometimes pretentious and over-emphatic, *Espoir* remains an impressive film, worthy of Malraux's great models, Eisenstein and Dovzhenko, worthy above all of the great book on which it is based. In October 1945, it won the Prix Louis Delluc, which is awarded to the most original, most creative French film of the year. No one doubted that this choice was a good one, though there were those who resented the fact that Malraux had become one of the closest collaborators of General de Gaulle.

Two years after its appearance in France, *Espoir* was shown in the United States. It had no success, but the great critic James Agee wrote fearlessly: 'Homer might recognise in this film, it seems to me, the only work of our time that is totally in accord with his own.' We are assured that André Malraux warmly appreciated this article, but omitted to point out that the reference was to a blind poet.

PART V

THE POWER OF THE SWORD

25 The camp

DEFEATED. He was on the defeated side, with the Spanish people, crushed by a coalition of the Axis powers, Moorish battalions, Salazar's régime, the Spanish bourgeoisie and Church – and the complicity of an idiotic France and an England which – including Winston Churchill – was then more concerned with the dangers that a victory for the 'Reds' might bring to the exploitation of the Rio Tinto mines than with the fatal risks involved in the rise of fascism.

When one has so forcefully and so frequently declared, through Garine in *Les Conquérants,* or Garcia in *L'Espoir*, one's determination to reconcile the people and victory and to be at last on the victorious side; when to achieve this, one has taken, as did Manuel, the hard path of subjecting oneself to the discipline of Stalin's party and chosen with him to make war rather than revolution, defeat takes on an even more horrible face. When, on 26 January 1939, he hurriedly recrossed the Catalan frontier in order to escape the advance guards of that same Yagüe that he had arrested at Medellin thirty months earlier, when he heard the gunfire of the last fratricidal battles between Colonel Casado and the Communists in a Madrid besieged by the Franco forces, when he read the accounts of the Caudillo's entry into the Spanish capital, what could André Malraux think? 'Generosity is being the victor . . .' muses Hernandez before the firing squad at Toledo; and Durruti himself said: 'We're ready to relinquish everything but victory . . .'

It was all over, but there was still this film to finish – the film that was supposed to drag the Americans out of their neutrality . . . And then, of course, they were getting closer to war, the first whiff of which he had felt in the summer of 1939. That summer that did not pass without a still more terrible blow to Malraux and his comrades: the signing on 23 August 1939 of the German–Soviet pact. Stalin with Hitler . . . That evening, Malraux dined with Max Aub, who had worked with him on *Sierra de Teruel,* and who had just been with him when the film was shown to Juan Negrin. They talked about the pact: 'Revolution at such a price, no . . .' said Malraux.[1]

Yet Malraux refrained from breaking with his allies from the Spanish war. Defeat had not led him to believe that the horrors of Nazism could be balanced out by those of Stalinism. As late as May 1939, he took part in an International Antifascist Conference, in Paris, side by side with Aragon, Paul Langevin and Marcel Cachin, the founder of the French Communist Party. He still believed that the struggle against Nazism could be carried out most effectively from their side – and his experiences in Spain left him with no illusions about the true nature of Nazism. Yet did this conference help to detach him from this cause? In his account of it, Ehrenburg notes sadly that 'the speeches seemed empty repetitions of things heard long ago'.[2] In May 1939, two months after the entry of the German tanks into Prague, what was the use of speeches? Or, indeed, of an unconditional alliance with a power whose national interests were to prevail, for a long time at least, over any other consideration?

Thirty years later, André Malraux had this to say about his views at the time:

> I was not so naïve as not to understand Stalin's reasons, and even to approve of them, from an ideological point of view. But you see, the French people was mobilised, thrown into a war that the Moscow pact had accelerated and aggravated by allowing Hitler to throw all his forces against us . . . If the rapid defeat, which we could not foresee, had not occurred, our proletariat would have undergone the same holocaust as twenty-five years earlier. Imagine a de Gaulle at the head of the French army, galvanising the struggle on the national territory in 1939 . . . The French proletariat

would have taken a terrible beating! So you see, Stalin's calculations meant less to me than that probability . . .[3]

So, however severely he viewed the pact and what it involved in the short term for the French masses, Malraux – in whom one can detect a rather abstract internationalism giving place to a more concrete patriotism – refused to make any public condemnation of it. To his friend Raymond Aron, who in October 1939 urged him to put his prestige and influence in the service of a necessary clarification, he replied: 'I will say nothing, I will do nothing against the Communists as long as they are in prison . . .'[4]

Malraux also refused to break with his Soviet friends, at a time when he was not only denounced by the right, but vilified in almost all left-wing circles. Ilya Ehrenburg recalls, not without a certain emotion, that during his stay in France in the winter of 1939–40 (he was writing his novel *The Fall of Paris*), he did not receive many visits – other than from Rafael Alberti, Jean-Richard Bloch (both Communists) and Malraux.[5]

Just after the signing of the pact, André Malraux and Josette Clotis set out for Corrèze. At Beaulieu-sur-Dordogne there was a hotel they particularly liked, 'Le Bordeaux', run by their friend Mme Fournier. Above all there was an admirable Romanesque church, with one of the finest tympanums in existence, 'the only one in which, behind the arms of Christ stretched out to embrace the world, the sculptor had depicted the arms of the cross like a prophetic shadow'.[6] It was, too, within sight of this masterpiece that Malraux retired, in order at last to write *La Psychologie de l'art*, which had been haunting him even before his departure for Spain – and which he had not forgotten even in the midst of the battle (as the dialogue in *L'Espoir* between Scali and old Alvear shows). His defeat as a man of action made it all the more pressing and necessary to carry out this project.

Yet on 1 September, he knew that there was no time left. In the morning, he had passed two of the old women who worked in the hotel on the stairs, 'pattering up to their rooms with tears streaming down their long-suffering faces':[7] Poland had been invaded by Hitler – and call-up notices had already been

pasted up in front of the church at Beaulieu. 'Every time I try
to finish *La Psychologie de l'art,* a new war breaks out,' he wrote
to a friend at the time. They returned to Paris, via Moulins,
where they heard the news of the first battles. On 8 September
they were in Paris: Simone de Beauvoir, then a friend of Josette
and André, records the former chief of the *España* squadron
'trying to organise help for those foreigners who are being
forcibly conscripted into the Foreign Legion'.[8] He also looked
after Spanish friends that the French government was throwing
into camps like that at Vernet, and arranged to send help to
Juan Negrin's son in London.

'When you have written what I have written and there is a
war in France, you join it.'[9] This was how Malraux sums up his
state of mind in September 1939. So he tried to join up, pre-
ferably in the airforce: he had after all proved himself – whether
or not his experience at Medellin and Teruel was relevant to the
conflict that had now broken out. Apparently, it was not. Why
wasn't a Spanish *coronel* good enough to make a French lieutenant? Because the French army was that great stupid, inert
body that was to be routed eight months later by the tanks of
Rommel and Guderian. And for the same reason André Malraux who, with little inclination to play at soldiers in a barracks
in 1922, had managed to get himself exempted on rather flimsy
grounds, found himself seventeen years later deprived of the
right to fight.

Having been rejected by the air ministry, he thought for a
time of joining the Polish army. ('You'll see me in a *chapka* yet,'
he wrote to his friend Louis Chevasson.) But first he tried to get
into the tank corps – which for him had the double prestige of
his father, for whom he still felt a certain admiration, and of
T. E. Lawrence – adding that he wished to join as a private,
like the author of *Seven Pillars of Wisdom.*

He was accepted at last by the tank corps. And it was not to
be the least extraordinary of his innumerable transformations.
One must picture this famous writer, nearly forty years old,
who had recently had the rank and responsibilities of a prestigious if not important command, who treated as equals
several ministers and half a dozen Academicians and dined at
the most fashionable Paris houses, standing in a line of volun-

teers in the barracks square at Provins, opposite a local sergeant . . .

He was 'spotted' of course. The fact that he had had his tunic made at Lanvin's did not make it easier for him to pass unperceived. There was a sergeant in his unit who 'saw him coming', Malraux-the-Red, the revolutionary and, naturally, antimilitarist writer (he had not read *L'Espoir*). Albert Beuret – for that was the sergeant's name – summoned Malraux for a twenty-mile walk, at night. They set out, kitbags on their backs. Did the revolutionary give in? Certainly not! Malraux kept walking. At dawn, it was the sergeant who stopped and held out his hand to the writer. They became the best of friends.

The tank unit to which Malraux had been drafted was called D.C. 41–Ei–1. It was made up of elements from different regiments and was based at Provins, a charming town near Paris. He remained there from mid-November 1939 to 14 May 1940. Why? They visited the cafés, took the turret-guns to pieces and greased the caterpillars. The officers even found an exciting new task for their men: the search for four-leaf clovers![10]

It was an odd crew that the friend of André Gide and Paul Valéry found himself joining. There was Bonneau, the self-righteous pimp; Léonard, the fireman from the Casino de Paris, who, one night, one single night, had slept with the star of the show; and Pradé, the peasant from Lorraine, whose brother had served in the International Brigade in Spain ('And when you come back from there, you can give up any idea of looking for work!'). For Malraux, it was a change from the offices of the *NRF*; it was a change, too, from the little restaurants of Valencia and the studio at Montjuich . . . But, after all, we have seen him act the fool with the mechanics of the *España* squadron. He certainly must have amused Bonneau and Léonard, if not Pradé, who, with his flat face and his slanted eyes, reminded him so much of an Asiatic.

In the barrack-room at Provins he wrote several letters to friends in which he describes himself an 'an apprentice tanker', and assured them that 'the experience is oddly interesting. Not always fun . . . How different these men are from those of my other war! But it is something to talk about . . .'[11] And another day, he notes: 'everything is fine except that it is difficult to

write . . .' During his seven months at Provins, where he had
been spotted by Sergeant Beuret, not a single officer showed the
least interest in this famous recruit: no captain or colonel suggested an exchange of views or a better use of his gifts. It does
not say much for the leadership of the French army in 1940.

Were they still looking for four-leaf clovers, Malraux, Bonneau and Léonard, on 10 May, when von Manstein threw his
tanks across the Ardennes? Gamelin's response was to send
those armoured divisions which he had managed to scrape together, against the advice of every leading figure in the army,
towards Belgium.

Malraux was not part of this armada that slowly ground its
way across the roads of Flanders. The fine account in *Les
Noyers de l'Altenburg*, which Malraux takes up again in the
Antimémoires – the driver of the leading tank guided by strings
attached to his arms, the fear of ditches, the fall, the death-like
stupor, the return to life – all that, which the reader assumes to
be autobiographical, is the work of a novelist, inspired by an
adventure of a similar kind experienced by his father, Captain
Malraux, in 1918, by his own 'return' to life in 1934, over
Algeria, and by his discovery of the world of peasants and
ordinary people in 1940. In an interview with me on 29 January
1973, Malraux remarked:

> 1940? It was pitiful . . . The tanks we had at Provins were
> not fit to be taken outside the training ground. In May we
> did a few manoeuvres on foot, with anti-tank devices. We
> did a bit of shooting. I was very slightly wounded on 15 June.
> The next day we were taken prisoner like infantrymen,
> about halfway between Provins and Sens, where we were
> heading . . .

So there he was beneath the towers of Sens Cathedral, seventy
miles south-east of Paris, where, for the first night, the prisoners
slept – later, they were moved to a warehouse. There he found
himself in an amorphous herd of defeated men, whose anger
was stifled only by fatigue. It was not the former school court-
yard where, in *La Condition humaine*, Katow and Kyo held the
cyanide tightly in their hands. It was more like a cattle-market
surrounded by barbed wire, filled to capacity with exhausted

animals. There were over ten thousand 'hungry, haggard men in the grips of dysentery'.[12]

André Malraux did not attempt to give too apocalyptic a description of this experience. On 27 July, after six weeks of internment, he wrote to a friend: 'The conditions in the camp are tolerable . . . I wouldn't recommend it for a holiday, but one mustn't exaggerate . . .'

There were only two topics of conversation: the date they would be freed ('A month? You're crazy. They'll let us out in one or two weeks. What can they do with us here?') and the ideal menu. Hungry people are always like that. They try to outwit their hunger by dreaming of banquets, by composing fabulous menus. ('You know what I like best – a partridge stuffed with pâté de foie gras . . . At home . . .')

Some of the prisoners refused to take part in these games. One of these was the poet Jean Grosjean,[13] who wandered through the camp, stepping over outstretched bodies dreaming of fresh cream and hot pâtés. He came across somebody who seemed, like him, in search of conversation, and who suddenly asked: 'Why have we lost the war?' They went on talking. They saw each other again. Grosjean was struck by the fact that his companion did not see the war in wholly European terms, but talked of Asia, the Near East and the United States. Three days later, he learnt that his companion was Malraux. One day, towards the end of the month, they found one of de Gaulle's first statements – which the armistice press published for a week.[14] Malraux liked it. Grosjean did not.

The local farmers asked for volunteers for the harvest. Several of the prisoners, including Malraux, saw it as an opportunity of enjoying a relaxation of surveillance. The volunteers numbered eleven, including André Malraux, Jean Grosjean and Sergeant Albert Beuret. They were drafted to a farm in the little village of Collemiers, where they were placed under the surveillance of a dashing Lt Metternich. They were not very comfortable – they slept in the straw. 'I wouldn't put my horse there!' exclaimed the German lieutenant, who got them beds. But most of them were thinking of how they would get away.

But for Malraux this problem had an added dimension. His brother Roland had come to warn him at the end of September that the Germans had decided to give at least a show of freedom to certain writers in order to show the American public how 'liberal' they were and that his name, together with Gide's, was on the list. The Germans would be looking for him. Rather than take part in such an operation, he had to escape.[15] Malraux took his problem to the village mayor, who was responsible for their presence, and offered to give him the money he would need to pay the ransom that the Germans would demand. The mayor rejected this curious offer: he would be content if half the 'harvesters' were still there in the cold season. As for the others, he would arrange something . . .

Clara, who had now finally separated from André,[16] found herself brought back once again, she says, into her husband's life. She and her brother-in-law Roland brought the prisoner clothes, shoes and some money.[17] Although the shoes produced by this family plot were too small, he set out without hindrance, accompanied by the Abbé Magnet, who offered him temporary hospitality at his home in the Drôme. A quiet episode in his life with which, not without a certain wit, he opens the otherwise action-packed *Antimémoires*: 'In 1940 I escaped with the future chaplain of the Vercors . . .'[18] This priest, who died in the Maquis, learnt from the fifteen years that he had been hearing confessions that 'the fundamental fact is that there is no such thing as a grown-up person . . .'[19]

26 Interlude by the sea

WHERE had André Malraux taken refuge in this defeated, invaded France? He had gone to what was then called the 'free zone'. The defeat of her armies had split France in two. By the terms of the armistice agreement of 22 June 1940, the German army took possession of the so-called 'occupied zone' (the north-east, the north, the west and the Atlantic coast). The other zone (the east, the centre, the south) was termed 'free': a government presided over by Marshal Pétain, one of the victors of 1918, ruled it under the constant pressure of the Nazis who, in November 1942, when the American and British allies landed in North Africa, finally crossed the demarcation line and invaded the whole of France. The entire country was now subjected to their brutal military administration.

The Jews were the first to suffer. They were forced to wear a yellow star, which the Germans regarded as a sign of disgrace, and many of them were deported in groups to the extermination camps. As a result of these cruel conditions, the rift between André and Clara became permanent. Clara, endangered by the anti-Jewish measures, went into hiding in the Toulouse area, then in Lot, where her husband came to live after 1942. However, they did not see each other again until after the war and then only to arrange a divorce. Clara joined the Resistance much earlier than André and carried out many missions, despite the risks she was running, not only for herself but also for her young daughter Florence. One evening, near the Spanish frontier, she thought she had fallen into a Gestapo trap: for once she regretted having given birth to the little girl sleeping in her arms on a station platform.

For some time, André Malraux's lot was to be an easier one
than Clara's. In the so-called 'free' zone, until November 1942,
an 'Aryan' did not need to feel too worried by the Nazi presence.
He could move about as he wished, and relations were maintained with foreign countries, in particular with the United
States, which had an ambassador at Vichy, the seat of the Pétain
government.

The atmosphere of defeat was heavy, German power seemed
overwhelming, the division in the country and in people's
minds was made all the more cruel in that, in occupied Paris, a
small fraction of the French intelligentsia collaborated with the
Nazis. But a sort of life went on, burdened with material cares.

As André Malraux was making for the free zone, in October
1940, Josette gave birth in a clinic in the Paris region – it is said
that she was so short of money that she had to leave the baby in
the clinic as security. The child was named Pierre-Gauthier.
Parents and child were reunited shortly afterwards and settled
on the Mediterranean coast.

About 20 November, Malraux moved in with Josette's family
at Hyères. With Clara then refusing a divorce, the situation was
not one to delight a provincial family: an illegitimate child, an
unmarried couple . . . And Malraux found himself once again
in an atmosphere similar to the one he had known in 1922
among the Goldschmidts at Auteuil. Minus the comfort, for the
Mediterranean zone was then short of supplies – with Gallimard's now under the control of the occupiers, Malraux was
cut off from all earnings from his books and was reduced to
poverty.

In December 1940, André Malraux set off for Nice, looking
for his friend Gide, and perhaps too – in view of the attitude of
Josette's mother – for lodgings some distance away from
Hyères. One day, in a tram in Nice, he felt someone tap his arm.
It was a young American called Varian Fry, who was then running the Emergency Rescue Committee at Marseilles. The task
of this organisation was to help refugees in difficulty and above
all to organise the departure from France of public figures
whose lives might be endangered if they remained. Fry had met
Malraux in March 1937 in New York during his propaganda
visit on behalf of the Spanish Republic. Malraux told him that

he had just escaped from a prisoner-of-war camp. Fry offered to get him out of the country – to which Malraux gave an evasive reply and talked rather of his need of money.[1] That, apparently, was no problem. The obliging Mr Fry acted as go-between with Random House, Malraux's American publishers, who were able to send him regular payments of money that would enable him to live fairly decently.

But his contacts with Varian Fry, which continued on a regular footing in the Committee's Marseilles offices in the rue Grignan, took on a more political form. Victor Serge, another 'interesting' refugee, who eventually took up Fry's offer to cross the Atlantic, often dined with Fry and Malraux. Serge had broken with Malraux when, in 1937, Malraux had refused to intervene on his behalf when he was detained in the USSR. Now, however, Serge had agreed to heal the breach.

Their thoughts were not only of the past. Since the American agent had the means of communicating with London, Malraux handed him a letter for General de Gaulle, offering his services to the 'Free French' forces who, he tells us in his *Antimémoires*, could not have had many airmen at their disposal. When he received no reply, he supposed that, like Pierre Cot, the former Air Minister of the Blum government, and a close friend of the 'Reds', he had been rejected by the leader of 'Free France' on account of his political commitments. Hence his somewhat reserved judgements on the leader of 'Free France' during the next few years – despite his approval of one of de Gaulle's first speeches at the end of June 1940.

Malraux adds that it was not until twenty years later that he got the true explanation of the silence from London: the messenger chosen by Fry (his secretary, Mme Bénédite) had been arrested by the police in a raid and had swallowed the message in the police van before she could be searched.[2] Thus Malraux's first attempt to contact de Gaulle misfired. But it must be remembered that, for Malraux, it had been rejected or ignored.

So he turned back to literature. For over four years he had corresponded with Robert Haas, his editor at Random House. Having struck up a friendship with Haas during his visit to America, in March 1937,[3] he sent him in January 1941, a few extracts from the book he had been writing over the past eight or nine months, under the title *La Lutte avec l'ange*. They consisted of 'The Ditch', an account of the fall of the tank he had been in into a trap, his subsequent 'Return to Life' and 'The Camp', an evocation of the life of the prisoners at Sens in June 1940, with which he was to open his book.

Malraux asked Haas to sell these pieces to 'some review that pays well' and to show them to a number of readers he trusted: Archibald MacLeish, Haakon Chevalier, the translator of *La Condition humaine*, now a professor at the University of San Francisco, José Bergamin, his Spanish friend, now a refugee at Mexico City, and Victoria Ocampo, editor of the Buenos Aires review *Sur*.

André Malraux did not allow embarrassment to stand in the way of the requests he made to his American publisher, who was now sending him seventy-five dollars a month. A few months later he wrote:

> I do not wish to ask any service of you that is not absolutely necessary or for any financial help that I cannot hope to repay. The greater your confidence in me during these 'troubled times', the more aware I am that I must avail myself of it only in cases of direst need and to the extent that my royalties will enable you to recover the advances you have been so kind as to send me.[4]

Since the end of January 1941, Josette, André and their young son had escaped from the uneasy hospitality of Mme Clotis and chosen to live in a delightful spot, Roquebrune Cap-Martin, where a friend of André's, the painter Simon Bussy, placed his villa at their disposal.[5] (It is said that Rudyard Kipling and T. E. Lawrence had stayed there. A small world!) Their stay at 'La Souco' (the name Bussy had given his villa) was temporarily interrupted by the return of the owner, from April to October 1941. During these six months, Josette and André had been able to rent another villa nearby, 'Les Camélias' at Cap d'Ail, near Saint-Jean Cap-Ferrat.

On 15 July, at Monte Carlo, Malraux had a long conversation with Roger Stéphane, who was to become one of the best 'Malrauxologists', and who describes him as being more optimistic and combative than depressed. He surprised Stéphane by approaching the problems of the war from a technological point of view. He spoke about the quality of the British bombs: 'He believes that German power has reached its height and is now on the decline . . . and that a German defeat would be a victory for the Anglo-Saxons . . . who will colonize the world and probably France.'

On the subject of the USSR, which the Nazi armies had invaded three weeks earlier, he felt sure that 'no German success in Russia is definitive, for one fine day anti-tank equipment will beat the tanks'. He believed in 'the solidity of the Soviet régime, thanks to some extent to the OGPU . . .' 'In the USSR,' he assured Stéphane, 'the police does not play the repressive role that it plays in fascist régimes: on the contrary, it constitutes the backbone of resistance.' 'Malraux did not conceal his wish to re-enter the war,' adds Stéphane, who presents him as highly sceptical about Marxism. Why, then, was Malraux closer to Communism than to fascism? Because 'Communism is open to the world, fascism is closed.'[6]

Two and a half months later, on 30 September 1941, Stéphane, who was going to Montpellier to join the 'Combat' resistance movement centred there, called on Malraux, who was still living at Cap d'Ail. There was no question, it seemed, of common action. Malraux expressed the fear that his young friend 'who was already under observation, would be caught', but 'approved of his desire to act'. He set little store by nationalism, which is 'a feeling, an idea, not a régime', and expressed doubts about the chances of a revolution in which 'the proletariat would eat less, but would have more dignity'. In fact, according to Stéphane, Malraux believed in an American victory that would bring in 'a European New Deal, a federal Europe, excluding the USSR'.[7]

A few days earlier, in mid-September, Jean-Paul Sartre had come from Paris (on bicycle) with Simone de Beauvoir in search of allies to form, the author of *La Force de l'âge*[8] assures us, a resistance movement to be known as 'Socialisme et Liberté'. Eventually they tracked down André Malraux. The travellers had thought of appealing to Martin du Gard, Gide and Malraux. Gide, who was the first to be approached, was the most evasive, suggesting that they visit his old companion of the antifascist committee of 1936–9. He wrote on this matter to Martin du Gard: 'I don't know what the effect will be, for Malraux does not like Sartre's writing at all. But Sartre has been warned . . .'[9]

Simone de Beauvoir gives this rather laconic version of the meeting:

> Malraux received Sartre in a magnificent villa at Saint-Jean Cap-Ferrat, where he was living with Josette Clotis. They lunched on Chicken Maryland, exquisitely prepared and served. Malraux heard Sartre out very courteously, but said that, for the time being at any rate, action of any sort would in his opinion be quite useless. He was relying on Russian tanks and American planes to win the war.[10]

Russian tanks? By attacking the Soviet Union, Hitler had given the war the world-wide dimensions that Malraux anticipated in June 1940. From a personal point of view, André Malraux felt very strongly that the noose was closing about him and about all those who were regarded as friends of the Soviet Union. In early June, he had written to Robert Haas: 'I may well have the opportunity of shaking hands with you before the end of the year.'[11] A month later he warned Haas: 'Soon it will be no longer possible to do anything for anyone.'[12]

Had Malraux at this time been asked to play an active part in the Resistance by leaders of networks who knew of his antifascist past and the proof that he had given in Spain of his gift – or taste – for action? Towards the end of 1940, he had been approached by a delegate from the network of the Musée de l'Homme, Boris Wildé, whom he had politely turned away. Shortly afterwards, at Roquebrune, the left-wing writer-dandy Emmanuel d'Astier (who was forming a team with their mutual friend Corniglion-Molinier) came to see him. Some time later, d'Astier set out for London in a submarine. Malraux had replied: 'I am marching, but I march alone.'[13] Another approach was made to Malraux shortly afterwards by Claude Bourdet, co-founder of the resistance movement 'Combat'. Again Malraux listened, adding: 'Have you arms and money? If you have, I'll go along with you. If not, it's not serious . . .' Bourdet could make no firm promises of arms or money.

The Malraux of those years, 1940–2, had rediscovered himself above all as a writer. For five years he had not spared himself as a political militant, he had made innumerable speeches and seen a good deal of action. He had fought in Spain to win. He had lost. He had fought in France and lost. He had not lost all faith in action, but he was tired of it, disturbed, more conscious of questions than of certainties. And what he had done had been done side by side with those who had seemed to him most effective, however unpleasant he may have found their doctrine, their theses and above all their methods: defeat had made their efficiency seem less admirable, and their methods more cruel. Now he felt a need to return to writing. And write he did. Between 1940 and 1943, there were three manuscripts on his table at once. First, *La Lutte avec l'ange*, the first two chapters of which, 'The Camp' and 'The Ditch', had been written in 1940 and offered to *Life* magazine, which had refused them. ('I am less well known than Herr Hitler, and less newsworthy,' Malraux dryly commented.)[14]

But he was not discouraged and, on 13 June 1942, wrote to his American publisher informing him that volume one of *La Lutte avec l'ange* (he did not yet say that it would be entitled *Les Noyers de l'Altenburg*) was finished. He told Robert Haas that he was publishing it in a de-luxe limited edition[15] and wondered whether Random House wished to do the same or to publish it in an ordinary edition, as volume one, or wait for the rest – 'two volumes at least'. He added, with touching good grace from someone who had been a publisher in his time: 'The main thing is that the present situation, whereby you have paid advances and possess nothing, should end.'

But *Les Noyers de l'Altenburg* did not take up all his time, or all his attention. Was this because Britain remained, until June 1941, the sole source of his hopes, the bastion of freedom, or because his hero in *La Lutte avec l'ange*, Vincent Berger, was born, spontaneously, as a sort of avatar of Lawrence of Arabia? Or rather because the problems of politico-military action, the results it yields, with all the bitterness, lies and deception it arouses, had haunted him since Spain, where he too had fought for something that had turned to ashes in his mouth?

Nevertheless, about the middle of 1942, he began a new piece of work, which he announced to his American correspondent thus:

> Having completed volume two [of *La Lutte avec l'ange*] and in order to get my breath back, I have written something else. It is called *Le Démon de l'absolu* and it is a book about Col. Lawrence. It is almost impossible to describe it in a few words, but I do not think I will be displaying undue pride if I say that it will be the most important book published on him so far: for nothing very important has been published about him. It will be finished in August . . . The book should sell very well, I think . . . I will then go back to volume two of *La Lutte avec l'ange*.[16]

A third manuscript was also occupying Malraux at this time. This was *La Psychologie de l'art*, which he had been talking about since 1935 and which had seemed, in 1939, to be his favourite project. But he was cut off from his sources, a long way from any museum worthy of the name, his library, his favourite 'advisers' – Drieu, Groethuysen. No good 'Imaginary Museum' can be created without a real museum to start with.

Malraux was not to be much luckier as a writer in the early 1940s than he was as a man of action in the late 1930s. He had practically worked out a system of getting his two works *Les Noyers* and *Le Démon de l'absolu* to the United States by the diplomatic channel – adding to Robert Haas that he would give the Library of Congress (then directed by his friend Archibald MacLeish) those of his manuscripts that were 'worthy of a state library'. But he had no sooner announced the good news to his publisher than, on 11 November 1942, the Germans invaded the free zone, thus cutting off all communication between France and the English-speaking countries. So Malraux's manuscripts did not reach either Random House or the Library of Congress. Only one copy of *Les Noyers de l'Altenburg* succeeded in reaching Switzerland.

Why did volume two of *La Lutte avec l'ange*, on which Malraux had been working since August, and *Le Démon de l'absolu*, which he said was already finished, remained unpublished – except for one chapter of the essay on Lawrence,

N'était-ce donc que cela?: already referred to? Were these texts 'destroyed by the Gestapo', as Malraux has often declared? His departures first from the villa 'La Souco' for the Chevassons' house in Allier, then for Corrèze, at the end of 1942, were not so hasty that he was unable to protect writings that were as valuable to him as his own life. Furthermore, we know from a witness that the 'Lawrence' had followed him to Corrèze. When, at the beginning of 1944, he joined the Maquis, his life became more eventful. But the Delclauxs, the very loyal friends with whom Josette and he were then living, could, if asked, have put these manuscripts in a safe place.

Did he himself destroy these works because he was not satisfied with them? It might be noted that he has always refused Gaston Gallimard permission to republish the pieces he spared from this autodafé – though he did use pieces from *Les Noyers* in his *Scènes Choisies*, published in 1947, and worked large sections of his unfinished novel into the *Antimémoires*. (From p. 26 to p. 109, the pages on his father's suicide, Nietzsche's madness, the discussion at the Altenburg, the Cairo museum and the museum at Aden . . .)

Les Noyers de l'Altenburg has never emerged from the humble condition of a ruined temple which the builder uses to quarry stones. Memories of the Cambodian adventure . . . People always quote the admittedly admirable scene in which the German soldiers bring back to their lines the gassed bodies of their Russian enemies. There is something of Tolstoy about these pages. But less attention is given to a number of other fine scenes, especially Vincent Berger's journey on horseback to Samarkand.

The first reader or first critic of *La Lutte avec l'ange* – Malraux had read extracts to him at 'La Souco' in 1942 – was Gide, who did not conceal a disappointment due as much perhaps to the fact that Malraux appeared to take little note of his criticisms as to the work itself. 'I recognized what he read to me at Cap-Martin,' he wrote dryly in June 1944, after reading the version published at Lausanne. 'I found all the weaknesses of form that I had pointed out to him earlier . . .' Since the vehemence does not carry the narrative forward as it does in *L'Espoir*, the defects of this breathless, vociferous and solemn style stand out all the more forcibly. But in the debate between perfection of form and creative impetus which, according to Malraux, so often opposed him to Gide, I find it easier to side with the author of *Les Noyers*.

The occupation of the southern zone by the German army in November 1942 condemned Malraux and his family to a more precarious life. A man could not be the former defender of Dimitrov and Thaelmann, or the ex-combatant in Spain, and expect to go free. He had to leave a region where he was too well known for his own safety. From 15 September to the end of October he spent several weeks with his friends Germaine and Louis Chevasson at the Château du Bon, a few kilometres from Commentry, in central France. His old schoolfriend was running a precision-tool factory that belonged to one of his Jewish friends – thus preventing the factory being placed under German sequestration.

This stay with Josette at the Chevassons' near the demarcation line gave him an opportunity of meeting a British officer representing the Buckmaster network in the *département*. Was it the first of such contacts? We have no information as to any previous ones. But everything seems to indicate that, from September 1942, Malraux was regarded in London backrooms as a potential agent. This does not mean that he was already working for the Resistance.

At the end of November 1942, Josette, André and little Gauthier left 'La Souco' and the Côte d'Azur for an area near the boundaries of Corrèze, Périgord and Lot, a sector where it was said that it was easy to hide and join the Maquis. It was also a region in which several of his friends had gathered around a delightful small town called Argentat, on the Dordogne: there was Emmanuel Berl, his wife Mireille (a witty singer who kept France singing throughout the Thirties) and his friend Bertrand de Jouvenel, the famous political scientist. The Malrauxs soon got to know the notary of Saint-Chamant, a neighbouring village, who offered to rent them the 'château' perched on the cliff, overlooking the tiny river, the station and the village.

There is something ironical about the fact that a man so concerned with aesthetics as André Malraux could have lived over a year and a half in this Disneyland castle, this fortress for an operetta Bluebeard, this Lorraine farmhouse that had somehow found its way into a Gascon landscape. But behind the house was an enormous tower, known as 'Caesar's Tower', which was not without style, and a strange little park *à la française* containing an odd statue of a priest in moss-covered stone; above all, there were some splendid trees around the house – horse-chestnuts, firs, birches and walnut trees (as at the Altenburg).

This hilly, wooded landscape delighted Josette, who was a true peasant girl at heart, and even André, who had begun to love nature – twenty years earlier, according to Marcel Arland, he 'cared only for a painted tree'. Though little given to shows of paternal affection (as Josette increasingly complained), he often set out to climb the hill opposite 'Caesar's Tower', holding Gauthier, nicknamed Bimbo, by the hand. The child thoroughly enjoyed himself out there. So did the father.

His study was situated (like General de Gaulle's at Colombey) in a rather ridiculous corner tower. In this pleasant circular room he continued to write, when he was not enjoying the company of Emmanuel Berl and his friends at Argentat. He had recently taken up again the manuscript of *La Psychologie de l'art* and was reworking *Le Démon de l'absolu* and *La Lutte avec l'ange*.

In 1943 he paid one visit to Paris. A friend saw him in a café on the Place Sainte-Clotilde, hiding himself with a sort of melodramatic naïvety ('Can't you see I'm plotting something? Please, don't recognize me . . .!'). He then met Drieu la Rochelle, one of the leaders of the pro-German intelligentsia, who found him 'desolate since he is no longer in Bolshevism' and half-heartedly *'gaullisant'*.[17]

A few friends sometimes came to Saint-Chamant. Gaëtan Picon, whom he regarded as the best critic of his work, spent three days there – at the hotel, since the 'château' had two lookout towers but no guest room. Malraux read him large extracts from *Les Noyers*, as he had done to Gide the year before. But Picon appreciated this work much more.

Every day the Malrauxs saw the Delclauxs, the notary of Saint-Chamant and his wife Rosine, a lively, exuberant, warmhearted friend. When introduced to Malraux in November 1942, Frank Delclaux had asked: 'What is your profession?' This did not exactly please Malraux. As for Rosine Delclaux, she often told him that she could understand his books only when she read them aloud, which made him laugh. But they were very loyal friends, in a period when nothing was more valuable.

The birth of Josette's second son Vincent, in November 1943, presented additional problems. The divorce with Clara had still not taken place – not only because she did not want it, but because André thought that it was not the right moment to separate officially from his wife, in view of the fact that her Jewish origin made her particularly vulnerable. Their eldest son carried the name Malraux, therefore, only because Roland, the elder of his half-brothers, had officially adopted him. When Vincent was born, the young man proposed to make the same gesture. But this time Josette refused, on the grounds that it might encourage André to postpone marrying her indefinitely.

But literary and family problems were not the only ones to concern the inhabitants of the Château de Saint-Chamant. The armies of the Third Reich and its allies were everywhere on the retreat, from the Ukraine to Tunisia – and the Maquis, hiding in the woods of Corrèze, were making their presence increasingly felt. Throughout 1943, André Malraux remained in contact with the British networks, for the good reason that his brother Roland, adjutant to Major Harry Peulevé, parachuted there by London, was the agent of General Gubbins's Special Operations Executive (SOE) at Brive. Without assuming any responsibility himself, the former head of the *España* squadron very often received his brother and his companions, exchanging information and operational ideas. But he was only on the fringes of active resistance until early 1944.

27 In the Maquis

On 21 March 1944, at Brive, a detachment of the Gestapo led by a local agent of the pro-Nazi militia entered the house of Armand Lamory, an employee of Maurice Arnouil, one of the leaders of the Resistance in Corrèze. The German police found four men there: the British major, Harry Peulevé, his adjutant, Roland Malraux, Charles Delsanti, a former police inspector at Ussel, and the radio operator, Louis Bertheau.[1] They were caught in the act of communicating with London and could offer neither resistance nor denial. First they were sent to the prison at Tulle, then sent either to Neuengamme or to Buchenwald, from where Peulevé returned, exhausted, to die ten years later.

When the chiefs of the SOE heard of the capture of their agents in the 'Nestor' network from one of Arnouil's adjutants – who had not been a direct target of the dragnet and had been able to escape – they appointed Jacques-Auguste Poirier, known as 'Captain Jack', to succeed Harry Peulevé. It was he who became the representative of the Buckmaster Network in the Périgord-Corrèze zone.

It was at this point that André Malraux joined the struggle. He had received the young Maquisards, who included his young brother, at Saint-Chamant and encouraged them by thus compromising himself. But he had not until now acted directly himself. If he could let them go to their deaths, how could he not now run the same risks himself? 'When one has written what I have written,' he said some months later, 'one fights.' He had done so already, and was to do so again.

At the end of March 1944, he quietly left Saint-Chamant

(shortly afterwards Gaëtan Picon received a letter that stated quite specifically, 'I no longer have an address . . .') and reached the Dordogne valley, where he knew several good locations for secret activities. First he chose the Château de Castelnaud, which overlooks one of the bends of the Dordogne, near the even more beautiful castle at Beynac and La Roche-Gageac. He was joined there by Josette and their sons, who had left Saint-Chamant two days after him. When her friends the Delclauxs asked her where she was going, she replied: 'The less you know the better, in case the police question you . . .'

Passing through Domme, the splendid village overlooking the valley, south of Sarlat, the Malrauxs called on their sister-in-law Madeleine, who had been married to Roland for only a year and who had been suffering great distress since her husband's arrest. She was expecting the birth of her son Alain in a few weeks. They remained in contact with her until André's capture.

Castelnaud was only the first of many places in the Périgord where André Malraux stayed over the next few months. He now went under the name of 'Colonel Berger' – after the hero of *Les Noyers de l'Altenburg*. During the four months he was to spend in the Maquis he went from one château to another, from Castelnaud to Urval in particular. There are over a thousand such châteaux in the Dordogne. That particular region is known as the 'Périgord noir'; it is a polygon formed by the valleys of the Dordogne and the Vézère – which flow into one another at Limeuil, another of 'Colonel Berger's' stopping-places – the Eyzies and Lascaux. The villages have such names as Rastignac, the name of Balzac's most famous hero, and Salignac (where Fénelon was born). The combination of literary associations and prehistoric sites was very much to Malraux's taste.

One mystery remains: how did André Malraux, a famous personality, but very much on the fringes of the Resistance movement (which, not without good reason, regarded seniority as a supreme value), and who had friends only by virtue of his political past, succeed in penetrating this complex network, and then emerge, in less than three months as a unifier? In history, a strong will goes a long way, as does that gift of the 'shaman' with his magical 'powers' of leadership that sometimes lead to power, which he had recently portrayed so brilliantly in

Les Noyers de l'Altenburg, in the character of Vincent Berger.

The fact is that he imposed his authority, not of course on everyone, but on a good many of the leaders of Maquis groups of a more or less spontaneous or autonomous kind, more or less loyal to one or other of the large organisations, the generally Communist-controlled F T P (Francs-tireurs et Partisans) and the generally Gaullist-controlled A S (Armée Secrète), not to mention the British networks of the S O E, headed in France by Major Buckmaster.

It was to the S O E that André Malraux says he attached himself at the beginning, if not from the contacts made in Allier in September 1942, at least since his brother and Harry Peulevé had contacted him at Saint-Chamant in autumn 1943. After the war, Colonel Buckmaster denied that the elder of the Malraux brothers had ever been a member of the S O E.[2] Yet it was through this channel that, thanks to his brother, he had at his disposal exceptionally reliable information as to the complex web of the Resistance in the 'R5' zone, which more or less covered Corrèze, Périgord, Lot and Bas-Limousin – the country of chestnuts, truffles and rye.

He had one ambition and it was a worthy one: first to federate, then to direct this constellation of Maquis groups. At the beginning of spring 1944 there were about 15,000 men, more or less armed, in this region: a potential force, and real enough to take on the occupiers on occasion. But these forces had their leaders. Malraux would never manage to impose his authority on most of them – Colonels Rivier, Vaujour and Guédin for the A S, Colonels Godefroy and Lescure for the F T P, not to mention the representatives of the 'Alliance' networks and, of course, Georges Guingouin, the powerful founder and Communist boss of the F T P organisations in Limousin.[3]

Malraux's strategy – which paid off for the 'R5' Maquis groups as a whole, as we shall see – consisted in playing one of his many contacts against the others, whether from a territorial, national or ideological point of view. In the whole of this zone he was the last to arrive. But he was also the only personality of any stature who (because he was 'new' and not involved in the quarrels that raged between networks and Maquis) had connections with both the British and the French, with both certain

Communists and most of the Gaullists, with the groups in the Lot, Corrèze and Périgord. He was as welcome among such Communist Maquisards of Lot as the brothers Brouel, near Cazals,[4] as among members of the Organisation de résistance de l'armée (linked to the AS) led by Lt Diener, a teacher who had regrouped about a hundred Alsatians and Lorrainers at Durestal.

About the middle of April, Diener, who went under the name of Ancel, heard about an 'inter-allied officer' who because of his connections with London would be able to help him obtain arms. He went to the Château d'Urval, where he was received by a tall, rather standoffish man, wearing a colonel's uniform, who impressed him considerably, talked of nothing but technology, figures, means of communication and transport, and introduced himself as 'Colonel Berger'. The visitor was assured that his unit would benefit from 'forthcoming' arms deliveries.

A month later, about 20 May 1944, Diener-Ancel saw the tall uniformed colonel known as 'Berger' arriving. The visitor had come to get information about the means at his disposal to protect a possible parachute drop of arms into the region of Domme. He then asked to inspect Diener's troops. The men were lined up, the tricolour hoisted and an attempt was made to play the *Marseillaise*: 'Berger' stood there saluting the flag with raised fist.

Despite these attitudes, despite his legend, despite a revolutionary past which nothing, not even the German-Soviet Pact of August 1939, had led him to question in public, Malraux was to turn increasingly towards the Gaullist tendency in the Maquis. Whether or not he was in a position to radio-control certain parachute drops in the spring of 1944 – it is now generally agreed that his influence in London was exaggerated – Berger-Malraux soon acquired among the Communists and, more generally, among the FTP the twofold reputation of trying to federate the military forces of the Resistance in the southwest and of favouring the supply of arms to the AS Maquis to the detriment of their own units.

So references to the work of Malraux as a Maquisard are distinctly hostile when they occur in texts emanating from the extreme left, such as the Maquis de Corrèze, and much warmer when they come from members of the A S, such as Bergeret and Grégoire, the authors of *Messages personnels*:

> I was always struck by the fearless way Malraux lived underground. For the whole duration, he stayed in châteaux with an insignificant guard and travelled the roads without taking the slightest precautions. We were still at the Eyzies when André Malraux summoned us, together with Martial, Colonel Louis, his chief of staff Philibert and Alberte. He had his command-post near Limeuil and had not changed his habits. One could ask anyone, the first kid one saw in the street: 'Where is the inter-allied command-post?' and he would reply, 'It's at the château, Monsieur!'[5]

A third type of evidence, ironically friendly, is that provided by Pierre Viansson-Ponté (now an editor of *Le Monde*), a brilliant observer who at that time was not content to be a mere witness:

> Anyone who met that strange Berger could not forget him. The Scarface hat or the beret stuck on his head, chainsmoking the English cigarettes found in the tips of the parachuted containers – an outward sign of importance in the underground – he talked on, facetiously and confidently about 'the chaps', 'Old Man Churchill' and 'that chap de Gaulle', punctuating his sentences every now and then with 'Your turn now', which it was as well not to take too literally as an invitation to reply.[6]

Malraux-Berger did accept 'replies', however, from a few well-armed questioners. But he knew how to disarm certain prejudices. In this way he managed to arrange peaceful coexistence with one of the 'Red' chiefs of the region, the famous 'Soleil', a Marseillais with a not very reassuring reputation as a bandit-chief, who operated near Villefranche-de-Périgord. 'Berger' went to meet him through dense forest, duly impressing him by his audacity and his sense of theatre. On that score there was no conflict between them.

One of Malraux's trump cards, in this difficult period of July 1944, when he no longer had to make his presence felt – this had been done – but to get himself recognised as the federator and intercessor with London of about one-tenth of the French Resistance in the countryside, was to be the presence at his side from 9 July of a professional who far outpaced any of his rivals in ability. Major Jacquot had been a member of the cabinet of the Minister of Defence – then Daladier – and knew more than anyone about the officer corps, those who had joined the Resistance and those who had not. He was, moreover, an intelligent man and a good tactician.

Berger's authority in the few weeks preceding his capture was based on an invention, that of the 'Inter-allied Command-post', which emerged fully armed from his fertile brain. Neither de Gaulle, the British nor the Americans, and certainly not the Communists, were aware of the existence of such an 'Inter-allied Command-post'. But on the basis of the presence of British officers like George Hiller, Cyril Watney (Michel) or Jacques Poirier (Jack) and, a little later, Americans like Lts Atkinson and 'Guy', Malraux gave his command-post, first at Urval then at Carennac, this imposing title. It was soon accepted by those currents in the Resistance that wanted the British and Americans to help them counterbalance the FTP after the Liberation. The 'Corps francs de la libération' was a creation that enabled Malraux to propose a way out for groups caught between the anti-Communist AS and the Communist FTP, and which refused to comply with the demands of either, equally intolerant, organisation.

The Normandy landing and the progress of the forces first of Patton and Montgomery, then of Leclerc, were to give credence to the notion of an 'Inter-allied Command-post', and the reaction of the enemy, in moving the SS Division 'Das Reich' through the Maquis groups of the Centre-West ('R5'), made everyone feel the need for outside support, for bigger supplies of arms and a coordinated strategy. Not that Malraux was capable exactly of providing any of these things. But from the end of June, he did serve as a kind of turntable and those under his command were happy to be so.

In his book *Inside SOE*, E. H. Cookridge, the historian of the British Secret Services, describes the situation thus:

On June 7, [the ss Division 'Das Reich'] passed Cahors and reached the River Dordogne at Souillac. Colonel Collignon, André Malraux, and other FFI commanders, went into action . . . André Malraux and his men followed the 'Das Reich' Division, but could not risk an open battle against Lammerding's eighty tanks and motorized infantry . . . Battling through a series of ambushes [the motorized units under ss Major General Von Brodowsky] reached Oradour-sur-Glane, north of Limoges, where Von Brodowsky perpetrated the most terrible massacre of the war . . . The 'Das Reich' Division arrived in Normandy, ten days behind schedule, completely disorganized, leaving many disabled tanks behind and with its men hardly able to fight. They could not be included in Rundstedt's and Rommel's defence plans. On Malraux's orders Cyril Watney had asked London to send RAF bombers and the German division was bombed throughout its progress north.[7]

Malraux has spoken on many occasions, in particular in a speech he gave on 13 May 1972 at Durestal, where the Diener-Ancel unit was based, of how his men put into practice the 'iron plan' which, involving the harassment of the ss Division and the sabotage of the railway tracks, played a useful strategic role in the battle of Normandy.

However, let us quote a contradictory witness who, not without bitterness, but not without some reason either, it would seem, reduces the brightness of Berger-Malraux's halo. This is the writer Francis Crémieux, who speaks as a Communist militant in a period of intolerance:

I saw Malraux again in July 1944 in Lot. The landing had taken me by surprise at Souillac, and I had joined the nearest maquis group. Without knowing it, I was under the orders of our adventurer.

At this time the FTP and Veny[8] were the most important formations in the department. A few detachments of the AS of Corrèze and of the ORA were fighting a war of their own. The 'Veny', abundantly provided with arms, money and fresh meat, were playing for high stakes. From time to time, they would make a few sorties to break the monotony of their lives. Meanwhile, the partisans were fighting and liberated the department.

Malraux, who called himself the inter-regional F FI, wanted to unify the military command of the department by entrusting it of course, as usual, to such creatures of his own as 'George the Englishman'. Thanks to Ravanel, the 'R4' F FI regional chief, and Jean Cassou, commissioner of the Republic, the operation failed.[9]

The polemical tone, the crude accusations made against the other side that they were content to 'play for high stakes' while his own men 'liberated the department', certainly weakens the value of this account as reliable evidence. But one can grasp through these few lines to what extent Malraux's personality was challenged, and certainly the ambiguity of his role is not exhausted by the different historical accounts of it at our disposal.

What is certain, on the other hand, is that by using his companions Cyril Watney, George Hiller, 'Jack' and Dick Atkinson, Malraux-Berger helped to organise and bring off what General Gubbins, the head of the s o e, described as 'the most important parachute dropping of the war, from Norway to Indo-China'.[10] It was on 9 July, during a meeting at which Malraux and Jacquot pooled their forces and plans, at the command-post of the a s-Corrèze at Chenaillers-Muscheix, that the s o e delegates were convinced they should ask London to start the operation that transformed the military situation in the region.[11] This is how the British historian Cookridge describes the situation:

On 14 July, France's National Day, in the bright light of a fine summer day, two hundred Flying Fortresses and Liberators, escorted by sixty Spitfires, appeared over the plateaux of Causse de Loubressac. For six hours the aircraft came and went in relays, dropping their cargo, so impatiently awaited and so joyously received by the maquisards. Defying German garrisons and patrols, 1500 Resistance men under the command of Colonel Collignon surrounded the dropping grounds covering twenty square kilometres. Women brought bed sheets and spread them out into huge white z-signs for every DZ. Farmers and tradesmen emerged from the villages with every available vehicle to collect the containers; the improvised transport included 180 oxen-drawn farm carts.[12]

It was as organiser of this unparalleled coup that, three days later, at Urval, Berger-Malraux gathered around him several of the Maquis chiefs for whom hitherto he had been no more than a contested partner. He now appeared if not as their leader, at least as their colour-bearer. For four years he had replied to those who tried to bring him into the Resistance (d'Astier, Bourdet, Crémieux, etc.): 'Have you any arms?' He had obtained those arms at last, and in abundance. He had won his gamble.

He had not been one of those 'few hundred men scrambling around in the woods with a few revolvers and a flag made of three pieces of muslin tied together', one of those men 'who kept France going with their bare hands', referred to in his speech of 13 May 1973 at Durestal. But he was to be one of those who in 1944 pointed their bazookas at the German tanks and transformed the Resistance into 'a struggle between submarine and battleship'.

Yet has the 'inter-Allied headquarters' ceased to be a myth? Let us say that it was a nebulous organism in which the Allies could contact one another, and which might prove useful when the need arose. Malraux and Jacquot set up no structures: but their command-post at Carennac or Magnague, near Martel, in Lot, became a 'sorting station' of the 'R5' zone, where a FTP officer was rarely seen, but which provided a meeting-place for important members of the AS such as Majors Collignon, 'Pernod' and 'Vincent', the organisers of the 'Gao Group' (Jugie and Puybaraud), the head of 'Veny' (General Vincent) and British and American officers of the SOE and OSS, such as Lake, Watney, Hiller, Poirier, Atkinson and 'Guy'. Was it simply a convenient fiction both for London and for over-autonomous Maquis leaders, which 'might serve' until the time came for old scores to be paid off? Everyone, including Malraux, had his own ideas on the matter.

28 The Gestapo file

AT THE time Malraux was snatched from the struggle, legend
has it that he was one of the leaders of the Resistance. In times
of war and trouble, legend is more important than ever. This
particular legend was strong enough in early summer 1940 for
a lot of young men, driven to join the unorganised Maquis
around the towns of the south-west (Bordeaux, Toulouse,
Périgueux, Agen) by German attempts to press them into forced
labour, to hear that Berger-Malraux was in command in that
region and to try belatedly to join those units that were supposed to be under his command.[1]

Let us hear what André Rudelle, one of the last men to see
Malraux before his capture at Gramat, has to say. It was he who
lent Malraux his car and tried to advise him to drive along the
country lanes rather than the highways, only to receive a reply
that seemed at the time sublime, but which proved to be stupid:
'The highways are made for fast driving!' At the time, they
were made above all for the Germans!

> On 22 July they had met again at the wood at Villelongue,
> near Rodez. 'Colonel Berger' and General Vincent had come
> to inspect some radio equipment belonging to the 'Veny'
> maquis and to organize its relations with the FTP.
>
> He was the kind of guy who preaches revolution. He men-
> tioned China and Spain. I only learnt his real identity on
> 18 August, at the liberation of Toulouse. But by his attitude,
> his physique and his style, I could see perfectly well that he
> was not a soldier. Too intelligent. He had a phoney uniform.
> His physique didn't go with it.

We'd met in a ruined farmhouse. I'd made an omelet over a wood fire. And being very clumsy, I burnt my foot. I remember being very shocked because Malraux began by talking about my burn with a 'now, now, young man . . .' and went on to talk about something quite different.

He was just as he is now, thin, a rounded forehead – one noticed only his forehead and his eyes. He was already round-shouldered. He talked and talked, about everything under the sun. Collignon, a career officer, vaguely acquiesced. A British major, George, understood nothing. General Vincent, an old professional soldier, was flabbergasted. I kept quiet for the first time in my life. Berger put the world to rights, alone.

So on 22 July he set out in Rudelle's old Citroën. In the front seat were two Maquisards, including the driver; on the back seat Major Collignon, Major George Hiller and himself, in uniform. The road was the N677. As they entered the little town of Gramat (Lot), shortly after 3 pm, flying the Cross of Lorraine pennant and the tricolour, they passed a German motorised column. Shooting broke out. The driver and bodyguard were seriously injured. Major Hiller was hit in the lower part of the abdomen. The car veered into a ditch.

The three officers and one of the Maquisards made for the field. Covered with blood, Hiller managed to slip behind a haystack (it was harvest time). Malraux dashed for the field. A bullet cut through the knee-strap of his right legging, he stumbled, and another bullet hit his right leg. He passed out. Neither Collignon nor the bodyguard were pursued, and Hiller was supposed dead. The Germans bothered only with Malraux, perhaps because he was in uniform.

Hiller spent eight hours behind his haystack, his belly open, trying to stop the haemorrhage by stuffing the wound with his tie and a couple of handkerchiefs. He was found during the night, seemingly breathing his last, by Captain Watney, who on Collignon's instructions had brought with him a medical student who had joined the Maquis, Georges Lachaize. They managed to take Hiller to the presbytery at Magnagues, where, gun in hand, they forced a surgeon from Cahors to operate on him.[2]

And what of Malraux? Let us turn to the *Antimémoires*:

> My prisons begin with a field. I regained consciousness on a stretcher laid on the grass and held by two German soldiers. Under my legs, the canvas was soaked with blood. They had made a makeshift dressing over my trousers. The British officer's body had disappeared. In the car were the still bodies of my two comrades . . .
>
> My porters went into the office of a garage. An NCO questioned the one who was escorting me. Then:
>
> 'Your papers!'
>
> They were in the pocket of my tunic, and I reached them without difficulty. I held out the wallet and said:
>
> 'They're false.'
>
> Without taking the wallet, he translated . . .
>
> An NCO beckoned me outside. The yard was full of soldiers. I was able to take a few steps. He made me face the wall, hands leaning against the stones above my head. I heard a command. '*Achtung*', and turned round: I was facing a firing-squad.[3]

(In an interview with Roger Stéphane,[4] he adds the following touch, which is not in the *Antimémoires*: 'So I started shouting at them: I'm no fool. I knew they wouldn't shoot before questioning me.')

In any case, the pretence was short-lived. He was taken to the Hôtel de France at Gramat, where he was subjected to an initial interrogation:

> 'Your name, Christian name, rank?'
>
> 'Lieutenant-Colonel Malraux, André, alias Colonel Berger. I am the military chief of this region.'[5]
>
> He threw a puzzled glance at my officer's tunic, which had no badges of rank. What moral did he hope to draw from that? I had been captured in a car that flew a tricolour flag with the Cross of Lorraine . . .
>
> 'What is your civilian profession?'

'Professor and writer. I have lectured in your universities. At Marburg, Leipzig, Berlin.'

'Professor' sounded serious. [6]

Two hours later, Berger found himself confronted by a white-haired 'Colonel',[7] but their conversations was somewhat vague. Would he be tried, killed? He had to spend the first night at Figeac, in a convent where the sister superior gave him a Bible – in the margins of which he was to note his thoughts about Josette and the children, and a reference to a 'Colonel Nietzsche' (!). But his fate remained very much in the balance. At Revel, he was taken to a general who assured him, as the colonel had done, that 'the Wehrmacht does not use torture' and added:

> In a way I pity you. You, the Gaullists, you are a bit like a French s s. You will be the ones to suffer most. If we should end up losing the war, you will have another government of Jews and Freemasons, at the beck and call of England. And it will be gobbled up by the Communists.[8]

He was taken to Toulouse, where he was taken first to a hotel a little too much like a nursing-home not to boast an executioner, then to the Saint-Michel prison, where he was shut up with about ten friendly prisoners who all told their tales of torture . . .

The door opened. 'Malraux, 6 o'clock.' It was time for his interrogation by the Gestapo:

> They handcuffed my hands behind my back. We went into the next room. There were doors open to right and left to reveal two men with their hands tied to their feet being battered by booted feet and a kind of bludgeon that I could not make out. In spite of the din, it seemed to me that I could hear the dull thud of blows on the naked bodies. I had already averted my eyes, from shame more than fear, perhaps. A man with curly blond hair, seated behind a desk, stared at me expressionlessly. I was expecting first of all an interrogation about my identity.
>
> 'Don't give me a lot of stupid answers: Galitzina is working for us now!'

What was he driving at? It could be a good thing that he was on the wrong tack. The important thing was to keep a a clear head in spite of the atmosphere, the uproar, and the feeling of having only one arm.

'You spent eighteen months in Soviet Russia?'

'I haven't spent more than three months outside France for ten years.⁹ That can easily be checked through the passport office.'

'You spent a year in our country?'

He was obliged to shout as I was.

'Never more than a fortnight. I gave the dates . . .'

'You said: for ten years?'

'Yes.'

'And you are thirty-three.'

'Forty-two.'

The Gestapo officer looked stupefied. He, 'Malraux, André', began to understand:

Thirty-three was my brother Roland's age. *He* had spent a year in Germany before Hitler and eighteen months in the Soviet Union. The self-styled Princess Galitzina was his mistress. It was his dossier that Paris had sent. Roland was in their hands. And if they had not yet located my dossier, it was because I always forget my name is not André. I have never been called anything else, but officially my name is Georges. So the armoured division had not passed on the complete interrogation report: it had merely sent for the dossier of André Malraux which the registry office had been unable to find because it does not exist . . .¹⁰

The interrogator referred to German prisoners held by the Maquis – Malraux had declared earlier to one of his questioners that they had been well treated. The German added, almost in passing, 'We've got them back.' He went on:

'So you admit that you are guilty.'

'From your point of view, there is no question about it.'

The German looked exasperated: 'We'll have to start all over again!' and sent him back between two guards.

He did not have to face torture.

'Match postponed,' he told his fellow prisoners on his return to the cell. 'They had the wrong dossier.'

No, it was not match postponed. He did not know that if he had been neither shot nor tortured it was also because others had acted on his behalf.

As soon as they had been warned of his capture, his friends had taken steps to avoid a summary execution, or an interrogation of the type practised by the Gestapo. René Jugie managed to warn Colonel Böhmer, the commanding officer of the garrison at Brive (with whom he had already made contact through Professor Fontaine, the chief medical officer of the nursing home near Clairvivre), that if Berger-Malraux was shot the forty-eight prisoners in the hands of the AS-Corrèze would suffer the same fate. And he backed up this ultimatum by submitting the list of prisoners in question to Böhmer.

Jugie then took further steps. The *Journal Officiel* of 18 December 1952 shows that on 9 August 1944 the sum of four million francs had been 'paid for the release of Colonel Berger'. This sum had indeed been provided by 'Léonie', the treasurer of the AS-Corrèze, to pay off members of the police or Gestapo agents they regarded as susceptible to this kind of initiative, and capable of acting on behalf of the prisoners. It has been established that it was not these moves that led to Malraux's release. But they may have been responsible, in part at least, for the rather exceptional way he was treated by men who were not noted for their clemency, and had not all read *La Condition humaine*.

Malraux has recounted his liberation from the Saint-Michel prison at Toulouse with a brilliance that perhaps owes something to the sense of exaggeration native to that part of Gascony. But there is no reason to doubt that his account is in the main true:

> All night long, troops passed by. One of the main roads ran along the front of the prison. In the morning, no breakfast. But around ten o'clock the rumble of lorries was succeeded by the hurried clatter of tanks. Either there was fighting to the north of Toulouse (but we heard neither guns nor bombers) or the Germans were evacuating the town.

And suddenly we all looked at each other, words and gestures suspended in mid-air: in the prison yard, women's voices were yelling the *Marseillaise* . . . There could be no doubt about it, the Germans had gone. Had the women found some keys? Men were running in the corridor shouting: 'Out! Out!' on the ground floor, a colossal wooden gong sounded slowly, then developed into a rapid tattoo. Suddenly we got it. In each room there was only one piece of furniture – a table, thick and heavy as in all the old prisons, perhaps dating from the Second Empire. All of us together took hold of ours, placed it upright against the door, and stepped back to the windows . . . At the fifth blow, our door burst open . . . Everywhere freedom was beating its impassioned gong. We . . . reached the yard in time to hear a few cries of pain and the gate of the prison slamming shut with a great clang above the receding noise of tanks and machine-guns. A dozen prisoners came back covered with blood or holding their stomachs before collapsing. Above us, the distant *Marseillaise* and the battering-rams; below, an unreal silence. Outside, shouts. Except for the fallen wounded, everyone had taken refuge in the big assembly-room: three or four hundred.

'Berger in command! Berger! Berger!'

The cry must have come from the occupants of the cells next to ours; everyone wanted to escape from this chaotic freedom, to act in concert: they were unarmed, and there were German tanks on the other side of the gate. I was the only prisoner in uniform, which gave me a bizarre authority . . .

'Doctors, step forward!'

He distributed tasks in case of a return offensive. Then:

'What happened?'
'We went dashing out, there were some tanks, they machine-gunned us.'
'And then?'
'Those who were able to came back.'
'And the tanks?'
'Don't know . . .'

It soon became obvious that the Germans had not finished evacuating Toulouse, that the prison was on their evacuation route, and that the passing tanks had seen the prisoners and shot at them. Either the tanks would ignore the prison or they would break open the gate.

If they got through they would massacre us . . . If our grenades set the first tank ablaze, the passage would be obstructed; those behind would not waste time on a siege.

The tanks passed the prison, giving them 'a farewell burst, just for the hell of it'. The clatter of the tanks stopped.

'Open the gate!' The first prisoners went out almost as if they were going for a stroll; but the frenzy of freedom sent the others shooting out from the porch like sinister school-boys. If more tanks arrived, the massacre would begin again.

No more tanks were to come.[11]

29 *The most Christian brigade of brigands*

As the Saint-Michel Prison at Toulouse was bursting like an
abscess, Paris was regaining its freedom in a frenzy of joy. How
could he wait any longer to see once more the rue du Bac and
the Louvre and the Champs-Élysées and the Tuileries without
swastikas, meeting once again 'Uncle Gide' and Groethuysen,
and Gaston Gallimard – and Josette too, who had left Saint-
Chamant, where she had been lying low after the ambush at
Gramat, and was now in Paris? So to Paris he went. We have
a curious echo of this very brief stay in Paris at the end of
August 1944 in an account of a meeting with Ernest Hemingway, who had arrived as a war correspondent on 25 August
with the French second armoured division and moved into the
Ritz. For an old companion from Spain, it cannot be said that
big Ernest's welcome was very fraternal:

> It was a story that Ernest loved to tell afterwards, and it
> got better with each passing year. He was sitting with his
> 'worthless characters' on the 'nice delicate old furniture' in
> his room. They were field-stripping and cleaning weapons.
> Ernest had his boots off and was wearing 'one of the two
> shirts' he owned. He was not prepared for the resplendent
> figure who came striding through the door. It was André
> Malraux in the uniform of a colonel, with gleaming cavalry
> boots.
> '*Bonjour*, André,' said Ernest.
> '*Bonjour*, Ernest,' Malraux replied. 'How many have you
> commanded?'
> Hemingway's answer was typically modest. '*Dix ou*

douze,' said he, with stupid insouciance. '*Au plus, deux cents.*'

Malraux's thin face contracted in the famous tic. '*Moi*,' he said, '*deux mille.*'

Hemingway fixed him with his coldest stare and said in level tones, '*Quel dommage* that we did not have the assistance of your force when we took this small town of Paris.' Malraux's reply is not on record. But one of the partisans presently beckoned Ernest into the bathroom. '*Papa*,' he whispered, '*on peut fusiller ce con?*'[1]

But the companions from whom he had been separated by the ambush at Gramat were demanding once again the man 'who had commanded two thousand . . .' On 1 September, at Aubazine, near Brive, he met his adjutant, Lt-Col. Jacquot, who meanwhile had signed in his name, with Colonel Böhmer opposite him, the unconditional surrender of the German Brive garrison. Thus the 'inter-allied command' of the Périgord-Corrèze-Lot zone, however ghostly it may have been, justified its creation – in the absence of its inventor.

However, between Toulouse and Périgueux a plan was being formed in the brains of a few Alsatians and Lorrainers who had long been engaged in the struggle: a doctor, Bernard Metz, a priest, Pierre Bockel, a teacher, Antoine Diener-Ancel, whom we have already met in the forest of Durestal and at the Château d'Urval, with Berger-Malraux.

All three had in mind an autonomous unit of compatriots whose principle objective would be the liberation of Alsace. For Metz the idea was rather one of 'redemption', a way of compensating for what they regarded as their compatriots' all-too-ready acceptance of the law of the occupier.[2] Diener had his men from Périgord. Bockel, whose command-post was at Isle-Jourdain, in Gers, could muster several hundred men from Agen to Auch and Muret. This amounted to almost 1500 well-disciplined men. They needed a leader who could not only command but who could also get the high ideal of autonomous unity recognised. Pierre Bockel had one name to offer, that of Colonel Detinger, who had recently been parachuted at Figeac, and who was Alsatian. But wasn't there a risk of them over-doing the Alsatian thing? Metz pointed out. Wouldn't it be

better to appoint a Maquisard? he added. There is that Colonel
Jacquot, at Brive, who has a lot of prestige. But most of the
officers criticised him for being 'left-wing', anti-clerical . . . At
this point Diener put forward his idea.

'Berger, who has commanded the whole of our sector, is on
good terms with London and has just been freed from Toulouse
prison. In fact, Berger is Malraux . . .' If Jacquot had just been
rejected on the grounds of being too left-wing, what would
they say of Malraux . . .? This 'Red' to command Alsatian
Catholics? But Metz was a passionate admirer of *L'Espoir* – and
Bockel thought highly of *La Condition humaine*. They gave in,
got Colonel Detinger to give up his command, and set out for
Aubazine to find Malraux and Jacquot, who both agreed to
serve as leader and adjutant respectively.[3]

Malraux, a Fleming from Paris, who had played in turn the
roles of Indo-Chinese, Russian and Spaniard, now found himself leader of an Alsatian crusade . . . The idea appealed to him.
He believed very strongly in signs and premonitions, loved to
play the magician, and was fascinated by Nostradamus. Malraux, who in *Les Noyers de l'Altenburg* had drawn a kind of self-
portrait in the character of the 'shaman' Vincent Berger, an
Alsatian, was now summoned by Alsace! 'I may tell tales,' he
sometimes says, 'but life is beginning to resemble my tales . . .'
The poet invents truth. This idea of belonging to Alsace, which
had suddenly occurred to him between the camp at Sens and
the chestnut woods of Saint-Chamant, had now become embodied in an offer that made him head of a band of ragged
warriors from the Upper Rhine.

Where did dream and literature end and reality begin? At the
Aubazine meeting on 3 September 1944 there was another con-
spirator, the novelist André Chamson, Malraux's old duelling
partner from the Twenties, a comrade from the antifascist
meetings and the Madrid Congress, and the editor of *Vendredi*.
He had taken to the Maquis in the Lot, where, as curator of the
national museum, he had been given the task of keeping many
of the nation's treasures out of the hands of the occupiers. Early
in 1944, he received a message from General de Lattre de
Tassigny – in 1939–40 he had been a liaison officer at his headquarters – asking him to muster 'some infantry', who would

join the troops scheduled to land in Provence. When, on 15 August, the de Lattre first army landed at Saint-Raphaël, Chamson knew he could count on several hundred men – a fact that he announced to de Lattre, at Aix, before returning to the south-west. It was at this point that he crossed Malraux's path once again. 'I have two battalions,' said Malraux, 'you have one. Taken together, three battalions is quite a force. Separated, they'll get nowhere . . .'[4]

In short, they met again at Aubazine, where it was decided to combine these various elements into a 'brigade'. Malraux got this idea, reminiscent to some extent of his Spanish days, generally accepted. 'We liked the word all the more because it had a corrosive effect in certain command posts and headquarters,' writes Bernard Metz.[5] The so-called 'Alsace-Lorraine Brigade' (commanded by Malraux the Parisian, Jacquot from the Vosges, and Chamson from Provence) wended its way towards the Rhône to link up with the first army in lorries sent by de Lattre to Chamson.

Between Autun and Lyon, Chamson announced his arrival to de Lattre. 'Chamson is sending me his three hundred tramps!'[6] exclaimed the general. But de Lattre was astonished at the unit that he was being provided with, and to find at its head not one writer but two . . . 'I formed the Brigade, Jacquot got it moving, Malraux gave it a soul!' Thus, without excessive modesty, André Chamson sums up the escapade.[7] In any case, by the end of September, at Besançon, the 'Alsace–Lorraine Brigade' comprised a little over 2000 men.

Malraux, now at the head of the 'Brigade', found himself a new personality. Pierre Bockel had first met him at Tulle, the town of the hundred inhabitants hanged by the Germans, and he had struck him as being hieratic, sarcastic and inaccessible. Two weeks later, at Besançon, Colonel Berger suddenly took the priest by the arm. He was aware of Bockel's influence and needed to exert his own over him. For hours on end, in a street of the old town, he unburdened his heart: 'What significance can man's history have if there is no God?' And Pierre Bockel describes this meeting thus: 'Extraordinary as it may seem, I have always felt since that night that it was through what Malraux said to me that I felt what my own faith might be . . .'[8]

The volunteers of the 'Brigade' were committed to fight
'until the liberation of the national territory'.[9] There was no
shortage of opportunities to fulfil their contract. On 26 September, they were attached, for 'operational' purposes, to the first
armoured division (General Sudre), which was moving through
the Vosges in the direction of the Moselle. For more than a
week, Malraux, whose command-post was at Froideconche,
and his men were involved in costly battles in the region known
as 'Bois-le-Prince', where, confronted by cadets from the school
for noncommissioned officers at Colmar, they lost a hundred of
their men. On 7 October, they captured a well-defended position, the Hauts-de-la-Parère, an operation that cost them further
losses. Colonel Jacquot was wounded for the first time in the
fighting.

They were badly armed and equipped, and dressed in the
most motley fashion. Some of them, right up to the Alsatian
October, were still wearing the summer shorts they had worn
in Aquitaine. But they were possessed of a native fury which,
on the Vosgian hills of Luxeuil that gave access into Alsace,
made them unusually tough adversaries. And they were led by
men whose boldness sometimes verged on provocation.

Colonel Jacquot, wounded three times in two months, was
nicknamed the 'sieve'. Malraux liked nothing better than standing on some high point during the worst of the shooting, dis-
playing the courage which, he said one day to Saint-Exupéry,
was merely 'an expression of the feeling of invulnerability' –
but it always had a prodigious effect on those under his command. Reporting for *Combat* in the Brigade's sector in November 1944, Jacques-Laurent Bost expressed surprise at seeing so
many officers in the firing line. He received the answer that it
was one of the requirements of a type of fighting based on
moral values.

The relations between superiors and subordinates in this unit
were of no ordinary kind. Recruitment had, to say the least, been
very varied, and little notice had been taken of personal records.
Among the volunteers were a good many of those known as
'Rhine gypies': in the view of more respectable folk, they had
only the vaguest notion of private property. After being
wounded on one occasion, Jacquot was transported by two

privates to the hospital where he noticed that his watch had disappeared. This did not prevent him – on the contrary, firm anticlerical that he was – referring to the unit of which he was second-in-command as 'the most Christian Brigade of Colonel Malraux'. It is quite true that the Catholic and Protestant chaplains, Bockel, Frantz and Weiss, played a rather exceptional role in this 'brigade of brigands', as André Malraux, who was delighted with his men's 'savage' virtues, liked to call it.

Malraux-Berger must have had a rather special view of his role to address his men after a particularly bloody day's fighting with these words, halfway between the sublime and the callous: 'I salute those who fell yesterday and those who will fall to-morrow.'[10] And it is not entirely surprising if certain officers saw fit to use elsewhere the professional qualities that they regarded as too valuable to be employed for largely mythical ends.

From the military point of view, the Brigade's activity was spread over five months (September 1944–February 1945) and can be divided into four periods: (a) the operation at Bois-le Prince, in the Vosges, its cruel baptism by fire; (b) the march on Dannemarie and the taking of the town (20–28 November); (c) its participation in the defence of Strasbourg against von Rundstedt's offensive (20 December 1944–10 January 1945); (d) the thrust towards Colmar and Sainte-Odile (February 1945). After which, the Brigade marched without firing a shot through Bad-Württemberg to Stuttgart (March 1945).

A little has already been said about the Bois-le-Prince operation. It was severe enough for the unit to be withdrawn after two weeks. On 10 October, the Alsace–Lorraine Brigade was sent to Remiremont to rest. At the beginning of November, it moved on Altkirch, to prepare for its participation in a new operation, in which it would be attached to the fifth armoured division in the unenviable role of support infantry.

It was there, on 11 November 1944, that André Malraux heard the news that hit him more cruelly than any other in a life that had seen a good deal of tragedy: the death of Josette Clotis. After two short visits, in August and October, to Paris – where André, accompanied by Pierre Bockel, had seen her again – Josette had returned with her two sons to her friends the Delclauxs, at Saint-Chamant, in Corrèze. Her mother had joined her there. The atmosphere at the 'château' was none too relaxed. Mme Clotis made life very difficult for her daughter, as regards both the upbringing of the children and the legal situation vis-à-vis André.

On 11 November, Mme Clotis was to return to Hyères, on the Mediterranean. Josette and her friend Rosine Delclaux accompanied her to the station of Saint-Chamant to see her off. Josette and Rosine helped Mme Clotis into the compartment with her luggage. When the signal was given for the train to leave, the two young women were still in the carriage. The train had already begun to move when they sprang up. Mme Delclaux managed to jump in the same direction as the train. But Josette, impeded by the thick wooden soles that were worn at the time, jumped the wrong way, stumbled and fell under the wheels of the train. She was taken to a clinic at Tulle, half an hour's drive away by car. She died ten hours later, horribly mutilated, but retaining consciousness to the end.[11]

Although a telegram reached him on the first day, a very rare event at the time – Winston Churchill's visit to Alsace had brought about an improvement in communications – André Malraux did not reach Tulle until the evening of the following day, 12 November. Malraux was convinced that he would see Josette alive and made no attempt to hide his despair from his friends at Saint-Chamant, to whom he entrusted the care of the two children. Three days later, he was back in Alsace, after a brief stop in Paris. A photograph of him, taken as he was leaving the *Combat* offices, where he had called on Albert Camus and his old friend Pascal Pia, shows how obviously grief-stricken he was at the time.

It was in this state of mind that he was to assume responsibility for the most difficult operation so far entrusted to the Brigade: the capture of Dannemarie, between 21 and 28 November, while General Leclerc's second armoured division, advancing by forced marches from Baccarat to Dabo and from Schirmeck to Molsheim, took Strasbourg on 23 November. Between Altkirch and Dannemarie, enemy resistance was at its fiercest. On 25 November the Brigade reached and occupied Carspach. The following day they moved on to Burnhaupt: the

Brigade came up against stubborn defence from two German battalions, one of which, dug in at Ballersdorf, the last village before Dannemarie, inflicted losses of over fifty men.

The weather was extremely cold, and moving over the frozen ground or perched on the tanks of the fifth armoured division – an exposed position in either case – the men of the Brigade suffered more than they had ever done. It took them seven long days to cover less than as many miles, and to reach Danne-marie. The attack began on 27 November. Major Ancel was wounded at the beginning of the action. An armoured train was defending the small town. It retreated during the night and Malraux's men, who had entered the town square the night before, controlled it by the morning of 28 November. The Belfort Road was open.

Two months later, at the request of a visitor, Malraux de-scribed the battle of Dannemarie. 'What struck me,' observed the visitor, 'was how much Malraux admired his men. He admired them even more than he loved them. They obviously astonished him. He told me how exhausted men volunteered to remain alongside those who came to relieve them in order to increase the fighting strength of the group . . .'[12]

Early in December Malraux was able to reach Strasbourg, where he set up his headquarters at Roseneck. He then pushed on to Sainte-Odile, not far from his 'walnut trees of the Alten-burg'. Malraux then got something done that Leclerc, excellent Catholic though he be, had not achieved: the resumption of worship in Strasbourg Cathedral, which he assigned to Pierre Bockel. And he was also able to bring to light the marvellous Grünewald altarpiece, which he admired more than any other and which had been hidden in the cellars of the Haut-Koenigsburg. He set foot on Alsatian territory, trying hard to master his own feelings.[13]

Had the time come to examine fifteenth-century altarpieces and pulpits and to look around the old museum?

Only ten days before, at Strasbourg, Field Marshal von Rundstedt had begun the Ardennes offensive, 'Hitler's last throw of the dice'.[14] In order to contain the German thrust at the point at which, in 1940, von Manstein had burst through Gamelin's disposition, Eisenhower decided to shorten his front and to cling on to the Vosges, which inevitably involved Strasbourg – Strasbourg, where the people of Alsace had been celebrating their liberation for the past month! How could Strasbourg be handed back to the enemy, with all the reprisals that would ensue! What might seem reasonable to an American strategist – and, indeed, was – seemed intolerable to most Frenchmen and not only to the intolerant de Gaulle, who appealed to Churchill to help him convince Eisenhower. Before the Allied commander was able to alter his decision, de Gaulle had taken his own and, since the Leclerc division had been transferred from this front to the Ardennes for the past two weeks, entrusted the defence of Strasbourg to de Lattre.

Thus, from 28 December, the Alsatian brigade, attached to the first Free French Division, was given the task of covering the southern approaches of the city, between the villages of Plobsheim and Daubensand and the Rhine – a distance of nearly ten miles. It was supported in the west by an advanced unit of General Patch's seventh army and in the south by the first Free French Division. But during the night of 2–3 January the neighbouring American regiment pulled back towards the south-west, leaving at the disposal of Malraux's unit an artillery group with a battery of 105-millimetre guns and an anti-tank battery: 'But the lack of artillery support was cruelly felt,' an officer of the brigade, Lt Octave Landwerlin, noted in his logbook. 'The pillboxes that the enemy had not had time to blow up were for the most part flooded. The exhaustion, the cold and the harassment from the enemy were hard to bear.'[15]

On 5 January, the enemy pressure was still increasing; it was felt both in the east, along the Rhine, and in the south, where the Germans were still in complete control of Colmar, which they were using as a departure base to take the defenders of Strasbourg in a pincer movement. General Von Maur issued an order of the day: 'The swastika will fly again over Strasbourg.' Lt Landwerlin again notes in his logbook the following orders received from the colonel commanding the brigade: 'You will hold your position whatever the cost until ammunition runs out. In the event of your situation becoming impossible, you will retreat into the city of Strasbourg where we will fight whatever happens, street by street, house by house. Strasbourg will in no circumstances be abandoned.'[16] Barricades had been erected, composed among other things of tramcars filled with paving stones.

From 7 January, the Brigade was subjected to terrible pressure from the enemy, using their 'Tiger' tanks. On 9 January, short of ammunition, in a temperature under 18° centigrade, on the frozen arms of the Rhine, a whole battalion of the brigade seemed lost. They crossed the river at a ford swept by a freezing current, thus avoiding encirclement – an episode in the style of the Long March, for which Malraux, quite rightly, was given credit.

The defence of Strasbourg – the assailants began to withdraw from the beginning of February – was carried out by a large number of units. But the part played by the Alsace-Lorraine Brigade, to the south of the town, in the Plobsheim, Obenheim and Gerstheim sectors, was certainly an important one, and recognised as such by the commander of the first army. And yet Roger Stéphane, arriving in Strasbourg on 25 January to meet Malraux, observed that 'nobody has heard of the Alsace-Lorraine Brigade' and had difficulty locating it in the neighbouring village of Illkirch.[17]

The 'Brigade' had not yet completely fulfilled its mission. As we have seen, its men had committed themselves to continuing the struggle until the total liberation of the national territory. For these Alsatians (many of them were from the Upper Rhine, Thann – Bockel's native city – was the true heart of the enterprise) the recapture of Colmar was a major objective. Of all the operations this one was the simplest. It took place in mid-February. It was followed by the even easier crossing of Baden, at the beginning of March, the entry into Württemberg and the ceremony at Stuttgart where General de Lattre decorated Malraux and his companions.

What role did the command of the 'Brigade' play in the life of André Malraux? To begin with, it represented four months of extremely dangerous fighting. ('His' Spain had lasted seven months, 'his' Maquis a little over four months.) But this time, the devotee of victory, the theoretician of efficacity, had won. He was at last on the winning side, and not by chance. This time, the adventure did not end in a car crossing the Pyrenean frontier through a flood of terrified refugees, nor lying on a stretcher, under the eye of an ss officer. And yet without the stretcher, and even without the car in Catalonia, there might have been no 'Brigade', no Colonel Malraux-Berger crossing the Rhine.

But the Alsatian adventure occupies a special place in his flamboyant career: it was the golden age, the time of concrete triumph. If there are periods in such a life, as there are in the life of societies, this one was for him the classical age, the 'siècle d'or'. The capture of Dannemarie, the defence of Strasbourg, the entry into Colmar could have been carried out by any regular army colonel or by some lucky leader thrown up by the resistance. But, for Malraux, they constitute the moment when, like Clemenceau on the night of the 1918 armistice, he could say 'I would like to die tonight.' Was this because what he had accomplished was exceptional? It certainly was that. But also perhaps because of what he was later to do in the RPF, as a minister, and so on.

For an intellectual, the peak could not be the mere fact of action, even when it was to action that he first devoted himself, finding in his art merely a compensation for his failures as a manipulator of history. Roger Stéphane has given us an account of the admirable agility, firmness, clarity of Malraux's intelligence at this climactic moment in his life. On 2 February 1945 Stéphane interviewed Malraux at Illkirch, near Strasbourg. Malraux talked for several hours. Stéphane provides an obviously faithful account of his intellectual, moral, aesthetic and political positions at that time.[18] We must content ourselves here with a few extracts:

> Intelligence is the destructiveness of comedy, plus judgement, plus the spirit of hypothesis . . .
>
> An important date occurred in the history of liberal Europe when a certain gentleman, instead of saying 'I am seizing power because I have the majority,' said 'I am seizing power because I have my hands on the controls.' This gentleman was neither Hitler, nor Franco, nor Mussolini, but Lenin . . .
>
> When one has written what I have written and there is

fascism somewhere, one fights against fascism . . . I know I
will not be a fascist, because I know what I am and that's
enough for me . . .

A Marxist? I'm a Marxist in the way that Pascal was a
Catholic. He died in time . . . Philosophically, I'm not at all a
Marxist . . . What matters more than anything to me is art.
I am in art as one is in religion . . . But art solves no problems. It merely transcends . . . If art is merely a matter of
beauty, then Goya is not an artist. There is something to be
said about ugliness in art. And it will be said.

But the two most curious features of Malraux's conversation
in February 1945 are political. When Stéphane spoke to him of
Le Temps du Mépris (which Malraux describes as a *navet*, a dud)
and referred in particular to the preface, which is an apologia
for fellow-travelling, Malraux interrupted him: 'I would not
withdraw a comma of that preface today.' When Stéphane went
on to express surprise that Maurras had not been condemned
to death,[19] Malraux had this comment to make on de Gaulle:
'One cannot practise the politics of Bainville and then condemn
Maurras to death . . .'[20] An odd remark in view of future
developments.

Book 3

METAMORPHOSES

PART I

FASCINATION

30 The turning-point

IN FEBRUARY 1945 Malraux declared that he 'would not with-draw a single comma' from the text in which, ten years earlier, he had expressed his allegiance, not to the Communist Party, but to its values. Nevertheless, he had just carried out against the Communists the most important action of his political life – not perhaps, for himself, for his image or for his men, but for the political development of France in the wake of the Libera-tion. André Malraux had spent many hours of his life on plat-forms and in front of microphones. None of his speeches was to have as much influence on the development of his country as the one he delivered at the congress of the MLN (Mouvement de Libération nationale) that met at the Mutualité on 25 January 1945.

Thirty-seven years later, when speaking of de Gaulle's visit to Stalin in December 1944, he told me: '*If de Gaulle could go to Moscow at that time, it was because I adopted the attitude I did with the Communists . . .*'[1] This is fantasy, of course. But as always there is some truth in what he says. De Gaulle's visit to the USSR was presented as an exercise of independence vis-à-vis the Americans. It could be so only if the French government were free in its movements from Communist pressure. Otherwise, it would be no more than tribute paid by the vassal to his lord. De Gaulle was indeed free when he chose to go to the USSR. But he was free, not because Malraux, six weeks later, refused to allow himself to be 'burgled' by the French Communist Party. It was because de Gaulle had dissolved the Communist militias – with the connivance of those PCF leaders most attentive to the wishes of the Soviet Union. But it is true that Malraux's behaviour in the Maquis, in the Brigade and at the January congress expressed or perhaps sublimated the attitude of a large section of the Resistance that enabled de Gaulle to act as he did.

In the interview with Roger Stéphane that I have already quoted, Malraux replies to the Communist plan to merge the various resistance organisations thus: 'I am quite willing to form an alliance, but I have no desire to be burgled.'[2] Such language may come as a surprise from the man of 1935–6, from the fellow-traveller, from the chief of the *España* squadron who had chosen to equip his unit, two thirds of which was composed of Communist militants or sympathisers, with a Party Political Commissar. In order to understand why he said what he did, we have to remember three things.

First, the sincere internationalist of the 1930s had experienced a new, very powerful sense of country as the result of the shock of defeat, the occupation and the Nazi repression. Secondly, more as a result of circumstances than deliberate choice, he had found himself in the Anglo-Gaullist branch of the Resistance, in objective conflict with Communist organisations. (Similarly, when he landed in Barcelona in July 1936, he might, by force of circumstance, have espoused, like Orwell, the cause of the POUM, and broken with Moscow and its friends.) Thirdly, his experiences in the Resistance had taught him how far the party's technique of infiltration could go. An incident related in the *Antimémoires* gives us some idea of his state of mind at the time of the Liberation:

Six months earlier I had had a secret lunch in a country bistro with four non-communist delegates whose groups were soon to be merged to form the French Forces of the Interior. Having settled the matter – without controversy – we discussed the future autonomy of the Resistance, then went our ways. I walked through the rain with the Paris delegate along a provincial Station Road. We had done some fighting together. He said without looking at me: 'I've read your books. I must tell you that at the national level the Resistance movements have been infiltrated through and through by the Communist Party . . . (he put his hand on my shoulder, looked at me, and stopped) . . . of which I have been a member for seventeen years.'[3]

What exactly was this MLN that held its first conference in January 1945, as the war was still dragging on in certain parts of the country? Above all, it was a constellation of the 'Libération', 'Combat', and 'Franc-tireur' movements of the southern zone, which had merged fifteen months earlier under the name of MUR (Mouvements Unifiés de Résistance) and a few other organisations (Défense de la France, OCM, Libération-Nord). The Resistance had another branch, the 'Front National', which had mainly emerged from the FTP, and which was sufficiently controlled by the Communist Party to include such 'safe' Catholic personalities as François Mauriac, Father Philippe and Mgr Chevrot.

The aim of the Communist Party was to bring the whole of the Resistance under the 'Front National'. However complex this would make the Front, it was simply, in the view of certain of its leaders, a problem of infiltration. Hence the strategy of unifying the Resistance movements that its friends and delegates were to present at the MLN congress – where the Communist Party had a few secret supporters.

When, on 26 January 1945, about two thousand delegates representing about a million members and a considerable moral force met at the Mutualité, two main opposing trends emerged from the MLN congress. The first was that of the supporters of the merger with the 'Front National'. The main advocates of this line were the non-Communist progressives, Emmanuel d'Astier, a friend of Malraux, and Pascal Copeau, son of the prophet of a new theatre and greatest French actor of the first part of the century, and two more or less secret members of the Communist Party, Pierre Hervé and Maurice Kriegel-Valmiront. Was what they had in mind simply a recruiting operation for the Communist Party? It was not as simple as that. Some of them, including Hervé and Kriegel, hoped to renew the Party by grafting the Resistance on to it, to change its direction by this massive influx of essentially patriotic forces. Like Charles Tillon, the head of the FTP, they were probably thinking of a

PCF in which the letter 'F' would be underlined in red and in which there would be a revival of internal discussion – in this they were in agreement with men like d'Astier and Copeau. It was as much a question perhaps of infiltrating the Party through the Resistance as infiltrating the other groups through the Party.

The other tendency was characterised both by a refusal and a hope. A refusal of the merger which, according to them, would bring the whole of the Resistance under the control of the Communists; and the hope of creating, in order to counterbalance the power of the PCF, a 'French labourism': an old dream . . . Some, such as Daniel Mayer, secretary- general of the SFIO,[4] proposed quite simply that the MLN should join their party *en bloc*. Others still were already preparing formulas overtly based on the person of General de Gaulle. Yet others, such as the young François Mitterrand, were still looking for a way.

And then there was Malraux, appearing quite suddenly as in the Resistance, in uniform, forelock dishevelled, with his peremptory gestures and his trenchant words, for all the world like some technician irritated by amateurs ('Let's be serious, we have no time to lose, those of us who are still fighting at the front, etc . . .'). What did he want? 'Not to allow himself to be burgled,' of course: it was this that placed him immediately in the ranks of the opponents of the merger. But he was also a character in search of a role. The images of the Maquisard, the prisoner of the Gestapo, the colonel, superimposed upon those of the antifascist leader and the veteran of the Spanish Civil War were beginning to add up to quite a panoply. It was this – plus his talent – that was to place him at the head of those opposing the plans of the PCF.

He needed one more transformation: he had to become the man who, after defying Hitler, said no to Stalin. He was not subject to the inferiority complex he describes in the *Antimémoires*:

> Although most of the Congress members were ex-fighters, their deeds of valour did not exempt them from the feeling of inferiority that the Girondin feels towards the Montagnard, the liberal towards the extremist, the Menshevik towards anyone who declares himself a Bolshevik.[5]

Malraux spoke on the third day of the congress, back again on the platform where he had defended Thaelmann, Dimitrov and a Spanish Republic dominated (in 1938) by the Communists. He was wearing a khaki tunic with five bands, a crossbelt and riding boots. He was very pale and, as the reporter from *Combat* noted (beside a headline announcing that the Red Army was speeding up its advance and laying siege to Breslau), 'animated by the same passion with which he commanded the Alsace–Lorraine Brigade at the front':

> The MLN is one of the forms of consciousness of this country, but it is also very vulnerable and in many ways dying . . . In so far as it was a truly active movement, it was made up of a number of men who happened to have remembered the saying of Monsieur Hitler, the most intelligent thing he had ever said in his life: 'When men want to fight and they have no weapons, weapons grow out of their hands . . .' What was the Resistance? A general mobilisation of French energy. What must it become? A second mobilisation of energy, as hard, as firm as the first.
>
> The government of General de Gaulle is not only the government of France but the government of the Liberation and the Resistance. So it is not for us to question it . . . It is right that the government should say: war and revolution are antinomic. When there are all the problems of foreign policy, when France must feed the allied armies or put its trains at their disposal, it is inevitable and indispensable that all energies should first be directed towards military victory and that the revolutionary problem should be left till later.[6]
>
> But there is one point on which we will not compromise, that is to say that if this point were abandoned, whoever among us is in the government should leave it, whoever among us is fighting should give up the struggle – unless he is in the army – whoever claims to represent the government should cease to represent it. This point is the essential *donnée* of the revolutionary will, it spells the end of capitalism: the nationalisation of credit is the key . . . One can destroy the system of capitalist credit within the framework of law and order, if the government of France demands law and order . . .

Malraux then came straight to the point:

> We must carry out a profound reformation of the spirit
> of the movement. The Communist Party for example is not
> an organism dedicated to persuasion, but an organism dedi-
> cated to action. And we here today must not forget that we
> too are an organism dedicated to action . . . If we wish to
> maintain the mobilisation of energy that we have represented,
> we must use similar techniques to those used by the Com-
> munists, that is to say we must observe within our move-
> ment a discipline equal to that of the Communist Party . . .
> however harsh and however difficult that may be.
>
> Although I believe that the overwhelming majority of us
> is against the idea of a merger, I also believe that this same
> majority wishes to find the point on which a unity of action
> on the part of all the Resistance groups could be established
> . . . Today, it seems to me, we are faced with exactly the same
> problem that faced us in the early days of the Resistance. We
> must start again from the beginning. Either we do not wish
> to do so and we will quietly take the path of negotiation, in
> which case we will add new corpses to the old ones, or we
> have a serious desire to act. So here and now we must say
> together, without illusions: 'A new resistance is beginning.'
> And I say to all of you who were capable, when you had
> nothing, of making the first resistance, will you, yes or no –
> and I say yes – be capable of doing the same again when you
> have everything in your hands?[7]

He was warmly applauded. It was his intervention that
delivered the final blow to the pro-Communist champions of
unification. Was this 'new resistance' that he urged on his comrades directed against the Communist Party? The homage paid
to his former brothers-in-arms scarcely conceals his intentions.
Pierre Hervé's comments in the Communist weekly *Action*
were no more soothing than his own speech:

> Is what is being proposed a new party, which, combining
> an ideology of planning with notions of authority and seek-
> ing support among the middle classes, would begin as neo-
> socialist and end in neofascism? Is that what the Resistance

is to become? . . . To provoke demagogy and anarchy is, in the last resort, to usher in the reign of the saviour: dictatorship . . .

It breaks one's heart to think of his magnificent books, which taught us a morality of grandeur . . . 'Sensitive souls' have a levity in adventure that enables them to believe that all that matters is the sincerity of the moment . . .[8]

Malraux, too, felt the bitterness of the situation:

On my way back to the front through the snow-covered countryside of Champagne, I thought of my Communist comrades in Spain, of the epic of the Soviet achievement, in spite of the OGPU; of the Red Army, and of the Communist farmers of Corrèze, always ready to help us in spite of the *Milice* on behalf of this Party which no longer seemed to believe in any other victories but those won by subterfuge.[9]

The congress voted for the 'Malraux motion' against the merger of the MLN and FN by 250 votes to 119. Talking to Stéphane, some days later, in Alsace, Malraux said: 'I could have been president of the MLN, if I had wanted to.' To which his visitor replied, with the noble impertinence of youth: 'So what?' However, he went on to ask Malraux if he had any political plans. And Colonel Berger replied: 'I have no wish to be Léon Blum (you know what I mean).' Not to wish to be Léon Blum is to wish to be quite a lot. Perhaps too much for others to enlist you when they are neither desperadoes, adventurers, nor saints.

On 25 January 1945, André Malraux did not present himself to the non-communist resistance as a saviour, or as the inventor of a French-style labourism. In a political congress, even composed of a majority of simple souls, a soldier, even a member of the FFI, can only impose his authority when all seems lost.

But Malraux had defied the power of French Communism, which, as we know, was not without support and allies. He had lit a counter-fire. He had drawn the attention of those who sought strength and courage for a particular strategy. And he had broken forever with the comrades of his youth. Was it to become a leader, or to find one?

31 Those who fell

IT WAS as a wounded man that Malraux made his break with
the past and set out on what he may have seen as a new adventure, as if to cauterise his pain with risk. The war that had ended
for France on the winning side, and for him in the exaltation
of those values of collective action that had occupied his mind
for the last twenty years, left him in profound disarray. On
8 May 1945, as the French people were noisily hailing the enemy
capitulation, he was walking about Paris, gloomy and almost
silent, with his friend Claude Gallimard.[1] He could see another
war coming, he said. Did he mean the 'new resistance' of which
he had spoken from the platform of the MLN Congress? Or the
Red Army at the frontiers? He was not only 'a man for history'.
He was also thinking of those who had fallen in this war, of the
men and women who had died, and for what? So that his
former allies and companions should become for him the worst
imaginable threat?

But above all he was thinking of Josette Clotis. He had met
her twelve years before at *Marianne*, where she wrote reports
on day-to-day events that were not really of much interest.
She had published two or three slight novels, one of which,
Le Temps vert, had a certain charm of its own. She was very tall,
slim, with a pale complexion and hair of a reddish brown. He
remembered her grey-green eyes, her figure, her laugh: she was
beautiful, though she did not exploit the fact. She could be very
funny, too, and was good at telling stories. She was also clever
enough to know when to keep quiet – not a bad qualification
for living with Malraux!

But she was no naïve or blind admirer: 'I will read André's books when there are fewer little Chinese and more Paris street kids around,' she once said. As for ideology: 'The only politics I know,' she would say, 'is the politics of the hawthorn . . .' She was of Catalan origin, from the Banyuls region – and her father, a senior civil servant in the Finance Ministry, had been posted to Hyères, where he was regarded as a figure of some importance and was to be elected mayor.

She loved the land, plants and animals, and was certainly very happy at Saint-Chamant: she tried to persuade André to buy a château just outside Paris. And he, who at twenty-five would have echoed Jarry ('The country? Oh, yes! Where roast chickens run around alive'), he too had come to love the land – at about the same time that he learnt patriotism.

Josette's death – a horrible, lonely death, which occurred even before he had been able to give her the joy of marrying her – affected him more than he imagined a mere personal event could ever do. He had never given anyone reason to believe that he had been affected by any of the other trials he had undergone. But this time he did not hold his feelings back. When, in the *Antimémoires*, he spoke of Lawrence he said: 'He does not seem to have experienced the death of a beloved woman. It strikes . . . like lightning.'[2]

He had lost his two brothers. The younger, Claude, an amazing character, a born adventurer, bold almost to the point of madness, a member of a network whose main task was blowing up German ships in the Seine estuary, was captured on 12 March 1944 (the date of his execution is not known). A few days later, on 21 March, Roland, André's companion in Corrèze, was arrested at Brive, imprisoned (and probably tortured) at Tulle and deported to Neuengamme with his comrades Peulevé,[3] Delsanti and Bertheau.

Roland had died in conditions so absurdly tragic that they seem almost to have been invented by Kafka. In April 1945, certain Nazis (including no doubt Himmler) had the idea of using the deportees as a bargaining counter that could be exchanged with the Allies for a free passage into neutral territory. So about twenty thousand survivors made their way to Lübeck and were packed into three cargo-boats ready to be shipped to

Sweden in the event of the negotiations succeeding. After making the whole journey on foot, Roland Malraux and his fellow-prisoners were piled into the hold of the *Cap Arcona,* the largest of the three cargo-boats, which was anchored about three miles off Lübeck.

On 4 May, the American airforce located these ships flying the swastika, flew over them and demanded their surrender. Instead of hoisting the white flag, the Nazi guards took to the lifeboats and tried to escape. The American bombers opened fire. Of some ten thousand unfortunates herded into the holds and between-decks of the three ships, only two hundred survived, suffering from terrible oil burns. The German guards were shot. A few days later the war ended.

André had great affection for this younger brother who, strangely enough, played an important role in his life on at least two occasions. First in 1939, when Roland returned from Moscow, where he had been correspondent of *Ce Soir* (Aragon's pro-Communist newspaper), in complete revolt against what he had seen – his 'return from the USSR' seems to have affected André Malraux far more strongly than Gide's. Secondly, in 1943–4, when Roland's entry into active Resistance considerably hastened André's own.

One of Roland's fellow-deportees described him, stoical, devoted, doing his utmost to get a doctor friend a job that was to save his life. 'He called himself a Communist. He was above all an aristocrat,' this friend remarks in a letter to André Malraux.

Roland was a very handsome man – wintry blue eyes in a Botticelli face. He had great generosity: as we have seen he adopted his brother's eldest son so that he could bear their name, and had offered to do the same for the second. What had happened between them at the beginning of 1944 that led Roland to remark of his brother to Clara, who had taken refuge in Lot not far from their Corrèze Resistance headquarters – and with whom the two younger Malraux brothers had always been on good terms: 'So you haven't realised that he's utterly inhuman'?[4]

The tone in which André Malraux speaks of his brother in the *Antimémoires* would lead one to believe that at the time of Roland's arrest their affection was totally unimpaired. Indeed, we know that in 1948 André Malraux was to marry his sister-in-law Madeleine.

The struggles of the Resistance had robbed him of another companion, one he also regarded as a brother: Raymond Maréchal. One can hardly forget the role played by the original 'Gardet' of *L'Espoir* in Spain, from Medellin to the Teruel Sierra. Malraux had met him at the beginning of the war in Madrid, walking about with a copy of Baudelaire under his arm. 'What are you doing with that?' asked Malraux. 'I brought it with me when I left Paris . . .' 'Good, then we'll work together . . .'[5] Maréchal became the chief of the squadron's gunners. On his return to France in 1937, after being severely wounded in the Sierra, he was one of the first to join the Maquis and Malraux was not surprised when he met up with him again in a sector near his own, in Haute-Corrèze, on the boundaries of the Périgord, between Beaumont and Durestal.

He had become an expert at harassing German convoys. In July 1944, at a time when he had just knocked out two enemy columns from the escarpments where he and his men were hiding, the peasants around him complained that they had no sugar. He learnt that a supply column would be passing through the area with a lorry loaded with sugar. He took up position, attacked it from the rear and drove up the convoy to block it. But the Germans had an armoured car that pushed Maréchal's car off the road. He jumped out and dashed into the fields with his three companions. The Germans had a machine-gun and shot them down like rabbits. The burial was to take place at night. The women of Corrèze – those dark women who crop up so often in Malraux's memories of the war – held vigil through the night from dusk to dawn, at the gravesides. And the next day, when the graves had been filled in, a tiny pile of sugar was found beside each cross . . .

At the beginning of the war Malraux had lost his most intimate friend of the Thirties, the Dutch writer Edgard du Perron, the dedicatee of *La Condition humaine*. Du Perron, three years Malraux's junior, was born in Java, into a family of French Huguenot origin that had made its fortune in the colony and in which, according to Clara Malraux, 'the servants were whipped.'[6] In 1921 he left the island and went to Paris, where despite his wealth he lived very modestly. He met Malraux in 1926 at the time of *La Tentation de l'Occident*: they were both obsessed by Asia.

The epigraph of du Perron's key-work, *Le Pays d'origine,* is a quotation from Malraux: 'One must seek within oneself something other than oneself if one is to look at oneself for long.' Eddy du Perron had been looking at Malraux for a long time – under the name of Héverlé, Malraux is one of the main characters of this obviously autobiographical novel. Close as these two writers may have been, what differentiates them is the nature of their pessimism. Malraux's pessimism is active, 'optimistic', one is tempted to say: beyond despair is action, and in particular political action. Du Perron is concerned above all not to betray his free will and his own truth and consequently refuses such action. Is this scepticism or despair? 'For me,' wrote du Perron, 'there is no place in any society.'

'He was my best friend,' wrote Malraux in the *Antimémoires.* 'He did not believe in politics, but he believed in justice.'[7]

What du Perron admired in Malraux was his ability to snatch from despair reasons for acting. But of the characters created by his friend more or less in his image, the one he preferred was old Gisors – the character in which the Dutch writer found reflected his familiar demons of renunciation and doubt.[8] He was absorbed in the search for a more profound 'knowledge of his singularity', as Malraux puts it. Nevertheless, he remained a close friend of Malraux, even if he could not follow him.

This noble individual, warm-hearted in spite of his pessimism and totally generous in spite of his painful egotism, met a peculiarly appropriate death. In May 1940, as the Nazis were entering Holland, he killed himself. What Malraux has written on the grandeur of suicide, especially in the *Antimémoires,* owes as much to Eddy du Perron as to Fernand Malraux. But it may owe even more to Drieu la Rochelle.

We have already discussed the strange friendship between the authors of *L'Espoir* and *Gilles,* the two symmetrical books of the struggle for and against fascism. The fact that Drieu took no part in the Spanish Civil War in no way diminishes the enthusiasm of his commitment to Franco's side. On this matter, Malraux simply observes that 'For France, Drieu fought. To the death. Not for Spain.'[9] Drieu's choice of fascism was strong enough for him to speak of Malraux and Aragon as 'Russian agents' and to see *L'Espoir* as no more than 'reportage . . . sacrificing to Soviet fashion . . .'.

Both men were to overcome these contradictions – even under the occupation. They met in July 1941 at Cap d'Ail, when Malraux criticized Drieu firmly, but not harshly, for having taken over the direction of the *NRF* in occupied Paris and refused absolutely to collaborate with the review in any way. In December 1942, Drieu published an article in which he recalls that in 1936 he had replied in the affirmative to a journalist who had asked him if he would go so far as to kill Malraux. Describing his state of mind at the time, he adds: 'If I met him in a battle, I would have to shoot at him and perhaps I would not have the right to prevent others from shooting him if, in certain extreme circumstances, he were taken prisoner. If I didn't think that, I wouldn't be taking Malraux seriously and that would be to insult him . . .'[10]

On 8 May 1943, Drieu notes in his journal that he had seen Malraux in Paris, a Malraux 'who no longer believes in anything, denies the power of the Russians, thinks that the world has no meaning and is moving in the most sordid direction: the American solution. But that is because he has himself given up being something in order to be a mere *littérateur* . . .'[11] But he was very moved that his friend should ask him to be the godfather of his second son. And when, in April 1944, Drieu was reflecting on a life that he was planning to end shortly afterwards, and taking stock of his friendships, he wrote: 'I die friendless.' But he added: 'I have respected Malraux. He is fooled neither by himself nor by others. Brother in Nietzsche and Dostoevsky.'[12]

At the beginning of March 1945, Drieu – who had already made a suicide attempt in August 1944 – killed himself. In his will, he made Malraux his literary executor and specified that he wanted his funeral to be attended only by women, with the exception of two friends: Bernier, a former member of the Surrealist group, and Malraux, who carried out the task that Drieu had entrusted to him with a painstaking conscientiousness that won the admiration of their common publisher, Gaston Gallimard.

32 The meeting

ONE thing is certain: it was not in the snows of Alsace, at the end of 1944, that they met. Another (no less imaginary?) story is even more appropriate to these myth-makers: de Gaulle and Malraux are supposed to have sat side by side at the three-screen showing of Abel Gance's extraordinary film *Napoleon* in 1936, 'and both men stood up together to applaud the show – and themselves – in a sort of delirium.'[1]

But the conversation that forged the alliance must be situated in early August 1945, in the solemn and unspectacular offices of the Ministry of Defence in which de Gaulle was then housed and as the result of a Pirandellian intrigue of which Malraux, in the *Antimémoires*, gives a version confused enough to be true.

Corniglion-Molinier, Malraux's companion from the Yemen adventure, now an FFI general and a member of the 'entourage', introduced his friend to the General's closest colleagues, Gaston Palewski and Captain Claude Guy. This was followed by a dinner at Palewski's. Malraux talked of mass education by radio, public opinion polls and Indo-China: this was in March 1945, the Japanese had just destroyed the French colonial system and, according to the *Antimémoires*, he spoke to Palewski and Corniglion about Ho Chi Minh, whose name was still unknown except to his comrades and to one or two specialists in the Colonial Ministry.

Malraux dazzled his audience. His name began to crop up more and more. One summer's evening he was visited by 'one of my regular contacts',[2] who said simply: 'General de Gaulle asks you in the name of France if you will help him.' 'It goes without saying,' Malraux replied. 'I was surprised but not excessively so – I have a tendency to think myself useful . . .'[3]

It was not until five months later, in the course of some conversation, that he guessed 'for no apparent reason' that de Gaulle 'had *never* summoned me' – that they had been 'characters in a curious intrigue, which he probably suspected before I did . . . When his supposed message was delivered to me, he must also have been given mine . . .'[4] But there had been the speech at the MLN congress which, coming from so markedly political a character, might be regarded as an appeal and was taken as such by some of the General's advisers. Above all, the Prince's entourage included that same Corniglion who, though he had become a general, was still none the less the Niçois of Italian origin who loved astonishing coups (the Queen of Sheba!), amusing schemes and stupendous gambles. And he was a close friend of both 'characters' . . .

Malraux's first appearances on de Gaulle's staff were uneventful enough. Claude Mauriac, François' son who at the time shared responsibility for the General's secretariat (which he was later to head), notes that on 9 August he saw Malraux, about whom he was writing a book.[5] 'I was astonished by his youthful and ordinary appearance,' he writes. 'Naïvely, I expected his prestige and genius to illuminate his face.' Eleven days later, he saw Malraux again in the office of de Gaulle's aides-de-camp. 'Nothing but generals!' Malraux sighed with embarrassed irony. 'It is to the General, to him personally, that I am attached . . .'[6]

The meeting took place, Malraux writes, on 10 August:

> I had retained an exact memory of his face: in 1943 Ravanel, then chief of the *groupes francs* [Resistance commandos], had shown me a photograph of him that had arrived by parachute. It was a head-and-shoulders picture; we did not even know that General de Gaulle was very tall . . . What struck me now were the ways in which he did not resemble his photographs. The real mouth was a little smaller, the moustache a little darker. And the cinema, although it conveys all sorts of expressions, has only once caught his dense heavy gaze . . .

'First of all, the past,' he said.
A surprising introduction.[7]

In fact, it was not in the least surprising. Between the authors
of *Fil de l'épée* and *Le Temps du Mépris*, there must have been
several misunderstandings to clear up . . . For this historian in
power, confronting his Communist allies, the 'past' meant:
'How do you stand with them now? How far have you gone?
What is left?' A crucial question. Furthermore, this 'past' was
an acknowledgement of achievement. De Gaulle's 'you exist
for me' (for good or bad) and 'tell me about yourself' could not
fail to seduce a man like Malraux, for de Gaulle was not acti-
vated by mere curiosity, but by a concern for all that was most
noble and serious. De Gaulle's approach was a typical stroke of
genius.

Malraux's account in twenty lines ('I engaged in a struggle
for . . . let's call it social justice. Perhaps, more precisely, the aim
was to give man a chance . . . When a weak France finds herself
face to face with a powerful Russia, I no longer believe a word
of what I used to believe when a powerful France faced a weak
Soviet Union. A weak Russia wants popular fronts, a strong
Russia wants people's democracies . . .') is perhaps a little over-
conciliatory. But it is a valid interpretation.

And then he told de Gaulle exactly what de Gaulle wanted to
hear from a man like him – that 'the essential lesson of the last
twenty years has been the primacy of the nation'; that 'in this
context it wasn't Marx who was the prophet but Nietzsche . . .';
that the resistance is against 'the Russian element in French
Communism'; that the French nation as a whole senses that 'we
are going through the most violent metamorphosis the West
has known since the fall of the Roman Empire' and has no
wish 'to face it under the guidance of M. Herriot'. Full marks!
Did he say what he did simply to please de Gaulle? Rather
because he believed it too.

And then they spoke about the Revolution, Mirabeau,
General Hoche, of whom the General remarked 'at the time he
was poisoned he was going astray . . .' Malraux pretended to be
surprised. 'Dictatorship . . .' the General added, by way of
explanation. He raised his forefinger: 'Make no mistake: France

no longer wants Revolution. The time is past.' Having made this clear – and such an idea would no longer disappoint the Malraux of 1945 – they talked about intellectuals with unruffled irony. 'At the present moment,' said Malraux, '*You are not getting through to them.*' And, concluding his father confessor turn, the General asked: 'What struck you most when you came back to Paris?' 'The lies,' replied the writer – or to be more precise in this case, the novelist.

Had Malraux been won over? Not yet. His first reaction was to think about the man who had not so much received him as listened to him – and for that reason seemed highly intelligent. What stayed in Malraux's mind was:

> This remoteness, all the more curious because it appeared not only between himself and his interlocutor but between what he said and what he was. I had already come across this intense presence that has nothing to do with words – not in military men, or politicians, or artists, but in distinguished men of religion, whose affably commonplace words seem to bear no relation to their inner life. It was this that had reminded me of the mystics when he had spoken of Revolution . . .
>
> He established with the person he was talking to a very powerful contact, which seemed inexplicable when one had left him. A contact above all due to a feeling of having come up against a total personality . . .
>
> I was trying to get to the bottom of a complex impression: the man lived up to his myth, but *in what sense*? Valéry lived up to his, because he spoke with the vigour and penetration of 'Monsieur Teste' – slang and fantasy to boot. Einstein was worthy of Einstein by virtue of that simplicity, as of a rumpled Franciscan, which in fact the Franciscans lack. Great painters are themselves only when they talk about painting. The only figure whom General de Gaulle then called to my mind, by way of antithesis rather than resemblance, in the way that Ingres brings to mind Delacroix, was Trotsky.[8]

Some weeks later, on 6 November, in a conversation with his colleague Claude Mauriac – by this time Malraux had also joined the General's staff – he described his first conversation with de Gaulle:

> A prodigious ruminant . . . as unshakable as a rock. Fascinated by principle and for that reason invulnerable in an unprincipled world . . . Positive: the extraordinary care he brings to reconstructing the machinery of the State . . . Negative: this fascination with the Rhine, which is no longer an issue . . . And the ignorance he has about the people . . . What a weakness never to have had a meal with a worker!. . .[9]

At this point, in fact, Malraux had not been subjugated, any more at least than Gide or Bernanos had been a little earlier. And a good deal less than François Mauriac. While thoroughly involved in the game of sharing the responsibility of power, Malraux admired, but not without losing his judgement. Gaston Palewski remembers Malraux's contributions to the 'morning meetings', at which the General's work was prepared. Far from confining himself to the cultural field, he threw himself enthusiastically into political discussion. But the spirit of 'opposition', of 'unorthodoxy', in the group was represented not by Malraux, but by an ex-schoolmaster who had been recently introduced to the staff – Georges Pompidou.[10]

The most interesting thing that Malraux said on 6 November to his young colleague concerns his own attitude: 'We must have the courage to face up to the Communists . . . We have a tough time ahead of us. There'll be quite a fight. That is my only excuse, my only reason, for being in this office.'[11]

He launched into the 'fight' as a minister. On 21 November 1945, after offering his resignation, de Gaulle was called upon by a unanimous vote in the Chamber of Deputies to form a new government made up 'equitably' of the MRP (Christian Socialists, SFIO (Socialists) and PCF. André Malraux became Minister of Information. He had ceased being a semi-official person. The author of *Le Temps du Mépris* and *L'Espoir*, the advocate of Thaelmann and the admirer of Trotsky took on responsibilities at the most public level: he became General de Gaulle's spokesman. And when one is Malraux, no task could be more demanding.

Why? One must not forget that he enjoyed being a minister (of Charles de Gaulle, of course, not of just anybody). The man who had known poverty now liked comfort. The man who had been something of an 'outsider' liked respectability. The man who had been charged and found guilty in a court of law liked power. A man of lofty thoughts – who also exalts the values of action and efficacy – naturally wishes to exercise power, providing it does not mean that he must abandon his ideas. We have seen Malraux's ideas of the 1930s crumble and re-emerge, transformed, as a result of the struggle in Spain, Stalinist strategy, the infiltration tactics of the Resistance and the balance of power in the world and in France at the end of the war.

The government in which he found himself had a majority of Socialists and Communists; it was the most 'left-wing' government that France has ever known. All the portfolios concerned with industrial production, including armaments (which had been given to Charles Tillon, the head of the FTP in the Maquis), were in the hands of the PCF. And on the social front, the first de Gaulle government was already going beyond what had been achieved by the Popular Front. What was being carried out was the programme of the Resistance – and, to some degree at least, the nationalisation of credit which, at the MLN congress, on 27 January, Malraux had seen as the key to any left-wing politics in the France of the Liberation.

It goes without saying that the sudden contract that had just bound Malraux to de Gaulle went well beyond, on the human plane, a common wish to realise a certain programme. And although it is possible to explain André Malraux's entry into de Gaulle's second cabinet[12] on rational grounds, we must go beyond that and discover why the author of *L'Espoir* had vowed allegiance to the author of *Fil de l'épée*. Was it because Malraux saw de Gaulle as the embodiment of history in the process of being made, as he had seen Trotsky? Was it because Malraux felt that although he had never eaten with a worker, de Gaulle belonged nevertheless to that 'famille Michelet'[13] which Malraux was using more and more as a reference point, in place of such concepts as 'class' or 'mass' (which, in any case, had never meant a great deal to him)? Was it because he glimpsed in de Gaulle (he knew his books and the speeches he had made in

London and after the Liberation) a synthesis of the man of action and the artist that responded symmetrically to that other synthesis – of the artist and the man of action – towards which he had always striven?

Was it because he too was a gambler, a man who took up a challenge, and at a time when the only challenge worthy of him was one he could address to Stalin, de Gaulle was the only partner with whom such an adventure could be attempted? Was it because, like Lawrence and Vincent Berger, this adventurer of fraternity needed a leader, a figurehead, a 'Prince', an elder brother dedicated to some great plan? Some light is thrown on his choice in a remark he later made to his friend Nino Frank: 'Adventure no longer exists except at the level of governments.'[14] Taken with his words 'it is too late to act upon things, one must act upon someone' and Hamlet's 'rightly to be great is not to stir without great argument', we have three very good keys to an understanding of the post-war Malraux.

In short he was enfeoffed to the General, who accepted this new companion with enthusiasm. The way was so uncertain that those who offered themselves were welcome. But for de Gaulle, there was more to it than that. Malraux was not one of his favourite writers – he preferred Montherlant, Bernanos and Mauriac. However, no accession to his cause could have affected him as much, because the author of *La Condition humaine* was not only a great artist of international reputation, whose influence was greater than that of any of his rivals, with the exception of Gide, but also a man of action (if only in an amateur capacity). And, what is more, a symbolic representative of that internal resistance with which he had never been able to associate himself completely.

Malraux still admired the Communist system, Stalin's Machiavellian tactics and the Red Army. But he believed that the new balance of forces in Europe had changed the very nature of Communism, and that the weight of the USSR emerging from the war made it objectively imperialistic. In a conversation with de Gaulle and Léon Blum, a few days after he joined the government, he said:

How can you expect true Communists not to take us for

another Kerensky or Pilsudski government? It's simply a question of who shoots first: it's no longer a state, it's a Western gunfight. Remember the Popular Front . . . It worked . . . because the Soviet Union was weak. With the Red Army and the Stalin of today . . .[15]

He remained attached to the preservation of the Soviet Union, but feared its expansion: 'Everything for Russia, nothing by Russia,' he said to Stéphane in Alsace.[16] He was haunted by the sudden revelation, in the spring of 1945, of the overwhelming power of this Red Army, which he had so praised in 1935, so yearned for in Spain and hoped to join (or so he said) in 1942 . . . He was no less haunted by the Communist use of infiltration techniques before, during and after the Resistance. In the *Antimémoires*, he writes of the MLN congress that most of the officially non-Communist delegates with whom he had dealings later proved to be members of the Party: though speaking in terms of formal membership, the figure of ninety per cent is exaggerated.

He was also obsessed by the fascination that the PCF exerted over intellectuals. In his conversation with de Gaulle in August, Malraux put the situation quite brilliantly. 'Literature is full of tender souls for whom the proletariat are noble savages. But it isn't easy to understand how Diderot could possibly have believed that Catherine the Great had anything to do with Liberty . . .'[17] And his conversation with Stéphane in Alsace is studded with jibes against left-wing intellectuals, from the 'intellectuals of the Café de Flore' (which for him, at this time, meant Albert Camus) to the intellectuals of *Les Temps modernes*, Sartre and Merleau-Ponty, with whom he had just refused to collaborate.

Once again, Malraux saw the problem in terms of morality and 'virility'; it took more courage to oppose the powerful Communists than to fight their intimidated enemies, just as ten years earlier it had taken more courage to oppose fascism than to denounce its divided enemies. His political strategy was beginning to resemble what he had recently said to Claude Mauriac: 'We must have the courage to face up to the Communists . . . There'll be quite a fight. That is my only excuse,

my only reason, for being in this office . . .' This type of statement does not, to say the least, reflect a meticulous analysis of
economic or ideological factors: but Malraux's 'politics', like
those of d'Annunzio, Montherlant or Jünger, have often been
based on this type of semi-ethical, semi-aesthetic argument.

In short, he is not so much anti-Communist as hostile to the
hegemony of the strong. And the Party, so unaccommodating
with its adversaries and above all so intolerant of anyone who
might be regarded as a defector, continued to put up with him
for a little longer. We have seen how after the MLN congress
Pierre Hervé, who can bite when he wants to, took Malraux
to task more in sorrow than in anger: so did a press not noted
for its tender-heartedness.

Was he an anti-Communist? At this time, neither de Gaulle
nor Malraux was an anti-Communist in the sense that Winston
Churchill or Arthur Koestler already were. They were certainly
on their guard against the Party, against its encroachments, its
claims to embody the *whole* of the Resistance and to assume the
essential functions of power. They were certainly on a slippery
slope – and Stéphane (like Claude Mauriac) asked him some
penetrating, almost prophetic questions on the subject. But it
seems to me that it is all too easy to judge these attitudes
twenty-eight years later.

The de Gaulle–Malraux relationship was based not upon a
negative or defensive theme, but on similar views of history,
on a shared ethic and, still more important, aesthetic of public
life, on a respect for a great cause, a 'great argument' that
resulted from an isolation that they had both borne impatiently.
It was not until later that they were united in a witch-hunt.

33 *A Minister for two months*

I BECAME Minister of Information. An instructive job: my
chief task was to prevent each party from grabbing all the
bedclothes. Thorez observed the rules of the game, putting
the Communist Party at the service of national reconstruction. But at the same time the Party was infiltrating furiously; Marcel Paul's reports were blatantly false. And in this
tripartite government, false Communist statements gave rise
to false statements on the part of the Socialists and the MRP.[1]

André Malraux was given too little time to prove himself in
this task of objective clarification. He chose as aides two men
of some substance. The minister's secretary-general was Jacques
Chaban-Delmas, a young FFI general who had been one of the
leading 'Free French' military delegates in occupied territory
and was beginning to make a name for himself: his *directeur-de-
cabinet* was Raymond Aron, one of the few men who could not
say with Gide that 'when one is with Malraux, one does not feel
very intelligent.' They had met as early as 1927. Then, Aron's
books on German philosophy had made him an intellectual
leader of the young generation. In short, this minister ran no
risk of sinking into somnolence.

Malraux set the tone when he had to appear before the
Chamber to defend his budget: 'To an interruptor from the
extreme-right who threw the word "liberty" at him, the minister replied: "Liberty belongs to those who have won it!" '[2]

Shades of Garine and Garcia . . . But General de Gaulle's
Minister of Information did not often have the opportunity of

acting out a scene from *Les Conquérants*. His two main tasks were first to communicate to public opinion the decisions and intentions adopted or expressed in the meetings of the Council of Ministers – a responsibility simplified (or, for him, complicated) by the presence of the General himself, who was hardly noted for his taciturnity; and, secondly, to allocate the paper rations among the various newspapers. In actual fact, this second task should have occupied him much more than the first. In the opinion of many of the paper users of the time, Malraux showed little application or competence in this field.

Though somewhat limited in his role as official spokesman by his monumental boss, he certainly found some consolation in transforming his ministry into the beginning of what, thirteen years later, would become the ministry of Cultural Affairs, and tried to put into practice his three main ideas: popular culture through the image, mass education by radio and the widespread use of public opinion polls. The sociologist Jean Stoetzel was given the first state money ever to be used for a public opinion poll in France – thus bearing partial responsibility for an epidemic that has affected the public life of that country ever since.

And he was able to give no more than a foretaste of another of his pet schemes – the 'imaginary museum' that he wished to set up in every place of work and education through the medium of reproductions of masterpieces, printed according to the methods of his friend Fautrier. The first series of such works was already being planned: Renoir's *Le Moulin de la Galette,* Watteau's *Pietà d' Avignon* and *Enseigne de Gersaint,* and Cézanne's *Château noir.* Only the first of these was printed and distributed: those who visited André Malraux's house at Boulogne, from 1946 onwards, could not fail to notice in the hall the fine life-size reproduction of Renoir's work.

But it was politics that preoccupied the Minister of Information above all. He was in the thick of discussions on the Constitution and proposed a presidential-type system, directly inspired by that of the United States, in which the head of the executive would not be responsible to parliament.[3] Cyrus Sulzberger, the correspondent of the *New York Times*, was granted an interview with Malraux on 8 January 1946. Sulzberger notes that Malraux expressed himself with great verve and seemed 'very assertive and sure of his opinions', but that his grasp of contemporary history seemed rather shaky. (Malraux told him that he had met Tito in Spain – in fact, the future Yugoslav leader had never set foot in Spain, being based at the time in France, mainly at Marseilles, where he was in charge of organising the recruitment and transport of volunteers for the International Brigade.)

In his diary for 9 January 1946, Sulzberger wrote:

> Visited André Malraux, now de Gaulle's brilliant minister of information. He is extremely nervous and rather dissipated looking: very thin, with dark shadows under his eyes and a long nose and face. He smokes American cigarettes constantly and refuses to sit down, walking about all the time . . . He said . . . The strength of the Communists was greatly exaggerated . . .
>
> Malraux thinks the Communists do not wish to really get power in France. He does not foresee any Communist effort at an armed *coup d'état* . . .
>
> Right now the Communists are insisting on a pre-war type of governmental philosophy with the executive powers controlled by the assembly . . . De Gaulle wants an American-type democracy and more executive power for the president. Malraux expects a very serious crisis long before May when the constitution will be completed. He does not know whether de Gaulle will resign and form his own party or not. He says it is possible but not probable . . .[4]

Shortly afterwards, the General's spokesman was informed – he was one of the first to learn of the decision announced by de Gaulle to his ministers on Sunday 20 January. This is Malraux's version:

> After ministerial meetings I used to stay behind with him to draw up the official communiqué. One day,[5] as we were going down the imitation marble staircase of the Hôtel Matignon, he said to me:
> 'What do you think you'll do at the Ministry of Information now?'

'Make a ministry of it, General. It will be finished in six weeks.'

'I shall have gone by then.'[6]

And so in the armour room of the Ministry in the rue Saint-Dominique the announcement of his departure was made before his assembled ministers. The only immediate comment came from the Communist leader Maurice Thorez: 'Voilà qui ne manque pas de grandeur!' This should not be seen as the hypo-critical homage of a man well satisfied. Thorez was too astute for that; he was very well aware of the risks created by the new situation – for him and his friends, as well as for the nation as a whole.

Most of de Gaulle's friends did not react in this way. Malraux and Claude Mauriac, for example, deplored the fact that he should have taken his leave with so much apparent unconcern: 'The annoying thing is not so much his departure,' André Malraux remarked some days later to his young colleague, 'as the letter that accompanied it . . . that deplorable paragraph . . . I took the liberty of telling him that the man of 18 June could not take his leave with a letter to President Gouin.[7] He agreed, but nothing came of it . . .'[8]

The departure, which de Gaulle regarded as a mere tactic (he was convinced that he would be recalled), caused a political earthquake. Should the government, the régime, be changed? Or should they simply paper over the cracks and appoint at the head of a virtually unchanged ministry a 'successor' to de Gaulle? The idea was debated inside a committee of the Christian Socialist MRP, whose leader, the foreign minister Georges Bidault, got up to denounce 'Malraux, this condemned man, this former convict!'[9]

Without waiting to learn whether General de Gaulle's spokes-man would become the spokesman of M. Félix Gouin, André Malraux regained his freedom. With his *Moulin de la Galette* rolled up under his arm, he returned to Boulogne-sur-Seine, where he was first of all the guest, and later the husband of his sister-in-law Madeleine. He was now, on top of everything else, a forty-five-year-old ex-minister.

34　Crusade in the Métro

WOULD he have resigned if it had been entirely up to him? He once remarked that he was in art as one is in religion, and there was that *Psychologie de l'art* that had been awaiting him since 1 September 1939 at Beaulieu-sur-Dordogne. He did try to get back to it, but there was the 'historic destiny' of Charles de Gaulle. There was, too, that whole constellation around him that was not yet the Colombey party, nor as yet that of Marly (the General's first place of retirement), for it was by no means sure what the 'king in exile' wanted. He did say or write to a number of friends – such as his former BBC spokesman, Maurice Schumann – that his retirement would be only for a time and that, in a few months . . . But those who wanted to bring him back to power were acting, at this time, on their own.

André Malraux joined the 'Study Committee for the Return of General de Gaulle', largely made up of the intellectuals of Gaullism, from Raymond Aron to Michel Debré, and the weekly lunches of the Gaullist 'barons', attended among others by Gaston Palewski, Jacques Chaban-Delmas and Georges Pompidou.

It was at this period, in late February 1947, at Boulogne, that I met him for the first time. I had just returned after a long stay in Indo-China and a mutual friend, Georges Manue, had already written to him by way of introduction. Accordingly, I was invited to the large house in Boulogne to talk to Malraux about what was happening in Hanoi and Saigon. Of course it was Malraux who did all the talking. He talked of nothing but Indo-China, and mainly from a strategic angle. He referred of course

to the need for agrarian reform and to the priority that should
be given to the problems of the peasants' standard of living.
But he also suggested the regrouping of the whole expedi-
tionary corps in the ports (Haiphong, Tourane, Cam-Rahn,
Saigon, Cap Saint-Jacques). The French could then say to the
Vietminh: 'Gentlemen, here we stand. Come and get us, or let
us negotiate . . .' This thesis was soon to be sustained by Pierre
Mendès France and François Mitterrand. The adventurer and
revolutionary of 1925 had been forgotten, in favour of the
statesman.

But de Gaulle, waiting in the shadows, was to fascinate him
more and more. A little later (in March 1946) he confided to
Claude Mauriac:

> I have known a relatively large number of statesmen but
> none has anything like his greatness . . . We must never for-
> get that he is a man of destiny . . . We are engaged in a tragic
> adventure. We must assume the risks that this involves . . .
> The truth is that we are witnessing the end of Europe . . .
> Europe's only chance – a Western block formed around
> France and England – no longer exists . . . Confronted by
> monstrous empires, we are doomed to be vassals, and a
> policy that does not take these new facts into account is
> absurd . . .

Despite the epic pathos of the beginning, this statement is
closer in the sudden humility of its conclusion to those of
Robert Schuman than to the General's nationalistic harangues.
Malraux goes on, in rather heretical vein:

> It is deplorable that de Gaulle should have crystallised
> against him all the forces of the left. This would not have
> happened if I had met him earlier. The great weakness of that
> great mind lies there . . .

And Claude Mauriac adds this comment:

> Never was he more committed. Never did he accept the
> risks of the adventure with as much calm. Did the value of
> the cause that he had chosen seem to him less important (as
> it did to Garine) than the struggle that it involved? . . .

However, he did not involve himself in any plots and scarcely wished to. Until de Gaulle broke his silence, he said, it was the duty of his supporters – especially his former ministers – to remain silent . . .[1]

During this period, Malraux was not often to be seen at Marly or Colombey. He was working on his essay on art, and published his *Esquisse d'une psychologie du cinéma* and his *Scènes choisies*, in which he included two large extracts from *Le Temps du Mépris* – as if to rehabilitate a book he pretended to despise, and perhaps, too, to show that although his political strategy had changed, he had not abandoned his essential ideas.

On 4 November 1946, at a solemn session of the new-born UNESCO in the great hall of the Sorbonne, he was given the opportunity of addressing to the world a message in which this internationalist turned nationalist suddenly spoke in a passionately European language. It is a fine speech but, coming from an author who had fought for universal values, it is somewhat defensive and pessimistic:

> What are the values of the West at the present time? We have seen enough to know that they are certainly neither rationalism nor progress. Optimism, faith in progress, are American and Russian rather than European values. The first European value is the will to consciousness. The second is the will to discovery. It is that succession of forms that we have seen in painting. It is that permanent struggle of psychology against logic that we have seen in the novel and that we see in the forms of the mind. It is the refusal to accept as dogma an imposed form, because, after all, navigators may have discovered parrots but parrots have never discovered navigators.
>
> The strength of the West is an acceptance of the unknown. There is a possible humanism, but it must be said, quite clearly, that it is a tragic humanism. We are confronted by an unknown world; we confront it with consciousness. And in wishing to do so we are alone. Let there be no misunderstanding: the will to consciousness and the will to discovery, as fundamental values, belong to Europe and to Europe alone . . .

The art of Europe is not a heritage, it is a system of will
... We are not on a field of death. We are at the crucial point
at which the European will must remember that every great
heir ignores or despoils the objects of his heritage, and really
inherits only intelligence and strength. The happy heir of
Christianity is Pascal. The heritage of Europe is tragic
humanism ... Despite the most sinister appearances, those
who will come after us may regard contemporary anguish
with stupefaction; the Europe of the fall of Rome, the
Europe of Nicopolis, the Europe of the fall of Byzantium
may seem to them mere ripples beside the determined spirit
that says to the huge, threatening shadows that are beginning
to spread over it: We shall use you, as we have used everything else, to drag man once more out of the clay.

But the time for a new choice was approaching. De Gaulle
had worked out a strategy that would bring him back to power,
either legally – for this he was counting on the constitutional
referendum which, it seemed to him, would sound the death
knell of 'government by parties' – or by a . . . less legal way.
   The strategy consisted of two operations, each in two stages.
The first operation took place in 1946. It involved blocking the
adoption of a constitution that would mean that France would
be governed by a 'convention' of the kind set up in Year I of
the Revolution. In order to avoid this General de Gaulle made
speeches first at Bayeux (in June), then at Épinal (in September).
On the first occasion, his plea for a strong republic, with a
powerful executive (the Fifth Republic in embryo) helped to
'sink' the government's bill. But the second time he did not
succeed in blocking the road to his successors. A bill establish-
ing 'parliamentary sovereignty' was adopted on 13 October.
The ways of strict legality were closed.
   At this point, the second operation was put into action – and
it is here that Malraux reappears. On 21 February 1947, he was
visited at Boulogne by Cyrus Sulzberger. The American journalist found him even more nervous than at their first meeting,
chainsmoking and making 'all kinds of strange noises' as he
talked. Malraux, it appears, did not have the time to work at
his 'history of art', because, 'these are not times for that'.

The visitor, who regarded Malraux as 'obviously close to de Gaulle', and as exerting 'great influence' over the General, quotes him as making some highly optimistic statements: the pressure of public opinion will force the president of the Republic to give the premiership to de Gaulle, who will accept it only on condition that he has full powers for two years. A referendum for a new constitution will be presented to the French people: if de Gaulle wins, he 'will come in as a dictator'. Malraux adds that de Gaulle has more chance of taking power than the Communists, because the conquest of power in France by the Communists would trigger off a world war for which 'Russia is not yet ready'.

For these reasons, or for others, the ex-Minister of Information was not in favour of the rapid creation of a great Gaullist party, but was trying, like Claude Mauriac (or so he told him), to moderate the General's impatience. But on 7 April 1947 they crossed the Rubicon. At Strasbourg – for Malraux the most symbolic of all cities – Charles de Gaulle announced the foundation of the 'Rassemblement du peuple français'. Malraux was on the balcony of the town hall behind the General, who declaimed the following:

> The Republic that we brought out of the tomb in which the despair of the nation had buried it . . . will be efficiency, concord and liberty or it will be mere impotence and disillusion, until it disappears by a gradual process of infiltration beneath a certain kind of dictatorship, or loses in anarchy the very independence of France . . . The time has come to form and organise the Rally of the French People which, within the law, will promote and bring to triumph, above differences of opinion, a great effort of common salvation and the profound reform of the State. Thus, tomorrow, in a harmony of action and will, the French Republic will build the new France.[2]

'Infiltration', 'a certain kind of dictatorship': de Gaulle had chosen his target. From the outset, the RPF declared itself for what it was, an anti-Communist counter-attack. Malraux, who accepted the post of 'delegate for propaganda' – an odd title for someone who had gone to Berlin in January 1934! – did not even deny it. He invented a formula: 'Before, one defined one's position in relation to the Communists. From now on, one will define one's position in relation to the RPF' – which merely presented the same truth in a different light. But he did not find much to reply to Claude Mauriac, who objected that the real virtues of the French people were not to be found in such company . . .

The atmosphere that de Gaulle created and sustained, not only for the benefit of his followers, but in all his public speeches of the years 1947–53, is that of world-wide catastrophe. War was certain, mathematically inevitable . . . France was lost – unless the General returned to the helm, and even then it might be too late. What is more, this belief in impending catastrophe was held quite sincerely by de Gaulle – and by Malraux too. All the conversations between the General and Claude Mauriac, the most faithful witness of the development of his thinking in the late 1940s, are filled with this mixture of bitter contempt and overwhelming pessimism – to which Malraux adds his own touch of personal pathos: the aesthetic of the Apocalypse.

So Malraux was now a 'companion' – as de Gaulle chose to call his supporters – and delegate for 'propaganda' of a party whose mass membership consisted of twenty per cent workers, disappointed or frightened by the Communists, and eighty per cent old Vichyism, an alliance of the frightened bourgeoisie and nationalism, that 'closed' value that he had so often and so harshly condemned. He did not feel too much at ease there at first. At Bordeaux, when de Gaulle went to speak on May 1947, Malraux tried to convince Mauriac to join the RPF. I heard the reluctant François Mauriac laugh quietly to himself and murmur: 'And to think that I am now on the left of Malraux!'

But what, in fact, was Malraux's own position in the RPF? How did he see the movement and his own role in it? People have often quoted his formula 'the RPF is the métro', which does not mean that this organisation was involved in underground activity, but that its support lay mainly in the lower-middle-class and white-collar workers. This may well have been the impression given at the public meetings addressed by Malraux and General de Gaulle. It was not true of the upper echelons of the party which, with a few exceptions, were those of a party of the traditional right, in ideas, behaviour, style and financial support. To this was added a new element, that of the 'knights of the round table' of the Gaullist Resistance.

It cannot be said that, during the two years in which he took an active part in the movement – from spring 1947 to summer 1949 – André Malraux was in an isolated and incongruous position in the only party he had ever belonged to.[3] As 'delegate for propaganda', he was in direct contact with General de Gaulle who, from 14 April, had taken over complete control and responsibility for the movement, following developments very closely from his office in the rue de Solférino.

Assisted by a powerful team, Malraux worked hard at his job. Everyone, from the secretaries to party leaders, called him familiarly 'André'. In his offices near the Opéra, at 19 boulevard des Capucines, Malraux had succeeded in creating an atmosphere of fraternity that he finally took for fraternity itself; and perhaps, on occasion, he actually believed that he had gone back to the time of the squadron and Raymond Maréchal . . .

At first, the 'propaganda' took the form of an information sheet entitled *L'Étincelle* (*The Spark*) – one wonders whether Malraux felt any embarrassment at appropriating the name of Lenin's newspaper. Soon, however, this organ came to be regarded as somewhat lightweight and a new weekly, *Le Rassemblement*, was started by a group of journalists who, with Camus and Aron, had helped to make *Combat*[4] the best French paper of the immediate post-war years. *Le Rassemblement* was no better for that – and no doubt remains an embarrassing memory for these talented men. Less disappointing for Malraux – and for those who valued what he did and wrote – was the review *Liberté de l'esprit*, which he founded a year later with Claude Mauriac. It was there that he published *Le Démon de l'absolu*.

What Malraux had been involved in was not so much 'propaganda' as the presentation of a big spectacle: André Malraux 'directed' Charles de Gaulle. One thinks of Eisenstein and Alexander Nevsky . . . But the great Russian director was at his best when directing the dead. For three years, Charles de Gaulle was a huge Gallic druid confronting the Tartars and Helots of the system. Music, lighting, crowds in the shadows giving vent to their hopes and anger, platforms draped with the tricolour and balconies looking down over the yelling multitude, strong-arm attendants and short, sharp slogans – everything was done to give the great ceremonial a sacred, militant, sonorous character and to keep the crowds up to scratch. But to what end?

There are two levels at which one may interpret the RPF and Malraux's role in it. Let us take the higher level first. It is expressed in a long interview that André Malraux gave in February 1948 to James Burnham.[5] Malraux provides the following definition of 'Gaullism':

> What Gaullism wants above all is to give France an architecture and an efficacity. We do not say that we will succeed, but we do say quite categorically that our opponents will not do this. Do not forget that Gaullism is not a theory like Marxism or even fascism, it is a movement of public safety . . .
>
> There is no true democracy where there is a strong Communist Party . . . There was no need for Stalin in 1944 to throw his party against the revival of France. Today, a reviving France can only be drawn into the orbit of the Anglo–Saxons, of the United States in particular. It is therefore indispensable for the Russians that France should not revive . . .

Hence the need to muzzle, by means that cannot be those of 'true democracy', and with a view to 'public safety', the party that is opposed to the revival of France.

On 5 March 1949, in more strident manner, he addressed those 'intellectuals' – left-wing intellectuals, of course – who at that time were harassing him, denouncing him and calling him a turncoat if not actually a fascist, and who had come in large numbers to the Salle Pleyel to heckle him.[6] Denouncing Stalinist 'mystifications' and the trials by 'abjuration' to which he and almost all his companions of the antifascist struggles of 1933–9 had been subjected, Malraux declared:

> A few years ago it was difficult to deny that Trotsky had created the Red Army: for *L'Humanité* to be fully effective, the reader must not read any other newspaper . . . Our

essential problem is this: How can we prevent psychological techniques destroying the quality of the spirit? . . . Almost all of you, in the intellectual sphere, are liberals. For us, the guarantee of political liberty and the intellectual liberty lies not in political liberalism, which is condemned to death as soon as it is confronted by the Stalinists: the guarantee of liberty is the power of the State at the service of all the citizens.

The vehemence of the tone comes naturally to him: there are people who order their breakfast with the voice of Cassandra. But this vehemence was increased by the catastrophic vision of things that he then shared with the General – and also by the trial to which he had been subjected by most of those who were or, in his view, ought to be his friends.

A few days earlier, on 18 February 1948, he spoke for the second time at the Vélodrome d'Hiver, and there were many of us who, having missed the meeting of July 1947 where he had developed his extraordinary verbal Apocalypse, did not wish to miss this particular performance. We saw him emerge, cleverly haggard-looking under the spotlights, Oedipus with his eyes still open, but his brow, almost shattered by history, yet ready nevertheless to confront a cruelly tragic destiny, a hand placed allegorically on the shoulder of de Gaulle–Antigone – unless it was he playing Antigone to the hero . . . He spoke of the rose-trees growing in the park at Versailles, of Goya and de Sade, of the Tartars, of Piero della Francesca and Tolstoy. We were not sure whether the appropriate response was to abandon ourselves to the flow of words, show concern or simply admire . . . François Mauriac, his chin resting on his left hand, was taking notes:

This son of adventure had arrived at the same point as Barrès, that great sedentary bourgeois: an appeal to the soldier . . . It was against the formidable Stalin that this age-less David was launching his attack. He fought against Stalin much more than he fought for de Gaulle. Shall I say what I really think: I think André Malraux is proud enough to regard Charles de Gaulle as a card in his own hand . . .

And he concluded this article entitled 'The Life of a Gambler' thus: 'He feels alive only in those brief moments when it is given to him to play double or quits with his destiny.'[7] A platform was then arranged for him. In October 1948, under the title 'Interrogation à Malraux', Emmanuel Mounier's review *Esprit* published one of the most fascinating critical dossiers that have ever been devoted to the author of *La Condition humaine*. The theme of course was: Why had the antifascist fighter of 1936 engaged in this struggle, in a movement that nobody (or almost nobody . . .) called fascist, but the whiff of which so offended the nose of Mounier and his friends?

This number of *Esprit* certainly provided a platform for Malraux's friends, for Gaëtan Picon, for example, who made it clear that Malraux, a friend (but not a hostage) of the Communist underdogs, came out against them only when they were in a position of power that in many ways was totalitarian. Roger Stéphane repeated what the chief of the Alsace–Lorraine brigade had told him three years before: 'When one has written what I have written, one cannot be a fascist . . .'

But there were other, more searching observers. For Albert Béguin, Malraux:

> by adhering to a doctrine of authority . . . has carried the logic of his pessimism to its logical conclusion. His political opponents attribute this latest choice to a revival of heroic romanticism and an appetite for power. This is to misunderstand both the very real greatness of Malraux and the tragedy of his personal problem. Not that the romantic taste for adventure is alien to him, any more than the desire to act on crowds or to sway minds. But Malraux is not subject to vulgar ambition. For he is, in one sense, the only authentic French fascist. For, in this country, where fascists are regarded as reactionary, conservative, inflexible, he is virtually alone in following the classic path to fascism: the path of the revolutionary, who remains a revolutionary, but who, by experiencing failure or by innate propensity, comes to despair of men.

Emmanuel Mounier was less cruel. He called his essay 'Malraux or the impossible decline':

If Malraux, as he is so fond of saying and as the quality of his work would lead us to believe, has remained in himself faithful to all his past faith, one imagines that he is not making things very comfortable for himself today. If he really thinks that he can triumph, by the sheer single-mindedness of his solitary energy, over the accumulated mediocrities to be found in those last-ditch 'rallies' that the European petty bourgeoisie, at the end of its inventiveness and vitality, sees as heroic marches, one cannot deny that he is still battering on the frontiers of the impossible. But if this hypothesis, by which Malraux is saved from the charge of decline and facility, is true, would he not find in this paradox of action, in that obscure and lyrical ellipse from revolution to conservation, food for his old love of extremes and the absurd? The lyrical illusion has several faces. Hearing sometimes the disturbing pathos that emerges from his public declarations, one wonders anxiously whether some obscure alliance of unused fervour and invincible despair is not brewing that will throw the living forces of *L'Espoir* against the frail Europe of the conspirators of fear.

Writing in the Communist weekly *Action*, Pierre Hervé made this comment on Mounier's article – a good example of the tone adopted at the time by spokesmen of the PCF, a very different matter from that of the congress of the MLN:

> One really wonders why Mounier looks with such obstinacy for mid-day at 2 pm. Whoever said or thought that Malraux is, literally speaking, either a conservative or a reactionary? He is a fascist. Do you hear, Mounier? Fascist! ... Why do you omit the essential fact? Fascism, with all its terror, its concentration camps and its murderers?

Fear? It is true that it was then at the centre of everything and that one could easily define the RPF in terms of fear – by the fear that inspired it and by the fear that it inspired. There is a novel by Graham Greene called *The Ministry of Fear*. A good title for this strange and banal Assembly.

Panic! Such was the climate of the time, in that year of 1947–8, that de Gaulle and Malraux chose to speak in the accents of 1940 when confronted with the great fear that Communism – the Red Army as well as the PCF – inspired. It is impossible to understand the incredible adventure of the RPF if one does not try to situate it in the climate of the period, that of the rupture between East and West, the beginnings of the Cold War, the Prague coup, the signing of the Atlantic Pact, the trial-assassinations in the People's Democracies (those of Petkov, Rajk, Slansky), monstrous purges aimed in particular at the veterans of the Spanish Civil War.

It was the period when books by Koestler and Kravchenko gave an unflattering if not slanderous view of Soviet justice, with its apparatus of police terror and concentration camps – a view that was tragically familiar to those who had survived the Nazi camps and did much to feed the anti-Communist fever in conservative circles.

It was the period when, in the Chamber of Deputies, the Communist Jacques Duclos welcomed Robert Schuman, the head of the government, with the cry, 'Voilà le boche!' and when his comrades yelled 'Heil Hitler!' when Jules Moch appeared in the Chamber. It was the period when half the French intellectuals regarded as 'slimy rats' those who so much as doubted the democratic virtues and aesthetic genius of Stalin. It was a time worthy of the wars of religion.

But fear was not only felt and exploited by the leaders of the RPF. They also inflicted it. Before being tamed by politicians anxious to use it as a battering-ram to open the gates of Parliament, the RPF had been, for some of its creators – and for Malraux above all – an insurrectional movement. He said so over and over again. In the interview with Burnham quoted above Malraux had declared it to be a principle that 'true democracy' was not possible in the presence of a 'Stalinist Party'. He believed and said quite unambiguously that every means was justified in opposing terror, and that the system would be overthrown only with daring. And he quoted Danton and Saint-Just in the conviction that, confronted by the 'Tartars', he could be what the great figures of the Convention had been when confronted by Brunswick.

On 13 January 1948, in a conversation with Cyrus Sulzberger, he declared that the Communists 'will attempt an uprising in Italy and in France between 20 February and 1 March and will disrupt production by a series of strikes and incidents that will last for four months. They will begin by derailing a large number of trains during the first five days in order to bring about a shortage of raw materials and will also attempt a series of political assassinations.' Malraux added that their 'shock troops' numbered over eighty thousand trained men, but that the Gaullist Rassemblement also had a private army of its own.[8]

A few days later, he addressed several British correspondents, including Nora Beloff. Although she wrote her memoirs some twenty years later, she remained struck by what he had said, and the tone in which he had said it. He had spoken of a 're-organisation of the Resistance' against Communism, of a 'return to the Maquis'. He had set up a blackboard and launched into a veritable 'Kriegspiel' of arrows and circles. 'He seemed to be close to hysteria,' adds the correspondent of the *Observer* – a paper not very sympathetic to the RPF, it is true, but one that was well aware of Malraux's past.[9]

A past that seemed to have swallowed up, as in the night, his anticolonialist preoccupations. Whereas General Catroux[10] left the movement in order not to be associated with a strictly imperial policy – de Gaulle fully supported the war in Indo-China, having opted for d'Argenlieu's policy of no compromise against the conciliator Leclerc – not a word of objection to these aberrations is on record from Malraux. It is in the *Antimémoires*, not in the RPF, alas, that a more sophisticated view is to be found. The 'delegate for propaganda' did not even try to promote the tactically moderate views that he had expressed to me just prior to the creation of the RPF, but instead placed his talent, his name and his fame at the service of a war directed against the Indo-Chinese people – it was enough to make the young man of 1925 blush for shame.

He was tragically conformist on this point,[11] but did he stand out on others? Much has been said of the coexistence within the RPF of a legalist tendency expressed by Soustelle and an insurrectionist tendency represented by Malraux. Arbitrating in this conflict, de Gaulle, a man of authority but not an advocate of the coup d'état, came down in the end on the side of the former, and Soustelle slipped into the corridors of parliamentary power. It is no accident that Malraux has always refused to be a candidate for parliament.[12]

But Gaston Palewski, de Gaulle's right hand in London, now denies that Malraux was more 'illegalist' than his 'companions': 'You know, I advised the General whose brother had just been elected chairman of the Paris Municipal Council, to move into the Hôtel de Ville . . . An event that would not pass exactly unnoticed.'[13]

What we can be sure of, however, is that André Malraux saw his participation in the RPF as a struggle, physical as well as moral, against the Communists. He has spoken of none of his 'companions' with more warmth than the leader of the strong-arm men of the 'Service d'ordre'. This side of things is related in a curious book entitled *Croisade à coups de poings* (*Crusade with Punches*),[14] written by one of his former bodyguards, René Serre. It is worth dipping into. On page 135, for example, the author takes us to Marseilles where, during a conference of the RPF in 1948, the Communists, who were very well organised in the Bouches-du-Rhône, tried to sabotage a meeting:

> 'Gaullism is a school of energy!' cried André Malraux. These words marked the beginning of the fight. The whistles and missiles that had punctuated the earlier speeches were forgotten. Now the real fun began . . . I landed a punch at the chief of the Communist Service d'Ordre and brought this man-to-man duel between professional fighters to a speedy end with a hefty right punch . . . A second attacker kicked me in what is usually the most sensitive part of the human body. I took the blow smiling. The athlete's box was doing its job. The astonished Communist decided that it would be advisable to get out, which he did, followed by part of my shoe . . .

It was at this point that Malraux was exclaiming: 'We have given this country a certain number of ideas it needed!' Ideas? One might well prefer the fights over the Sierra de Teruel.

In any case, it was during this conference at Marseilles that the veteran of antifascism had his greatest triumph as an orator. It was the archetypal speech of his RPF period: Malraux recapi-

tulated all the themes that, from the Vélodrome d'Hiver to
Nancy, had punctuated his speeches. However, the selfindul-
gent aestheticism that often made his speeches inaccessible to a
large public was here reduced to a minimum.

He opened with the theme of propaganda, 'which is neither a
technique, nor a special skill', and which he would like to erase
from the vocabulary (not that he did).

> Our propaganda is that poster by Rodin depicting a
> Republic shouting her hopes in the destiny of France from
> the rooftops. And it is no use slashing the poster! Only the
> best posters are slashed! There are no more beautiful faces
> than those that bear wounds!

The second theme was anti-Communism:

> There can be no democracy where some of the participants
> cheat. Upsetting the chessboard is not just a rather special
> way of playing chess. There is no free play with the Stalinists,
> whose sole aim is to see that the pseudo-democratic game is
> run in France in the exclusive interests of Russia!

The third theme was that of the ideological content of the
Gaullist campaign:

> We then gave for the first time a serious content to the
> idea of general interest: on the one hand, a powerful arbitra-
> tion, and on the other, a real amalgam in which the nation
> can recognise itself . . . We have brought back to a country
> that had forgotten it since the death of Hoche and the death
> of Saint-Just this idea of the general interest on which France
> will, in the future, be based.

The prose became more purple as the speech moved towards
its conclusion:

> You French faces that surround me, on which I see again
> those Gothic faces beside me in captivity, in which I see
> again the simple faces of the soldiers of Verdun, those faces
> that are those of France herself – let the Stalinist journalists
> laugh! – a great honour is being done you: it has been given
> to you to raise with your perishable hands this great body of

France that lies groping in the shadows, observed by a world so often fascinated by it . . . France is like those great iron statues of ancient times, buried when the conquerors had passed on, and which a thunderbolt suddenly unearths, in times of disaster. This statue has been tragically unearthed . . .

And how did Malraux conclude? The day before, the General had asked him: 'What are you going to say?' And Malraux replied: 'I shall talk to them about chivalry!' The General pursed his lips sceptically: 'Try, Try . . .' This was the result, greeted by an outburst of applause:

> In the name of all of you, my companions in propaganda, I wish to repeat what we have tried throughout this year to make France understand: that the man who is about to speak is for us first of all the man who, during this country's terrible slumber, maintained her honour as an invincible dream; but he is also the only man in centuries of whom France could say, for years, beyond the miserable passions that surround him today: 'There is no spinning-girl in France so poor that she would not spin to pay his ransom!'[15]

What of Malraux's eloquence? The funeral orations of the 1960s, those for Jean Moulin or Georges Braque, for example, are beautiful pieces of French prose, written and then chanted by an old-style tragedian. But the orator of the 'Rassemblement' was a different matter altogether, though similar in one respect at least to that of the Popular Front. Nothing was written down beforehand. He had no plan. A few key-phrases, a few heroic slogans, serve as leitmotifs for the speech. With these few ideas in his head – his parallel between Goya and the Grand Turk, between the Marquis de Sade and Maurice Thorez, between the cathedrals and abattoirs of Chicago, or as here between de Gaulle and François I he was off: the words flowed, the voice rose as it gathered emotion. And in the half light, three thousand astonished faces drank this potion unheedingly – they became drugged.

Once he was on the platform, he was no longer very clear what he was saying. But because he is Malraux, and is sometimes touched with genius, and always has a fantastic ability to summon up images and ideas, it is not impossible to read some of the transcripts of these moments of trance. The hypnotist is too great a writer for a sort of literature not to emerge from these demonstrations.

There is also the savage humour, which sometimes takes on a pathetic form. Of President Auriol, first head of the fourth republic, who had declared that he would not bring de Gaulle to power, since he was not Hindenburg, Malraux remarked: 'M. Auriol informs us that he is not Marshal Hindenburg. Indeed, we are well aware that he never won the battle of Tannenberg.'[16]

The RPF reached the height of its success in the local elections of October 1947 (thirty-eight per cent of the vote). By the time of the Marseilles conference in April 1948 it was already well into the decline that became obvious in 1951: at the legislative elections, the most important test, it hardly obtained twenty-one per cent of the vote, and was on the way to being 'absorbed' by the system – an operation that M. Pinay carried out with the delicacy of an undertaker carving the chicken at a funeral meal.

Malraux did not wait so long before moving off. At the end of 1949, he was much less involved in 'propaganda', and in 1950 illness isolated him from the movement. He was still to appear on important occasions at the General's side, but two years' experience seems to have taught him that he had followed the wrong trail. Why? Because he saw that the movement that he had wanted (or hoped!) to be 'left-wing', supported by the best that France could offer in intelligence and talent, and resolutely rejecting the parliamentary way, was in fact a right-wing organisation, snubbed and more often despised by the intelligentsia (real or supposed), that had been taken over for electoral purposes by the old professionals of conservatism.

On 17 May 1947, he had said to Cyrus Sulzberger: 'The RPF is doomed if it does not succeed in rallying the left.' He added: 'We are embarrassed by certain of our right-wing sympathisers, but we can do nothing about it.' It was then that he made the strange declaration already referred to: that 'if there was a Trotskyist movement in France today that stood some chance of success, instead of the tiny handful of Trotskyites bickering with the Communists, I'd be a Trotskyite and not a Gaullist'.[17] One of the most irritating aspects of the RPF, for him, was the slippery slope towards parliamentarianism. Though, at first, he was well satisfied with their success in the local elections of October 1947, which gave the movement credibility and provided them with town halls that might later prove to be working bases for rallies and meetings, he constantly warned his fellow-members against the poison of parliamentarianism. At Saint-Maur, on 5 July 1952, he became the prosecutor at the trial of the movement's parliamentary members, already regarded as 'dissidents'. 'I speak,' he said, 'in the name of the militants, of those for whom mystique is more important than tactics.' It was too late. And he knew it.

But there was something else that he found very irritating. However much he affected to despise the intellectuals, to pour scorn on Sartre's *Les Temps modernes* and the 'clientèle of the Café de Flore', none of the truly creative writers of post-war France followed him. Those who had been Gaullists, like François Mauriac, had turned away. Those who were in the official left refused all contact. And yet he tried to attract the progressives. In the spring of 1947, Arthur Koestler brought to him a group composed of Simone de Beauvoir, Jean-Paul Sartre and Albert Camus, who, Koestler assures us, 'had not taken too much persuading to meet Malraux . . .'[18] They started talking. 'The proletariat . . .' Camus began. 'The proletariat? What's that?' interrupted Malraux. 'I can't have people throwing words like that around without defining them . . .' Camus became impatient and got bogged down in his definition. Sartre became angry. It was a disaster – and the effects lasted a long time.

Camus, who was not an ungenerous man, was to write his *L'Homme révolté* without mentioning Malraux. Yet he knew that the manuscript of *L'Étranger*, the book that had made his fame, had been sent to Gallimard's in 1942 by Malraux, accompanied by these two words: 'Very important.' And he had not forgotten his own adaptation of *Le Temps du Mépris*, which he and his company had performed at Algiers in 1937 . . . (But when he received the Nobel Prize, in 1957, Camus stated: 'I should give it to Malraux.') As for the *Temps modernes* group, their hostility to Malraux continued to grow – right up to the venomous pages devoted to him by Simone de Beauvoir in *Tout compte fait*, published in 1972.

He was still there, the 'companion' Malraux, at the Vélodrome d'Hiver, on 22 February 1952, beside a de Gaulle suddenly aged by the blighted hopes of his movement. And he was still there on 6 May 1953, when Charles de Gaulle, drawing the lesson from local elections that had proved a disaster for the 'Rassemblement', decided that the RPF would no longer take part in either assemblies or elections:

> The efforts I have made since the war . . . have not, so far, succeeded. I recognise this quite clearly . . . But it is more than ever in the public interest that the Rassemblement, having withdrawn from the electoral impasse, should organise and extend throughout the country . . . Such a regrouping . . . runs the risk, alas, of appearing as a serious shock in which, once again, the supreme law would be the salvation of the nation and the State. Our illusions have failed. We must now prepare the remedy.[19]

André Malraux the writer was now free to return to his profession. Claude Mauriac tells how he met Malraux in January and November 1952, and in October 1953. At the first meeting, he had to wait two hours before the name of de Gaulle came up in the conversation (and there was no mention at all of the RPF). The two names of François Mauriac and the Catholic philosopher Gustave Thibon cropped up together. 'I don't trust that fellow,' said Claude Mauriac. 'Which one?' asked a sardonic Malraux.[20] At their second meeting, the General was referred to only once.[21]

The thing that most strikes one in these conversations, so brilliantly reported by Claude Mauriac, is the atmosphere of holiday, of release, of escape towards oneself. The preacher of the 'crusade with punches' was now simply André Malraux, writer.

35 The desert and the spring

THE crossing of the desert: this was how André Malraux referred to the period that began, for those Gaullists who remained faithful to their leader, with the General's admission of failure in his speech of 6 May 1953. For five years, de Gaulle and those who refused to rub shoulders with the parliamentary 'system' lived in retirement, cut off and in some cases forgotten. Charles de Gaulle took the opportunity of accelerating the writing of *Mémoires de guerre,* the first volume of which appeared in 1954.

André Malraux was living at Boulogne-sur-Seine, in the large brick house in which he had stayed in 1946. He had married Madeleine in March 1948, at Riquewihr, as an act of homage to Alsace. The comrades of the Brigade were there, with Canon Pierre Bockel (although the marriage was a civil one) and Diener-Ancel at the head. He seemed happy with this gentle, beautiful woman, who played Schumann and Stravinsky so well (not to mention the thirty-six or so notes of music written by Friedrich Nietzsche), with Josette's two sons, Gauthier and Vincent, and the son of Madeleine and Roland, Alain, born a few months after his father's tragic death.

Thus relieved of some of his responsibilities and illusions, André Malraux found himself, perhaps for the first time in his life, free to write at leisure – except for the years 1941–3, the period of 'La Souco' and Saint-Chamant, when his leisure had to be paid for by concerns of an equally absorbing kind. Everything seemed to point towards a period of intense literary creation. He had to write his great novels in the time he could snatch from his activities as publisher, militant and combatant (1937–9). He could now benefit from relative isolation, financial security and a decade of extraordinary experiences (1939–49) – war, resistance, brigade, party struggles at de Gaulle's side – to make of *La Lutte avec l'ange*, beginning with *Les Noyers de l'Altenburg*, his greatest work of fiction.

Must we conclude that he was capable of truly creative work only when spurred on by dangerous or frenetic action? That comfort condemned him to the essay and when he was not undergoing risks or being involved in some struggle or other he was good only for making magnificent comments in the margin of someone else's work? He is a curious case of creativity under constraint. Did Retz write any differently? Or T.E. Lawrence, whose last ten years produced nothing but his correspondence?

Even at the level of the essay, it cannot be said that serenity brought abundance. Almost the whole of *Les Voix du Silence* was written and published before the summer holidays of 1953–1958: *Le Musée imaginaire* was published by Skira in 1947; *La Création artistique* in 1948, *La Monnaie de l'absolu, Saturne* and the essay on Goya in 1950; the first edition of the writings collected under the title *Les Voix du Silence* appeared in 1951 and the first part of *Le Musée imaginaire de la sculpture mondiale* ('Le Statuaire') in 1952. From the period of the crossing of the desert, in fact, we have only the second and third parts of *Le Musée imaginaire de la sculpture mondiale* ('des bas-reliefs aux grottes sacrées' – 'le monde chrétien'), a few brilliant but short essays, *Du Musée*[1] and *Le Portrait*,[2] and *La Métamorphose des Dieux*, the peroration of *Les Voix du Silence*, in 1957. Not a negligible list, it is true, unless it is compared with that of the 1930s – publishing at Gallimard's the monumental *Tableau de la littérature française*, addressing meetings at the Mutualité, dashing off to Berlin, fighting in Spain and writing his two greatest novels.

He spent those years from 1953 to 1958 in seclusion, besieged by innumerable images, which he cut out and reassembled, scissors and glue in hand, delighted, absorbed, fascinated by this play of hands and divine inspiration, that combined material activity and meditation, a puzzle in which the virtuosity of the layout artist is added to the unifying, adventurous genius of the aesthetician. Was he ever happier than when surrounded by these inoffensive, provocative collages and montages?

There is, then, the great aesthetic sequence, debatable in many respects and, indeed, much debated, that appeared under the general title of *Les Voix du Silence*. It is too little related to the events of our subject's biography to deserve a lengthy examination here. Begun in 1935, interrupted by two stays in the country (in 1936 and 1939), taken up again between 1941 and 1944 at Roquebrune, Cap d'Ail and Saint-Chamant (at the same time as *La Lutte avec l'ange* and the essay on Lawrence), continued in 1947–8, after the illness of 1950 and finally in the 'desert' in 1953, then interrupted, but still not completed, in 1957 with *La Métamorphose des Dieux*. The whole work is based on a hypothesis. It is the hypothesis that underlies the beliefs of Scali in *L'Espoir* and the great discussion at the Altenburg: that man exists as a coherent, permanent, universal concept.

In spite of Möllberg,[3] the negator, and against the opinion of the majority of the delegates to the Altenburg congress, Berger-Malraux believes that, from the Eyzies bison to the *apsaras* of Angkor Vat, from the angel of Rheims to Goya's tortured prisoners, a genius, a common project exists, certain ends converge, without ever becoming fixed or petrified. A man creates the work – but the work becomes multiplied and proliferates, different from itself and from its creator, from one metamorphosis to another. This essay was written specifically against Spengler and Möllberg; it is about the fluid immortality and convergence of civilisations, about the metamorphosis of societies that attempt at the level of art the synthesis that Malraux found lacking on the political plane between the individual and fraternity, pessimism and hope, lucidity and faith in creative history.

At one moment, he was calling upon his fellow-countrymen to rally, with bare fists if necessary, around the 'supreme' value represented by the nation. At another, he was sitting in his villa at Boulogne-sur-Seine, besieged by a multitude of images that he stuck like butterflies into the pages of his phosphorescent essays, writing: 'the imaginary museum is the suggestion of a vast possible projected by the past, the revelation of fragments lost from man's obsessive plenitude, brought together in the community of their unconquered presence . . .' And recalling that 'Rome welcomed in her Pantheon the gods of the defeated,' he quotes the Chinese epitaph on enemy heroes: 'In your next life, do us the honour of being reborn in our midst.'[4] Specificity on the one hand, plenitude on the other. A closed universe or an open world, nationalism or humanism, the 'companion' and the essayist pursue an odd coexistence in the early 1950s.

Claude-Edmonde Magny's penetrating article on *Le Musée imaginaire,* published in *Esprit,*[5] points out better than the indignant nit-picking of specialists the vices, or rather the contradictions, of the whole enterprise.

> The trouble about discontinuous thinking that leaps perpetually from one idea to another is that it sometimes gets out of the author's control: by refusing to present his credentials to anyone, the author finally becomes the dupe of his own creation.
>
> Malraux's ideas have no depth; like his characters, they are pure positivity. They emerge fully armed from his brain, instead of being conquered at great cost from error and stupidity . . . What is missing in Malraux perhaps is that he has never been stupid in his life, never formed some foolish idea which he then, with great difficulty, had to set about correcting . . . As a result, his most dazzling flashes of inspiration leave us unconvinced . . . It is usually said of him that 'he has ideas'. It would be truer to say that his ideas have him . . .

Another strange thing about *Les Voix du Silence,* a work that tries desperately to unify and claims to bring together the innumerable elements of the human genius into a limitless assembly, is that, like the novels, it has the most disjointed form. It is written in a 'vertical' style, made up entirely of repeated 'fortissimi'; it is all beginnings and ends, juxtapositions of aphorisms and dazzling hypotheses.

The technique of the novel imposes or justifies this dislocation of these juxtapositions – though not such a sustained tension. Malraux the novelist sets in opposition characters that are, like those of Dostoevsky, conflicting lobes of his own brain (Garcia, Scali, Magnin) and brings them to life in discussion – of Bernanos he remarked that he composed scenes before creating his characters, and the same could be said of Malraux himself. In the novels, this discontinuous, jerky writing makes an important contribution to the overall effect. But the use of the same antithetical, frenzied and divisive style in his essay exhausts the reader as well as dazzling him and contradicts, by its very brilliance, the thesis that he is supposed to be proving.

To discover the Malraux of those years, we cannot do better than seek him in the man reading, pen in hand, the masterly essay that Gaëtan Picon devoted to him[6] and turning the harsh light of his intelligence upon himself. Claude Mauriac remembers him, working with his publisher, Francis Jeanson, choosing illustrations for the book that appeared in spring 1953.[7] Selfcriticism and selfdefence, page against page, body against body, theme against theme, lucidity confronting generosity, a dialogue between living people that is an extension of those of Scali and Alvear, Gisors and Ferral, Walter and the delegates at the Altenburg. A creative criticism that reveals a Malraux at the height of his understanding of himself and of others, a marvellous aesthetician of the novel. There is this, for example:

> If there are men for whom the state of floating memory with which life is coloured is a consoling state, and others for whom it is a permanent threat, the difference between these two types is one of the most profound that can exist between men . . . It is useless to stress what a fairly precise knowledge of this question would bring to an analysis such as yours. Well beyond the 'constructed character'; for such a character may be so on memories of happiness, or against enemy memories. I'm convinced that the creative process of the novelist is bound up with the nature of the past that inhabits him or eludes him – and which separates irreducibly the technique of Stendhal and that of Dostoevsky.[8]

There was, Malraux goes on, a scene on this subject in the lost part of La Lutte avec l'ange, which would have said a great deal on the role of dreams in the work of this daydreamer, whose art and life are certainly, as Picon writes, 'a methodical organisation of courage'.

Malraux stands, at the moment at which the RPF disappeared, and with it the least happy period of subjection in a life that has never ceased to build itself against fate and against acceptance, in the plenitude of his lucidity. Whereas Kyo's voice isolated him, because it was heard through his ear, as by others, and not through his throat, the different gaze of the critic and the friend link Malraux with others – and with himself. He enjoys a fraternity of the intelligence that has survived the lost fraternity of action of the 1930s and extends the attempt at unification made in *La Lutte avec l'ange* and *Les Voix du Silence*.

It was a curiously leisurely life he led at this time. In 1952, he took to the road again, revisited Greece and Egypt, and rediscovered above all the country whose culture which, with that of India, was more important to him than any other, Iran. It was his fourth visit to that country: he took a great many notes for *La Métamorphose des Dieux* and saw again friends of twenty years' standing.

In January 1953, he was invited for the third time to New York. This time accompanied by Madeleine, he had been asked to participate in an international conference on the history of art and museology, organised to mark the occasion of the opening of new galleries at the Metropolitan Museum. When asked if he agreed with Rebecca West that America's cathedrals were her railway stations, he replied pleasantly, satisfying at once his duties as an aesthetician and a conference guest: 'No, her cathedrals are her museums.'[9]

He put the finishing touches to a fine study of Vermeer, which he wrote in collaboration with Paul Claudel. He gave interviews, a great many interviews, all centred on the same themes, the values that the West must in his view defend – consciousness, lucidity, fraternity, the need for historical continuity. Let us take the interview he gave to *Les Nouvelles littéraires* in 1952, in which he defines what he calls his 'two obsessions':

> The fatal flaw of many European intellectuals is masochism, a smug resigning of intelligence to the benefit of stupidity in the guise of strength . . . Let us render

to History what is History's and to man what is man's.

My second obsession is that we are living – and not only we Frenchmen – at a time when men are replacing the decisions that they ought to be taking with the expression of their problems at best in terms of tragedy, but more generally in terms of comedy . . .

It was also a time when he finally wrote about the hero who had haunted him more than any other: Saint-Just. For Albert Ollivier's fine book,[10] André Malraux wrote one of his most dazzling prefaces, the one at least that most throws light on himself. He praised the advocate of the 'general interest', the archetype of those 'who strive for glory' and 'a few eternal dreams'. It was natural that Saint-Just should find a defender in the 'companion' of the RPF who had been inveigled into an adventure whose motives were perhaps no worse than those of Robespierre's lieutenant – he had so often compared the 'Rassemblement' to the First Republic . . . And Mauriac had not been alone in seeing him as the archangel of the new terror. 'Saint-Just would have accepted his friend's dictatorship, providing it assumed a Roman colouring . . .' wrote Malraux. He was thinking of another, but there were those who might well think it of him.

He had not broken with Charles de Gaulle, whom he sometimes visited at Colombey or the rue de Solférino. But the 'general interest' became embodied for a time in another personage who, it seems, would also have had a place in the Committee of Public Safety: Pierre Mendès France, who for seven months, from July 1954 to January 1955, offered France some bold solutions to its suffocating problems.

The General conceded that if nothing serious could be done within the rotten framework of the parliamentary institutions, the efforts of Mendès France, his former Economics Minister (1945), might be regarded with some sympathy (for now, that is . . .). Malraux found himself freer to say, in several articles and statements, particularly in L'Express, how interested he was in the dual struggle of this Jacobin against the decline of the country and the guerrilla warfare being carried on inside parliament. He praised the 'energy' of this government, he spoke to

L'Express of 'our left', yet added firmly that he was 'nothing but a Gaullist'. He went on:

> The left must get out of the habit of playing to lose, as if the right could be defeated only by the Soviets; as if the left had been created only to defend its fine feelings or to represent once more the noble tragedy of the fall.[11]

And how could Malraux, however much he had agreed to keep silent at the time of the RPF, not look with respect on Pierre Mendès France's operation in snatching France out of the Indo-Chinese mire? He admitted this all the more clearly in that the General himself agreed.

But at the end of 1954, history returned with a vengeance into the sphere of the aesthetician: Algeria revolted. It cannot be said that André Malraux's life was transformed by the event. There is nothing to indicate that he was closely involved, from the first few years of the war, in the activities of his liberal friends, those in *L'Express* for example, with whom his daughter Florence, an intelligent young woman who was very absorbed by the problems of decolonisation, was associated. Nor, for that matter, was he closely involved in those of his Gaullist friends who had taken part in the debate – Jacques Soustelle, for example, was appointed Governor-General of Algeria in 1955, and was originally assisted by a liberal team. When, late in 1955, there began to be talk of brutality, concentration camps and torture, friends of Malraux appealed to him, as they also did to François Mauriac, Albert Camus and Jean-Paul Sartre. When confronted with torture, the author of *Le Temps du Mépris*, the former anticolonialist of Indo-China, returned. It was a return to the source.

Let us hear what he said in the spring of 1958 to Jean Daniel,[12] one of those who then urged him to return to his original fight against the colonial system:

> Terrorism? It's hearsay. But hearsay can be important. Terrorism is hope . . . Without hope terrorism dies. Of itself. Either the Americans land and bridges are blown up and railway tracks torn up in Corrèze. And that means something. Or the Americans don't land, and then it's repression,

it's the population against us, it's what Baudelaire calls the 'irremediable'. With the irremediable there is no possibility of terrorism.

At the elementary stage it's the father or the mother killed or humiliated. Or even the friend. Above all the friend . . . But even if the friend is killed, without hope there is no terrorism . . . Hope is not the certainty of immediate success, for oneself, for the terrorist himself. I have seen maquisards die in joy, knowing that the whole maquis group was about to be crushed. Hope is the irresistible movement of history, it is the ineluctable future. Quite obviously, the FLN has not lost hope. Indeed, I don't believe it possible to create a situation in which it will lose hope. Not at the moment, at any rate.

At the moment, you know, we are not decolonising, we're consolidating, we are holding a situation with whatever lies to hand, we are at war because nothing was thought out in advance . . . And so for lack of an ideology, we let things take their course, even to the point of torture . . .

Jean Daniel then asked: 'From your point of view, torture and terrorism are just hearsay?'

You could put it like that, but you have to be careful here too! Torture has far-reaching implications. The whole system is in question. Even, let us not baulk the word, civilisation. The police state is round the corner. After that, night falls.

Did Malraux, personally, think there was a solution to the problem?

Of course, I have my own, let us say, provisional solution. In order to let Europe survive, while at the same time giving in to nationalism, a pilot-zone must be created at once. Not as Lacoste[13] is doing it, of course. And then a contract must be signed with the Sultan of Morocco and Bourguiba. Without such a contract nothing is possible. Within this zone everything can be done: Stakhanovism, agrarian reform, kibbutzim, model Arab villages, dams, the lot. What's more, you revive as much as you can of Arabic and Muslim culture, so much so that even in Egypt people will be talking of this pilot-zone as of a Mecca . . . We would make the Algerians proud to cooperate with France and make all the other Arabs of Algeria and elsewhere jealous of the inhabitants of this zone. This would not preclude any negotiation or any political act. But it would create a mystique of achievement. The only weapon we can use against the FLN 'temperament'. Later we could build up a French North African Federation, because for once the peoples of North Africa would have seen the benefit they could derive from us. At the same time, France would revive, because she would be given an aim.

It is not revolution that Malraux is proposing for North Africa, any more than for Indo-China in our interview of 1947. It is active, thorough-going, publicity-conscious reform. His attitude may be debatable in substance. But at the beginning of 1958 he had recovered something of his moral stature, of his historical situation.

In April 1958, *La Question*, the book in which Henri Alleg (a Communist militant working with the Algerian FLN) denounced the torture to which he had been subject, was seized by order of the authorities. A number of left-wing groups tried to organise an appropriate reply to this gesture – meanwhile more and more information was coming out about the killing by paratroops of another Communist militant, Maurice Audin. Several famous writers were invited to make a collective protest. Albert Camus refused, but despite, fundamental disagreements, Malraux agreed to sign, together with Mauriac, Roger Martin du Gard and Sartre, a 'solemn address' to the President of the Republic (then René Coty):

The undersigned:

– protest against the seizure of Henri Alleg's book, *La Question*, and against all the recent seizures and infractions of freedom of opinion and expression,

– demand the clarification in conditions of absolute impartiality and openness of the facts reported by Henri Alleg,

– call upon the public powers in the name of the Declaration of the Rights of Man and of the citizens' rights to condemn unequivocally the use of torture, which dishonours the cause it claims to serve,

– and appeals to all Frenchmen to join with them in signing this 'solemn address' and sending it to the League of the Rights of Man, 27, rue Jean Dolent, Paris 14e.

ANDRE MALRAUX
ROGER MARTIN DU GARD
FRANÇOIS MAURIAC
JEAN-PAUL SARTRE

L'Express and *L'Humanité* on 17 April and *Le Monde* on 18 April published this letter, which aroused considerable feeling. Did Malraux consult de Gaulle before embarking on so momentous an intervention? It is difficult today to prove the matter one way or the other. But it must not be forgotten that in the spring of 1958, the General spoke with particular freedom about the situation in Algeria and the prospects that were opening up there. Furthermore, the crimes of the Fourth Republic could not entirely be for him, those of France . . .

PART II

POWER

══

36 At the right hand of the master

For André Malraux, the Fifth Republic began in front of a
Tintoretto, near a window in Venice that opens on to the
Grand Canal and from which one can see both San Marco and
San Giorgio. He had not given up all hope of a restoration, but
he was not thinking of de Gaulle. Let us turn to the *Anti-
mémoires*:

> People say that he always knew he would return to power.
> Was he sure that he would return in time? I remember, some
> time before Dien Bien Phu,[1] being with some friends . . .
> Elizabeth de Miribel[2] asked me how I thought the General
> would come back. 'Through a conspiracy of the military in
> Indo-China,' I answered, 'They think they're using him but
> they will get their fingers burnt.' It was not the Indo-China
> army, and when my prophecy proved almost right I was
> staying in Venice, absolutely certain that nothing was going
> to happen.[3]

But it *was* the military in Indo-China – transported by the
State, with all its wounded pride and its unsatisfied thirst for
revenge, to the shores of the Mediterranean, a few miles from
Metropolitan France – that struck. Exasperated at being unable
to take sterner measures with the FLN, and blaming this fact on
a régime too exhausted by internal quarrels (including those
that de Gaulle and the RPF had done their best to bring about)
to regain the energy needed to implement Draconian measures,
this army in search of victories called on General de Gaulle.
Would they get their fingers burnt?

The exhausted Fourth Republic surrendered. In Algiers, the 'Committee of Public Safety' placed itself in a state of insurrection, but under the orders of General Salan, whom the premier, Pierre Pflimlin, had appointed his Delegate-General. From outside the plot, where Malraux at first was, it was difficult to see to what extent General de Gaulle was inciting the plotters and to what extent he was containing them. In the *Antimémoires* Malraux offers this ingenious summary:

> The only thing that emerged clearly from this chaos was that a muddled but resolute movement had aircraft and fighting men at its disposal against a government without either an army or a police force. Pflimlin's representative, Salan, had started the cry of 'Vive de Gaulle',[4] and it was no longer expected of the General that he should stop the paratroops but that he should prevent civil war – which looked as though it was about to begin, like the civil war in Spain, like the October Revolution, with the cinemas open and the sightseers strolling in the streets . . .
> Two days after my return, he summoned me.[5]

Did he go to this meeting with a light heart? What did he think of this confused operation, in which the role of the General was, to say the least, ambiguous? Malraux must have known that the General was annoyed with his faithful Gaston Palewski for refusing the Rabat embassy some months earlier: it would have made such a good observation post and, if necessary, more than that . . . Perhaps he shared the bitterness of a few old 'companions' who, at the end of May 1958, expressed their views thus: to think that we have organised so many meetings, made so many plans, so many preparations and efforts to bring about a return of the General to power and that this should be accomplished by a commando of colonels, for the most part anti-Gaullist . . .

So he is face to face with de Gaulle again. Our task is to rebuild France, says the General, of course. But he cannot do it without the French people. 'If they want to go back to sleep . . . I cannot do it without them . . . They don't want colonels.' The 'gist' of what de Gaulle said, according to Malraux, is this:

> As for the colonial question . . . I shall have to tell every-

one concerned with the Empire that colonies are finished. Let us get together and create a Community . . . Let them create States – if they can. And if they agree. Those that don't can go. We won't stand in their way.[6]

Malraux cannot resist making a sketch of the great man in the hour of his return from Elba:

And perhaps History brings with it its own physiognomy. His had become tinged, over the years, with an apparent benevolence, but it had retained its gravity. It seemed not so much to express his deepest feelings as to enclose them. Its habitual expression was one of courtesy – and sometimes humour. At these times his eyes would simultaneously light up and grow smaller, and his heavy gaze would be momentarily replaced by the twinkle of Babar the Elephant.[7]

What role would Malraux play in the entourage of the sovereign, advancing impassively into the fray? When, on 1 June, de Gaulle formed his ministry, Malraux found himself 'ministre délégué à la présidence du Conseil', a sort of Minister without Portfolio, with special responsibility for information as in November 1945, and for 'the development and promotion of French culture'.[8] He was disappointed. In his *Express* 'blocnotes', François Mauriac was to write a little later that Malraux would have liked, in fact, to be Minister of the Interior. This remark was thought at the time to be a writer's dig at a power-hungry colleague. This was not at all the case. François Mauriac had got his information direct from his son, to whom Malraux had confided on his return from Venice that there were only two truly resolute men in France, and that in order to cut short the civil war they would need him, Malraux, in a position of great responsibility.[9] He mentioned neither the Ministry of the Interior nor that of War. But it was clear that he did not mean some relatively minor portfolio such as those of information or culture. What he wanted was to 'do' something, not to get people to talk . . .

But it was to Information that he went. He took the opportunity to appoint some talented men, in charge of television, for example, which he first thought of offering to Claude

Mauriac and which he finally gave to Albert Ollivier, the biographer of Saint-Just. And since all he could do was speak,
Malraux spoke – and brilliantly. On 24 June, he summoned the
press and, since he had no precise responsibilities, assumed all
of them for an hour, speaking on every aspect of policy.

It was a fine performance. Since the speeches in favour of
the Spanish Republic, the MLN congress and the RPF meetings,
Malraux had acquired a professional skill, which, however, in
no way diminished his enthusiasm. But what did he actually
say? First that 'General de Gaulle is not yet Napoleon III' –
which in relation to Algeria was not necessarily a compliment:
the second emperor's idea of an 'Arab kingdom' was much
more daring than those attributed to de Gaulle at this time.
And then he really got under way:

> A paralytic France wants to walk.
>
> What is needed is not to give yet another form to her
> paralysis.
>
> She wants to rediscover not her former weakness, but her
> hope. And the government intends to give her the means to
> do so now . . .
>
> When I said France, I meant the whole of France, includ-
> ing those who marched on 28 May from the Nation to the
> République.[10] I wish to speak of those who marched to
> proclaim their attachment to the French Republic and not
> to the Russian Republic.
>
> Today there are men who want a Republic without the
> General, and others who want General de Gaulle without
> the Republic. The majority of Frenchmen want both the
> Republic and General de Gaulle . . . It is the old people
> proud of its liberties but tired of our defeats. And I think it
> will hear me when I cry out to it on one of those squares that
> since the Revolution are part of its history: 'We are not your
> enemies!'

Was he harassed on the subject of Algeria? What was the
political significance of the demonstration of 'fraternisation'
between Europeans and Muslims on 16 May of the previous
year, which seemed suspect, because too well organised by the
supporters of integration?

Was this movement organised at first? Malraux agrees that it probably was, but goes on to retort:

> The battle of Valmy was certainly paid for, and the French army did not know. It is by no means sure that Danton did a disservice to France in doing so.[11] And although Valmy was paid for, Jemmapes and Fleurus were not, nor indeed was the huge, dense procession that followed the armies of the Republic across Europe.
>
> Even if it was begun by 'paying', by organising fraternisation, a moment came when it was no longer so. It was already no longer so on 23 May, and it would be ridiculous to say that it was still so when General de Gaulle arrived in Algiers . . . We have seen more Muslims acclaim General de Gaulle than there are *fellaghas* in the whole of Algeria . . .[12]
>
> For the first time a revolution in Islam has been carried out not against the West, but in its name, and there are shouts of 'Algérie française' as there were never shouts of 'British Pakistan'. I'm convinced that when someone cries 'Algérie française!' we are confronted by an immense historical movement, probably the most important with the revival of China.

Words verging on the delusional: two and a half years later, huge FLN processions were demanding independence. Four years later, it came.

He did not end, however, without daring to touch on the hitherto taboo subject: torture. 'No act of torture has occurred to my knowledge, or to yours, since General de Gaulle arrived in Algiers.[13] None must occur in future.' This gave him an opportunity to launch his new idea: 'In the name of the government I here invite the three French writers to whom the Nobel Prize has given particular authority, and who have already studied these problems, to form a commission that will leave for Algeria. I'm in a position to assure them that they will be given full authority by General de Gaulle.'

The idea did not lack style: Roger Martin du Gard, François Mauriac and Albert Camus summoned as witnesses of the morality (or immorality) of the French presence in Algeria . . . It fell flat, however: Martin du Gard was seriously ill;[14]

Mauriac was sceptical; and Camus was anxious not to be involved in any public 'campaign' at the side of the opponents of French Algeria. All three refused. Malraux continued to press Camus, hoping to persuade him in the name of de Gaulle to become a sort of permanent ambassador in Algiers of the French conscience. To no avail.

At this time, Malraux saw himself as a sort of link between de Gaulle and the left. More than that, he regarded himself *as* the left, the left-wing current which, by supporting the régime, made it a buttress against fascism. He believed in a de Gaulle who had intervened in order to save the Republic from the 'Nasserites' of the Algiers general staff, and was astonished that the left did not gather round him. Let us take another look at what he said to Jean Daniel, in late June 1958, a few days after his press conference:

> I am on your side, against the Nasserites . . . I cannot understand Mendès France and *L'Express*. What do you want? Tell me. Do you or do you not know that the régime is threatened? Right. The conditions in which the system has been defeated place the régime in danger. Agreed. But the conditions? Who created them? And, anyway, now they are what they are. Mendès ought to be thrown into the Seine . . . We are there, trying to do something. We are making progress.[15]

He thought he was helping to save the Spanish Republic when he formed an alliance with the Communists – which was probably justified. He now believed he was saving democracy by putting de Gaulle in opposition to the totalitarians. He was to be proved not entirely wrong. But he would not have got Algeria out of the mire with a few ingenious ideas and noble phrases.

Why was he sent on his travels? Simply to give him something to do? Or because this Minister of Information's contacts with the press worried too many members of the government – or simply because there was no one better qualified to represent France abroad? In any case, de Gaulle sent him to the Antilles and to French Guiana to win votes for the referendum by which the Gaullist constitution drawn up during the summer would be institutionalised or rejected. He then travelled on to Iran, Japan and India, where the new French régime was regarded as a sort of substitute fascism.

At Fort-de-France, a complicity among writers was established between the visitor and the poet Aimé Césaire, the mayor and popular leader. Martinique acclaimed him. But at Cayenne, he used a different style to confront the crowd standing in the hot night. His account in the *Antimémoires* has the power of a good western:

> . . . NO placards began to rise above people's heads, over the YES placards; and two banners slowly unfurled, twenty yards long, held at each end by poles: DOWN WITH – the startled crowds moved out of the way – FASCISM.
>
> Then DOWN WITH DE GAULLE.
>
> Then DOWN WITH FRANCE.
>
> I still had enough voice left to shout:
>
> 'If it's independence you want, you can have it . . . And who gave you the chance before de Gaulle?'
>
> There was applause as far away as my voice carried, and the crowd moved away from the men holding the poles. Beyond, a jamboree was beginning. From the right, in the distance, came the noise of shouting; demonstrators were trying to outflank the police in order to attack the platforms. Then I heard shouts close by, and the space around my booth was suddenly empty. A glittering object whistled past my left ear, crashed into the back of the booth, and fell at my feet. I picked it up and raised it above my head while I went on with my speech. It was a weapon I had never seen before: a piece of wood about fifteen inches long, with an enormous nail sticking out of it. More of them arrived. If the throwers came nearer, it would be easy for them to take aim and hit me. As I went on with my speech, I surveyed the security precautions: between the throwers and myself, the little girls who had brought me bouquets; to the right, some boy-scouts . . . Then a wild-looking procession came into view and paused, dazzled by the light. In front, an injured man dragged by four others (presumably on a blanket), blood-stained, his arms and legs dangling; behind him, with

the galvanic movements of crazed drunkenness and blood-lust, a hundred maniacs armed with nail-studded planks. They advanced towards me as I went on speaking, then veered towards the stands where a number of women were sitting. They seemed about to exhibit this twitching body as a kind of *Pietà*, when all at once their lunging advance was brought to a halt. The men carrying the body let it fall. In front of the platform a company of marines . . . were taking up positions at the double, their carbines at the ready.[16]

At New Delhi, the reception was more muted. Nehru welcomed him with this sentence: 'I'm glad to see you again. The last time was after you were wounded in Spain. You were just out of hospital and I was just out of jail . . .' There is something frightening about such skill. But not for Malraux – he admires it. After a while, the Indian prime minister was more ambiguous: 'So now you're a minister . . .' To which Malraux adds this comment: 'The phrase did not in the least mean: you're a member of the French government. In a slightly Balzacian and especially Hindu sense, it meant: so this is your latest incarnation . . .'[17]

And because the visitor had won him over, even though his title and his role may have irritated him a little, Nehru quoted, as a farewell present, a saying of Gandhi's: 'Freedom must often be sought behind prison walls, sometimes on the scaffold, never in council-chambers, law-courts or schools.'[18]

Before these exotic journeyings, André Malraux had practised his old job as delegate for propaganda by haranguing the crowd on 14 July, 24 August (the anniversary of the Liberation of Paris) and 14 September, in the Place de l'Hôtel de Ville and the Place de la République – a good opportunity, in terms of date and venue, to proclaim both the fidelity of the General and his companions to the republican régime, and his own obsessions:

We never better understood what the Republic meant to us than during the years of occupation. On the deserted pedestals, the old voice, then faceless, said: They could take away my effigies but no one has been able to replace them . . . It is in the power of no one to tear me from the hearts of

Frenchmen ... The memory of the republic was for us then, as it is for us today, as it always has been for France, the memory of the Convention, a nostalgia for the onward rush of a whole people towards its historical destiny ... Fraternity in effort and in hope.

Thus he made his lyrical contribution to the electoral triumphs that legalised the Gaullist republic in the autumn of 1958, a régime that he has defined by negation: 'It is not the Fourth Republic, plus General de Gaulle.'

From June 1958 to April 1969, Malraux was a member of the government of the Fifth Republic, while continuing obstinately to refuse General de Gaulle's offer of any parliamentary seat he chose to fight. In January 1959 he became a Minister of State; six months later he was put in charge of 'Cultural Affairs', where he remained (more or less) for the next ten years. His contribution to the government during those eleven years can be seen in two ways: as a specialist, or supposed specialist, with the task of carrying out certain functions in a particular sphere; and as a somewhat exceptional member, on account both of his own personality and of his uniquely close relations with the General himself, of the group collectively responsible for a certain policy. The word responsible is seriously meant here – when one remembers what happened in Algeria between 1958 and 1962, up to the end of the war, and the resolution of its aftermath.

Malraux will best be remembered as a minister for his running of Cultural Affairs. In the cabinet, he occupied a place that General de Gaulle has described in his *Mémoires d'Espoir* thus:

On my right, then as always, was André Malraux. The presence at my side of this inspired friend, this devotee of lofty destinies, gave me a sense of being insured against the commonplace. The conception which this incomparable witness of our age had formed of me did much to fortify me. I knew that, in debate, when the subject was grave, his flashing judgments would help to dispel the shadows.[19]

Yet what emerges from the evidence of most of his colleagues is that this walking phenomenon was, in the four hundred or so cabinet meetings in which he took part, a rather quiet, not to say unremarkable, member. The sketches of 'dyables' and 'farfelus' that he tirelessly drew to escape the eloquence of his colleagues are certainly evidence of the survival of the man of invention inside the bored minister. But it is surprising that the glittering personality that crossed the century accompanied by fanfares should have lived out his ministerial time under the Fifth Republic as an elder statesman digesting his all too excellent lunches.

In these twelve years, he appears to have moved or astonished his colleagues only on two occasions: in April 1961, at the time of the four generals' *putsch* in Algiers, when,[20] after declaring himself to be in favour of executing the organisers of the *putsch*, he offered to command a tank unit that would go into battle against them. The second occasion was in August 1965 when, on his return from Peking, he turned the salon of the Élysée Palace into an extraordinary shadow theatre – offering a version of his visit in which the novelist of *La Condition humaine* shared the honours with that of the visiting minister.

Apart from these two high points, and a few remarks like 'I'm the only one here to have no definition of culture to offer,' he proved 'not very talkative, rather terse – not to say cryptic',[21] emerging from his reserve only to approve without reservation the peremptory theses of the General, his neighbour.

Did he, however, allow certain misgivings to colour his reception of two of the General's most challenged policies – that concerning Israel from the 1967 conflict onwards, and that concerning 'le Québec libre'? It has been said that he did, but two at least of his colleagues (MM. Palewski and Peyrefitte) deny it.

Malraux certainly did express reservations on these two subjects, and on others, to close friends. In his private capacity he was known to receive certain of the General's expressions of anti-Americanism with a 'Now he's gone too far!'. But the minister was a tireless example of public loyalty.

37 *Algeria as remorse*

'THE most serious problem for any Frenchman and especially for me,' he said in 1960 when speaking of Algeria during a visit to America.[1] 'Especially for me?' If that had been true, it would have been seen to be – Malraux then being a very public man. After the period of 1958 when, as Minister of Information, Malraux tried for six months to comfort de Gaulle against the Algiers extremists and to give a republican, liberal style to a régime born of extremism and disorder, what did he do, what did he say, to show that he was attached to the idea of bringing peace to Algeria on the basis of political and military realities? What did he do, what did he say, that helped to punish or contain the crimes that were being committed there in the name of France?

'To put an end to the Algerian war, where is it better to be, in the Café de Flore or in the government?' he once asked, with the air of having said everything there was to say on the matter. As far as M. Michel Debré, the stubbornly 'Algérie française' prime minister, was concerned, he might as well have been in the Café de Flore . . . As far as André Malraux is concerned, it remains an open question. By his presence in a government that continued the war for four years, he lent his illustrious name and his revolutionary past to a policy that had long been overtly conservative. But the position he occupied also gave him the opportunity of giving assistance to certain Algerians – assistance which, while not insignificant, was well below that provided by his friend and colleague Edmond Michelet, de Gaulle's Minister of Justice from 1960 to 1963.

For two years, in 1959 and 1960, he devoted a good deal of his time to propaganda visits, notably to Latin America, in order to defend a policy whose secret face – an acknowledgement of the authenticity of the Algerians' cause and of other aims than those of reconquest – he no longer tried to reveal, as he had done in 1958. The speeches he made in Rio de Janeiro, Lima, Mexico City and Buenos Aires, for example, are conformist to a degree that, in view of Malraux's reputation, goes well beyond the requirements of ministerial solidarity. He could hardly campaign against de Gaulle, being in the government, but could he not reveal the still subterranean positive aspects of the strategy then being carried out by the General? If he wished at all costs to remain a minister, why did he agree to market such shoddy merchandise? He had turned down de Gaulle's offer of becoming a deputy. Could he not also have refused to become the commercial traveller for the most controversial aspects of de Gaulle's policy? This was how he addressed his Mexican audiences: 'The envoy of an old country of liberty has come here to say why and how each of her gestures, for almost two years, has not ceased to serve the same cause. The passionate anticolonialism of Mexico has found, I think, in what I came to say, both reasons for reflection and reasons for hope.' And to the Uruguayans, he said: 'My country is advancing in Algeria with a terrible wound in her side, but she is advancing as the fighters for liberty advanced.'[2]

To the Argentines, he declared that: 'Eight hundred thousand Frenchmen and a million Arabs have chosen France, against thirty-thousand *fellaghas* who think that Algeria is the FLN . . . To abandon Algeria would mean leaving those who are faithful to us to be murdered. France will not allow them to be murdered!' While the Peruvians were asked to believe that: 'only "thirty thousand *fellaghas*" believe that Algeria is represented by the FLN which, deprived of all legitimacy has no real audience . . . It is untrue . . . that it is enough to pick up a rifle to become the legitimate master of a country.'

Was he thinking of Gandhi's words that freedom was to be sought behind prison walls, not in council-chambers? Was it necessary to send the author of *L'Espoir* in the tracks of Bolivar and San Martin to make speeches that might equally well have come from Soustelle?

These propaganda tours by the former RPF specialist, punctuated with forecasts about the exhaustion of the FLN, about the divisions within it and the influence exerted over it by Peking and Moscow, read like cuttings from the right-wing press of the period. They are based on strange socio-historical postulates. The Persian branch apart, André Malraux has never shown the slightest interest in Islam, which for him, 'lacks form' and possessed only the negative strength of the oppressed. Any movement in an Arab–Muslim country can only, in his opinion, culminate in Kemalism; and in Algeria, Kemalism – laicism, modernism, feminism – is what, according to him, de Gaulle was promising. So . . . And he was off on clouds which, to de Gaulle and a possibility of the system he supported, and the thrust of Islamic nationalism stops, the whole Western world will cease to retreat . . .'[3]

The truth is that the problem interested him above all on one level (that of the survival of the régime) and only incidentally on another (that of its health). He saw in Algeria – whose history, culture and people he did not know, and whose art seemed to him to lack any particular merit – a permanent threat for de Gaulle and a possibility of the system he supported, and in whose efficiency he believed, being dragged into the mire. But he was seen to be more active in opposing the attempts of the Algiers factions to move ahead of Paris, than concerned to limit the 'blots' that this terrible war provoked. What he was to do in this latter sphere was concealed beneath a long indifference to the appeals of the tortured.

On three occasions, between 1959 and 1961, André Malraux, a member of the Michel Debré government, was requested by his former left-wing friends, by those who, like him, had signed the appeal of 17 April 1958, to make a gesture expressing his disapproval of the methods of war which he himself had said, 'dishonour the cause that they claim to serve'. In vain.

Indeed in 1959, the Minister of State was confronted by an affair similar to the one that had aroused the protest of the writer a year earlier. A book written by four FLN militants who had been tortured, entitled *La Gangrène,* was seized by the

Minister of the Interior of the Gaullist Republic, just as *La Question* had been seized by that of the Fourth Republic. In *Les Lettres nouvelles*, the review he edited, Maurice Nadeau addressed to him the following appeal:

> It is scarcely credible, André Malraux, that you could have read *La Gangrène* without there rising within you the generous indignation that made you denounce to the world the Nazi or Chinese butchers and take the side of their victims. It is no longer in Germany, in Spain, in China that torture is taking place, but on your own doorstep, in your country, and you seem to have said not one word against those whom you once condemned. We have been too well nourished on your works to think that their author could deny them today. They speak for you. They might even rise up against you.[4]

Malraux tried to fight back, and to this summons and to others that followed produced some odd replies. He claimed that these accounts of torture were fabricated by the Communist Party – though perfectly well aware that unlike Henri Alleg, for whom he pleaded at a time when he was not a minister, men like Bashir Boumaza and his companions, the authors of *La Gangrène*, were far from being Communists. At Mexico City, he riposted that during the Mexican war torture also took place – which was neither very courteous nor very skilful. His last argument was hardly better. When shown Sartre's latest declaration, he exploded: 'When Sartre was in Paris putting on plays passed by the German censor, I was facing the Gestapo.'

But the appeals increased and became more varied. When you are Malraux, you are of some importance to the world, and the world calls upon you to be yourself. Thus, on 23 June 1960, Graham Greene published in *Le Monde* an 'open letter' to André Malraux which could not simply be thrown away disdainfully without re-reading:

> . . . You may recall that we once met as members of a literary jury which, each year, awards a prize in memory of a heroic Frenchwoman who died in the camp at Mauthausen for the defence of French liberties . . .

What has urged me to write to you is a passage from an English newspaper. Here are a few sentences that are painful to read for those of us who love France and feel great respect for the head of your government.

Among the accused are M. Henri Alleg, who was forcibly removed from the dock for accusing those who had arrested him of murder.

At the end of 1957, declared Maître Matarasso, four intellectuals: M. Sartre, M. Mauriac, M. Martin du Gard and M. Malraux (at present Minister of Culture) demanded that full light be thrown on the subject of torture, impartially and with the greatest openness. It was absolutely necessary to put an end to the activities of those who tortured Alleg and assassinated Audin, he added, because other human beings were still being subjected to the same tortures.

At this point, the procurator of the Republic rose to his feet and interrupted: 'The defence has just insulted me. I demand that the counsel for the defence appear before the court.'

Then it was the turn of the accused to speak. One of them criticising the position of an in camera *hearing, declared: 'In this same courtroom, I was condemned to death by a Vichy court. At that time the hearings were in public.'*

That a defendant should be removed from the bar, that a procurator should demand the appearance of a defence counsel before the court and that a prisoner should quote Vichy as an example of justice carried out in public, such incidents provide the subject of a tragi-comedy of unbearable cynicism. It is hard to believe that such a court can exist when the leader of Free France is at the head of the government and the author of *La Condition humaine* is one of his ministers . . .

The circle of the Erinyes was closing in around him. In September 1960, an imposing group of artists, writers and actors came together to draw up and sign a denunciation of the continuation of the Algerian war and the methods being used in it, and supporting the 'right to disobedience' of young men called upon to take part in it. The protestors numbered 121, a figure that served them as a label. Among them was André Malraux's daughter Florence, a film-maker. Though deeply upset, he never flinched, not even when the government of which he was a member decided to ban those who had signed the 'manifesto of the 121' from all official functions and from the radio and television. To have the right to play tragedy, he had to approve at least by his silence the tragedy that was taking place in Algeria!

He was first of all a minister – at a time, it is true, when the government of which he was a member, at the instigation of the head of state and despite the prime minister, was at last taking the necessary steps and actively negotiating with those few *fellagha* adventurers who, according to Malraux in Mexico City, Lima and elsewhere, were doomed to isolation and thwarted ambition.

Within this government, where he emerged from his melancholy silence only to deliver a few unfortunate tirades, he did not remain inactive in the face of the spreading 'gangrene'. In *Tout compte fait,* Simone de Beauvoir accuses him of simply providing a front, as minister, for the practice of torture in Algeria. She was inadequately informed. On several occasions, at the request of Albert Camus or Jean Daniel, he got Algerian militants released from the worst of the camps – though these actions were conducted with discretion.

There were also actions like the unreserved support he gave to Jean-Louis Barrault in putting on Jean Genêt's *Les Paravents*, a 'scandalous play' against the Algerian war, which the friends of M. Debré, the prime minister, would quite happily have had banned had it not enjoyed the protection given to the directors of the Théâtre de France by the Minister of Cultural Affairs.

The episode of the trial of the 'Jeanson network'[5] remains ambiguous. Against the firm advice of his client, Maître Vergès, Francis Jeanson's defence counsel, revealed before the court the friendship that had existed between the two writers from the outbreak of hostilities. Since his entry into the struggle, Jeanson had refused to ask anything of Malraux. The minister did not protest against the use made of his name and held no grudge against Francis Jeanson on account of it. Indeed, when visited by Jeanson in 1966, he said: 'During that war, there were those who spoke and those who acted. I don't have to tell you with whom my sympathies most lay . . .'

Then there were the more flamboyant phases of this struggle, those in which Malraux found himself once again in harmony with the atmosphere of the antifascist struggles. On the occasion of the generals' *putsch* of April 1961, Malraux was not content to declare in a cabinet meeting that he would ride 'in the first tank' against the rebels. He became a *communard* against the Versailles of Algiers and locked himself up with a few dozen volunteers in the Ministry of the Interior (where the minister, Roger Frey, was too worried to be indignant at his colleague's intrusion, and where his chief private secretary, Sanguinetti, remarked ironically: 'Well, well! So Malraux has come to save us!'). And he recruited volunteers, as he had done for the Alsace–Lorraine brigade sixteen years earlier. A picturesque incident, perhaps, but a good memory for those of us who were there.

This behaviour aroused the symbolic personage within him. It was perfectly natural that in the following year the OAS[6] terrorists, the last-ditch defenders of French Algeria, chose him as one of their targets. On 7 February 1962, a plastic bomb was placed on the sill of a ground-floor window of the house in Boulogne where he had been living for fifteen years. It was a five-year-old child, the owner's daughter, who was hit by the explosion and lost an eye.

Six weeks later, the Évian agreements, which ended the war, were signed. It was in the United States, as the guest of President Kennedy, that André Malraux made his first public comment on the settlement: 'France has chosen self-determination because it has chosen justice, but justice does not consist in abandoning the innocent, nor in betraying the faithful. The Évian agreements were difficult agreements, and your press was right to describe them as "the most poignant heroic act of a long-drawn-out work". Their application will also be difficult and it will require all one's energy and that of our former opponents.'[7]

True; he had told his left-wing detractors that de Gaulle would make peace. But he had stopped saying it for so long and seemed so resigned to an endless war that he refrained from jubilation. Algeria as anguish was replaced by Algeria as remorse.

38 The art of statecraft

ONE December day in 1945, Emmanuel Berl was asked what Malraux's functions were as Minister of Information. 'Oh, that's quite simple,' said Berl. 'He tries to put disorder into a ministry that doesn't exist . . .'[1] In 1959, he was given a Ministry of Culture – he who, when asked in 1952 about the possibility of the state giving a 'healthy' lead to the nation's artistic life, exclaimed: 'Good God! Let's hope the state will direct nothing in art! . . . The state is there not to direct art but to serve it! . . .'

It was on 24 July 1959 that André Malraux, 'ministre d'État chargé des Affaires culturelles' since the formation of the Debré cabinet six months earlier, was at last given the administrative organisation that would enable him to carry out a 'cultural policy'. The mission entrusted by General de Gaulle to one of the greatest writers of the time and one of his few intimates aroused lively interest and a good deal of hope.

According to his terms of appointment, his task was 'to make accessible the major works of mankind in general and of France in particular to the greatest possible number of Frenchmen, to ensure the largest audience for the cultural heritage and to encourage the creation of the works of art and of the minds that enrich it'.

As Minister of Culture, André Malraux avoided confining himself within too brilliant and too restrictive definitions of 'culture'. But he did sum up his project in a few naturally striking formulas: 'The collectivity has now recognised its cultural mission. The masses have a right not only to schools, but also to theatres and museums. We must do for culture what Jules Ferry did for education.'

Jules Ferry? M. Malraux could certainly allude to the founder of compulsory education in France without looking ridiculous. But one objection certainly comes to mind. Ferry had based his actions on an ideology, on an ideal that was both very broad and very precise, composed both of republicanism and laicism. The battle he launched had clear objectives: he had to convince the French of the virtues of the Republic, of the need for schools that would teach history and the practice of history. It was a question of training citizens and giving the Republic republicans. What did M. Malraux offer in exchange for this austere faith? What ideology, what enthusiasm, other than a sort of egalitarian and nationalistic aestheticism? André Malraux was to seek feverishly – and in vain – for a 'French way of culture', halfway between the Western market system and Soviet statism.

With what means? What exactly did a cultural policy mean that had no jurisdiction over books, schools, radio, television, the socio-educational activities of youth, or cultural relations abroad?

A man of culture, haunted by catastrophe and a sense of tragedy, by death more than by the art of living, nourished on revolutionary history but fascinated by literary glory, a determined antifascist who had turned into the bard of the RPF, openly contemptuous of 'psychology', which left him unaffected by bureaucratic cunning and all the more at the mercy of the games of bureaucrats, he lent his weight on the whole to freedom and innovation, but in so sporadic or unpredictable a way that the most well-intentioned action often led to a sorry outcome. He lent his authority to the boldest initiatives in favour of contemporary art. He encouraged artists, writers and critics such as Henri Seyrig, Gaëtan Picon and Georges Auric to take on responsibilities for cultural policy – but they seldom remained for long. Generally speaking, Malraux's actions took the form of brilliant gestures that had no sequel or bold decisions followed by sudden retreats.

However eager he was to initiate a particular policy – cultural centres, the national inventory – did he really want to fight to get them carried out? Malraux, more than anyone, had the ear of General de Gaulle and was still an old friend of Georges Pompidou, yet how many times did he give up the fight before ever really striking a blow in favour of a particular project or a particular collaborator?

And then there were his working methods, his contempt for personnel problems, which made him attach little importance to the choice of collaborators and be scarcely aware of changes in his staff, his long absences, the difficulty that this eloquent man found in communicating with his staff otherwise than by short impersonal notes. One of his chief assistants had only one short interview with him in three years. Most of the theatre people, notably Barrault after the Odéon affair, were never granted the favour of an audience . . . The personification of power may have its advantages, providing its holder assumes the role of an organiser rather than that of an intermittent symbol.

Did a knowledge of Sassanid art and Ming China prepare him for the administration and organisation of cultural life in the France of the second half of the twentieth century? Because he had a greater liking for the painting of ancient Asia than for that of contemporary Europe, for the art of museums rather than that of the galleries, for dips into the distant past than for prospecting the present, we should, perhaps, in the case of a man like Malraux, speak of a defensive rather than offensive conception of cultural action.

He loved painting, sculpture, architecture. He also loved glory. And he wanted painting, architecture or sculpture to increase the glory of France. Hence a policy of large exhibitions, visits, international exchanges and historical speeches that took him from Cairo to Tokyo and involved long journeys for the Mona Lisa and the Venus de Milo, with all the nationalistic exaltation that this policy of prestige brought with it.

Some of the large exhibitions organised by the Minister of Cultural Affairs – the Spanish 'Golden Century', the Tutankhamun, the Picasso, the Persian art exhibition and above all, perhaps the finest of all, the exhibition devoted to the European sixteenth century – brought to the museums a very wide, delighted public.

But would one not have expected of so prestigious a minister, and one so attentive to national prestige, a systematic policy of buying masterpieces, in particular those by French artists that had once been sold abroad? Apart from a few fine eighteenth-century pictures (in particular a Chardin), with which the French museums were already well provided, it was rather the opposite that happened. Thus Claude Monet's *Falaise* left France, and above all Cézanne's *Grandes Baigneuses* was sold to the National Gallery, London, for some 7·5 million francs. This took place in a Gaullist France, usually so combative in matters of prestige, whereas, at the same time, the canton of Basle was mobilising for, and achieved by referendum, the release of funds that made it possible to prevent two of Picasso's pictures leaving Switzerland! It is true that the sanctions against more covert losses and the state's rights in the sale of an important work of art were strengthened. But the smallness of the sums given for the buying of pictures for the national museums led 'under Malraux' to a loss rather than an enrichment.

Of Malraux the aesthetician, and more particularly of the aesthetician in power, it can be said that he was a man of the known, of the documented and, more specifically, of the 'photographable'. Of the dozen or so decisions that reflect favourably on the 'Malraux era', three stand out: the setting up of the inventory of national monuments and artistic riches, the work done on seven famous monuments for which special regulations were passed, and the setting up of 'protected areas'. To this should be added the establishment of a special service for excavations, although the funds allocated to this organisation were too inadequate for it to be really effective.

Praise has often been accorded other achievements of these ten years: the reorganisation of the Invalides, the preservation of parts of the Marais, the re-pointing of the façades of some of the most beautiful buildings in Paris. (An operation decided upon by Pierre Sudreau, a senior civil servant in the previous republic, but carried out – very well carried out – under the rule of M. Malraux.) But what of the fate of Les Halles? Of Maine-Montparnasse? Who better than André Malraux could have alerted the authorities to the serious mistakes that were being made in these famous parts of Paris? If 'cultural agitation' was justified, it was certainly in this sphere, where the needs of technology and short-sighted financial gain were given primacy over any other consideration. M. Malraux did nothing to prevent these depredations. The face of Paris will bear their traces for a long time to come.

If André Malraux, Minister of Cultural Affairs, had been asked what he would most like to be judged by, he would no doubt have replied, 'The cultural centres.' But were they his invention? They were a fine, generous idea in any case, based no doubt on memories of visits to the Soviet Union, the Popular Front and revolutionary Spain. The Fifth Republic, the masses, France, the revolution, art, de Gaulle, cathedrals, grandeur, all this was to be thrown into the melting pot that would bear witness to French 'pre-eminence': 'For the cost of twenty-five kilometres of motorway,' said André Malraux to the Chamber of Deputies on 27 October 1966, 'France may, in the next ten years, become once again, thanks to the cultural centres, the first cultural country in the world.' From Caen to Thonon, Rennes to Firminy, Saint-Étienne to Ménilmontant, Amiens to Grenoble, these 'cathedrals' of subversion were erected in which people were called upon to do something new themselves.

The strangeness of the enterprise would no doubt have doomed it to remain a ministerial pipedream if one man had not taken his minister literally, believed in what he said and devoted himself to carrying it out with tireless devotion. That man was Émile Biasini. This former civil servant in the Colonial Ministry, who possessed powers of imagination rare in a civil servant, set out by providing himself with a doctrine. In a source document entitled *Action culturelle, an I*, he made a highly spirited statement of what he meant by cultural action, declaring that his aim was 'to transform a privilege into common property'.

The implementation of such a programme presupposed the agreement, if not the actual encouragement, of the local communities. Travelling up and down the country, appealing to municipal councils, encouraging potential organisers, negotiating with mayors, collecting promises (which, strangely enough, were kept), M. Biasini gradually wove his tapestry,

combining the use of buildings and already well-known organisers in more specific projects: at Amiens and Grenoble, there
appeared in turn a certain aesthetic and a style of direction,
with a certain kind of cultural action in view.

In April 1964 the Maison de la Culture at Bourges was
solemnly opened by the minister. The speech he made on that
day was to be repeated, with minor variations, in the same in-
cantatory, resounding, prophetic style:

> Culture is the totality of forms that have proved stronger
> than death ... All the young men of this city must be brought
> into contact with what is at least as important as sex and
> blood, for there is perhaps an immortality of the night, but
> there is surely an immortality of men ... To take up again the
> meaning of our country is to wish for all what we have been
> able to bear within ourselves. We must be able to gather
> together the greatest number of works for the greatest num-
> ber of men. This is the task that we are trying to carry out
> with our perishable hands.

In April 1968, at Bourges, the movement reached its height:
a conference of provincial theatres assembled, in a single week,
7500 theatre lovers, organisers, speakers and spectators. The
old brick building skilfully redesigned to serve its various purposes – theatre, concerts, exhibitions, lectures, television – was
the scene of hundreds of suggestions, refutations and discussions. As he entered the building, the visitor was confronted by
two declarations engraved on the wall. On the left were these
words of Malraux: 'There is not, there will not be a Cultural
Centre on the basis of the State nor, indeed, on the basis of the
municipality. The Cultural Centre is you. It will come into
being if you want it!' And on the right were these words of
M. Armand Biancheri, a schools inspector: 'At once an institution and a challenge to all institutions, the Cultural Centre bears
contradiction, that is to say movement and life, within itself.'

But a month later it was May 1968, the student tornado, and
the cultural centre was well and truly turned into a forum.
There were indignant protests. André Malraux became once
again Georges Pompidou's minister. One director of a cultural
centre was silenced, another was thanked for his cooperation.

The director at Bourges was sacked. Having sown the seed, André Malraux did not always care for the fruit it bore.

Serious criticisms now began to be levelled at André Malraux's project. Where did cultural action begin and where did it end? The fact that the problem should have been posed with such abusive emphasis in May 1968 does not make it any the less permanent. All art is not culture and not everything that is called culture is art. Hence the false position in which the organisers and artists involved in the programme found themselves. What rites ought to be celebrated in these 'cathedrals' of culture?

What was it all leading to? someone involved in one of these cultural centres might well ask. Should he have been given this reply from the minister: 'Come with us and make this symbolic gesture addressed to the world that will show that France has become once again the first cultural country in the world'? This formula, inspired by an overwhelming sense of nationalistic competition, certainly cannot be taken as a definition of this generous, disordered enterprise, affected as it was by both the powerful imagination of one man and the centralising poisons of the system, and also by innumerable contradictions, including the one referred to by Jean Vilar, between 'a disinterested action and a society based on interest'.

Malraux doesn't really like the theatre, which has treated him very badly. The production of La Condition humaine, in 1954, at the Théâtre Hébertot, upset most of his admirers. On this point – as on some others, which reflect little credit on it – the Fifth Republic reminds one of the Second Empire. It is true that in the early days of the régime, when endowing the Comédie Française with a new general administrator, M. de Boisanger (a diplomat whose past gave no indication that he was a suitable candidate for the honour of opening the way to a theatrical revival), Malraux made some eloquent statements on the need to restore tragedy to its rightful place. Some months later, M. de Boisanger was 'liquidated' (the word is vulgar, but the event was even more so). The same period saw the slow decline of Jean Vilar's Théâtre National Populaire, which the minister responsible hardly ever honoured with his presence! What can be said about the destruction of the

Ambigu, that jewel of Parisian theatres, now transformed into a car park? What can be said, indeed, of the disarray of the capital's theatre?

But the saddest affair of all, of course, concerned the Odéon. On 21 October 1959, the old theatre, nobly renamed 'Théâtre de France', was opened in the presence of General de Gaulle. The directors Jean-Louis Barrault and Madeleine Renaud were set up as the torch-bearers of the French theatre. Nine years later, a ministerial decision removed them from a theatre which, in the meantime, had experienced some vicissitudes. Why was this decision made? Because Barrault, in May 1968, had done things and said things that were thought to be inconsistent with his responsibilities.

Confronted by the long-haired crowd that had invaded the Odéon from 16 May, caught up in the vertigo that everyone experienced in those feverish weeks, harassed, exhausted, drunk like everybody else with words, Barrault had mounted the stage and between two harangues from the spokesmen of the 'mass', admitted the vanity of his earlier work and the inanity of the régime's cultural policy. 'Yes, Barrault is dead,' he declared, 'but you have before you a living being. What is to be done?' It was the time, it should not be forgotten, when General de Gaulle was absent from Paris and a number of ministers were hiding under the table. Jean-Louis Barrault learnt that his declaration had been taken very ill indeed by 'the minister', as soon as the wielders of power found the courage once more to 'judge' and condemn. What had Malraux decided?

In his *Souvenirs pour demain*,[2] Barrault recounts the sequel thus:

> 5 July. I can resist no longer and I myself take a short letter to the Palais-Royal, rue de Valois, that I wish to leave on Malraux's desk:
>
> > Monsieur le Ministre,
> > I have the honour to request the favour of a private interview, which will enable me to speak to you about the future of the Théâtre de France, its company and its director.

I hope to maintain with you the excellent relations that we have always had.

In the hope of receiving a favourable reply . . .

The ushers, who have known me for years, some of them from the time of Jean Zay (1938), received me with great kindness. They looked me straight in the eye.

I set out for the Palais Royal. André Malraux was getting out of his car. I went up to him. 'Monsieur le Ministre, I have just left you a letter I have taken the liberty of addressing to you.'

He nodded two or three times, gave me a sidelong look and grinned malevolently. He said nothing, turned away and disappeared. This time it is clear! . . .

Six weeks later, Barrault received the following letter:

Monsieur,

At a time when the new statutes of the Théâtre de France are about to be published, I have to inform you that in view of your various declarations, I consider that you can no longer continue to carry out the direction of this theatre, whatever its future may be. Yours faithfully,

ANDRÉ MALRAUX.

André Malraux's entourage has given a version of the adventure much less favourable to Barrault, stressing in particular that the director of the Théâtre de France had said some extremely malicious things about the minister responsible for it, and had assured the British press that the invaders of the Odéon had been sent by the government . . .

This is, of course, a particularly sordid episode, made up for by other gestures. But when, after ten years of activity (or presence) at the head of a ministry, André Malraux resigned in order to follow de Gaulle, it was necessary to take stock of what had been achieved under his rule. It was tempting to attribute the failings to the ill-defined character of an organisation which, from being the secretariat of state for the fine arts, had become a ministry of cultural action; it succeeded, only to a certain degree and by fits and starts, in slipping between the areas occupied by those two colossi of cultural diffusion, the Ministry of Education and the television service. Any attempt to introduce French people to culture without the unstinting support of the instrument that opens up the way to it for them (as children) and that dispenses it to them daily (as adults) is doomed to failure.

One may be severely critical indeed of the way in which education is dispensed to our fellow-citizens. One may be still more severely critical of the content of this education. One may regard as very cruel what is offered to them on the television: but how are we to regard a minister of 'cultural action' who has responsibility for the Record Office but not the slightest influence over the programmes imposed each evening on ten million Frenchmen and Frenchwomen?

There were plenty of other anomalies. At this time, the minister had no responsibility for books (it was thought that if he had it might have embarrassed a minister who was also a writer) or for relations abroad, except through exhibitions, ministerial visits and inaugurations of monuments dedicated to Goethe or Chopin . . . While M. Malraux himself, in an interview with the English-speaking press in 1964, expressed marked disdain for sport as a possible responsibility for a Minister of Culture.

The most obvious defect in the organisation of cultural affairs lay, as we know, in its budget. It was not enough to compare what earlier régimes had done for culture and what the Fifth Republic allowed M. Malraux to do: the enterprise was of a different nature, the man responsible an utterly exceptional personality, his place in the state unparalleled, the national and international ambitions of the régime out of all proportion to what they had formerly been. The figure for culture remained at 0·43 per cent of the national budget: it had increased less quickly than that of the principal items in the budget, military expenditure not included. In terms of finance this hardly measured up to the ambitions of the original conception. It must not be forgotten that André Malraux had constant access to the two leading members of the régime. Who could have altered this state of affairs, if not he? One of the most serious criticisms that can be made of the Fifth Republic's first

Minister of Cultural Affairs is his timidity in this respect. Witness this remark made by a treasury official in 1967 to a senior civil servant of the Ministry of Cultural Affairs: 'These plans are fine. But if we are to follow them, your case must be pleaded more vigorously at the top . . .'

These ten years of 'cultural action' will remain one of the most ambiguous adventures in the life of André Malraux. It was no ordinary adventure, any more than the event that was to reveal its contradictions in all their starkness: the movement of May 1968. It is not entirely paradoxical to suppose that it was in the spring of the barricades that the enterprise initiated in July 1959 bore its revolutionary fruit, setting André Malraux, 'cultural agitator', against M. Malraux, minister.

The intermittent, precarious character of André Malraux's work as minister at this time was due, partly at least, to a series of ordeals in his private life. The death of his two sons in spring 1961, a long illness in 1965 and the separation from his second wife, shortly afterwards, seriously undermined his energy, his balance and his tenacity.

Gauthier Malraux was just over twenty-one and his brother Vincent barely eighteen. Early in the morning of 23 May 1961, they left the island of Port-Cros, where they had just spent a long weekend. They went back to Hyères to collect their fast car and set out for Paris. In Burgundy, not far from the place where Albert Camus had been killed the year before in another speeding car, the young men overturned. It was five o'clock in the afternoon. Gauthier, it seems, was killed instantly. Vincent died at Autun hospital where he had been taken in a coma. André Malraux arrived next morning and had the bodies taken to the church of Saint-Germain de Charonne; after a religious service, celebrated at the father's sudden request by his friend Pierre Bockel, a companion of the Alsace–Lorraine Brigade, the two boys were buried beside their mother Josette in the nearby cemetery.

'It takes sixty years to make a man, and then he's only fit for dying.' André Malraux, who wrote that, was now sixty. He was a minister, and content – if not happy – to be so. He had a strange fondness for honours, the motor-cycles that surrounded him when he travelled, banners, *Marseillaises* and military salutes, cabinet meetings that bored him, and speeches, even those of others . . .

The face had become heavier, drawn downwards. He had once looked like a Dominican heretic who had escaped the executioner's fire and was still haunted by the smell of the stake. He now looked more like a prior by Memling or Roger van der Weyden, one who had now sadly lost his faith but still clung to the advantages of office and who, to while away the time, had become the protector of philosophers and fresco-painters.

The bluish-green eyes no longer looked at a bee on the wall behind the person he was speaking to, but at the shadow of a bee beyond the wall. The forelock no longer fell forward. It had disappeared, freeing the pasty-coloured brow. Constantly kneading his right cheek and the corners of his lips, the still elegant hand busied itself illuminating the odd capricious word or taming his over-exuberant eloquence.

A whiff of brimstone, incense, and whisky floats around this Garine-minister, and his distant gaze seems to seek, in the gardens of the Palais-Royal, Cambodian *apsaras* disguised as soldiers of the great Revolution.

FOR General de Gaulle's minister, 'friend of genius', protector of the arts, one mission followed another, especially since misfortune had struck and he could no longer bear to be at home, either at Boulogne, which he left after the assassination attempt of 1962, or in 'La Lanterne', the attractive residence provided for the Minister of Cultural Affairs on the edge of the park at Versailles. He travelled from Moscow to Washington – where the Kennedy household, already noted for its love of the arts, received him warmly. At the White House, John Kennedy treated him to a biographical account that reflects very favourably on the French information service in the United States: 'We all wish to take part in the innumerable adventures that life offers, but M. Malraux beats us all. We are the descendants of pioneers who were themselves men of great vitality. But Malraux directed an archeological expedition to Cambodia, was in touch with Chiang Kai-shek, with Mao Tse-tung, took part in the Spanish Civil War and in the defence of his country, followed General de Gaulle, and was at the same time a great figure in the creative sphere. I think he leaves us all far behind. So we are very proud to have him among us.' Accordingly, six months later, Malraux returned to the United States – with the Mona Lisa.

The job of a Fifth Republic minister also had its more austere moments. He could take no pleasure in reciting the 'funeral orations' of the great men for whom he wrote some of his finest prose. When one has the sacred horror of death that André Malraux has, one does not speak of it lightly. And he did not praise Le Corbusier without himself feeling sorrow, however forgetful he had been, as Minister of Cultural Affairs, the master of state commissions, of the creative genius of the Swiss architect.

Jean Moulin[1] had been dead for twenty years, and André Malraux had known him only when he had been on the staff of Pierre Cot, the Minister of Air, in 1936. But the grandeur of his role, the horror of his execution, the symbolic character of the sacrifice of the 'unifier' – everything combined to give a particular intensity to the speech of remembrance he gave when Jean Moulin's ashes were transferred to the Panthéon.

It was very cold that day in the rue Soufflot. General de Gaulle was there, immensely tall in the long greatcoat that covered him from top to toe. Malraux moved forward over the huge platform to the microphone like an exhausted automaton. He clutched his notes as if holding on to a lifebuoy. His broken voice floated on the icy wind like a drowned man buffeted by the waves:

> Enter here, Jean Moulin, with your fearful retinue. With those, like you, who died in the cellars without having talked; and even, what is perhaps more agonising still, with those who died after having talked; with all those in prison stripes and shaven heads from the extermination camps, with the last stumbling body of the dreadful files of *Nacht und Nebel* who fell at last under the rifle-butts; with the eight thousand Frenchwomen who did not come back from the labour camps, with the last women who died in Ravensbrück for having sheltered one of our men! Enter with the race that was born in shadow and disappeared with the shadow – our brothers in the Order of the Night . . .
>
> It is the funeral march of the ashes which you see before you. By the side of those of Carnot with the soldiers of the Year II, those of Victor Hugo with the Misérables, those of Jaurès watched over by the spirit of Justice, may they lie here at rest with their long retinue of disfigured shades . . .[2]

Another fine piece of prose, conquered by a life like his – by lives like theirs. Conquered like liberty. Around us, from the entranced crowd there arose like a lament, gradually swamping the band, the 'Song of the Partisans'.

Malraux's life was also, in the 1960s, that of a Gaullist militant, one of the General's faithful supporters and one of those whose help he needed in times of crisis. We have seen him in 1960 when the barricades were going up in Algiers; in 1961 at the time of the *pronunciamiento*; in 1962, when the régime confronted the leftist coalition, at the referendum that would transform the system into a semi-presidential one; in 1965, when the General chose to ask for a second mandate and nearly lost it; in 1967, when the left failed to defeat him in the legislative elections; in 1968, when a handful of students very nearly overthrew the sun-king; in 1969, when de Gaulle's rule finally came to an end.

The oddest episode in this oddest of ministerial careers took place in autumn 1962. After the assassination attempt at Petit-Clamart and the end of the Algerian war, the General decided to consolidate the régime by requesting, through a referendum, that the president of the republic should be elected by universal suffrage. In the cabinet, Malraux was one of the most ardent supporters of this idea. So there he was, thrown into a new enterprise which, in many respects, recalled the RPF, except for the fact that the Gaullists were now in power and had unlimited resources at their disposal, including the state propaganda machine.

On 30 October, two days after the referendum gave General de Gaulle a majority that he himself described as 'poor and uncertain', André Malraux, at a meeting in the Palais de Chaillot, launched the Association for the Fifth Republic, which its founders, most of them former members of the Resistance networks and nostalgic for their underground days, immediately baptised 'A$_5$R'. This would have been fine for a secret service. But it was not so good for a mass movement. This organisation, into which Malraux was supposed to infuse his lyrical enthusiasm, was in fact the resurrection of the 'Association for the Support of General de Gaulle', created in 1958 to deal with any 'trouble' that might arise in the seizure of power. It was itself a creation of the RPF, whose earliest and staunchest supporters had been members of 'Free French' networks.

The meeting of 30 October 1962 was a swindle. Once again, Malraux had forged ahead without ensuring rearguard support.

The more prudent, more temporising elements in the régime – those around Georges Pompidou, the new prime minister – warned the General against this adventurous, chivalric style. The French were grateful to him for bringing an end to the Algerian war, but they had no wish to stir up the conflict on the home front. The time had come for the warrior to rest.

So the General remained silent. And the meeting of the 'New RPF' fell flat. Before some 2500 people, the meeting was opened by an (American!) film to the glory of the head of state. Malraux mounted the platform. He had nothing to say. So he gesticulated, railed and condemned. An admirer, Morvan Lebesque, a biographer of Camus, describes Malraux's half-hour appearance on the television screen thus: 'It was a painful spectacle, both for his friends and his opponents. M. Malraux's opinions are not in question: he developed them with moving sincerity and raised the level of the debate to heights at which his party usually finds it difficult to breathe.' But Morvan Lebesque refuses to recognise in 'this orator in close-up, ignorant of the elementary rules of television, shot from a caricatural angle, deformed and grimacing . . . a man whom we have admired, who remains in so many respects admirable. Who was responsible for this frightful spectacle? The man himself, if it is true that one is never betrayed other than by oneself? Or television, which makes so many imbeciles likeable, but which might have ridiculed a Pascal or a Dostoevsky?'[3]

In 1965, when de Gaulle's presidential term was coming to an end and a new candidate had to be chosen, the question that everyone was asking was: will the general, who is now seventy-five, go on? Early in June, the President of the Republic called to the Élysée four men whose verdict he awaited. They were two prime ministers, past and present, Michel Debré and Georges Pompidou; the chairman of the Constitutional Council, Gaston Palewski, oldest of his political advisers; and André Malraux. There were two cleverly phrased, adroitly motivated affirmatives that might just be taken as warnings: those of Gaston Palewski and Georges Pompidou. And there were two resolute, fearless, unequivocal affirmatives, those of Michel Debré and André Malraux. This sudden note of caution, however, might well have led the General to prolong his reflections.

But, after all, that majority was not like that of the country, poor and uncertain. It was enough, it seemed, to confirm him in his decision, which he kept to himself for some time.

Thus, committed as much as ever to the political struggle, Malraux had to take part in the campaign, in particular at the meeting at the Palais des Sports where, after the General's failure to obtain an absolute majority in the first round, all the companions were gathered round the microphone, snatching one by one at the voting results of the second round for the old disappointed sovereign. It was again Malraux who loosed the sharpest arrow at the leader of the opposition, François Mitterrand.

This left is not on the left because the left cannot be defined by governments that have been unable either to make war or to make peace, because the left is the immense dream of the left that dreams and accomplishes nothing and lastly because a left-wing government can be defined neither by Suez, nor by Sakhiet,[4] nor by Dien Bien Phu.[5]

40 *The China visit*

LEGEND has imposed its version of the visit. In the summer of
1965, André Malraux was sent to Peking by General de Gaulle,
on the grounds that he was a former companion of the Chinese
revolutionaries, in order to consolidate, ennoble and place on a
personal footing the links forged the year before between
France and China, at the political level, by the recognition of
the People's Republic of China. He saw Chairman Mao again
and, after a series of interviews with the Chinese leaders, transformed official relations between two republics into friendship
between two great men.

The reality is rather different, though not entirely commonplace. A sick man, listening to the advice of his doctors and
dreaming of one of those long voyages that stimulate him to
write, set out on a sea cruise. He chose to go to Singapore, a
city linked to his past on three accounts, and to sail on the
Cambodge, a name that could not fail to revive memories. Early
in July, in Singapore, he received a letter from General de
Gaulle – who already knew of his friend's wish to extend the
voyage to Peking – giving him a mission to go to China in the
name of the French government. This letter was accompanied
by a message that he was to hand to the Chinese Head of State,
Liu Shao-ch'i.[1] Meanwhile, the Quai d'Orsay would prepare,
with the Chinese authorities, a welcome for the French Minister
of Cultural Affairs. It was at Hong Kong, about 17 July, that
the minister received the invitation from the Chinese authorities. He left for Canton on 20 July and from there for Peking,
bearing General de Gaulle's message to Liu Shao-ch'i.

Two years later, the *Antimémoires* provide an account of this journey,[2] cut with some long flashbacks – including the magnificent description of the Long March. I shall not attempt a systematic breakdown of this account, but I shall try to place side by side the poetic evocation of the novelist and the statements and actions of the minister, and to fill out as best I can the memories of an autobiographer whose memory is clearly that of a 'conqueror', eager to recognise as his what belongs to him only by virtue of the right of conquest of the imagination, dream and a category that for him transcends any conflict between the true and the false and which he admirably calls 'le vécu', the 'lived' or 'experienced'. On 15 July 1965, André Malraux's knowledge of China was limited to his brief stay in Hong Kong in August 1925, his brief visit in 1931 to continental China and, of course, what he had read about it (above all, Edgar Snow) and, lastly, what he had written about it, which is sometimes quite brilliant. There is also his legend, based on his own statements or writings and on the imagination of others, independent of him but authenticated by him: this legend tells us that he was one of the protagonists in the revolutionary struggles in Canton and Shanghai – and now it was the legend of the minister, the messenger of the republic and General de Gaulle. But supposing it was not a legend? And supposing, by virtue of being 'lived', the legend had become true?

When he speaks again of landscapes, streets, photographs of faces that he has observed often enough and well enough to describe them, and which he turns into images by which Western man pictures to himself what it was like over there, how could his 'memory' not come into play? It is clear that when he says he 'recognises' Gallen in a photograph of fifty officers in the Canton Museum of the Revolution,[3] he is rediscovering a face that he has seen on a hundred documents. And who could doubt that, when confronted by Mao himself, he 'recognises' this illustrious face?

Those who witnessed this visit and, at some stage or other, were involved in André Malraux's activities, noted that he made little attempt to play the old soldier or specialist with his hosts. He listened much more than he spoke, sparing his guides and interpreters remarks of the 'in-my-time' type. Indeed, the *Antimémoires* are written in a rather evasive tone as far as the past is concerned. Apart from a brief reference to 'stories I heard in Shanghai before 1930' that betray more confusion of memory than desire to mislead, Malraux abuses the reader only by a sort of artistic drapery, a historico-fictional backcloth held up at the back of the stage, because it is expected of him, and because the attitude of 'return' is more interesting than the surprise of the tourist. Was it not his friend Groethuysen who said that one should only arrive somewhere for the second time?

Where a more critical reading is called for is in the conversations that Malraux had in Peking, first with Marshal Chen-yi, Minister of Foreign Affairs at the time,[4] then with the prime minister, Chou En-lai, and lastly with Mao Tse-tung – with President Liu Shao-ch'i standing discreetly at his side. If one contrasts the version of these conversations given in the *Antimémoires* with accounts reconstructed from other witnesses, it is not to give some paltry lesson in exactitude to the writer – or even to the minister. It is primarily because it is fascinating to observe how the truth is reshaped by a highly literary imagination – and also because the imagination of the greatest artist may sometimes be less rewarding or, quite simply, less interesting than the truth itself.

Let us take the first conversation that André Malraux had in Peking, that with Chen-yi. From his account, it appears that 'in the Marshal everything springs from convention' and that his statements in conversation are like 'gramophone records'.[5] This is as an odd criticism because it refers to a conversation of great interest (on the Chinese intervention in Vietnam, on the relations between Ayub Khan[6] and the Americans, on Siberia and the USSR); but Malraux does not relate the funniest moment, it is true. He speaks at the beginning of a 'preliminary exchange of courtesies' – which is a good deal less amusing than what actually took place:

Malraux: I salute the soldier and the poet![7]
Chen-yi: I'm not a soldier any more. And I have no time to write poetry . . .

Malraux: It's the same with me: all we sign nowadays is autographs . . .

Nor does Malraux recount two curious exchanges of views about Marxism and about the Canton uprisings (perhaps, despite their reputation, the *Antimémoires* are a homage to the art of understatement!).

Malraux: I've studied Marxism too . . .
Chen-yi: Yes, there is a Socialist tradition in France. I'm thinking of Saint-Simon . . . [if this is only a 'gramophone record', it's a funny one . . .]
Chen-yi: Canton is a holy place of the Revolution . . .
Malraux: I spent six months there in 1927. I was in prison in 1923 with Ho Chi Minh . . .
Chen-yi: Ho Chi Minh was Marxist before we were! From 1919, with us it was 1921 . . .
Malraux: He was in Paris in 1946. On leaving he said: 'My greatest regret is not having met Malraux!'

Did he deliberately tone down the conversation with Chen-yi in order to bring out the extraordinary brilliance of the interview with Mao Tse-tung? The fact is that in his meeting with Chou En-lai, which took place a week later on 2 August, in the Palace of the People, the visitor again considerably reduces the published account and speaks again of 'putting a record on'. He must be alone among all Chou En-lai's visitors to find him boring . . . But he has special and very strange connections with him. In the scene as described in the *Antimémoires*,[8] Malraux refers to it briefly: 'He knows as well as I do that in the United States he is thought to be the original of one of the characters in *La Condition humaine*.' (Why in the United States? Because it is W. M. Frohock who has most clearly formulated the hypothesis. But it is not original. Many French commentators have seen Kyo as a reflection of Chou En-lai.)

But, although Malraux 'recognises' him too ('Chou En-lai has changed little . . .'), he is disappointed – Chou En-lai irritates him. Did he expect some complicity, some recognition of fraternity, an 'Ecce Homo' from his 'model'? He describes his attitude as 'amicably distant', sees him as 'neither truculent nor jovial: faultlessly urbane' and 'as reticent as a cat', a 'studious cat' with 'thick eyebrows, pointed towards the temples like those of the characters in the Chinese theatre'.[9] Malraux does not like him. Would he have liked Kyo had he become a minister?

The account of the conversation in the *Antimémoires* is insipid. That is what happens when one is not Kyo: the poet takes his revenge on you by turning you into a Marxist M. de Norpois. What we know of the conversation from other sources is more interesting. Let us begin with the end:

> Malraux: I have seen your name written on the walls of caves in Yenan . . .[10]
> Chou: You also have a knowledge of Marxism . . .

Then he talked of certain cultural projects (a history of the Long March that Abel Gance had just filmed, in two versions, an exhibition in Paris of Chinese art 'like the one Taiwan is presenting in the United States' – 'those are stolen objects!' interrupts Chou En-lai, displeased . . .).

And they talked about Indo-China, which allowed Malraux to throw out the most wildly improbable idea that ever emerged from the brain of a novelist, that of a new partition of Vietnam on the basis of a north–south line, along the Annamese Cordillera – thus leaving the mountains to the Communists and the ports to the others . . . To which Chou En-lai can only murmur, with the mild surprise of a faultlessly urbane cat: 'I am not aware of such a project.'

It is quite natural that the visitor should have wished to tear from the pages of history any record of such a half-baked notion. What is surprising is that he should have regarded as lacking in interest what Chou En-lai said to him about relations between China and the United States, four years before Henry Kissinger's visit to Peking. 'We help Vietnam unreservedly. But that does not prevent us from negotiating with the United States: in fact, contacts between us have never ceased since August 1952.'[11] It was only to be expected that the prime minister should be a doubly grey eminence and that only one individual, the legendary Chairman Mao himself, should stand out from the Chinese backcloth.

As for the meeting with Mao Tse-tung, things are a little more complicated. There are three versions – not counting the Chinese, of course, which must be rather short – three French versions, therefore, in existence: there is the one held by the Quai d'Orsay, the one Malraux gave, on his return, to the cabinet meeting of 18 August 1965, which contains a few additional details, and that of the *Antimémoires*, the most decorative one. We will begin with the last, without fear of later disappointment. Here again, the truth is worth its weight in artifice.

We know the fine account of the visit to the great man, the letter handed to President Liu, who was already shadowy enough to give Mao time to emerge into the limelight, Malraux's comments on Yenan, 'the museum of the invisible' and on the Maquisards of all revolutions, the shafts that Mao directed against Stalin, his information on the role of the workers, who were 'more numerous than is usually thought' in the Long March, the description of the peasants' poverty at that period by the former leader of Hunan . . . Then Malraux says:

> 'You are in the process of restoring Greater China, Mr Chairman; that is evident in all the propaganda pictures and posters, in your own poems, in China herself, with the military adjuncts of which tourists are so critical . . .'
>
> 'Yes,' he replies calmly.
>
> 'You are hoping that your . . . ancient agriculture, in which manual labour is still so widespread, will catch up on mechanisation?'
>
> 'It will take time . . . Perhaps decades . . . You have shown your independence with regard to the Americans.'
>
> 'We are independent, but we are also their allies . . .'
>
> '*Our* allies! Yours and ours!'
>
> As much as to say: a fine lot they are![12]

Malraux is then bold enough to bring up the problem of the opposition. Is it still powerful?

> 'There are still the bourgeois-nationalists, the intellectuals, and so on. They are beginning to have children . . .'
>
> 'Why the intellectuals?'

'Their thinking is anti-Marxist. At the time of the Liberation, we welcomed them even when they had been involved with the Kuomintang, because we had too few Marxist intellectuals. Their influence is far from disappearing. Especially among the young . . .'[13]

The French ambassador, Lucien Paye, who accompanied Malraux, intervened: 'The young I have come across in the course of my travels . . . are nevertheless deeply devoted to you, Mr Chairman.' Mao replies: 'One can see things in that way also . . . You have seen one aspect. Another could have escaped you . . . Youth must be put to the test . . .'[14]

They spoke of France, and to the Chinese leader who accused the European Communist parties of having become 'social democratic parties of a new type', Malraux declared that 'individually, most of the Communists would like to have you kiss them on one cheek and the Russians on the other . . .' This remark made Mao Tse-tung and his companions roar with laughter. 'Soviet revisionism is an . . . apostasy,' said the Chinese leader. 'It is moving toward the restoration of capitalism . . .' André Malraux challenged this with some quite brilliant arguments, though admitting that the metamorphosis from Stalin to Brezhnev was as radical as that from Lenin to Stalin. 'In other words,' said Mao, 'you think they are not revisionists, because they are no longer even Communists!'[15]

Before taking his leave, Malraux predicted the restoration of 'the China of the great empires'. Mao replied:

'I don't know; but I do know that if our methods are the right ones – if we tolerate no deviation – China will be restored to greatness.'

Once more I am about to take my leave of him: the cars are at the bottom of the steps.

'But in this battle,' he adds, 'we are not alone.'

'Not for the first time.'

'I am alone with the masses. Waiting.'

The tone is a surprising one, in which there is bitterness, perhaps irony, and above all pride . . .

Little by little we approach the front steps. I look at him (he is looking straight ahead). What an extraordinary power of allusion! I know that he is about to intervene anew. Through the young? Through the army? No man will have shaken history so powerfully since Lenin. The Long March portrays him better than any personal trait, and his decision will be brutal and ruthless. He is still hesitating, and there is something epic in this hesitation . . . Overhead, an aeroplane flashes past. With his hand to his forehead in the age-old gesture, the Old Man of the Mountain watches it recede, shading his eyes from the sun.[16]

It is no use commenting ironically on these predictions ('I know that he is about to intervene anew . . .') written after the event.[17] The drawing is very fine, 'hardly finer than what was said', and what was heard – with little more ornamentation – by the ministers gathered around General de Gaulle ten days later. The illustrious colleague had chosen to be brilliant. He was; he did not fail the expectations of his audience. Even Raymond Marcellin, who, it is said, did not take kindly to this praise of Revolution – however far away the revolution may be, and however artistically ambiguous the praise . . .

First, André Malraux defined his 'mission' – an exchange of information at the highest level, an evaluation of what France represented for the masters of China. An attempt to sound out what they expected from the rest of the world. Then he undertook to draw a portrait of Mao, to give an account of his career, to define his power and that of the Party. And he gave an account of his three interviews which he summed up thus: Chen-yi, the trial recording; Chou En-lai, the record: Mao, history.

His account of the interview with the leader of the Chinese revolution differed very little from that provided by the *Antimémoires*, except that he did not intersperse with it the account of the civil war and Mao's reflections on it – which were more or less borrowed from books by Edgar Snow. He recounted to his colleagues that he had begun the conversation with the comment 'Rome is replacing Sparta' which, if that was in fact what was said, must have left Mao perplexed. He also suggested that the old leader and his entourage reminded him not so much of the first Bolsheviks as of the court of Louis-Philippe . . .

He stressed the fear of 'revisionism', the idea of material progress, the very Chinese and independent aspect of Mao's thinking and his serenity. He also remarked that at several points during the conversation Mao Tse-tung had consulted Liu Shao-ch'i – an observation that naturally disappears from the *Antimémoires* version, written as it was after the fall of Liu. There was nothing, in fact, that might lead one to invalidate the account published two years later.

But what was really said? As far as one can piece together the evidence, the interview was rather less epic, rather more down to earth. When, the following day, he was presented with the official typescript from the 'Department', which becomes a diplomatic document only after it has been given the approval of the interested parties, Malraux simply said: 'I shall add to it.' He did add to it. It may be a pity that he did not publish the more naked, but also more fascinating, text of what was said on 3 August 1965. Let us attempt to re-establish the substance from the fragments of the substance.

Mao: You went to Yenan?
Malraux: Yes, I saw the caves. One can understand why you won the war. They tell a lot about courage and austerity.
Mao: It is the maquisards who win wars . . .
Malraux: I too have commanded a Maquis group . . .
Mao: The French people managed to overthrow the monarchy!
Malraux: Then the soldiers of Year II became those of Napoleon . . . How did you manage to infuse yours with so much courage?
Mao: We were equal among ourselves, and we gave land to the peasants.
Malraux: Agrarian reform?
Mao: . . . And, what is more important still, practice in democracy.
Malraux: And in this way you won your campaigns. But Chiang Kai-shek held the cities.
Mao: We wagered on the Chinese people, on the majority.
Malraux: In 1934, Gorky told me that you would not be able to capture the cities . . .

Mao: Gorky didn't know China . . .

Malraux: Yet you did have your defeats.

Mao: Yes, we had to abandon southern China. But we transformed these defeats into victories . . .

Malraux: The Long March! That was an adventure of epic proportions . . . But what do you think of the destiny of the world?

Mao: For China, the problem can be summed up thus: socialism or revisionism. There are strong tendencies in our society that are driving towards the second way . . .

Malraux: How can you combat them?

Mao: By destroying corruption.

Malraux: Your aim is to recreate a Chinese China, totally?

Mao: Yes, and it will take a long time. There is revisionism, the bourgeois, the writers . . .

Malraux: Why the writers?

Mao: We inherited them from the Kuomintang. We hardly had any among us!

Malraux: In the USSR, do you really believe that they wish to return to capitalism?

Mao: The mess they're making there will lead to it. Kosygin is worse than Khrushchev!

Malraux: In the industrial sphere, you have won the game. But what about the agricultural sphere?

Mao: We haven't won anywhere. There are too many contradictions . . .

Malraux: In the plan, do you give priority to agriculture? And do you expect to reform the people's communes?

Mao: Technical, not structural, reforms.

Malraux: In agriculture, do you think it more important to develop areas or yields?

Mao: Yields.

I have not repeated here the passages reported above on the French Communists, on the 'allies' of France and China, on the attitude of Chinese youth (including Lucien Paye's intervention), which were important moments in the interview. In short without the novelist's 'pathetic trimmings', historical flashbacks (whether or not put into the mouth of Mao – who, in any case, had made them to Edgar Snow, Agnes Smedley or Ann-Louise Strong), it is like an engineer's working drawing compared with a Baroque canvas. One may prefer the drawing.

Malraux himself has explained the discrepancy between the *Antimémoires* version and the account pieced together by professional witnesses in an interview with Henry Tanner, the *New York Times* Paris correspondent, in October 1968:

> I went to see Mao for reasons of State. Our delegation was therefore present . . . What happened is that we were alone at the most personal, most human stage . . . He wanted to talk about the past . . . so he let all the officials go away . . . and as he walks like . . . a bronze emperor . . . with stiff legs . . . there was room to move and I was alone with the translator and him . . . In the conversation he did not speak Chinese, he spoke in Hunan dialect, the translator was a translator of Hunan, so that when he wanted to be understood by me alone, he spoke in Hunan . . .

He adds that 'when one studies the typescript produced by the French and Chinese Ministries of Foreign Affairs, it will be seen that my text is extremely close to the typescript . . . Of course, there is always the polishing up.' (About the same time, a devoted female admirer of the book remarked to Malraux, 'the only trouble is that Mao Tse-tung talks rather like Malraux . . .' To which Malraux retorted, 'You would rather he spoke like Bettencourt?')[18]

When the writer comes to the aid of the minister, it is not only a matter of 'polishing up' but also of 'colour' – as Barrès said of the Goncourts. Should one prefer the laconic old man with an expert knowledge of agrarian reform to the 'bronze emperor' facing the setting sun? When history offers in turn the sketch, the report and the poem, why should the historians complain?

Nothing much remains of this fine journey. For Malraux at least – except a reputation that reached as far as the ears of Mr Nixon, the least likely man in the world to decipher a single line of Malraux, and eighty-five pages of the *Antimémoires*. The Peking leaders were something less than enthusiastic about these pages, which would explain, in part at least, their subsequent silence on this visit, whereas they speak quite readily in China of the visits of MM. Couve de Murville, Peyrefitte, Bettencourt . . .

Official Chinese thought was already severely critical of *Les Conquérants* and *La Condition humaine*, an epic of metaphysical defiance, a praise of death as far removed as possible from the Chinese attitude (which is as much Confucian as Marxist) and a description of a revolution that appears to be the work of foreigners. Perhaps, too, the Peking leaders did not appreciate that Malraux should allow the legend of his participation in their revolution to be perpetuated.

The China of Malraux's novels is urban, cosmopolitan, metaphysical and emotional; the native revolutionaries are all terrorists seeking foreign aid. What more disconcerting image could Malraux have suggested to the Chinese leaders, who wanted their revolution to be rural, intensely Chinese, optimistic and impelled by the 'masses' themselves? But how unjust, too, is this lack of understanding, when one thinks of the innumerable non-Chinese who have learnt to respect China through the pages of Malraux's books?

That is why I feel I must quote what a high-ranking Chinese diplomat said to me when I asked him in 1972 what, all things considered, his country thought of Malraux. He laughed a little, with the laugh that means that the subject is a delicate one. Then, after a pause, he said: 'For us, he is a friend of China. He was on our side in the most difficult times . . .'

41 *Rear-guard action*

THIS André Malraux, who had been close to the Soviet Union
only when it was besieged and threatened by fascism and who
discovered and 'wedded' the French nation only in defeat, was
not the man to abandon the General when his power was on
the wane. We have seen him give public voice to his loyalty at
the time of the *putsch* and the *pronunciamiento*, and also when,
in 1965, the General was wondering whether or not he ought
to retire.

Then came May 1968. Three weeks of student demonstrations and strikes almost succeeded in overthrowing the régime.
Confronted by the young people and workers the régime
wavered between the old repressive reflexes of the police apparatus and the temporising tactics of ex-schoolmaster Pompidou.
The Fifth Republic lost its nerve and, in the last days of May,
saw its founder disappear, only to emerge from a helicopter
among his pretorians, on foreign soil, an *émigré* furtively outside himself as much as outside his country. It was a false exit,
yet a more effective one than that of 1946. Between noon on
29 May and 6 pm on 30 May – as in those atemporal, historical
dreams in which the sleeper thinks he sees in turn Alexander
the Great, Madame de Pompadour and Bismarck – France went
through two or three pseudo-revolutions. Cuba? The Commune? Moscow? But the Restoration was already under way.

Of all the bewildered, disloyal or obstinate staff that swarmed
for a few days over what already seemed to be the spoils of the
Fifth Republic, only the prime minister and the Prefect of
Police were still standing. As for André Malraux, he was too

eager an observer of events, too fascinated by revolutionary adventures, not to rediscover on the Paris left bank in May 1968 something of the Madrid or the Toledo of August 1936 – minus Stukas and Franco. Rather than hide himself away or draw up the ministerial lists of the General's successors, he analysed what was happening.

Six months later, the Paris correspondent of the *New York Times*, Henry Tanner, asked him if he did not think that he had been on the 'wrong side of the barricades'. He replied:

> Thirty years ago, I wrote a book called *L'Espoir* . . . It begins with the formless revolution I call 'the lyrical illusion' and becomes the application – principally by the Communist Party, but not only by it – of the revolution. For me, the lyrical illusion is something in the revolution that must be overcome . . . May was nothing more than an immense lyrical illusion, the problem was to discover what would emerge from it . . . The imagination in power means nothing. It is not the imagination that seizes power, but organised forces. Politics is not what one desires; it is what one does. The important thing is not to cry 'Long live liberty'; it is to make sure that liberties are achieved by the state. May was no more than a raw material . . . What the young people expected of us, above all, was a hope, beneath the malaise that they feel even more than we do, and which is at bottom of a religious nature, because we are in an unprecedented situation of rupture between man and the cosmos, between man and the world . . .

In this interview, he referred to the description of the crisis that he had given during an electoral meeting held by the Gaullists on 20 June in the Parc des Expositions. In face of the events, it is the only interpretation that a public figure of that time can re-read without embarrassment:

> This chaos . . . would like to be fraternity . . . What the students, the real ones, expect from us first of all, is hope. But besides this hope, there is the most fascinating of negative feelings, the old nihilism that suddenly reappeared with its black flag, and which no longer has hope in anything but destruction. We are not confronted by the need for reforms,

but by one of the most profound crises civilisation has ever known.

When he began his speech, he had said that he would speak on that day only at a historical level. He had nevertheless to bring in electoral polemics. Imprisoned in his old slogan as in a yoke of simplifications ('Apart from the Communists and the Gaullists, there is nothing!'), he goes on to attack the PCF as in the good old days of the RPF. But there, too, what he says of the Communists of 1968 reveals an unusual lucidity for someone in his situation:

> Disturbed by their leftist companion-enemies who had appeared for the first time, by their rightist companions, whom they thought they still needed as a mask, they, like everybody else, felt the revolutionary onrush beneath which the masses swamped the CGT,[1] and the CGT the Communist Party . . . I heard Canon Waldeck Rochet,[2] sheathing his claws, give a benign speech that would not have disgraced the teachers of the School of Wisdom . . .

The General obtained his reprieve on 30 June. Was Malraux really pleased at the election of a Chamber that emphasised still more the Restoration style of the neo-Gaullism that appeared after the barricades? Those weeks were to give him yet another opportunity to express, strangely enough, his sense of loyalty. When Georges Pompidou was eliminated by the old demiurge, irritated at having been saved by this creature of clay, Malraux participated with all the members of the government at the farewell dinner given on 10 July by the disgraced victor. He rose, glass in hand, and declared: 'Monsieur le deputé du Cantal, I drink to your destiny!'[3] It was enough for Pompidou to add the adjective 'national', six months later, to trigger off the great schism that was to contribute to de Gaulle's overthrow. Malraux had been the unconscious instrument in the initiation of an act of parricide; in the spring of 1969 he did his best to counter its effects.

Was he one of those (with Couve de Murville, Michelet, Schumann) who tried to dissuade the General from facing the risks of a referendum? It seems unlikely. He probably approved the 'double or quits' then attempted by de Gaulle, in order to escape from the humiliating situation of a doomed man saved by his own people in the name of conservatism, and in order to rediscover himself purified, strengthened, recrowned by the plebiscite. When his friend Georges Pompidou declared that he was ready to assume the succession, that is to say, to provide a stronger alternative to de Gaulle, Malraux quickly saw the danger that this operation might represent for the General. He tried to convince 'Dear Georges' to stand down, to declare his determination not to be in any sense the heir of the royal remains. To no avail. 'Monsieur le deputé du Cantal' saw his national destiny far too clearly. He was not going to give it up.

André Malraux gave these private approaches the most public and most solemn form on 23 April 1969 at the Palais de Sports: 'There is no post-Gaullism against General de Gaulle . . . One may found a post-Gaullism on the victory of Gaullism. One could not found one on its defeat!' Pompidou commented: 'One has to be Malraux to see a continuous line between 18 June 1940 and this referendum . . . To set out from the Resistance and arrive at regional reform: even Malraux's genius is not enough to do that!'⁴ One might add that one has to be Pompidou to see a continuous line between 18 June and his own history . . .

Since then, in an interview in *L'Express* in 1972, André Malraux has declared that General de Gaulle committed political suicide in 1969. That he had 'willed' his defeat, his execution, at the hands of the French people. Having experienced certain episodes of the General's political agony – he saw him three times during the last days, between 20 and 27 April then on 11 December 1969 at Colombey – Malraux is certainly well placed to speak of it. Nevertheless, he is not entirely convincing. Certain of the old man's confidences to others, to Michelet, to Schumann, and the temptation he felt to postpone the referendum show a man ready to play 'double or quits', playing for high stakes and prepared for the worst – this is *not* to say that he sought the worst.

General de Gaulle's retirement was Malraux's. Being 'a minister of the General' was not just to be anybody's minister. When one is Malraux, the comparison does not even arise.

When questioned one day about a book in which it was said that in order not to offend him M. Pompidou refrained from offering him a post when he was forming the first ministry of his seven-year term, Malraux burst out into a sort of laugh: 'Could you see me staying with "them" after the General's departure? It is as if we had won the Spanish Civil War and Negrin had asked me to become a colonel in the Guardia Civil.'[5]

There were feelings of loyalty, the aesthetic attractions of retirement, his criticisms of Pompidou from the point of view of Gaullist 'chivalry', simple fatigue and, lastly, the exhaustion of the 'cultural' project since May 1968. In short, Malraux returned to private life, though he kept a few gestures in reserve for future use.

After the age of adventure, the age of fraternity and the age of power, there began for him too the time of memory.

PART III

MEMORY

====

42 *The true, the false, the 'lived'*

'WHAT books are worth writing, apart from memoirs?' asks Garine in *Les Conquérants*, written in 1928. In February 1945, to Roger Stéphane, who had asked him if he kept a journal, Malraux replied: 'That's all very well for people who like to contemplate their past.'[1] In June 1965, it was 'to contemplate his past', to resuscitate it and perhaps to 'polish it up' that he set out for Asia on the *Cambodge*, towards the source of his youthful adventures, a schoolboy's exercise book under his arm.

Three years later he was to say to Henry Tanner that he 'did not know' when he set out that he would write 'this' book (he is speaking of the *Antimémoires*), let alone whether he 'could' write it. He began it on board the *Cambodge* – the first page bears as an epigraph the words 'Off Crete'. He likes to write at sea. He had two weeks before him. When he arrived in Singapore, he had begun the work. It took him another two years, exactly, to complete this evocation of his past (but, as he said at the time to Emmanuel d'Astier, 'If I count the flies and mosquitoes buzzing around the lamp, it took much longer...'). He had managed to write again – for seven years or more he had written nothing but speeches. For him, it was a victory. He had thought himself stricken with literary impotence. He had overcome it.

He entitled his book *Antimémoires*, so as to make it quite clear that it was not an account of his life – it was neither Chateaubriand's *Mémoires d'outre-Tombe*, nor Rousseau's *Confessions*, nor Gide's *Si le grain ne meurt*, nor Sartre's *Les Mots*. He explained his intentions very well to Emmanuel d'Astier at the time the book was published:

> Man does not construct himself chronologically: the moments of a life are not added to one another in an ordered accumulation. Biographies that proceed from the age of five to the age of fifty are false confessions. It is experiences that situate man. I think that one can rediscover a life through one's experiences, and not present experience as the crowning of the narrative . . .
>
> The *Antimémoires* reject biography, deliberately. They are not based on a journal or on notes. Setting out from the decisive elements of my experience, I rediscover a character, and fragments of history. I recount the facts and describe the character as if it did not concern myself. From time to time, I am reminded of certain episodes: I simply add them.[2]

He said it, he wrote it: 'What matters to me that matters only to me?' What is the use of relating that 'miserable little pile of secrets' that is a man's life? Again to d'Astier, he says:

> It is my one true book . . . I'm thinking of Proust. *Du Côté de chez Swann* made a new attempt to do anything resembling Chateaubriand impossible. Proust is an anti-Chateaubriand. Chateaubriand is an anti-Rousseau. I would like to be an anti-Proust and situate the work of Proust in its historical context.

To another questioner, he went on to develop the comparison with the author of *À la recherche du temps perdu*: the idea of the fatality of time. Except that for Marcel Proust it was a beneficent fatality, time offering the writer the material of which the work, which alone survives, is made. For Malraux, this fatality is maleficent, time destroying the accomplishments of action and even, through old age and death, the conquests of consciousness.

The *Antimémoires* are quintessential Malraux, the most perfect fusion-confusion of the true and the imaginary, experience and dream, lived raw material and the art that transforms it. Neither in *Les Conquérants*, nor in *L'Espoir*, nor in *Les Noyers de l'Altenburg*, nor even in that enormous novel of artistic creation *Les Voix du Silence*, has he better played this game of masks and things, of memory and that super-memory that is the imagination, so arbitrarily and diabolically entangled are history and fiction. And he has done this with such boldness that no one can now say to him: but this isn't true! True, false? China, Spain, the Resistance? We come back to the words of Clappique in *La Condition humaine* (it is not for nothing that he irrupts into the *Antimémoires*, for he is anti-history): 'It is neither true nor false, but lived . . .'

In order to cover his tracks still more, Malraux placed as an epigraph to his book this tiny 'Buddhist text': 'The elephant is the wisest of all the animals, the only one who remembers his former lives; and he remains motionless for long periods of time, meditating thereon.' His former lives . . .

In a prefatory note that is no less subtly evasive, Malraux says: 'This book forms the first part of the *Antimémoires*, which will probably comprise four volumes, and will be published together after the author's death . . . The passages of this volume whose publication has been deferred are of an historical order.' Does this mean that the rest is not? Or that what is being presented here is merely the surface of history? Or that the 'serious things' occur and are said only beyond death?

On 29 January 1973, André Malraux confided to me that he might change his mind on this matter and that other fragments of the *Antimémoires* – those, for example, on which he was then working and which describe his most recent experiences 'at the threshold of death', his stay in December 1972 at the hospital of Salpêtrière – might be published during his lifetime. 'But there are those who have confided in me – John Kennedy for example – whom I could not betray . . .'

The curious thing is that this book, which transfixes the history of the century like a sword through the entrails of a bull, and which aroused such a wide-ranging response in the European and American press, was virtually ignored by the 'politicians'. Was this because the word 'Antimémoires' was taken literally to mean anti-reality? By approaching the question of truth as he does, André Malraux has deflected the attention of historians from his book, impregnated as it is with history – from the Resistance to the Long March and from his discussions with de Gaulle to the descriptions of the deportees. He laid the stress on Proust, rather than on Michelet or Retz. He was taken at his word. It is a pity.

When one thinks that he could be regarded as a great expert in Chinese affairs after having written two perfectly fictional novels on the Kuomintang and that when he presents very convincing descriptions of great statesmen and major events of our time he is treated for all the world like a Proust, one has a right, I think, to reflect on the tribulations, in literature, of the notion of truth.

It is curious that the historians did not notice to what extent this narrative technique, coming from a novelist trying to bring a world to life through his own experiences, paid homage to the disciplines of history – not, of course, in the sense of respecting the fact, which serves here only as a recognition-point, but in the relation between the individual and the event. Are these 'anti'-memoirs because chronology is rejected? No. Rather because the individual is not central, is not the culminating point of the historical process, and because it is the event that brings the individual to life, rather the reverse. Around Chateaubriand, or Retz, or even Lawrence, the action is ordered and history constructed. Malraux's 'I' is not that of the protagonist of Corneille's tragedies, the pivot and organiser of the action. It is that of the privileged 'confidant' of Nero or Theseus. He is in History, by vocation. But although he sometimes distorts it, he refrains from placing himself in her place – History has the last word. Why, then, should one expect exactitude from him? True, false? Before we can decide, we must establish a wish to have us believe. Is this the case? Try to throw doubt on the absolute veracity of the conversations with Mao Tse-tung or Nehru as reported in the *Antimémoires*, and he will simply show surprise and refer you to the Chinese, Indian or French archives. But ask him to elaborate on a particular phase of the battle that ended for him and his men at the bottom of a tank trap and he will protest: 'All that is fiction . . . It is taken from *Les Noyers de l'Altenburg*, which is simply a work of the imagination . . .'[3] Yet in *Les Noyers* the scene in the ditch follows very shortly after that of the camp, an obviously autobiographical evocation of a crowd of prisoners. So where does the document end and the dream begin?

Another point. In the chapter added to the paperback edition of the *Antimémoires*, one of the speakers (it is difficult, as in *Les Chênes qu'on abat*, to distinguish whether it is Malraux or the other person – de Gaulle in the first instance, Méry in the second – who is speaking) declares that the biographers of Ho Chi Minh have emphasised Hanoi's difficult relations with France and the United States, but not those with China and the USSR. Having myself written a biography of the Vietnamese leader that in no way skates over this kind of problem, I protested. He replied: 'But it is Méry speaking!'

43 The death of the Father

ON 10 November 1970, at about nine o'clock, shortly after conveying the news to the President of the Republic and before making it public, Charles de Gaulle's family told André Malraux that the General had died during the evening of the previous day at Colombey, from a stroke.

Malraux had not seen him again since that day on 11 December 1969, when they had had a forty-minute meeting that became the original material of the book to be called *Les Chênes qu'on abat*. A few days after the conversation at Colombey, the General had once again expressed his attachment, his affection even, on the occasion of the death of Louise de Vilmorin, with whom André Malraux had been living for three years. It was a very brief message, but an exceptional one on the part of the old man – in view of the situation: 'In your suffering, I think of you. Faithfully, Charles de Gaulle.'

The following day two funeral services were held for General de Gaulle: the one he had wanted, at Colombey, for his family, the village people, his companions and the people of France and elsewhere, and the one that had been wanted for him, at Notre Dame, before M. Pompidou and thirty or so heads of state from all over the world.

In the village church where the pale head of Charles de Gaulle loomed every Sunday over the services with a formidable and distracted air, the family, the parishioners and some two hundred and fifty surviving members of the Order of the Liberation were gathered together. Malraux was not there. Shortly before the service was due to take place, a loud screech of brakes was heard in the square. Emerging from the car that had just brought him from a brief visit to Mme de Gaulle, André Malraux stood there, a ghost of unsure step, his hair blowing about in the wind; he disappeared into the tiny nave and seemed to throw himself forward as if for a charge. He moved up the centre aisle, like a blind prophet, almost stumbling over the stand that had been placed in front of the altar to contain the coffin. He looked dazed, as he stood there opposite the great plaster Christ that looked down over the choir. People had to move up to make room for him and they saw him there, stooping, preoccupied, when the doors of the church opened again to let the coffin, borne by twelve young men of the district, pass through.

Did he like this carefully concerted simplicity, with its three-fold reference to the family, history and the village? Was this how the inventor of the ceremonies of the RPF, who had wanted fanfares at the burial of Georges Braque and had assembled a crowd of thousands to salute the ashes of Jean Moulin, was this how he had expected the funeral of Charles de Gaulle to be?

'It was the funeral of a knight-at-arms,' he said to AFP correspondent Jean Mauriac. 'There was just the family, the Order and the parish. But the General's corpse should not have been in a coffin, but placed like that of a knight, on wooden logs . . .'[1]

In his account of that day, there is a fine moment. The crowd is pressing forward to reach the cemetery. An old peasant woman wants to pass. But a marine, who has been ordered to let no one through, bars her way with his rifle. The old woman struggles with him and shouts: 'He said everyone, everyone!' Malraux intervenes. The marine swings round without a word and, as he lets her pass, seems to present arms to the people of France[2] as the good woman clumps her way towards the coffin.

André Malraux had now lost the man who most strongly marked and orientated his life for fifteen years — more than any other man had done. How different they were, the huge graduate of Saint-Cyr, who had entered history through refusal, and the swaggering, self-taught adventurer, noisy challenger of bourgeois society, who had been made a minister by his friend!

Did Malraux really believe that he was the friend of Charles de Gaulle? When the *Mémoires d'Espoir* appeared in 1970 and he read the sumptuous paragraph that was devoted to him ('On my right I have and will always have André Malraux . . . Friend of genius . . .'), he was so overcome that he ran straight to his friend Manès Sperber to read it to him. However exceptional the signs of friendship, trust and respect shown him by the General, he remained convinced that he was there only as a sort of specimen of the intellectual class, as a historical monument, as the guarantee, too, of a certain populism; that de Gaulle regarded him as a picturesque amateur and, as writers, admired Montherlant and Mauriac more.

Apart from these few lines from the *Mémoires* and the place he accords Malraux – de Gaulle had too great a sense of the state and his own role to be associated in the government with anyone whom he regarded as an incompetent flatterer – we know very little of what the founder of the Fifth Republic thought of Malraux. Their conversations, as reported in the *Antimémoires*, give little inkling of their relations – and still less is revealed in that essay on the approach of death that Malraux entitled *Les Chênes qu'on abat*, published in 1971 in advance of volume two of the *Antimémoires*, of which it is no more than a chapter. It is an eloquent title: the plural says a great deal. It is, of course, a quotation from Hugo, but there are other expressions in his poems just as suitable to honour the disappearance of a great man. Malraux wanted this plural – it associated him, on the same level, with the fate of the stricken sovereign. And the dialogue that he 'relates' is put together in such a way that it is often impossible to know who is speaking – as, sometimes, between Garcia and Scali in *L'Espoir*. This is how Malraux's 'super-memory' works.

Why should one question the accuracy of the account of this 'interview'? Also present that day at 'la Boisserie' was M. Geoffroy de Courcel, who notes, without acrimony, that the conversation lasted for about forty minutes, adding that since the visitors left at about 3 pm the description of the host contemplating the stars as they left, even on a foggy December day, must be pure imagination. There are people who see stars at noon: they are those who, on 18 June 1940, believed in something.

This is, more or less, what the critic Murray Kempton says: 'To read de Gaulle and Malraux even here together when everything had passed them by is to understand the command that fantasy will forever be able to place upon us: both of them are so much more wonderful than anyone real . . .'[3]

What is described here is the nature of a bond between two men at the end of their careers, fascinated by History, haunted by the limits of action and obsessed by death, two men who have passed through the 'what is to be done?' that had occupied their lives to a 'what is the point?' Malraux says as much when he speaks elsewhere of 'my bloody and vain life'. When the General says (or when Malraux says that the General said): 'My only international rival is Tintin', he gives some idea of what, for them, History is made of: the dreams that Chateaubriand saw as the raw material of the government of the French people.

They stand there before the deserted landscape around Colombey. The flow of the centuries slowly jostles them towards death and this diminished horizon tells them that they will leave. What they say to one another is sometimes of a solemn vacuity that is nothing short of astonishing. But they do speak to one another and it is perhaps this that the book expresses most of all for André Malraux, who for forty years, has suffered from the anguish of being unable to communicate with others, and who is there, towards the end, with the man of History, talking with him.

There is this bond of words spoken now and deeds accomplished in the past. There is that enormous and durable complicity between two individuals from two totally opposed cultural worlds – the one born in the nation and for the nation, within order and for order, in the Church and unable to conceive of moving away from it; the other, the outsider, the cosmopolitan, the rabble-rouser, the creator of a ramshackle air squadron, the man of disorder.

With the coming of the war, the General discovers the limits of order and the writer becomes aware of the vices of disorder. The meeting took place, for the one, at the frontier between the national institution and the true nation; for the other, at the frontier between formless fraternity and the real nation – the

nation that is made up not of ideas, but of men, not of words
but of everyday sufferings, humiliations, lacks, frustrations. 'I
married France' – this Gaullean, not to say Gaullist turn of
phrase, so like that of the founding father, is rather more
sonorous than need be. And it was not so much France perhaps
that Malraux married at that time as the French in France – a
people who had become a mass of humiliated, alienated and
exploited proletarians.

I am not trying to find a Malraux faithful to himself in spite
of himself, moving quite naturally from the struggle for the
proletarian class to that of the proletarianised nation. He has
himself accepted and admitted the transformation when, for
example, he says to the radio reporter Julien Besançon:

> During the war, I found myself confronted on the one
> side with the proletariat, on the other with France. I married
> France. Others married the proletariat, usually in the hope
> that they would have a mistress. And so did we . . . Yes, I
> subordinated France to social justice. At the present time I
> am subordinating social justice to the nation, because I think
> that if one does not gain the support of the nation one will
> not have social justice, one will simply make speeches . . .[4]

As we know, the transformation took place before the meeting with de Gaulle, during his time with the Maquis groups
and the formation of the Alsace–Lorraine Brigade. Even in
1942, Malraux is still talking of fighting at the side of the Red
Army. In 1943, he is in contact with those networks that are
in communication with the British and Americans, joins a
Maquis group of strictly Gaullist obedience, then forms a unit
inspired principally by the theme of the reconquest of national
territory; and when he makes his political 'comeback', at the
MLN congress, it is in order to block a Communist policy, in the
name of national independence. It was not until six months
later that he discovered de Gaulle, but everything was already
orientating him towards a man who had travelled in the opposite direction, who had broken with class allegiances in order
to refound the nation on those for whom the war and the
occupation had been, for various reasons, a personal insult and
an intolerable frustration.

Between General de Gaulle and Malraux there were in fact three points of convergence: France, which the one discovered and the other bore within him; decolonisation, familiar to the writer, but a revelation to the General; and the fact that they were both intellectuals. The word 'intellectual' may be taken here to define men whose action is guided by certain ideas, who display a love of style and who conceive of history in similar ways – men who might have the same understanding of books – if not of Flaubert and Dostoevsky, at least of *Mémoires d'outre-tombe*, *War and Peace* and *The Decline of the West*.

Was the author of *L'Espoir* shocked, disappointed, indignant, to see Charles de Gaulle, visiting Spain a few months before dying, shake hands with Francisco Franco? He has refrained from commenting publicly on that visit.[5] While travelling in the Mediterranean some months later, Malraux refused to land at Cadiz, announcing that he had too many friends killed there in the resistance to Franco to be able to set foot on Spanish soil as long as this régime was in power.

However, they had in common that fundamental thing: the confusion, more conscious on the part of the General, more insidious in the writer, between reality, the raw material of political analysis, and its representation, the raw material of political art. De Gaulle wishes to act – and can act – only at a certain altitude; he takes facts as they are, but makes them what he wishes them to be. If he is a realist, he is certainly a realist of the imaginary.

Malraux, too, is perfectly capable of dismantling the mechanism of a political event, but he is more eager to reassemble it as he wishes – and in doing so deploys all the resources of an unrivalled imagination. He, too, is an imaginative realist and has defined adventure as the realism of fairytales – but he might have given the same definition of all action.

Halfway between the poetic dream that interprets life and the fact on which action is based, these two 'daydreamers' travelled the same road. Death chose to separate them.

44 The survivor

THE departure of Charles de Gaulle might have made Malraux a mere survivor, one of those 'disinterested' individuals whose existence no longer has meaning. 'This is the end of this man's time, and of mine,' Malraux was to say a year later before the television cameras. Yet there were a few things left for him to accomplish. Moreover, *La Métamorphose des Dieux* and the *Antimémoires* were still unfinished books; he was still working on them in the great house of the Vilmorins, at Verrières-le-Buisson, surrounded by his pictures – his Braque, his Fautriers, his Poliakov and his cats, in the blue drawing-room of the witty woman, now dead, to whom he wished to remain close.

To *La Métamorphose des Dieux* he expected to add a double sequel, '*L'Irréel*' and '*L'Intemporel*'. He was working on these in 1973 while writing a sequel to the *Antimémoires* which he published in 1974 under the strange title *La Tête d'obsidienne*. The book, which was received with a good deal of reserve and disappointment, offers a vivid and pungent portrait of Pablo Picasso as a symbol of the victory of man, maker of art, over death. But the Malraux rhetoric is heavier and more nebulous than ever. As strange as the title are the author's introductory words: this book is a fragment of *Le Temps des limbes*, the first part of which was published as the *Antimémoires*. The second will be entitled *Les Métamorphoses*. When categories are confused to this point in an immense imaginary representation of the real, anything can become anything. The important thing is that Garcia's wish, 'to transform into consciousness as broad an experience as possible', is realised. But is it transformed into consciousness or into artistic obsessions?

His experience, his field of experience, could be broadened still more. He had, for example, merely scratched the surface of Latin America. When confronted by the Mayas, he had been reminded of the Sassanids. In Brazil, he had done little more than explain how French generals were fighting for the emancipation of Algeria. Now he linked himself to those same left-bank intellectuals, whose manifesto-mania he had so often derided, by signing, together with Sartre and Mauriac, a demand for the release of Régis Debray, then imprisoned in Bolivia. It was a generous gesture, because although he had sufficiently proved that he could risk his life when necessary, he had not always been ready to risk his reputation when this meant acting like others.

A television journalist questioned him on this matter. Why did he associate himself with this cause? 'Because the Western world today is full of people who spend their time talking and never put into practice what they say. Debray did his best to carry out what he thought. Debray behaved with, shall we say, responsibility. Bravo!' 'If you had been the same age, would you have done the same thing?' 'I did do it.'

And then there was Bangladesh. Again a colonised Asian people (colonised this time by other Asians) that rose up and was apparently subjected to the fate of the workers of Shanghai called upon to fight by Kyo and his associates. The West remained silent, perplexed. The Pakistani oppressors placed such good soldiers at the service of American strategy, and are such good buyers of French arms! André Malraux was no longer a minister. He could affirm what seemed to him the greater truth and the starker injustice.

He let it be known that he was ready to set out for East Bengal and stand side by side with the Bangladesh rebels. One day, he explained that it was in order to join the fighting. Another, to set up a school of guerrilla warfare in Calcutta. Another, to practise his profession as a revolutionary writer. Naturally enough, these statements caused some amusement. There is something absurd about the idea of a short-winded, half-crazed seventy-year-old leading a military action. But anyone who has not seen an anonymous crowd of pastry-cooks, town-hall clerks and plumbers setting out for war has no idea of how unfitted for action people called upon to die can be.

When, on 17 December 1971, a letter from André Malraux to President Nixon was published in *Le Figaro*, it was the same day that Pakistan recognised its defeat and accepted the emancipation of Bangladesh. It was a strange apostrophe, and one that arrived too late, as if he had joined the Resistance the day de Gaulle entered Paris. It is strange indeed that a man can challenge the American strategy indirectly responsible for the situation in Bengal, while standing by for years, without murmuring a word, as the same American power massacred the Vietnamese people, with whom he was at least linked by old ties. He does, it's true, refer briefly to the Vietnamese tragedy in this letter to Richard Nixon. And then:

> You will remember our conversation with General de Gaulle . . . You did me the honour of talking to me about American policy. I said to you: 'The USA is the first country to have become the most powerful in the world without wanting to. Alexander wanted to be Alexander, Caesar wanted to be Caesar. You had no wish to be the masters of the world. But you cannot afford to be so in an absent-minded way . . . It is not fitting that the country of the Declaration of Independence should crush the wretched struggling for their own independence . . . It is not I who should be saying what I am saying today; it is you . . .'

(The affair continued to fascinate him, even after the end of the war, and over a month later he was still talking in my presence about the strange campaign, and about the surprising inactivity of the Pakistani airforce.)

Because he was André Malraux, one of the most famous men of his time, a former minister of de Gaulle's, he needed the agreement, before acting, of the power without which any initiative in Bangladesh was unthinkable: that of New Delhi. Mrs Indira Gandhi, the prime minister, asked him to be patient. She would be passing through Paris, she said, after London and Washington. They would talk about it: it was extremely generous of him, the friend of her father, Jawaharlal Nehru, a hero of the *Antimémoires*, to take up the cudgels for the friends of India. But the conversation in Paris between a Malraux tired of waiting and an Indira Gandhi determined to hold him back and aware that 'her' war would be over in ten days, was a particularly melancholy comedy. The image of André Malraux leaving the drawing-room of the Indian Embassy, where Mrs Gandhi had just received him, is one of the most pathetic in the career of this man doomed to pathos. The livid complexion marked by violet trails, staggering, his hand gripping the curtains, unable to speak a word, neighing with sorrow – he is the vanquished man, deprived of his will for dignity. He referred to the Indian prime minister as 'that woman' and, with all his pain and genius, he failed to make these words sound other than vulgar.

That he should have felt cheated by an Amazon's cunning of the death he hoped to find there is merely a hypothesis. Who can ever know whether someone else – or even himself? – really seeks death? Perhaps he was more like the de Gaulle he has described the night before the referendum of April 1967, not so much a suicide as caught up in, and accepting in advance, the ultimate consequences of a fatal game. A few weeks later, in any case, as Mrs Gandhi was celebrating her victory, he confided to a friend: 'Why go there now? They have no interest in killing me any more . . .'

It was a way out, on the ancient earth of Asia, beside a crucified people, in the midst of voluntary companions . . . He had to give up the adventurer's death, that of Perken, the tragic man who dies both at the centre of his destiny and outside it, and the death of the hero, the being from elsewhere, invested with an uncertain mission written on wind-swept sand.

In the first few days of 1972, he resigned himself to not dying in Bengal. I asked him if Mr Nixon had replied to his letter in December. 'Oh, yes, oh yes!' he replied, with a sententious murmur that ill concealed important news. Three weeks later, he was invited to Washington, where, after John Kennedy, he was to confront Richard Nixon. Was he fully aware of the contradiction involved in the (former) friend of the Vietnamese revolutionaries being the guest of a head of state who was mercilessly crushing beneath his bombs the sons of his former companions? After all, de Gaulle did go to visit Franco! Further-more, Malraux told me that if one was going to stop the Vietnam war, one had more chance of doing so by going to the White House than writing an article in *Le Nouvel Observateur*.

It was not as a friend of the Vietnamese, but as an 'expert' on Chinese questions that Richard Nixon had invited him to Washington, just prior to his Peking visit. 'He wants to meet someone who knows Mao,' said Malraux as he left Orly. 'There aren't that many of us . . .' Even at this level of 'knowledge', the knowledge to be obtained in an hour-long official interview through the medium of translators, Malraux was not just any one of Mao's visitors. In the United States, there were about thirty men, from John Service to Edgar Snow, much better informed as to what the leader of the Chinese revolution might have to say, ask, suggest to an American visitor than the author of *La Condition humaine*. But these were the 'witches' that Mr Nixon had so long hunted . . . Malraux was a witch exorcised by honours.

What did he say to him? We shall have to wait for volume two or three of the *Antimémoires* before we have the visitor's version. Meanwhile, we must content ourselves with the inter-view he gave to Jean Mauriac, for the France-Presse agency, after the conversation with Mao:

> The mistake of the Americans is in believing that the Long March happens every morning. To visit Mao thinking of the Long March would be as if one had seen Stalin while think-ing of the bank raids. Stalin said to me: 'We thought that we would be saved by the European revolution. But it is the European revolutions that will be saved by the Red Army.' Mao thinks that the Asian revolution will be saved by Chinese apples and the rice fields . . .

Moving suddenly from this rather heavy-handed economism to the role of keeper of supreme secrets, André Malraux con-fided to his interviewer:

> An agreement has existed between Peking and Taipeh for at least five years, bound up with the death of Chiang Kai-shek. But they didn't expect Chiang Kai-shek to live so long.

I'm convinced that this agreement contains terms by which Nationalist China will become Chinese once more on the death of Chiang Kai-shek. It will, of course, take a subtle form. But you can expect subtlety where the Chinese are concerned. That is what I told Nixon . . .

In the autumn of 1971, shortly before playing the role of world oracle, André Malraux had met two intelligent television producers, Françoise Verny and Claude Santelli. 'Why don't we do a big thing together? I just sit there in front of you and tell you everything . . . The *Antimémoires* spoken . . .' So they went to Verrières, and sometimes in the fine garden in which Louise de Vilmorin wanted to be buried beneath a cherry-tree, sometime in the blue drawing-room, surrounded by favourite cats, whisky and tea, they recorded for hours and hours: Alexander, Trotsky, Mao, de Gaulle . . .

They talked of Nietzsche and of his walking-stick, which Hitler had taken possession of – his own way of being Nietzschean; of Stalin and Gorky; of the Maquis among the dwarf oak-trees, horse-chestnuts and heather where the wretched adversaries of the 'Das Reich' division trained. They talked of God, and Malraux said that it did not seem to him possible, as an agnostic – not an atheist – to find 'any other answer than a religious one' to the problems of the world today . . . He went on in this style, in the grips once more of Pascal – then suddenly said to his guests: 'No, stop the cameras, I don't want to depress them any more than necessary.'

So they recorded in this way about a hundred hours, the equivalent of two thousand pages of text. 'They'll only keep ten hours of it,' he told me in January. 'Enough to make the French disgusted with me forever . . .' In fact, nine broadcasts of fifty minutes each, under the proudly Hugoesque title, 'La Légende du siècle' were shown to several million French citizens, between April and November 1972. Sometimes they saw him dumbstruck, beating the air with hysterical forearms, confused. Sometimes, too, he could be brilliant and amusing, as when he recounted his visit, as a sort of teller of good fortune, to the geishas of the Japanese emperor, or his encounters over Spain with Italo Balbo's airmen – too human at such close range to be shot down, or the burial of Khrushchev, when a woman covered the thick-set body with a final umbrella . . .

He was well received. It is not often that a genius, wounded, chilled, but surviving his ordeals, expresses himself so well in front of so many. Was it a farewell? He made no attempt to make it seem so. After the thwarted plans of an epic death in Bengal, after acting as extraordinary adviser to the most powerful man in the world at the moment he was throwing himself into the strangest enterprise of his life, after this long dialogue with the silent multitude of citizens, what was left for him to do or say? About the Charles de Gaulle of *Les Chênes qu'on abat,* he confided something like this to a friend, shortly after the publication of the book:

> All that remained to him was to meditate on the past, which is always, more or less, to meditate upon death; not one's own decease, of course, but death as a metaphysical problem. The past lay before him; to write one's 'memoirs' is to live six hours a day with the past. What I learnt with him, namely that the past is something that helps to decide the future; had disappeared.

Is this, in a way, a self-portrait of the Malraux of 1973 who, rushed into the Parisian hospital of La Salpêtrière in November 1972, and given up for dead, re-emerged three weeks later, lively, buzzing with innumerable plans, receiving dozens of visitors, fearlessly writing his memories of this 'house of the dead', finally setting out for Bangladesh in April, presiding over the great retrospective exhibition that the Fondation Maeght devoted to him from July to October 1973, at Saint-Paul-de-Vence? Of the Malraux of 1974, who publishes articles on 'art pompier' in *Le Figaro,* spends a month in Japan, revisiting Kyoto and Nara, and sends hundreds of kindly letters to young writers and old friends? A life so rich in metamorphoses ought not to include fewer resurrections.

45 Garine in glory

HE WISHED to enter History, if possible by breaking in. He
did. He wanted glory. He won it. He wanted power. He
received the reflection of it, which he savoured, together with
the honours, fortunes and worldly respectability that go with
it. He refused, of course, to become an Academician, and it is
common knowledge that if the Nobel Prize for Literature was
withheld from him it was because he was for so long a minister
in a government regarded as semi-fascist by a few puritan pro-
fessors of the Stockholm jury. What other French writer, since
Victor Hugo, will have so animated, stirred, directed, orientated the art and life of the collectivity, the colour of its towns,
the chances of being a man and an artist in one's own country?

A writer with no followers, a 'loner' who has kept aloof from
literary diplomacy and commerce since 1939, a writer of indefinable influence, though one that obviously goes beyond the
influences he appears to have exerted, in spite of himself, on
Camus, Sartre and the current of tragic existentialism of the
1940s. Contemptuous of fashion and of stylistic or formal
experiment, and quite happy to play the role of the man of
action who has somehow wandered into literature, of the
'serious' man fallen prey to the futile malice of word-spinners,
he is for many people, as for François Mauriac, 'the greatest
living French writer and certainly the oddest.'[1] But he himself
has always questioned his greatness as a writer.

He presents his writing to friends for their opinion, with a
modesty bordering on humility – and these friends are invariably surprised at being regarded as arbiters. He is being
perfectly serious when, as so often in conversation, he places

Bernanos and Montherlant above himself as a writer, regarding his own work as artificial, second-hand, clumsy, envying the superb ease of writers who were so by the grace of God. His most highly-wrought books from the formal point of view – *La Voie royale, Le Temps du Mépris, Le Noyers de l'Altenburg* – have, at various times, run the risk of being disowned (which has in fact been the fate of *Le Royaume farfelu*). His own favourite books are the least complex, those in which he expresses himself with ease and fluency, *L'Espoir* and the *Antimémoires*, those in which he yields up what is for him the essence, in which experience strengthens and grounds expression, in which the writing is or is intended to be merely the reflection and interpretation of action.

He always wanted to be someone who not only 'doesn't speak in order to do nothing', as de Gaulle put it, but who tries 'to do' before talking; someone who not only makes his actions agree with his words, but also makes his words an extension of his actions. He was not trying to establish a pre-eminence of the writer who acts over the writer who stays at his desk – on the contrary, he puts Faulkner above Hemingway. But the writer who places the values of action very highly condemns himself to act or lose his *raison d'être*. As a combatant of the Spanish Civil War, as a Maquisard and as the founder of the Alsace–Lorraine Brigade, he acted. Why did he act? In Spain, he twice helped to defend Madrid; in Périgord, he helped a few hundred men to delay the northward progress of the 'Das Reich' division, thus saving thousands of British and American lives in Normandy; at the head of the Brigade, he was one of those who spared Strasbourg an intolerable recapture by the Nazis at the end of December 1944.

For good or ill, he played a crucial role in thwarting the Communist attempt to gain control of the whole of the Resistance at the beginning of 1945; he helped to harden the attitude of the régime towards the Algiers *putschists* and to cover de Gaulle's left flank when the General was caught between two fires during the negotiations that led to the independence of Algeria. Not all his actions belong to the world of the shadow theatre – or were an attempt to prove his virility, as in the case of Hemingway or Montherlant.

'A great writer whose greatness concerns the life he led,' wrote Mauriac. None the less, what he has done, even in so finished a work as *La Condition humaine*, proves above all that man can go further than himself when he is searching for that which transcends him, and is bound up with that which surrounds him. The great adventure of his life was not flying over some ruin in the Yemen, or over some Spanish city, or the capture of some hill in the Vosges, but the crossing of the frontier between the worship of difference and the discovery of fraternity. It is this that makes the preface to *La Temps du Mépris* his key-text, his central testimony. There Perken and Garine, the adventurers, the 'loners', the missionaries of the absurd, find themselves again in a community, and in doing so create the type of man that Malraux was in Spain, in the Resistance and in the Brigade, the totally lucid militant, the man whose experience, broadened to include the collectivity, is immediately transformed into consciousness.

The fact that Communism should have been the focus and the locus of this long process of maturation should be neither exaggerated nor minimised. It would be mean and untrue to present the period of fellow-travelling as a passing phase, an 'artistic subject handled powerfully and brilliantly, but without sincerity', as is suggested, and finally rejected, by Gaëtan Picon. Nor should it be seen as a miscalculation, an error of maturity and proof of the weakness of André Malraux's political grasp. One does not fight for ten years without learning something of the virtues and vices of one's fellow-combatants. But virtues and vices do not remain inert. Some grow stronger and others weaker, according to historical situations.

A comrade from the battle of Teruel holding his own against fascist assailants by sheer obstinacy and a sense of organisation does not incur the same political judgement or arouse the same tactical reaction as the Communist minister of 1945 attempting to monopolise the sacrifices of his militants in the service of a particular ideology and global strategy. It is striking to observe to what extent Malraux adjusted his attitude to the PCF to the radical historical mutation that transformed the sacrificed opponents of fascism into consumers of power.

When Gaëtan Picon suggested, in his *Malraux par lui-même*,

that he 'broke with the Marxist concept of the class struggle,' he replied in a brief marginal note that he had never seen it as the key to history. And he added, 'I had never accepted it as such.'[2] As a key to history? Where does anyone see anything of the kind in Malraux? At all events not in *La Condition humaine*, nor in *L'Espoir*, where the notion of class never appears, where the very few proletarians to be seen are either terrorists or anarchists. What we have are revolutions made by intellectuals without either country, roots or social environment, strangers to any 'class', any 'standard of living' (except the mercenaries of the *España* squadron, the only characters to possess an economic life, and the only ones more or less condemned by the author). And what historical essay by Malraux, even during the period of his alliance with the Communists (even the preface to *Le Temps du Mépris*), sees any other motive-force to history than heroism on the part of individuals or the community against political, far more than against social or economic injustice?

From Indo-China to Spain and the France of 1945, André Malraux has certainly not failed to plead for agrarian reforms and the nationalisation of credit, which shows him to be something more than a condottiere of revolt and is evidence of his social intelligence. But there is nothing to this that implies the least tincture of Marxism, and when Marshal Chen-yi, in Peking, referred to Saint-Simon when Malraux was speaking of Marx, he was as inspired as if he had referred to Fourier, Kropotkin or Georges Sorel. I have already quoted Malraux's riposte to Roger Stéphane asking him if he was a Marxist: 'As Pascal was a Catholic! He died in time . . .' And he added: 'Philosophically, I'm not at all a Marxist.' One may well wonder how this proposition accords with the previous one – but this is nothing new in Malraux. Perhaps one might attempt a synthesis by suggesting that Malraux is almost as Pascalian as Pascal was Catholic, and as far removed from Marxism as Pascal was from the religion of the Jesuits. But he must be seen above all as a Nietzschean, a Nietzschean haunted by Dostoevsky and the problem of evil.

Even more than Marx, Nietzsche represents the rejection of the ethical way, of the Christian aesthetic. But Dostoevsky,

above all that 'fifth Gospel', *The Brothers Karamazov*, brings him
back to it all the more strongly because Dostoevsky is the witness and interpreter of the Christianity of the Nestorians, discovered during his Siberian exile, a Christianity of the weakness
and vulnerability of God.

Can a certain appreciation of Dostoevsky exist without a
minimum of receptiveness to the strangest, most mysterious
aspect of Christianity, namely, the idea of the temporary defeat
of God and of the power of the Devil? To Bernanos, who asked
him in 1945 what he considered the most important event of
our time, Malraux replied 'The return of Satan' – to Bernanos,
who had said that to be a Christian was not to believe in God,
which was easy enough, but to believe in the Devil. In Malraux's mouth, was this Satan merely the wretched torturer of
Auschwitz and Oradour?

André Malraux, born into the Catholic religion, soon lost
any faith – despite, as Clara suggests, a few moments of
adolescent mysticism. He became very anticlerical in the early
1930s, yet in *La Condition humaine* expressed an overwhelming
thirst for transcendence and an obsession with Pascalian themes.
Is the man who portrayed in Guernico a Christian who seems
to be seen from the inside, who charged his *Les Noyers de
l'Altenburg* with a kind of spiritual anticipation in an atmosphere of neo-Christian charity, whose essays on art are a
homage to the collective, spiritual and humanist art of Gothic
Christianity, is he one of those vagabonds, those prowlers of
God of whom Rimbaud could be said to be the archetype? His
old friend Emmanuel Berl says: 'What I have in common with
Malraux is the rejection of the rejection of God . . .'[3]

His official position is the one he has often formulated: 'I am
an agnostic eager for transcendence, who has received no
"revelation".' On 25 August 1948, he wrote to his friend Pierre
Bockel, one of the chaplains of the Alsace–Lorraine Brigade:
'I emphasise my defence of that which is eternal in man,
whether or not I conceive it as bound up with revelation.' Let
us leave to the priest and friend responsibility for the religious
interpretation he gives these words.[4] But thirteen years later,
when planning an expedition to Bangladesh, he wrote to the
same friend that 'for obscure reasons', they would die 'together'

and that his friendship would help him 'to die nobly'.[5] This goes quite a long way: but one can imagine Romain Rolland or the intractable Martin du Gard writing that to a priest or a pastor without betraying their fundamental atheism.

There are other signs too. There is, for example, Malraux's reply to Pierre Bockel's offer to accompany him to Jerusalem: 'I could go to Mecca, to Benares. But to Jerusalem, no. I would have to go to Gethsemane – and there, fall on my knees . . .' And the priest commented: 'If he refused to go to Gethsemane, isn't it because he's already there?' and went on to quote from Pascal: 'You would not seek me if you had not already found me.' There is also this formula, spoken by André Malraux to the chaplain: 'I am an agnostic. I have to be something, for don't forget that I am very intelligent . . . But you know better than I that no one can escape God . . .'[6]

Lastly, there are his relations, on this subject, with de Gaulle. One could not read without surprise the passage in *Les Chênes qu'on abat* in which he puts into the General's mouth words that might cast some doubt on the religious faith of his inter-locutor. Yet he was convinced – he has told me so himself – of Charles de Gaulle's untroubled Christian faith. But there is the highly ambiguous incident reported again by Pierre Bockel. Taking this priest by the arm one day, the General said to him: 'You know Malraux very well, you ought to convert him: it would suit me very well . . .'

Was he a sort of fellow-traveller of Christianity? He was, in any case, fascinated by Christian metaphysics and also by sanc-tity, by individuals such as Bernard de Clairvaux, the creator of crusades, the brilliant preacher of Vézelay, who haunted him for so long, and St Francis, the gentle vagabond of Tuscany. Thus, towards the end of this tumultuous, ambition-crazed life, he caught a glimpse, beyond fraternity, of what he sometimes calls charity and sometimes gentleness:

But if you really must treat me like Dostoevsky and know 'my' saint, then it is obviously St John . . . The poet, the irrationalist? No, the man to whom we owe Christ, without whom the face of Jesus could not be deciphered, the man through whom we know that 'God is Love'. It's pretty banal to say that now, but at the time it was a rather new idea! You know, when I was a prisoner in Lot at the end of July 1944, it was St John that I wanted to read and I asked the Mother Superior of the convent in which we were staying for the night to lend me a copy of the Gospels. Well, it didn't work! I was not Dostoevsky . . . I got nothing out of it, apart from reading a fine piece of writing. What I hoped for did not happen – though I expected to be shot any minute![7]

'I am in art as one is in religion.' It is a celebrated formula and describes one possible Malraux. But when Roger Stéphane suggested complementing it with Gide's formula, 'There is no problem of which a work of art is not an adequate solution,' he rejected it out of hand (and Uncle Gide with it). 'Art resolves nothing,' he replied, 'it only transcends.' This was said in 1945. Would Malraux have spoken in this way a quarter of a century later? There is, through *Les Voix du Silence,* and even more through *La Métamorphose des Dieux,* a slow, strong rise in the vocation and power attributed to art, in its function as a bearer of freedom and continuity, as a manifestation of the universality of man and of his ability to triumph over destiny in a sort of universal transparency.

The early Malraux observes destiny, and in order to play with it draws a grinning caricature of it: the 'farfelu', the amorphous genius, the obese butterfly, fluttering and incapable, narrowly missing death and the mire. The second Malraux opposed destiny with history, a chain of human wills, a challenge to the irremediable – yet itself spotted with the dross of destiny, heavy with meaninglessness and misfortune. The third Malraux discovers that 'the sovereign rectification of the world is the privilege of art. Art is not the expression, but the Song of History . . . Destiny has given in . . .'[8] For art is 'anti-destiny'.

On his road, at war against the despairing absurdity of the condition of men, against the incommunicability that makes them strangers to themselves and irreducibly different, Malraux encountered fraternity. It took other forms, as we have seen, than that of antifascist meetings and battles in Spain. It was sometimes the search for a thought or a form, the meeting with a dead master or an old living friend, Masaccio, Michelet,

Groethuysen, Drieu la Rochelle, Martin du Gard, the Goya of the House of the Deaf Man or the Braque of Varengeville, the long collaborative labour with Gide on *Le Tableau de la littérature française*, the collective search for items in an exhibition of Persian art, the discovery of some foreign author hitherto unknown in this country, introduced and illuminated by some brilliant text, as were William Faulkner and D. H. Lawrence.

Fraternity was above all that of the combatant and the militant, of the bombardments of Spanish airfields, of the Maquis in Corrèze and in the snows of Alsace. He had proved to himself that man could transcend himself; he proved it to himself again through others. And through them he discovered that man is neither alone nor entirely absurd, that if action is a denunciation of the void, common action is a denunciation of solitude. The cyanide offered by Katow, the parachute that he himself gave in Spain to Raymond Maréchal, and his brother Roland, arrested by the Gestapo, passing on to him his job and his responsibilities in the network – all these actions form a chain of wills and sacrifices that testify to 'the honour of being a man'.

Yet action never gave him what he expected of it. He demanded not only that it should be a rather superior form of entertainment, a denunciation of the absurd and the void, a refusal of death, but also that it should bring with it harmony, reconciliation with oneself. He had learnt its limitations – not so much because of his relative inability to act (there is always the element of the 'farfelu' in him), but above all because action divides as much as it unites, because it is too 'Manichean' (the word is his) not to run the risk of bringing consciousness and experience into conflict. He sought extreme consciousness at the peak of experience. He did not find it there. There lies his failure.

Yet we have to admit that the Malraux plunging into divisive and devouring actions is more creative than the author of *La Métamorphose des Dieux,* who has entered 'into art as into religion' and is surrounded by the gentle peace of the monastery that for him is represented by the museum. The furious Malraux in quest of an absolute through an action that cannot give it him, pursuer of himself (and beyond), captures his masterpieces. The Malraux pacified by the 'Voices of Silence' that come to him through art is surrounded by the serenity of a necropolis. His search for immortality, beyond transcendence, takes him to the man of stone, to the world of statues.

His subject is not the artist, but the hero. It is curious nevertheless that in five or six great novels, peopled by some of the most intelligent and cultured characters of contemporary literature, André Malraux never tried to create a great painter, a great sculptor or a great poet, though he was a friend of Braque and Valéry. We see only anthropologists and aestheticians, picture dealers and archeologists, teachers, critics and composers of film music – who have all, when he takes them up, abandoned their art or their work for action, or renunciation.

Through his essays, he pits himself against Goya and Mantegna, Michelangelo and Rembrandt – and in doing so he participates in a creative metamorphosis. But he himself never creates one of those artists in quest or in possession of that transcendence that art carries within itself – his characters are always on the fringe of art, in quest of heroism, amateur researchers in quest of adventures, lost intellectuals in quest of fraternity. Malraux never attempted to create a figure like Thomas Mann's hero in *Death in Venice* or Marcel Proust's Elstir, a great artist confronting the problems of artistic creation. His heroes – with the exception of a few speakers at the Altenburg who, like Möllberg, are anti-heroes – are all in the grips of action and in quest of heroism, some of them even of victory.

Perken's grandeur derives from defeat. Garine's does not. And the grandeur of Garcia or Manuel derives, on the contrary, from their hope in victory – whatever they do to attain it. With Vincent Berger, there is a return to inevitable defeat; but it is done through a shaman figure, a man whose mysterious 'powers' have no need, perhaps, for power. There appears another dimension to the adventurer, whose failure no longer provides a defence against his own nothingness. Lawrence – because he is bound up with a history, a dual history, that of his country and that of its allies – is in a different situation from Mayrena, and since Garine, Malraux has had other experiences

that the death of the hero does not doom to absurdity. For
– less than art, perhaps, but more at least than adventure
– the fraternal struggle contains its plenitude and its continuity.

A struggle against the irremediable defied by heroism, denied
by fraternity, transcended by art? I am not trying to offer '*the*'
definition of the life of André Malraux ('My bloody and vain
life'), which has not come to the end of its acts of defiance and
its metamorphoses. We shall ask for one from his best interpreter, Gaëtan Picon:

> Scenes, characters, ideas, dramatic figures: their voice is
> that of the passions of a life . . . The work reveals to us not
> so much what its author is as what he conceals and what he
> conquers: what he wishes to be. From anguish, through
> courage, to exaltation, it is always, for Malraux, a question
> of escaping from oneself, of exchanging a subjectivity for
> something exterior and objective. He has a passion for his-
> tory, for the event, the act, ideas, problems, artistic styles,
> great cultures; all forms of a single passion for the im-
> personal. This solitary by instinct and fate needs to be
> surrounded and sustained, loves whatever binds him to
> others: speaking, appearing, acting, thinking; distrusts
> whatever encloses him within himself: feeling . . . One can-
> not pay too much heed to the passionate preference he
> lavishes on the plastic arts: this may be, among other things,
> because canvases and statues are at the meeting-point of
> gazes, and books at the point where daydreams diverge.
> Impatience with the event, disgust with slack periods, a call
> to great circumstances, this tendency to submit everything
> to an illumination that amplifies it and to a rhythm that
> accelerates it: this is again a recourse against oneself, a need
> to be distracted from self. Rather than a vocation of instinct,
> rather than the expression of an indivisible and irresistible
> personality, heroism is, in this case, response, will.[9]

Yet there is a point at which the will to heroism breaks down:
death, with its weight of the irremediable, which 'transforms
life into destiny'. Sartre defines Malraux (and Heidegger) as 'a
being-for-death'. To which Malraux replies: 'And supposing

instead of saying *for*, one said *against*? It only appears to be the same thing. . . .'

Summoning up his will against death, he finds two ways. The immortality of the man of stone and the metamorphosis of ever-changing art cannot appease his needs, because the given is stronger here than the gained. There remains the construction of a life organised as a representation for a double defiance of death. The *Antimémoires* erect, *against* a life, a formidable buttress of creative will and poetic imagination: they are 'anti' as in anticlinal. Thus this life already created as a tragedy, built as a rampart, modulated as an act of defiance, will find an endless echo by being transformed into a work that is still being written.

Malraux has not acted in order to find in action the source of an inspiration. He has written because action, even when fraternal and collective, gave him neither a response to a certain need for an absolute, nor the fulfilment that conquerors seek. His life is not a pretext, it is an end in itself. His work is compensatory.

A life constructed as a work and a work breathing like a life are the two forms of an intense organisation of self, first as will, then as representation.

Notes

1 A SON OF THE WAR

1 André Malraux, *Antimemoirs*, trans. Terence Kilmartin, London 1967, New York 1968, p. 16. Page references throughout are to the Penguin paperback edition.
2 Clara Malraux, *Memoirs*, trans. Patrick O'Brian, London and New York 1967, p. 344.
3 *Antimemoirs*, p. 10.
4 *L'Événement*, August 1967.
5 *L'Événement*, August 1967.
6 A. Vandegans, *La Jeunesse littéraire d'André Malraux, Essai sur l'inspiration farfelue*, p. 35.
7 *Memoirs*, p. 203.
8 G. Gabory, *Mélanges Malraux Miscellany*.
9 Interview given by André Malraux to the author, 30 June 1972.
10 *L'Événement*, August 1967.

2 CLARA

1 *Memoirs*, p. 154.
2 ibid., p. 159.
3 ibid., pp. 162–4.
4 ibid., pp. 165–6.
5 ibid., p. 171.
6 ibid., p. 185.
7 ibid., pp. 184–5.
8 ibid., pp. 193–4.
9 ibid., pp. 221–3.
10 Interview given by André Malraux to the author, 30 June 1972.
11 *Memoirs*, p. 175.
12 *Le Disque vert*, March–April 1923.
13 Fifteen years later, he asked his friend Corniglion-Molinier:

'What dowry did your wife bring you?' 'Debts . . .' 'Lucky
bastard!' Malraux retorted.
14 Gaëtan Picon, *Malraux par lui-même*, p. 80.

3   THE SMALL CHANGE OF REVOLT

1 *Memoirs*, pp. 244–5.
2 ibid., p. 220.
3 Quoted in A. Vandegans, *La Jeunesse littéraire d'André Malraux*,
p. 221.
4 *The Royal Way*, trans. Stuart Gilbert, pp. 34–6.
5 *Memoirs*, p. 247.
6 ibid., p. 251.
7 Perken refers to this figure in the passage from *The Royal Way*
quoted above.
8 Walter Langlois, *L'Aventure indochinoise d'André Malraux*, p. 8.
9 *Correspondance*, published by F. Garnier, p. 215.
10 *Memoirs*, p. 249.

4   THE FOREST

1 *Memoirs*, pp. 253–4.
2 Pp. 54–64.
3 *Memoirs*, p. 262.
4 The three western provinces of Cambodia, in which all the
temples of the Angkor complex and its dependencies are situated.
5 *The Royal Way*, pp. 76–7.
6 Langlois, *L'Aventure indochinoise d'André Malraux*, p. 280, note.
7 *Memoirs*, p. 264.
8 'L'art d'Indravarman', in the *Bulletin de l'EFEO*, 1919, pp. 66–90.
9 *Le temple d'Içvarapura*, p. 7.
10 *The Royal Way*, p. 13.
11 'La Légende du siècle', broadcast no. 2, May 1972.
12 *Memoirs*, pp. 270–1.
13 ibid., p. 273.
14 *The Royal Way*, pp. 110–11.
15 ibid., p. 111.
16 Langlois, *L'Aventure indochinoise d'André Malraux*, p. 26.
17 *Memoirs*, p. 281.

5   THE MAGISTRATES

1 *Memoirs*, p. 304.
2 ibid., p. 305.
3 ibid., p. 307.
4 *L'Aventure indochinoise d'André Malraux*, p. 28.
5 *L'Impartial*, 22 July 1924.

6 Quoted by Langlois, *L'Aventure indochinoise d'André Malraux*, p. 40.

7 ibid., p. 8.

8 *The Conquerors,* trans. Stuart Gilbert, pp. 54–6.

9 One of these photographs was of a bas-relief from Angkor that had nothing to do with the affair (Langlois, *L'Aventure indochinoise d'André Malraux,* p. 51).

10 *Memoirs,* pp. 327–31.

11 Max Jacob, quoted by R. L. Doyon, *Mémoires d'homme.*

12 Having had to deal with him, twenty-two years later in Saigon, in quite different circumstances, the author can corroborate that Maitre Béziat was a formidable opponent.

13 Quoted by A. Vandegans, *La Jeunesse littéraire d'André Malraux,* p. 220.

14 *Candide,* 13 November 1930.

15 Vandegans, op. cit., p. 249.

16 *Memoirs,* pp. 357–62.

17 ibid., pp. 362–4.

18 ibid., p. 368.

19 ibid., pp. 368–9.

20 Quoted by Langlois, *L'Aventure indochinoise d'André Malraux,* p. 62.

6 A FRENCH COLONY IN 1925

1 *Les Combats et les Jeux,* pp. 32–3.

2 Interview given by André Malraux to the author, June 1972.

3 *Les Combats et les Jeux,* p. 77.

4 ibid., p. 100.

5 ibid., pp. 118–21.

6 ibid., p. 158.

7 A FIGHTING NEWSPAPER

1 *Les Combats et les Jeux,* p. 104.

2 ibid., pp. 85–6.

3 ibid.

4 Quoted by A. Vandegans, *La Jeunesse littéraire d'André Malraux,* p. 244.

5 *Les Combats et les Jeux,* pp. 197–9.

6 *Les Combats et les Jeux,* pp. 177–81.

7 A. Vandegans, *La Jeunesse littéraire d'André Malraux,* p. 248.

8 Langlois, *L'Aventure indochinoise d'André Malraux,* p. 185.

9 *Les Combats et les Jeux,* p. 206.

10 ibid., pp. 214–15.

8 L'INDOCHINE ENCHAINÉE

1 *Les Combats et les Jeux*, pp. 194–5.
2 ibid., p. 228.

9 ASIA: THE DREAM AND THE REALITY

1 Classiques Vaubourdolle, 'Pages choisies d'André Malraux', p. 3.
2 Quoted in A. Vandegans, *La Jeunesse littéraire d'André Malraux*, p. 241.
3 Edmund Wilson, *The Shores of Light*, p. 573.
4 *La Lutte ouvrière*, 9 April 1937.
5 *Une Littérature de fossoyeurs*, p. 57.
6 Former companion of Leo Trotsky, friend of André Gide, Surrealist writer and military historian.
7 Interview given by Pierre Naville to the author, June 1972.
8 W. M. Frohock, *André Malraux and the Tragic Imagination*, Stanford University Press, San Francisco, 1952–67, p. 6.
9 *Les Combats et les Jeux*, pp. 241–2.

10 HOMECOMING

1 Interview given by André Malraux to the author, June 1972.
2 Interview given by Marcel Arland to the author, 2 February 1972.
3 *Memoirs*, pp. 366–7.
4 Interview given by Claude Gallimard to the author, 19 November 1972.
5 Meeting between Louis Aragon and the author, February 1972.
6 *Variétés*, July 1929.
7 *L'Europe nouvelle*, October 1926.
8 *Les Nouvelles littéraires*, 31 July 1926.

11 CONQUEROR AND FARFELU

1 'Farfelu' is a slang word, meaning dotty, fanciful, bizarre, much used by Malraux. (An early quasi-Surrealist fantasy is entitled *Le Royaume farfelu*.) Lacouture sees the word as representing the lighter side of Malraux's character, as opposed to the more serious, 'conqueror' side [Trans.].
2 *Mort de la pensée bourgeoise*, p. 187.
3 Published in 1929 in the review *Signaux de France et de Belgique*, then in 1967 in *Le Magazine littéraire*.
4 Twenty years later, in an afterword written for *Les Conquérants*, André Malraux wrote: 'If this book has survived, it is not because it depicted certain episodes in the Chinese revolution, but

because it showed a type of hero in whom ability to act, culture, and lucidity meet.'

5 The book by André Vandegans, often quoted in this work, illuminates this side of Malraux's character perfectly.
6 Interview given by Gaston Gallimard to the author, February 1972.
7 *La Revue européenne*, May 1927.
8 Interview with Frederic Grover, *Revue des Lettres modernes*, November 1972.
9 Grover, 'Malraux et Drieu', ibid., p. 68.
10 Which shows that 'lucidity' does not exclude a certain naïvety.
11 Grover, op. cit., p. 61.
12 On 20 December.
13 *L'Événement*, September 1967.
14 *Candide*, 13 November 1930.

12 THE PATHS OF GLORY

1 *Galerie privée*.
2 Interview given by Manès Sperber to the author, February 1972.
3 *25 années de liberté*, col. I, pp. 301-2
4 *Le Sabbat*, pp. 420-1.
5 He died in 1970. Malraux refers to him briefly in the *Antimémoires*.
6 Twenty years later, Picon was to write the best study of Malraux, *Malraux par lui-meme*, Paris, Seuil, 1953.
7 *The Journals of André Gide*, trans. Justin O'Brien, London 1949, vol. III, p. 267.
8 *Marianne*, 15 December 1933.

13 INTERLUDE OVER THE DESERT

1 My italics.
2 *Antimemoirs*, p. 68.
3 *Mémoire brisée*, p. 291.
4 Shiism, one of the two great traditions in Islam, is particularly strong in Persia.
5 *L'Intransigeant*, 10 March 1934.
6 Interview given by Georges Henein to the author, 17 March 1972 (*Le Canard enchaîné* is France's best-known satirical paper – trans.).
7 *Le Crapouillot*, June–July 1971.
8 *Antimemoirs*, p. 69.
9 ibid., pp. 71-2.
10 ibid., pp. 81-2.
11 *Antimemoirs*, pp. 73-7.
12 ibid., p. 77.
13 Published by W. Langlois in *Mélanges Malraux Miscellany*.

14 COMMITMENT ON THE SIDE OF THE COMMUNISTS

1 'Jean Paulhan à la *NRF*', no. spécial 'La mort de Groethuysen'.
2 Interview given by André Malraux to the author, June 1972.
3 December 1930.
4 Ilya Ehrenburg, *Truce: 1921–1933,* London 1963, p. 136.
5 *Marianne,* 29 March 1933.
6 J. P. A. Bernard, *Le Parti communiste français et la question littéraire,* p. 178.
7 Ehrenburg, op. cit., p. 275.
8 Who was, in fact, to be expelled shortly afterwards for Freudian tendencies . . .
9 The method used by the acquitted legionnaires.
10 Gallimard, 1935.
11 'Indochine S.O.S.', pp. ix–x.
12 *Marianne,* 20 December 1933.

15 A CONGRESS IN MOSCOW

1 *Memoirs,* p. 264.
2 'Autour d'un discours de Malraux', J. Leiner, *La Revue des lettres modernes,* November 1972, pp. 133–4 (documents translated by Hélène Reshetar). Nizan, a novelist and Sartre's closest friend, had joined the French CP. He left the Party after the Nazi–Soviet Pact of 1939, accused by his comrades of working for the police. He was killed in the battle of Dunkirk in 1940.
3 ibid.
4 *Commune,* September 1934.
5 'Autour d'un discours de Malraux', pp. 59 and 144.
6 ibid., pp. 147–8.
7 Interview given by André Malraux to the author, January 1972.
8 *Commune,* November 1934.

16 THAELMANN AND DIMITROV

1 J. Humber-Droz, *10 ans de luttes antifascistes,* La Baconnière, p. 112.
2 Interview given by André Malraux to the author, January 1972.
3 Henri Barbusse, poet and novelist, author of the most impressive novel in French on the 1914–18 war, *Le Feu,* became the leader of the Communist intellectuals after 1925.
4 Nicole Racine, 'Les Écrivains communistes en France 1920–1936', doctoral thesis, under the direction of René Rémond, p. 33.
5 *The Invisible Writing,* London 1954, pp. 246–7.
6 *Fin d'une jeunesse,* Paris 1954, p. 51.
7 September 1935.

8 8 November 1935.
9 Quoted by J. P. A. Bernard, *Le Parti communiste français et la question littéraire*, p. 187.
10 *Mémoire brisée*, p. 289.

17 THE MAESTRO OF THE MUTUALITÉ

1 The Mutualité is one of the largest halls in Paris, often used for public meetings, etc.
2 Which earned him a philippic from Thierry Maulnier in *Le Figaro* of 29 June 1935.
3 Based on notes made by a witness.
4 This took place two years after the arrest of Serge.
5 Interview given by André Malraux to the author, January 1972.
6 *Commune*, September 1935.
7 Ehrenburg, *Memoirs*, p. 317.
8 Lucien Rebatet, *Les Décombres*, Paris, Denoël, 1942, pp. 38–9.
9 Paris, Maspéro, 1967.

18 GIDE

1 Preface to *Les Chênes qu'on abat*, p. 7.
2 *Action*, no. 12, March–April 1922, p. 17.
3 *Le Disque vert*, February–March–April 1923, pp. 20–1.
4 *Journal*, vol. I, p. 45.
5 ibid., p. 11.
6 *The Journals of André Gide*, trans. Justin O'Brien, vol. III, p. 42.
7 ibid., p. 345.
8 R. Fernandez, *Littérature et Politique*, p. 283.
9 Gide, op. cit., vol. III, pp. 344–5.
10 ibid., p. 348.
11 *Terre des Hommes*, 1 December 1945.
12 Gide, op. cit., p. 346.
13 *Antimémoires*, p. 22. This passage does not appear in the English translation [Trans.].

19 T. E. LAWRENCE

1 *Malraux par lui-même*, p. 16.
2 *Antimemoirs*, p. 294.
3 From a suppressed introduction to the French translation of *Seven Pillars of Wisdom*, quoted by Claude Mauriac, *Malraux ou le mal du héros*, p. 170.
4 *Antimemoirs*, p. 294.
5 *Antimemoirs*, p. 65.
6 In his *Malraux et le gaullisme*, p. 275, J. Mossuz takes up one of Malraux's statements and situates the meeting in London. See

also the additional chapter, not included in the English translation, of the paperback edition of *Antimémoires*, p. 140.

7 *L'Express*, 22 March 1971.

8 ibid., p. 145.

9 The union of Asian lands once conquered by the Turks.

10 Published in a limited edition of eighty copies by the Éditions du Pavois, in 1946, then by the review *Liberté de l'esprit*, April–May–June 1949.

11 op. cit., p. 275.

12 P. 6. It will be noted that the final phrase was used by Malraux as the title of the book he was then writing.

13 *N'était-ce donc que cela?*, p. 18.

14 ibid., p. 6.

15 *Seven Pillars of Wisdom*, p. 349.

16 ibid., VI, p. 74.

17 The Deux-Magots is the famous café in Saint-Germain-des-Prés once, if not still, reputed to be the rendezvous of writers and intellectuals. The Hôtel Matignon is the residence of the French Prime Minister [Trans.].

18 Interview given by André Malraux to the author, 20 July 1972.

19 *Portrait de l'aventurier* (with a preface by Sartre), in which Stéphane traces a parallel between T.E.L., von Salomon and Malraux.

20 *Fin d'une jeunesse*, p. 156.

21 *Seven Pillars of Wisdom*, IX, p. 103.

22 R. Stéphane, *T. E. Lawrence*, p. 238.

23 ibid., p. 239.

20 TROTSKY

1 Interview given by Malraux to the author, June 1972.

2 Interview given by Pierre Naville to the author, 20 April 1972.

3 *NRF*, April 1931, pp. 488–507.

4 *Marianne*, 25 April 1934.

5 *La Vérité*, 27 April 1934.

6 ibid., 6 April 1934.

7 op. cit., p. 125.

8 The day after Malraux's visit to Royan, Trotsky warned his companions against a man who was in contact with the PCF and visited Moscow. This mistrust was regarded as 'exaggerated' by Trotsky's entourage.

9 Information given by Pierre Naville to the author.

10 Gide had just published his *Retour d'URSS*.

11 *La Lutte ouvrière*, 9 April 1937.

12 *New York Times*, 17 March 1937.

13 See another extract from this speech on pp. 221–2.

14 Cyrus Sulzberger, *A Long Row of Candles*, New York and London, 1969, p. 326.

15 Quoted by Maurice Merleau-Ponty in *Les Temps modernes*, no. 34, p. 176.
16 ibid., p. 180.
17 Interview broadcast on 9 September 1967.
18 In the version published in *Le Magazine littéraire*, July 1971, no. 54.

21 THE 'CORONEL'

1 'La Légende du siècle', April 1972.
2 Information from *El Sol*, 20 May 1936.
3 *Mémoire brisée*, p. 291.
4 This is the date he gives. Several newspapers of the period date his arrival as 23 July.
5 He died in 1972 in Mexico City, where he had retired.
6 The scene between Scali and the captured Italian airman who had taken off from La Spezzia on 15 July, p. 140.
7 Federación anarquista ibérica. Confederación Nacional de Trabajadores.
8 Hugh Thomas, *The Spanish Civil War*, London 1961, p. 225.
9 Janet Flanner, *Men and Monuments*, p. 39.
10 Julien Segnaire left the Communist Party ten years later.
11 Gallimard, 1952.
12 *La Rançon*, p. 50.
13 *Malraux par lui-même*, p. 90.
14 *Le Magazine littéraire*, no. 11, 1967.
15 Pietro Nenni, *La Guerre d'Espagne* [French translation], p. 163.
16 ibid., p. 163.
17 ibid., p. 165.
18 Unpublished letter from Georges Soria to the author. In *The Yoke and the Arrows*, 1957, p. 23, Herbert L. Matthews, the *New York Times* correspondent praises Malraux warmly as 'a true idealist and a brave man – my favourite Frenchman . . .'
19 'La Légende du siècle', April, 1972.
20 *La Révolution et la guerre d'Espagne*, Paris, 1961.
21 *The Spanish Civil War*.
22 No. It was Colonel Ascensio who commanded the column.
23 Six machines . . . the squadron never had more planes flying at once.
24 *Days of Hope*, trans. Stuart Gilbert and Alastair Macdonald, London, 1938, pp. 84–90.
25 Rpt. *Mort en Espagne*, Paris, 1937, p. 73.
26 Hugh Thomas, the excellent historian of the Spanish Civil War, speaking of the intervention of the *España* squadron, describes it curiously as 'French'.
27 *Journal*, p. 1195.
28 *Les Combats et les Jeux*, p. 189.

29 Conversation between the author and J. Segnaire, 19 August 1972.
30 *Days of Hope*, pp. 254–6.
31 ibid., p. 249.
32 Of alcohol, of course.
33 That of the mercenaries.
34 *Days of Hope*, pp. 250–6.
35 A suburb of Madrid.
36 *Days of Hope*, pp. 256–7.

22 THE VOLUNTEERS OF ALBACETE

1 The future head of the republican government in exile.
2 J. Delperrie de Bayac, *Les Brigades internationales*, p. 92.
3 ibid., p. 93.
4 *Days of Hope*, p. 417.
5 *Eve of War, 1933–1941*, London 1963, pp. 165–6.
6 He did so in the Maquis in Corrèze, where he had joined Malraux.
7 There is a photograph of this.
8 *Days of Hope*, pp. 413–17.
9 ibid., p. 364.
10 *Spanish Testament*, Left Book Club, London, 1937.
11 J. Delperrie de Bayac, *Les Brigades internationales*, p. 215.
12 *Days of Hope*, p. 377.
13 In particular by Broué and Temime, op. cit., p. 348.
14 Though in *L'Espoir* it takes place before the attack on Teruel and the descent of the mountain, with which Malraux had wanted to end the book.
15 *Days of Hope*, pp. 423–4.
16 Alfred Fabre-Luce, for example, in an article in *Le Monde*, 21 October 1971.
17 Hidalgo de Cisneros, *Virage sur l'aile*, pp. 316–17.
18 He asked me not to divulge his name.
19 Broué and Temine, op. cit., p. 348.
20 Interview with Roger Stéphane, October 1967.
21 Mauriac may shrug his shoulders. This time, Malraux is not 'romancing'. Queipo did dare to say that, and many other things too.
22 François Mauriac, *Mémoires politiques*, pp. 78–80.

23 'LIFE AGAINST DEATH'

1 Reported in *The Nation*, 20 March 1937.
2 *Starting out in the Thirties*, London, 1966, pp. 107–8.
3 Janet Flanner, *Men and Monuments*, p. 51.
4 ibid., p. 40.

5 In this respect, it is worth comparing the memoirs of the United States ambassador to Madrid, Claude Bowers, *My Mission to Spain*, with what his British colleagues, such as Sir Henry Chilton, wrote.
6 *Ce Soir*, 21 April 1937.
7 *Eve of War, 1933–1941*, p. 178.
8 Koltzov, *Journal*, op. cit., p. 431.
9 ibid.
10 Ehrenburg, op. cit., p. 178.
11 *World within World*, London 1951, p. 239.
12 Malraux's reply to this question (29–1–73) is as follows: 'Any psychoanalyst will tell you that when a novelist puts a moustache on a hero who more or less represents himself, it is because he is looking for a mask . . .'
13 *Days of Hope*, pp. 247–8.
14 A curious note informed the public that the order of the scenes had been altered in order to bring it more up to date.
15 On 29 January 1973, André Malraux gave me the following reply to the question: 'No. In the sense that I am not the sort of chap who goes around with a notebook in his pocket in order to jot down things as they happen. But I do scribble notes from time to time. The book was written very quickly, you know. Between the actual event and the publication of the novel there were first drafts, rewritings, moments of remorse . . .'
16 *Carnets*, La Table Ronde, Paris, 1947.
17 December 1937.

24 HOPES UNFULFILLED

1 *Sierra de Teruel*, Mexico City, 1968, p. 8.
2 Translated as 'Comrades' Blood' in the English edition [Trans].
3 *Petite Littérature du cinema*, pp. 30–1.
4 Pierre Galante, *Malraux*, p. 163.
5 *Le Magazine littéraire*, no. 11, 1967.
6 Galante, op. cit., p. 167.
7 I heard this phrase used myself.

25 THE CAMP

1 *Sierra de Teruel*, p. 14.
2 *Eve of War, 1933–1941*, p. 238.
3 Interview given by André Malraux to the author, 20 July 1972.
4 Interview given by Raymond Aron, 28 December 1971.
5 *Memoirs*, p. 476.
6 *Antimemoirs*, p. 228.
7 ibid.
8 *The Prime of Life*, trans. Peter Green, London 1962, p. 308.

9 *Fin d'une jeunesse*, p. 82.
10 'La Légende du siècle', May 1972.
11 Correspondence with friends who wish to remain anonymous.
12 J. B. Jeener, *Télé-7 Jours*, 29 April 1972.
13 He later became co-editor of the *NRF* and translator of the *Koran*.
14 Jean Grosjean remembers only that it was not 'l'appel du 18 juin'.
15 Interview given by Jean Grosjean to the author, October 1972.
16 They were divorced in 1945. Since then, Clara's life has constantly been difficult, though made more bearable by the affectionate presence of her daughter Florence (who, in 1970, married the great film director Alain Resnais). Clara Malraux had published several novels and a book on Israel (*Venus de toute la terre*) when, in 1963, under the general title *Le Bruit de Nos Pas* (*Our Footsteps*), she began a brilliant account of their years together – a work often quoted in this book. The fourth volume of this series appeared in October 1973, describing the storms in this marriage of two exceptional human beings. Particularly memorable is her husband's cruel remark: 'It is better to be the wife of André Malraux than a second-rate writer . . .' A fifth volume is due: *La Saison violente*.

Devoting a good deal of energy to defence and praise of Israel ('as important in my life as the Resistance in the Forties', she said), she is now a lively, vocal grey-haired lady, living in a tiny flat, in a working-class quarter. She is still obsessed or fascinated by the tempestuous man she lived and worked with.
17 *Les Combats et les Jeux*, p. 193.
18 Site of the bloodiest battle of the Resistance.
19 *Antimemoirs*, p. 9.

26   INTERLUDE BY THE SEA

1 Varian Fry, *Surrender on Demand*, New York, Random House, pp. 9–10.
2 *Antimemoirs*, p. 110.
3 W. G. Langlois, 'A. Malraux 1939–1942, d'après une correspondance inédite', *Revue des Lettres modernes,* Paris, 1972, pp. 95–127.
4 ibid., 9 June 1941.
5 Simon Bussy's wife Dorothy, an excellent English writer, is best known for her novel *Olivia*, translated by his friend Roger Martin du Gard.
6 Stéphane, *Chaque homme est lié au monde*, pp. 72–3.
7 ibid., p. 84.
8 *The Prime of Life*, p. 393.
9 *Correspondance Gide-Martin du Gard*, p. 237.
10 *The Prime of Life*, p. 394.

11 This idea of leaving for the United States appears nowhere else.
12 Langlois, op. cit., p. 116.
13 *L'Événement*, September 1967, p. 53.
14 Langlois, op. cit., p. 114.
15 Éditions du Haut-Pays, Laussane-Yverdon, 1945, under the same title, *Les Noyers de l'Altenburg*.
16 Langlois, op. cit., pp. 119–20.
17 Grover, 'Malraux et Drieu la Rochelle', loc. cit., pp. 88–9.

27 IN THE MAQUIS

1 Georges Beau et Léopold Gaubusseau, 'R5' (*Les SS en Limousin, Périgord et Quercy*), p. 204.
2 Interview given by René Jugie (Gao) to the author, 24 November 1972.
3 Guingouin was expelled from the French Communist Party after the war.
4 P. Galante, op. cit., p. 183.
5 Éditions Bière, Bordeaux 1945.
6 *Le Monde,* 27 September 1967.
7 E. H. Cookridge, *Inside S O E,* London, 1966, pp. 340–1.
8 An independent organisation directed by General Vincent, supported by the British.
9 *La Marseillaise,* 23 April 1947.
10 ibid.
11 Interview given by René Jugie (Gao) to the author.
12 Cookridge, op. cit., p. 329.

28 THE GESTAPO FILE

1 This was, in fact, what I did myself.
2 George Hiller, who never fully recovered from his wounds, died on 27 November 1972, as counsellor at the British embassy in Brussels.
3 *Antimemoirs*, pp. 167–9.
4 *Fin d'une jeunesse*, p. 52.
5 This was untrue, but it conformed to instructions to appear more important than one was in order to avoid immediate execution.
6 *Antimemoirs*, pp. 171–2.
7 According to the historians of 'R5', p. 407, Georges Beau and Léopold Gaubusseau, it was Major Fitschen. That Malraux should have transformed a major speaking to him into a colonel is only to be expected.
8 *Antimemoirs*, p. 182.
9 His visits to Spain never lasted more than two months.
10 *Antimemoirs*, pp. 191–3.
11 ibid., pp. 196–201.

29 THE MOST CHRISTIAN BRIGADE OF BRIGANDS

1 Carlos Baker, *Ernest Hemingway, A Life Story*, London 1969, pp. 497–8.
2 *L'Alsace française*, p. 9.
3 Interview given by General Jacquot to the author, 19 November 1972. The General added that his left-wing ideas were regarded as much more reprehensible by his colleagues than those of Malraux. After all, an intellectual . . .
4 Interview given by André Chamson to the author, 23 February 1972.
5 *L'Alsace française*, p. 13.
6 Interview given by André Chamson to the author, 23 February 1972.
7 ibid.
8 Interview given by Pierre Bockel to the author, 19 November 1972.
9 This formula was not offered them until 20 October. Before this, they were virtually 'francs-tireurs'.
10 Interview given by Pierre Bockel to the author, November 1972.
11 In the *Antimémoires*, André Malraux describes Josette Clotis' death as taking place at Brive. He is confusing this with an occasion when his wife stayed in a clinic in this town a year earlier for the birth of her second son.
12 *Fin d'une jeunesse*, p. 55.
13 But it was then that he wrote to her friend Rosine Delclaux that the music celebrating the entry of the brigade into a village 'seemed to him to have been played for Josette'.
14 Jacques Nobécourt, *Le Dernier Coup de dés de Hitler, la bataille des Ardennes*, Paris, Robert Laffont, 1973.
15 P. Galante, op. cit., pp. 212–13.
16 ibid.
17 *Fin d'une jeunesse*, p. 34.
18 ibid., pp. 40–69.
19 The trial of the director of *L'Action française*, accused of collaboration with the enemy, had just ended with a sentence of imprisonment for life.
20 Jacques Bainville (1869–1937) was then the best-known right-wing royalist historian, and had been associated with the Action française. He was supposed to have inspired the anti-Germanism of de Gaulle.

30 THE TURNING POINT

1 Interview given by André Malraux to the author, 20 July 1972.
2 *Fin d'une jeunesse*, p. 43.
3 *Antimemoirs*, p. 90.

4 *Section française de l'internationale ouvrière*, the French social democratic party, now known simply as the French Socialist Party [Trans.].
5 *Antimemoirs*, p. 90.
6 This is, word for word, the thesis of the Communists in Spain, which he had taken over as his own.
7 *Combat,* 28 January 1945.
8 *Action,* 16 February 1945.
9 *Antimemoirs*, pp. 91–2.

31 THOSE WHO FELL

1 Interview given by Claude Gallimard to the author, 21 November 1972.
2 *Antimémoires* (additional chapter in the French paperback edition), p 466.
3 Who was later transferred to Buchenwald and came out of it alive.
4 Clara Malraux, *Memoirs*, p. 230.
5 Interview given by André Malraux to the author, 29 January 1973.
6 Interview given by Clara Malraux to the author, February 1972.
7 *Antimemoirs*, pp. 365–6.
8 Eugène van Itterbeck, 'Une amitié d'intellectuels: du Perron et Malraux', *Septentrion*, no. 1.
9 Gaëtan Picon, *Malraux par lui-même*, p. 91.
10 *NRF*, December 1942, quoted by Frederic Grover, 'Malraux et Drieu la Rochelle', *Revue des Lettres modernes,* November 1972, p. 8.
11 ibid., p. 87.
12 ibid., p. 90.

32 THE MEETING

1 E. d'Astier quoting Abel Gance, *L'Événement*, September 1967.
2 Certainly Claude Guy, the General's aide-de-camp.
3 *Antimemoirs*, p. 95.
4 ibid., p. 110.
5 *Malraux ou le mal du héros.*
6 *Un autre de Gaulle,* p. 144.
7 *Antimemoirs*, p. 96.
8 ibid., pp. 97–105.
9 Claude Mauriac, *Un autre de Gaulle*, Paris, 1970, pp. 148–9.
10 Interview given by Gaston Palewski to the author, 23 November 1972.
11 *Un autre de Gaulle*, p. 148.
12 Not counting the provisional government.

13 The spiritual heirs of Jules Michelet (1798–1874), the great French historian. He is best known for his seventeen-volume *Histoire de France* (1833–67).

14 *Mémoire brisée*, p. 286.

15 *Antimemoirs*, pp. 106–7.

16 *Fin d'une jeunesse*, p. 43.

17 *Antimemoirs*, p. 102.

33 A MINISTER FOR TWO MONTHS

1 *Antimemoirs*, p. 105 – Marcel Paul (PCF) was Minister of Industrial Production (1945–6).

2 *Combat*, 1 January 1946.

3 G. Elgey, *La République des illusions*, p. 52.

4 Cyrus Sulzberger, *A Long Row of Candles*, pp. 271–2.

5 Probably Wednesday 9 January.

6 *Antimemoirs*, pp. 109–10.

7 The Socialist chairman of the National Assembly, who was to succeed General de Gaulle.

8 *Un autre de Gaulle*, pp. 174–5. In his letter to his successor, General de Gaulle painted an idyllic picture of the situation, declaring that 'the train was now on the rails' and that if he was now going, it was because the most serious problems of the Liberation and reconstruction had now been resolved.

9 Edmond Michelet, *La Querelle de la fidélité*, Paris p. 80.

34 CRUSADE IN THE MÉTRO

1 *Un autre de Gaulle*, pp. 174–7.

2 *Discours et Messages*, vol. II, pp. 54–5.

3 His name features on all the lists of committee members.

4 Some time earlier it had passed into the hands of a left-wing group led by Claude Bourdet.

5 Fragments of which were published in *Le Rassemblement* and in *Carrefour* (March 1948).

6 His address was included in *Les Conquérants* (paperback ed.).

7 *Le Figaro*, 19 February 1948: 'What a fine article your father has written!' de Gaulle remarked the next day to Claude Mauriac . . .

8 Malraux dispensed this 'information' again from the platform of the Vélodrome d'Hiver.

9 *The Transit of Britain*, London, 1973, pp. 41–2.

10 De Gaulle's representative in the Mediterranean, 1940–4.

11 Between 1948 and 1953.

12 Having invited him to do so, and being met by a categorical refusal, the General sent him the following message: 'Brutus always overcomes Caesar . . .'

13 Interview given by Gaston Palewski to the author, 23 November 1972.
14 Pp. 135–6.
15 *Le Rassemblement,* 24 April 1948.
16 Speech at Nancy, 25 November 1951.
17 Sulzberger, op. cit., p. 326.
18 Interview given by Arthur Koestler to the author, 20 November 1972.
19 *Discours et Messages,* vol. II, pp. 581–2.
20 *Un autre de Gaulle,* pp. 356–63.
21 ibid., pp. 386–9.

35 THE DESERT AND THE SPRING

1 Ed. Estienne, 1955.
2 *Femina illustration,* 1956.
3 The hero of *Les Noyers de l'Altenburg,* said to be a portrait of Frobenius, the great German ethnologist.
4 *The Voices of Silence,* trans. Stuart Gilbert, London 1954, pp. 361 and 640.
5 October 1948, pp. 516–34.
6 *Malraux par lui-même.* Nine years earlier, Gaëtan Picon had published with Gallimard's a first essay on Malraux.
7 *Un autre de Gaulle,* pp. 373–4.
8 *Malraux par lui-même,* p. 60.
9 Janet Flanner, *Men and Monuments,* p. 63.
10 *Saint-Just ou la force des choses,* Gallimard, 1954.
11 *L'Express,* 25 December 1954 and 29 January 1955.
12 Interview published later in *Le Temps qui reste,* Stock, 1973, p. 245.
13 Then Minister for Algeria.

36 AT THE RIGHT HAND OF THE MASTER

1 Spring 1954.
2 De Gaulle's secretary in London, who remained very close to the Gaullists.
3 *Antimemoirs,* pp. 110–11.
4 15 May 1958, two days after the movement began.
5 *Antimemoirs,* p. 113.
6 ibid., p. 114.
7 ibid., p. 116.
8 *Journal officiel,* 27 July 1958.
9 Interview given by Claude Mauriac to the author, March 1972. In fact, Malraux would have liked the General to give him responsibility for Algeria.

10 Malraux is referring to a left-wing demonstration against de Gaulle.
11 An old theory according to which Danton paid Brunswick to make sure that the Republic won.
12 There were more Frenchmen acclaiming Pétain in Paris, in April 1944, than there were true combatants in the Maquis.
13 The Minister's 'knowledge' was inadequate. Torture was not suspended. At most it was limited for a time, owing to the change of régime.
14 He was to die two months later.
15 Unpublished interview, 29 June 1958.
16 *Antimemoirs*, pp. 136–8.
17 ibid., p. 150.
18 ibid., p. 166.
19 Charles de Gaulle, *Memoirs of Hope*, trans. Terence Kilmartin, London 1971, p. 272.
20 Salan, Challe, Zeller, Jouhaux, who tried to revolt against de Gaulle's move towards Algerian independence.
21 Interview given by Gaston Palewski to the author, 22 November 1972.

37 ALGERIA AS REMORSE

1 Statement made to the newspaper *Novedades*, Mexico City, 9 April 1960; quoted by Jeanine Mossuz, *Malraux et le gaullisme*, Paris, 1970, p. 209.
2 ibid.
3 Interview given in Paris to foreign journalists, 2 July 1958.
4 *Les Lettres nouvelles*, 1 July 1959.
5 Francis Jeanson had set up a 'support network' for the FLN, many of whose members were brought to trial in 1960.
6 Organisation armée secrète.
7 Quoted by J. Mossuz, op. cit., p. 223.

38 THE ART OF STATECRAFT

1 *L'Aurore*, 10 October 1967.
2 Paris, Seuil, 1972, pp. 365–7.

39 WORLD-WIDE MISSIONS

1 Most famous of all French Resistance leaders, parachuted into France in 1942 to coordinate the underground movements under Gaullist leadership. Betrayed, arrested and tortured in June 1943, he died on the train in which he was being transferred to Germany [Trans.].
2 *Antimemoirs*, pp. 435–6.
3 *L'Express*, 1 November 1962.

4 The bombing by the French airforce in 1958 of an FLN camp in Tunisia, which killed eighty civilians and gave rise to the Anglo-American (Murphy–Beeley) 'good offices' mission. It spelled the end of the myth of 'Algérie française'.

5 *Le Monde*, 17 December 1965.

40   THE CHINA VISIT

1 A year before the Cultural Revolution of 1966.
2 *Antimemoirs*, pp. 368–432.
3 ibid., p. 380.
4 Died in 1971.
5 *Antimemoirs*, pp. 384 and 388.
6 Then the Pakistani head of state.
7 Chen-yi wrote short poems. He had published some as a young man.
8 P. 397.
9 Pp. 394 and 397.
10 According to the *Antimémoires*, he went there after this interview.
11 Before the Warsaw meeting.
12 *Antimemoirs*, p. 413.
13 ibid., p. 414.
14 ibid., pp. 414–16.
15 ibid., pp. 420–1.
16 ibid., pp. 426–8.
17 The meeting took place in August 1965. The 'Cultural Revolution' began in May 1966. The *Antimémoires* were published in September 1967.
18 A minister who had visited China some months earlier.

41   REAR-GUARD ACTION

1 Confédération Générale de Travail. The Communist-led trade union organisation.
2 The leader of the PCF at this time.
3 Pierre Viansson-Ponté, *Histoire de la République gaullienne*, p. 578.
4 Philippe Alexandre, *Le Duel de Gaulle-Pompidou*, Paris, Grasset, 1970, p. 366.
5 Interview given by André Malraux to the author, 29 January 1973.

42   THE TRUE, THE FALSE, THE 'LIVED'

1 *Fin d'une jeunesse*, p. 51.
2 *L'Événement*, September 1967.
3 Interview given by André Malraux to the author, 29 January 1973.

43   THE DEATH OF THE FATHER

1 *L'Express*, 13 November 1972.
2 Preface to *Les Chênes qu'on abat*, p. 13.
3 *New York Times* book review, 23 April 1972.
4 *Europe no. 1*, 4 March 1967.
5 On 29 January 1973, André Malraux told me: 'The General was no longer in power. He was no longer going there in the name of France. He had been touched by the letter that Franco had written to him at the time of his departure in 1969. And he wanted to see Spain. But if he had made this visit as head of state, I would not have been able to remain in the government. I would have gone. Quietly . . .'

45   GARINE IN GLORY

1 *Le Dernier Bloc-notes*, p. 235.
2 *Malraux par lui-même*, p. 94.
3 Interview given by Émmanuel Berl to the author, 3 August 1972.
4 *La Croix*, 25 November 1972.
5 Interview given by Pierre Bockel to the author, 19 November 1972.
6 ibid.
7 Interview given by André Malraux to the author, 29 January 1973.
8 Gaëtan Picon, *Malraux par lui-même*, pp. 113–14.
9 ibid., p. 117.

Index